Bernd Wübben

German Mergers & Acquisitions in the USA

GABLER EDITION WISSENSCHAFT

Bernd Wübben

German Mergers & Acquisitions in the USA

Transaction management and success

With a foreword by Professor Dr. Dirk Schiereck

Deutscher Universitäts-Verlag

Bibliografische Information Der Deutschen Nationalbibliothek
Die Deutsche Nationalbibliothek verzeichnet diese Publikation in der Deutschen Nationalbibliografie; detaillierte bibliografische Daten sind im Internet über <http://dnb.d-nb.de> abrufbar.

Dissertation Universität Witten/Herdecke, 2006 u. d.T.:
Wübben, Bernd: German cross-border mergers and acquisitions in the United States

1. Auflage März 2007

Lektorat: Brigitte Siegel / Anita Wilke

Der Deutsche Universitäts-Verlag ist ein Unternehmen von Springer Science+Business Media.
www.duv.de

Umschlaggestaltung: Regine Zimmer, Dipl.-Designerin, Frankfurt/Main
Gedruckt auf säurefreiem und chlorfrei gebleichtem Papier
Printed in Germany

ISBN 978-3-8350-0624-9

To Suzanne

Foreword

In early 2006 BASF AG, Ludwigshafen, acquired, in a prolonged and rather hostile transaction, the U.S. Company Engelhard Corporation in order to strengthen its competitive position in the world's largest economy. This sizable takeover follows even larger acquisitions by German companies in the United States in the past decade, such as by Daimler-Benz, Deutsche Telekom and Deutsche Bank. Due to increasing pressure from the continuous globalization of international capital and product markets, numerous medium-sized German companies also aimed at entering the United States, as it offers a more dynamic growth potential compared to many rather stagnant European markets. Accordingly, a transaction in the most important consumer market is expected to be particularly beneficial for German acquirers and should elicit positive reactions by investors. But did this actually happen?

Despite the high volume of cross-border transactions during the past decade, the number of studies analyzing the success of mergers and acquisitions activity is still limited, especially regarding transatlantic acquisitions involving U.S. target companies. In his thesis, Bernd Wübben provides empirical evidence to fill this gap. Based on capital market data and a survey of executives, his primary objective is to assess the overall success of U.S. acquisitions by German companies and to identify which characteristics of the acquiring and target company and the acquisition structure had a significant impact on the transaction success.

Another focus of the thesis is to describe from the perspective of a foreign acquirer special considerations for structuring and managing a cross-border transaction of a U.S. target company, mainly the legal, financial accounting, and tax implications.

Bernd Wübben fully achieves the objectives of this dissertation. The analysis contains many intriguing and surprising results, which make this thesis an interesting read that I highly recommend to corporate finance practitioners and researchers. I wish for the dissertation its due wide diffusion in corporate finance research.

Professor Dr. Dirk Schiereck

Preface

It is a pleasure to express my appreciation to those who enabled me to pursue and complete my doctoral thesis.

First, I would like to acknowledge the enormous debt of thanks I owe to my supervisor, Professor Dr. Dirk Schiereck, for his valuable advice, guidance and patience throughout our collaboration. I thank both Professor Dr. Thomas Armbrüster as the Chair of the Examining Board and Professor Dr. Alexander Bassen for their time and thoughtful assessments.

I am particularly indebted to Dr. Norbert Fischer of KPMG's German Practice in New York for his generosity and flexibility.

I am thankful to my parents for their countless and continuous contributions.

Finally, I wish to express my deepest gratitude to my love Suzanne, who is always there for me. Her unwavering encouragement, support and sacrifices were essential to this thesis, which I dedicate to her.

Bernd Wübben

Overview of contents

Contents

List of figures

List of tables

List of abbreviations

%	Percent
Adj.	Adjusted
ADR	American Depository Receipts
ADR	American Depository Shares
AG	Aktiengesellschaft ("Stock corporation")
AktG	Aktiengesetz ("German stock corporation law")
AML	Additional minimum liability
APT	Arbitrage Pricing Theory
AR	Abnormal return
ARB	Accounting Research Bulletin
b	Billion
BCL	Business Commercial Law
c.	Column
c-a ratio	Cash-to-assets ratio
CAPM	Capital Asset Pricing Model
CAR	Cumulative abnormal returns
CERCLA	Comprehensive Environmental Response, Compensation, and Liability Act
CFO	Chief financial officer
cont.	Continued
Corp.	Corporation
DAX	Deutsche Aktienindex ("German stock index")
DCF	Discounted cash flow
DGCL	Delaware General Corporation Law
DM	Deutsche Mark
DOJ	Department of Justice
EBIT	Earnings before interest and tax
EBITDA	Earnings before interest, tax, depreciation and amortization
EBO	Employee buy-out
Ed.	Editor
e.g.	Exempli gratia
EITF	Emergency Issue Task Force
EPA	Environmental Protection Agency
ERISA	Employee Retirement Security Act of 1974
EStG	Einkommensteuer-Gesetz ("German Internal Revenue Code")
et al.	Et alia
etc.	Et cetera

EU	European Union
EVA	Economic Value Added
f.	Following
ff.	Following pages
FASB	Financial Accounting Standards Board
FDI	Foreign direct investment
FIN	Financial Interpretation No.
FTC	Federal Trade Commission
GAAP	Generally accepted accounting principles
GDP	Gross domestic product
GmbH	Gesellschaft mit beschränkter Haftung ("Limited liability company")
H	Hypothesis
HGB	Handelsgesetzbuch ("German commercial code")
Hrsg.	Herausgeber ("Editor")
HSR	Hart-Scott Rodino
Hyp.	Hypothesis
IB	Investment bank(s)
IDW	Institut der Wirtschaftsprüfer ("Institute of Chartered Accountants")
i.e.	Id est
IFRS	International Financial Reporting Standards
Inc.	Incorporated
IFRS	International Financial Reporting Standards
IP	Intellectual property
IPO	Initial public offering
IRC	Internal Revenue Code of 1986, as amended
IRS	Internal Revenue Service
IT	Information technology
KGaA	Kommanditgesellschaft auf Aktien ("Limited partnership")
LBO	Leveraged buy-out
Lifo	Last-in-first-out
LLC	Limited liability company
LOI	Letter of intent
LP	Limited Partnership
M	Million
M&A	Mergers and acquisitions
MA	Market adjusted model
max.	Maximum
MBO	Management buy-out
min.	Minimum

MM	Market model
MSCI	Morgan Stanley Capital International
MTBV	Market-to-book value
n/a	Not applicable
Nf	Number of degrees of freedom
No.	Number
NOL	Net operating loss
OLS	Ordinary least square
p.	Page
pp.	Pages
PBO	Projected benefit obligation
pos.	Positive
PV	Present value
ROA	Return on assets
ROE	Return on equity
S&P	Standard & Poor's
SAB	Staff Accounting Bulletin
SARA	Superfund Amendments and Reauthorization Act
SDC	Security Data Company (by Thomson Financial)
SEC	Securities Exchange Commission
SERP	Supplemental Executive Retirement Plan
SFAS	Statement of Financial Accounting Standard
SIC	Standard Industry Classification
SOX	Sarbanes-Oxley Act of 2002
stat.	Statistic
Std.	Standard deviation
t	Trillion
TO	Tender Offer
U.K.	United Kingdom
UmwG	Umwandlungsgesetz ("Transformation Act")
U.S.C.	United States Code
U.S.	United States
USD	United States Dollar
Var.	Variable
Vol.	Volume
WACC	Weighted-average-cost-of-capital
WARN	Worker Adjustment Retraining and Notification Act of 1988

1 Introduction

1.1 Focus and goals of the study

The dynamic interaction of a continuous integration of global product markets, progressive technological developments, and heightened pressure from international capital markets vastly contributes to an increasing worldwide consolidation and concentration of industries.[1] In this rapidly evolving global competitive environment, German companies are faced with positioning themselves by expanding internationally in order to reallocate their resources, penetrate different regions, and to access new technology.[2] As an efficient and fast strategic alternative to organic growth, geographic diversification through cross-border mergers and acquisitions ("M&A") represents the predominant means for German companies to strengthen their global market position by seeking lucrative international growth opportunities.[3]

In this context, the United States as the world's single most homogenous market[4] became the major target country for strategic cross-border transactions by German companies during the past decade.[5] Alongside an overall high volume of worldwide domestic and cross-border mergers and acquisitions,[6] the importance of the transatlantic leap is highlighted by a drastic increase of German M&A activity in the United States in the late 1990s.[7] Numerous spectacular U.S. transactions during that period, such as the $40.5b *Daimler Benz AG-Chrysler Corp.* merger in 1998, which is so far the largest transaction by a German acquiring company, the *Deutsche Telekom AG-VoiceStream Corp.* acquisition in 2000 valued at $29.4b, and the $9b acquisition of *Bankers Trust New York Corp.* by *Deutsche Bank AG* in 1998 caught the public interest.[8] Following a decrease in the level of worldwide M&A activity in the years 2001 to 2003, the recently announced *Adidas-Salomon AG-Reebok Inc.* and *Fresenius Medical Care AG-Renal Care Group* acquisitions as well as the hostile bid for *Engelhard Corp.* by *BASF AG* provide an indication for the continuous importance of the United States for German companies in their pursuit of becoming global players.[9] A statement by Heinrich von Pierer, the former Chief Executive Officer of *Siemens AG*, summarizes the strategic necessity of a corporate presence in the United States: "Wherever it makes sense for us to do something in the United States, we do it. It is still the biggest market

1 See SHIMIZU ET AL. (2004), p. 308.
2 See GRUBE (2005), p. 60.
3 See KPMG (2005), p. 421; HITT (2000), p. 11f.
4 See LUCKS (2005a), p. 10.
5 Based on data obtained from Thomson Financial Securities Data Company.
6 For example, the total value of M&A transactions completed in the United States between 1998 and 2000 was with nearly $4t more than the total value of all deals completed during the preceding 30 years, see HENRY and JESPERSEN (2002), p. 60.
7 See LUCKS (2005a), p. 9.
8 See for example WARLIMONT (2000), p. 29; DRIES (1998), p. 7; DUNSCH (1998), p. 1.
9 See HEITHECKER (2006), p. 9.

in the world, and a very competitive market. Succeeding in the U.S. was critical to becoming more competitive as a company".[10]

A cross-border transaction in the United States not only offers tremendous business opportunities, it also involves unique challenges for a foreign acquirer that result from a combination of peculiarities of the U.S. business practices, customer preferences, country and corporate cultures, and regulatory and legal issues, such as antitrust laws, financial reporting requirements, tax implications, and labor laws.[11] Compared to domestic transactions, such differentiating aspects add a higher level of complexity to all phases of the transaction process, i.e. the strategic conception and structuring and management of the acquisition as well as the post-closing integration of the target company.[12] Unfamiliarity with the U.S. environment might create risks that, besides a generally higher information asymmetry in cross-border mergers and acquisitions, could negatively impact the overall success of a transaction.

Despite the strategic importance of the U.S. market and the high transaction volume during the past decade, there is neither a comprehensive description of the current U.S. institutional framework from the perspective of a German acquirer[13] nor a systematic assessment of the success and its determinants of the recent German cross-border transactions in the United States.[14] In particular large transatlantic acquisitions such as the *Daimler-Chrysler* merger are commonly cited in the press as major failures and examples of destroyed shareholder value.[15] Assessing the success of the U.S. acquisitions by *Siemens AG*, Klaus Kleinfeld, the company's current CEO, acknowledged that *Siemens* "made acquisitions where you questioned why they had been made".[16] The empirical evidence from studies by scholars and practitioners of cross-border transactions predominantly by Anglo-Saxon acquiring companies is ambiguous at best regarding whether geographic diversification generally

---

10 STEWART and O'BRIAN (2005), p. 116.

11 See MIDDELMANN and HELMES (2005), p. 687; SHIMIZU ET AL. (2004), p. 309; CULLIAN and HOLLAND (2002), p. 22.

12 See HALL (2001), p. 1.

13 LUCKS (2005a) for example provides a compilation of various aspects for transatlantic mergers and acquisitions from the perspective of German companies, including numerous case studies. Other authors focus on specific considerations for the cross-border transaction process, for example MIDDELMANN and HELMES (2005) for due diligence and HUTTER and LAWRENCE (1999) for applicable U.S. federal securities laws.

14 There are several studies examining the success of German domestic and cross-border transactions before the 1990s, for example by BÜHNER (1991). Due to a different interaction of endogenous and exogenous factors influencing the cross-border M&A activity during the past decade, the transferability of the findings and conclusions from such older studies is limited.

15 See ZSCHÄPITZ (2006); HENRY (2002). Also LUCKS (2005b, p. 11) recently posits that "large-scale transatlantic M&A projects have a particularly low success rate, destroying vast assets within national economies in their wake".

16 NOLAN (2005), p. 138. Klaus Kleinfeld was at the time of the interview Chief Operating Officer of *Siemens* in the United States.

achieved its presumed benefits[17] and generated value not only for the seller, but also for the shareholders of the acquiring companies.[18]

In this context, an evaluation of the institutional conditions and the success and its determinants of U.S. cross-border acquisitions by German companies is necessary and useful. Accordingly, this study aims at the following three main goals:

(i) To analyze from the perspective of a foreign acquirer the main considerations for the structure and management of an acquisition of a U.S. target, given that unlike the strategic conception and post-merger integration, the execution of a transaction is the most standardized phase within the acquisition process, thereby revealing the lowest variability between individual transactions.

(ii) To conduct an empirical analysis of the overall success of German acquisitions in the United States for the period 1990 to 2004.

(iii) To identify which characteristics had a significant impact on the transaction success, with a particular focus on various aspects of the structure and management of the cross-border acquisition.

1.2 Organization of the study

In order to achieve these goals, this study is structured in six chapters, as illustrated in Figure 1.1. Chapter 2 lays out the conceptual framework for this study. It includes a definition and categorization of mergers and acquisitions and the perspective for measuring their success, which is followed by a discussion of theories explaining the occurrence of mergers and acquisitions activity. After presenting the global and German transaction activity during the period from 1990 to 2004, the individual steps within the various phases of a standardized acquisition process are briefly introduced, including a discussion of specific aspects for cross-border acquisitions.

The third chapter elaborates on specific aspects for structuring and managing a cross-border acquisition of a U.S. target company, comprising the form, due diligence, tax planning, valuation, and principal documentation for the transaction. In addition, the U.S. regulatory framework of antitrust laws is presented. The chapter concludes with a discussion of the main implications from the local peculiarities for the acquisition structuring and management phase.

---

17 Such benefits might result for example from the exploitation of target country specific endowment factors or the transfer of imperfectly imitable resources of the acquirer, see SETH ET AL. (2000).

18 See KUIPERS ET AL. (2003), p. 1; BODNAR ET AL. (2003), p. 1. An overview of the findings in the existing body of research is provided for example by MOELLER and SCHLINGEMANN (2005), BRUNER (2004a), and CAMPA and HERNANDO (2004).

Introducing the success analysis, Chapter 4 provides a survey of the existing empirical research on the success of cross-border transactions. In order to avoid distortions from the influence of different institutional and economic environments, the reviewed studies are limited to those that analyze transactions during the period from 1990 to 2004. The main features and results of three main methodologies for measuring success are summarized, i.e. capital market based event studies, financial statements based studies, and surveys of executives. The evidence in the literature regarding potential determinants of transaction success is inductively condensed into 18 hypotheses, which are tested in Chapter 5.

The success of acquisitions by German companies in the United States during the years 1990 to 2004 is assessed in Chapter 5 from the perspectives of the shareholders and executives of acquiring companies. Based on the results of an event study and the responses from a survey of chief financial officers of German acquirers, determinants of cross-border transaction success are evaluated in a uni- and multivariate analysis, involving characteristics of the acquiring and target company as well of the transaction structure and management. Additionally, the observations from the event study are compared to a sample of domestic and European cross-border transactions by the identical group of German acquirers of U.S. targets. Chapter 6 concludes the study by summarizing the main findings and by suggesting topics for further research.

Figure 1.1: Organization of the study

1 Introduction

2 Conceptual framework

- Definition, categories, and measuring success of mergers and acquisitions
- Theories explaining merger and acquisition activity
- Merger and acquisition activity in the period 1990 to 2004
- Phases of the standardized merger and acquisition process

3 Special considerations for structuring and managing a cross-border acquisition of a U.S. target company

- Form of acquisition
- Due diligence and tax planning
- Valuation and documentation
- U.S. antitrust law and regulatory framework
- Conclusions and implications

4 Prior research on the success of cross-border acquisitions and its determinants

- Methodologies
- Overall transaction success
- Determinants of transaction success
- Conclusions and testable hypotheses for the study

5 Empirical analysis of the success of German acquisitions in the United States

- Methodologies and samples
- Overall transaction success
- Uni- and multivariate analysis of the determinants of transaction success
- Conclusions and implications

6 Summary and outlook

2 Conceptual framework

2.1 Introduction

This chapter provides the conceptual framework for the study. It defines and categorizes mergers and acquisitions, gives the perspective for measuring success of acquisitions (Section 2.2), discusses theories explaining the occurrence of merger and acquisition activity (Section 2.3), summarizes the global and German merger activity in the period 1990 to 2004 (Section 2.4), and describes the phases of a standardized acquisition process (Section 2.5). The theoretical basics of Sections 2.3 and 2.5 are laid out first without a distinction of the geographical focus of the transaction, before specific considerations for cross-border acquisitions are addressed.

2.2 Terminological basis

2.2.1 Definition of mergers and acquisitions

There are various expressions interchangeably used in the U.S. and German finance literature and among practitioners in connection with corporate mergers and acquisitions, including the terms takeover, transaction, consolidation, concentration, fusion, amalgamation, business combination, tender offer, and sell-off.[1] In the absence of a uniform definition, these expressions are generally subsumed under the generic term "mergers and acquisitions". In the United States the term M&A typically covers a wide range of corporate activities beyond the traditional means of strategic expansion like business combinations and strategic cooperations.[2] For example, COPELAND and WESTON (1988) stated that the "traditional subject of M&A has been expanded to include takeovers and related issues of corporate restructuring, corporate control, and changes in the ownership structure of firms."[3] Figure 2.1 displays the various areas of M&A that can be derived from this broad definition.[4]

1 See WIRTZ (2003), p. 10.; CUSATIS ET AL. (2001), p. 529; JANSEN (2001), pp. 43-46; WESTON ET AL. (2001), p. 5f.; ZIESCHANG (2000), p. 17.

2 See WESTON ET AL. (2001), p. 5f.; GAUGHAN (1999), p. 7; HERZEL and SHEPRO (1990), p. 3f.; COPELAND and WESTON (1988), p. 676.

3 COPELAND and WESTON (1988, p. 676). SUDARSANAM (1995, p. 1) offers a wider definition by interpreting M&A as a "means of corporate expansion and growth".

4 A description of all individual M&A areas is omitted. For a detailed discussion for example refer to JANSEN (2001), p. 45 f.; COPELAND and WESTON (1988), p. 676 ff.

Figure 2.1: Areas of M&A activity in a broad sense[5]

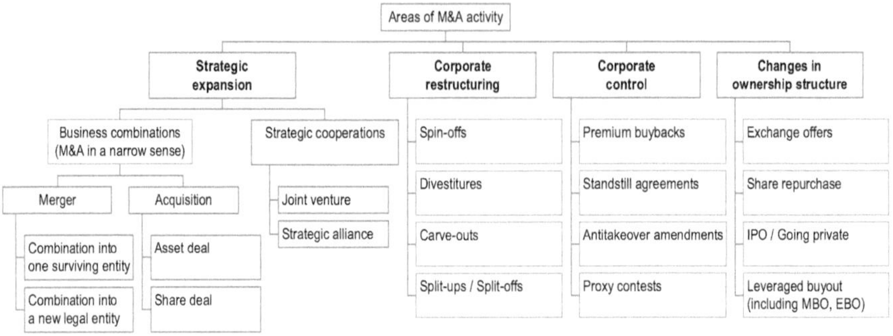

In a more narrow definition, which is frequently offered in the German finance literature, the term M&A is strictly confined to strategically motivated business combinations, i.e. transactions that result in the transfer of ownership as well as management and control rights from one company (the "target") to another (the "acquirer").[6] Such a transfer may be accomplished either through the (i) acquisition of assets or the majority of shares[7] of the target company and its subsequent integration of the target into the acquirer's corporate group, or through the (ii) merger of the acquirer and the target, which may or may not follow an acquisition.[8]

---

5 Source: presentation follows GAUGHAN (1999), p. 7; COPELAND and WESTON (1988), p. 676f. This presentation is based on the perspective of those companies engaged in M&A activity, for which M&A is a means of external growth as a strategic alternative to internal organic growth. Another perspective for a differentiation of M&A activities would be that of a service provider, for example an investment bank, for which M&A is a line of business, see BEITEL (2004), p. 32. Such a perspective is not adopted for this study; for a further discussion refer to ACHLEITNER (2002), pp. 152-164.

6 See for example WIRTZ (2003), p. 12: "Das M&A-Management umfasst den Prozess und das Ergebnis des strategisch motivierten Kaufs bzw. Zusammenschlusses von Unternehmen oder Unternehmensteilen und deren anschließender Integration oder Weiterveräußerung. Damit verbunden ist eine Übertragung der Leitungs-, Kontroll- und Verfügungsbefugnisse." Similar definitions can be found in LUCKS and MECKL (2002), p. 23f.; MÜLLER-STEWENS ET AL. (1999), p. 1. VOGEL (2002, p. 5) also includes rights in connection with contractual cooperations (such as alliances and joint ventures) as well as services rendered in connection with transactions. PICOT (2002) offers a definition of M&A that is more in line with the aforementioned broader context by including strategic alliances and joint ventures. All definitions have in common though that transactions merely pursued for financial investment purposes are not covered, see ACHLEITNER (2002), p. 141f.

7 In this context MÜLLER-STEWENS ET AL. (1999) point out that besides the transfer of ownership in the shares, the transfer of control and voting rights is also important. Some authors narrowly define an acquisition as the complete transfer of ownership in the target's shares, see for example ZIMMERER (1993), p. 4294.

8 See ACHLEITNER (2002), p. 141f. The author states that the term M&A comprises transactions on the market for companies, parts of companies, and participations. JENSEN and RUBACK (1983, p. 5f.) created in this context the expression of "the market for corporate control".

Within this study the definition of the term "mergers and acquisitions" follows the narrow interpretation of M&A, focusing only on companies as acquirers.[9] Strategic cooperations in the form of joint ventures or strategic alliances as an alternative to business combinations are not included in this definition and therefore are not further discussed.[10] Throughout this study, the terms "acquisition" and "transaction" are interchangeably used to refer in a generic sense to all transactions in which the businesses of companies are combined through the purchase of a majority of shares or assets or through a merger. In order to further specify the subject of this study, the definition of mergers and acquisitions is followed by a presentation of criteria employed for classifying different types of transactions.

2.2.2 Categories of mergers and acquisitions

Analogous to the definition of the term M&A, the literature offers various possibilities for categorizing transactions.[11] The most frequently cited criteria are the type of business combinations, strategic direction, acquisition structure, status of the target, attitude of the transaction, form of payment, financing of the transaction, and the geographical focus. Following is a brief discussion of these different criteria and the resulting dimensions of transactions as shown in Figure 2.2, as they become relevant for the analysis of the success of German transactions and its determinants.

Figure 2.2: Criteria for categorizing mergers and acquisitions[12]

Criteria for categorizing mergers and acquisitions			
Type of business combination	**Strategic direction**	**Acquisition structure**	**Status of the target**
• Acquisition • Merger	• Horizontal • Vertical • Concentric • Conglomerate	• Asset deal • Share deal	• Private • Public
Attitude	**Form of payment**	**Financing**	**Geographical focus**
• Friendly • Hostile	• Cash • Securities	• Equity • Debt • Hybrid	• Domestic • Cross-border

9 This definition follows for example GERPOTT (1993), p. 22. Accordingly, transactions by private persons, for example through a management buy-out, or by investor groups are not included in this definition.

10 For a discussion of these forms of cooperations for example refer to WIRTZ (2003), p. 14f.; VOGEL (2002), p. 12f.; JANSEN (2001), p. 50f.

11 For a more detailed discussion of these categorization criteria refer to JANSEN (2001), pp. 43-46; BREALEY and MYERS (2000), p. 912ff.; DUFEY and HOMMEL (2000), p. 963ff.; GAUGHAN (1999), p. 3ff.

12 Source: presentation follows BEITEL (2004), p. 34.

Both mergers and acquisitions[13] relate to changes in the economic control of an entity, but differ with regard to the retention of the legal existence of the target company.[14] A merger is the closest form of a business combination.[15] It combines the assets and operations of two companies either into one surviving company[16] or to establish a new legal entity.[17] As a result, the legal existence of at least one participating company is given up, with the shareholders of the transferring parties receiving shares of the combined company.[18] Mergers generally only become effective through an affirmative vote of the majority of the shareholders of both companies, as governed by specific laws or statutes of the states where the participating companies are chartered.[19] In an acquisition, the target company is integrated into the corporate group of the acquirer, with the legal existence of the target initially remaining unchanged.[20]

Based on the business sector and product or technology affinity of the involved companies, horizontal, vertical, concentric, and conglomerate transactions are distinguished (see Figure 2.3).[21]

Figure 2.3: Categories of mergers and acquisitions based on strategic direction[22]

		Products / Technology	
		Identical / similar	**New**
	Target is supplier / customer	Vertical	Vertical
Market	**Identical / similar**	Horizontal	Market-concentric
	New	Technology-concentric	Conglomerate

A horizontal transaction occurs between competing companies operating in the same industry and intends to achieve synergies and greater market power by consolidating resources.[23]

13 Within the confined discussion of this criterion, the term "acquisition" only refers to the purchase of shares or assets and does not include mergers.
14 See BUONO and BOWDITCH (1989), p. 60f.
15 See WESTON ET AL. (2001), p. 6.
16 See PAUSENBERGER (1989), p. 622. In the German corporate law this merger type is referred to as "Verschmelzung durch Aufnahme" and is regulated in UmwG Sections 4-35.
17 See GERPOTT (1993), p. 33. In the German corporate law this merger is referred to as "Verschmelzung durch Neugründung" and is regulated in UmwG Sections 36-38.
18 See VOGEL (2002), p. 6f.
19 An exception to this rule is the so-called "short-form" merger, which is permitted under U.S. state law without a vote of shareholders when all (or substantially all) shares of one corporation are owned by another corporation, see REED and LAJOUX (1999), p. 6. For a further discussion refer to Section 3.2.3.1.
20 A share acquisition is often combined in a second step with a merger of the target with the acquirer or its acquisition vehicle that was specifically incorporated for the purpose of the transaction.
21 See for example REINEKE (2001), p. 20; SETH (1990); SAUTTER (1989), p. 8. This classification, which was also adopted by the U.S. Federal Trade Commission, is frequently used in the literature and follows ANSOFF (1987, p. 184). KUMMER (2005, p. 39) remarks that this classification is of a mere technical nature and for vertical transactions does not distinguish between forward- and backward-integrations.
22 Source: presentation follows BECKER (2005), p. 65.
23 See BÜHNER (1990a), p. 5.

The potential for realizing synergies in these transactions is generally higher than in vertical acquisitions, in which the parties operate on different manufacturing and distribution levels.[24] Vertical transactions typically aim at reducing uncertainty and transaction costs in forward and backward linkages of the production chain, usually in client-supplier or buyer-seller relationships.[25] In conglomerate transactions companies in unrelated business activities seek to benefit from economies of scope and to diversify risk.[26] Conglomerate transactions were very popular in the late-1980s, but they have diminished in importance in the 1990s as companies have tended increasingly to shift their focus back on their core business to cope with intensifying international competition.[27] Concentric transactions are marked by acquiring a target, which operates in the same market as the acquirer, but with a product or technology portfolio that is unrelated to that of the acquirer ("market concentric") or vice versa ("technology concentric").[28]

An acquisition can take the form of either a purchase of assets ("asset deal") or shares ("share deal") of the target company.[29] An acquisition is typically structured as an asset deal when the target is a division of a corporate group and not a separate legal entity and when the transaction involves only part of a business, such as a product line.[30] It may also be desirable in case the acquirer wants to avoid assuming all of the target's liabilities. An asset deal requires the preparation of extensive documentation and payment of taxes for the transferred assets, which may be too time-consuming and costly for the acquirer.[31] Apart from tax considerations, in such a situation the acquirer typically prefers to structure the situation as a share deal, thereby also avoiding the obstacle of obtaining third-party consent for the transfer of an individual asset or a contract. However, a share deal may be difficult to consummate if it requires the consent of numerous shareholders of the target, while in an asset deal such shareholder consent is typically not required.[32] From the seller's perspective a share deal may be more beneficial than an asset deal if it is too difficult to use or dispose of the remaining assets.[33] Negative implications in a share deal may result from so-called "change in control" provisions,[34] for example by triggering special payments to the target's executives.[35] Table 2.1 summarizes the main advantages and disadvantages to be considered by the acquirer and the seller when determining whether to structure a transaction as an asset or share deal.

---

24 See SCHUBERT and KÜTING (1981), p. 29.
25 See PAPPROTKA (1996), p. 11f.; KIRCHNER (1991), p. 44.
26 See WIRTZ (2003), p. 19; BÜHNER (1990a), p. 6.
27 See UNCTAD (2000), p.101.
28 See ZWAHLEN (1994), p. 23.
29 See PICOT (2002), p. 26; MERKT (1994), p. 356f.
30 See HOLZAPFEL and PÖLLATH (2003), p. 103f.
31 See HOLZAPFEL and PÖLLATH (2003), p. 104.
32 See GAUGHAN (1999), p. 16.
33 See DEPAMPHILIS (2003), p. 516f.
34 "Change in control" may be defined in various ways, for example by focusing on a shareholder vote approving the sale, a sale of a required percentage of shares, or a turnover in the board of directors.
35 See MIDDELMANN and HELMES (2005), p. 675.

Table 2.1: Comparison of asset and share deals[36]

	Asset deal	Share deal
Advantages	• It is possible to acquire only part of a business • Previous liabilities of the target company usually are not inherited • Profitable operations can be absorbed by loss companies in the acquirer's group, thereby effectively gaining the ability to use the losses for tax purposes	• Lower capital outlay, since only purchase of net assets • Typically more attractive for the target shareholders, therefore probably lower purchase price
Disadvantages	• Overall more time-consuming and more costly than a share deal • Possible need to renegotiate supply, employment, lease, and technology agreements • A higher capital outlay is usually involved (unless the debt of the business is also assumed) • It may be unattractive for the target shareholders, thereby increasing the purchase price	• Acquirer is liable for any claims or previous liabilities of the entity • Difficult to consummate if large number of target shareholders • Increasing prevalence of change in control provisions

The status of the target, i.e. whether it is a privately owned or a public company, has a significant impact on the acquisition process, especially in case of a share deal.[37] The acquisition of shares of a public company requires compliance with federal and state securities laws and is potentially vulnerable to competing offers from third parties.[38] Accordingly, mechanisms to protect the transaction are typically more important for an acquirer in this case.[39] In addition, certain contractual provisions with the target shareholders do not apply in a public transaction, such as warranties and indemnifications or earn-out provisions[40] and other contingent considerations.[41]

In case the acquirer initiates the transaction, it can be distinguished between a friendly and hostile acquisition.[42] Friendly transactions start with negotiations between both parties, which typically result in the signing of a letter of intent[43] and the approval of the board of directors. A hostile acquisition (or "unsolicited bid")[44] is an offer to buy shares of a public company without prior consent of the target's board and is therefore undertaken against the wishes of

36 Source: own presentation.
37 An asset deal involving the entire assets of a public company is unusual.
38 See REED and LAJOUX (1999), p. 723.
39 See LAJOUX and NESVOLD (2004), p. 75f.
40 In an earn-out agreement, the selling shareholders are entitled to additional payments if the acquired target meets certain financial milestones after the transaction, see LAJOUX and NESVOLD (2004), p. 63.
41 See REED and LAJOUX (1999), p. 725f.
42 See BERENS ET AL. (2005), p. 33.
43 See JANSEN (2001), p. 184f. The letter of intent as an instrument of entering into the acquisition management process is discussed further in Section 2.5.3.1.
44 See BRUNER (2004a), p. 806.

the target company.[45] The price premium typically paid in hostile takeovers tends to be higher than in friendly transactions, for example due to takeover defense mechanisms of the target.[46]

In case the seller initiates the transaction, the target may be sold either via exclusive negotiations with a potential acquirer or via an auction, which can be either in a public (in this case the potential list of acquirers is anonymous to the seller) or in a controlled (in this case the seller pre-selects a list of potential acquirers) form.[47]

Acquisitions can be paid for either in cash or with shares of the acquirer, so-called "exchange offers",[48] depending among others on the financing possibilities for the acquirer and implications on taxation for both parties.[49] Cash transactions may be financed from internally generated or externally borrowed cash,[50] while exchange offers are paid for either through exchanging existing treasury shares or through issuing new shares.[51]

Transactions can be differentiated as domestic or cross-border, based on whether the acquirer and the target have their home operations in the same country or not. Typically, a cross-border acquisition of a foreign company adds complexity to the transaction process, especially with regard to the acquisition management and post-closing integration.[52]

2.2.3 Success of mergers and acquisitions

Similar to the definition and categorization of mergers and acquisitions, the literature offers various criteria for measuring the success of transactions, as shown in Figure 2.4.[53] Those measurement criteria differ generally in terms of the employed concept, dimension, timeframe, and gauge. Concepts for measuring success are either based on quantitative information, i.e. financial statements-, capital market-, or event-oriented data, or on qualitative information, which is obtained from interviews or questionnaires of people involved in or affected by an acquisition. Within the dimensions of success, number and content can be differentiated, resulting in the consideration of one- or multi-dimensional as

---

45 See REED and LAJOUX (1999), p. 7; JENSEN and RUBACK (1983), p. 6f.
46 See BEITEL (2002), p. 11. Such measures are discussed in Section 3.2.3.5.
47 See BERENS ET AL. (2005), p. 35f.
48 See BRUNER (2004a), p. 433.
49 See RAPPAPORT and SIROWER (1999), p. 148f.
50 Transactions primarily financed with debt are commonly referred to as leveraged buyouts, see JANSEN (2001), p. 57-60. In practice the term leveraged buyout ("LBO") is usually reserved for acquisitions of public targets in which the company becomes private (so-called "going private"); one version of the LBO is the management buy-out, in which the acquirer of the target is its own management, see GAUGHAN (1999), p. 10.
51 See SLUSSER and RIGGS (1994), p. 213f.
52 See LUCKS and MECKL (2002), p. 252f. This aspect is discussed further in Section 2.5.5.
53 See WIRTZ (2003), p. 395; VOGEL (2002), p. 276; GERPOTT (1993), p. 190.

well as financial, market strategic, or social aspects. With regard to the timeframe of measuring success, ex ante and ex post short-, mid-, and long-term views are possible. Success can be measured using various gauges, such as the internal goals of the acquirer, comparison to the acquirer's peers, or alternative investments. Typically, the average success rate of transactions is not the focus of an analysis from a business management perspective, but instead the high variance of the success dimensions and the related question "... why some [transactions] fail and other succeed."[54]

Figure 2.4: Criteria for differentiating success of mergers and acquisitions[55]

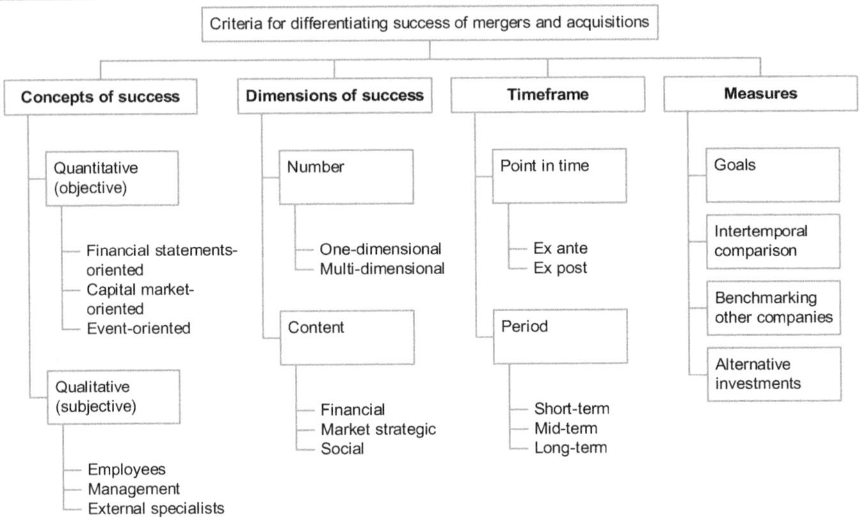

In a general sense, success is defined as the achievement of objectives.[56] Accordingly, in the context of M&A activity the measurement of success requires the formulation of the objectives of a transaction, which typically are derived from the acquirer's overall strategic goals. The acquisition objectives can be determined from various potentially incompatible perspectives, such as the acquirer's shareholders, employees, management, customers, and society, as shown in Table 2.2.[57]

---

54 SCHWEIGER and WALSH (1990), p. 47.

55 Source: presentation follows GERPOTT (1993), p. 190.

56 See KIRCHNER (1991), p. 90; LÜCKE (1983), p. 105.

57 See BERGER ET AL. (1999), p. 136. The potential conflict in the interests of shareholders and management has been expressed as the "agency-conflict", which is further discussed within the presentation of managerialism hypotheses for explaining M&A activity in Sections 2.3.2.1 and 2.3.3.3.

Table 2.2: Potential perspectives for evaluating transaction success[58]

Perspectives for evaluating transaction success				
Shareholders	**Employees**	**Management**	**Customers**	**Society**
• Creating additional shareholder value, for example through growth or realization of synergies	• Securing jobs • Increasing compensation • Improving career potentials	• Securing jobs • Increasing compensation, power, and prestige	• Improving access to products and services • Reducing prices • Increasing product offering and variety	• Securing location of companies • Securing jobs • Reducing bankruptcy risks

A transaction should be deemed a success if its objectives are met, as stated by CORDING ET AL. (2002): "Did we accomplish what we set out to accomplish, regardless of other exogenous or endogenous factors simultaneously at work?"[59]

The predominant focus in the finance literature for evaluating the success of M&A activity is to define the acquisition objectives on the basis of the shareholder value approach.[60] The key premise of this approach is to link the business goals of the company solely to the financial goal of the shareholders, which is the maximization of their share price.[61] Hence, within the shareholder value approach the success of an acquisition is measured by comparing the shareholders' value subsequent to the announcement or consummation of the transaction to a notional value that is calculated based on the assumption that the transaction had not occurred.[62] Depending on the status of the acquirer, shareholder value can be measured in two ways. In case the acquirer is a private company, there are various valuation methods

---

58 Source: presentation follows BEITEL (2002), p. 32.

59 CORDING ET AL. (2002), p. 6.

60 See for example BAMBERGER (1994), p. 12; GOMEZ (1992), p. 13; PAPPAPORT (1986), p. 12f. For a detailed discussion of the shareholder approach refer to COPELAND ET AL. (2000); RAPPAPORT (1986).

61 See LOVE and SCOULLER (1990), p. 5; RAPPAPORT (1986), p. 12f. CHAKRAVARTHY (1986, p. 448) points out a potential conflict of objectives from this perspective: "Creating stockholder value need not always converge with the interests of other stakeholders". For example, the demands of the employees for long-term job security can contradict those of the shareholders for cost reduction, which is generally seen as a measure for increasing shareholder value. JENSEN (1984, p. 110f.) defends the main focus on the shareholder: "Stockholders are commonly portrayed as one group in a set of equal constituencies, or 'stakeholders', of the company. In fact, stockholders are not equal with these other groups because they are the ultimate holders of the rights to organization control and therefore must be the focal point for any discussion concerning it."

62 See BAMBERGER (1994), p. 12f. RAPPAPORT (1986, p. 202) offers a different definition, based on the present value ("PV") of the combination of companies A and B compared to their stand-alone values: $Value_{Transaction} = PV_{AB} - (PV_A + PV_B)$. Accordingly, RAPPAPORT (1986) focuses on the value that is created for the combined company. As a result, an overall successful transaction can be value reducing for the shareholders of the acquiring company, if for example the acquirer pays a transaction premium that exceeds the present value of synergy potentials, see SIROWER (1997), p. 42ff. Since the main focus of this study is the success of German acquisitions from the perspective of the shareholders of the acquiring company, the implications of this equation are not considered further.

available,[63] while in the context of the shareholder value approach, discounted cash flow methods are predominantly applied.[64] In case the acquirer is a public company, the success measure is the reaction of the capital market, which is quantified by computing a so-called "abnormal return" using event study methodology.[65] The event study methodology is presented in detail in Section 4.3.1.1 and is adopted later for the purpose of this study of analyzing the empirical success of German acquirers in the United States.

Following the definition and categorization of mergers and acquisitions and their success is the discussion of the question why companies engage in transactions.

2.3 Theories explaining mergers and acquisitions activity

2.3.1 Overview

M&A activity is the result of the dynamic interaction of exogenous influences of the business environment and various endogenous motives of the acquiring companies. The general economic conditions and developments prevailing during the observation period of this study, i.e. the years from 1990 to 2004, are presented in Section 2.4 in connection with the description of the global and German transaction activity during that time.

Since there are no theories that explicitly address the occurrence of cross-border acquisitions, endogenous factors motivating companies to engage in transactions are explained by three general economical theories of a company's motivation to grow: new institutional economics, strategic management, and portfolio theories. Within the new institutional economics and its focus on various market imperfections, the transaction cost- and principal agent-approach are the two predominant theories applicable to merger and acquisition activity.[66] The strategic management literature[67] offers two differing perspectives explaining how companies achieve and sustain competitive advantages resulting in superior performance[68] and consequently higher value: the (i) market-based view, which focuses on the external market of a company, and the (ii) resource-based view, which in contrast focuses inwardly on a company's resources.[69] Further variations of the resource-based view are the capability- and knowledge-

---

63 See Section 2.5.3.2.

64 See COPELAND ET AL. (2000), p. 131.

65 See FAMA ET AL. (1969), p. 1ff.

66 See ACHLEITNER (2002), p. 48f. Another theory in this context is the property-rights-approach, but it does not offer important implications with regard to the explanation of merger and acquisition activity, see WIRTZ (2003), p. 25.

67 For an overview of the development of the strategic management research refer to for example MÜLLER-STEWENS and LECHNER (2001), p. 7f.

68 In this context performance is not measured as net profit but is based on the concept of economic rent, i.e. the earnings of a company over and above the cost of capital employed in their business, see MÜLLER-STEWENS and LECHNER (2001), p. 102.

69 See BAMBERGER and WRONA (1996), p. 386.

based view.[70] Another important explanation for M&A activity is offered by portfolio theory.[71] Figure 2.5 displays this systematization of economic theories relevant in the context of M&A, which are discussed further in Section 2.3.2.

Figure 2.5: Systematization of economic theories explaining external growth[72]

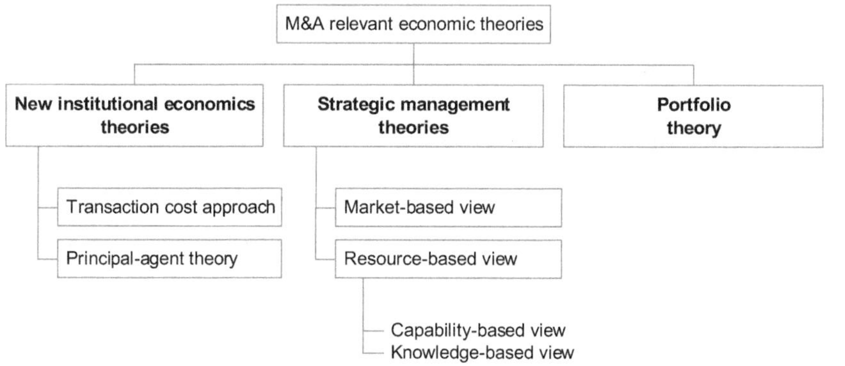

These economic theories serve as a basis to derive company internal motives that are simultaneously applied to domestic and cross-border transactions.[73] In the case of the separation of the acquirer's ownership and management, such endogenous factors may encompass potentially divergent and conflicting interests between the company's shareholders and its management, as discussed in Section 2.3.3.[74]

In order to explain the occurrence of cross-border acquisitions, the theories of direct foreign investment are also of particular interest, since acquisitions represent one vehicle amongst other alternatives for a company to enter a market in another country. Those theories are discussed in Section 2.3.4.

2.3.2 Relevant economic theories

2.3.2.1 New institutional economics theories

The transaction cost approach proposes that the comparative costs of conducting transactions through external markets rather than internally within a company determine the company's

70 See BEA and HASS (2001), p. 28.
71 See WIRTZ (2003), p. 51.
72 Source: presentation follows WIRTZ (2003).
73 See LAUSBERG and ROSE (1995), p. 178. For the purpose of this study, company internal reasons do not involve corporate expansions through cooperations or strategic alliances.
74 See VOGEL (2002), p. 32.

size and scope.[75] Transaction costs are defined as the "the ex ante costs of drafting, negotiating and safeguarding an agreement and, more especially, the ex post costs of maladaptation and adjustment that arise when contract execution is misaligned as a result of gaps, errors, omissions, and unanticipated disturbances; the cost of running the economic system".[76] The transaction costs perspective rests on the behavioral assumptions of bounded rationality, i.e. a company's capacity to act rationally is inherently constrained by its inability to gain complete information, and of opportunism, i.e. exchange partners pursuing their own interest may be willing to conceal information or mislead one another in order to gain an advantage.[77] As a result of these informational uncertainties and efforts to constrain opportunism, companies incur costs. Based on this theory, acquiring a target company is beneficial if it yields lower transaction costs compared to buying the desired products or services of the target on the external market.[78] Especially in cases of frequent and specific transactions with opportunistic exchange partners, companies engage in mergers and acquisitions in order to mitigate hold-up problems and under-investments.[79] Since such transactions typically occur upstream and downstream along the value added chain, the transaction costs approach mainly applies to vertical transactions.[80]

The principal-agent (or agency) theory[81] addresses the question of aligning the interests of two parties in contracting relations that are marked by uncertainty and information asymmetries between them.[82] In an agency relationship the principal is the contracting party with the lesser amount of available information.[83] With regard to mergers and acquisitions, such relationships may exist between the acquirer and the target, and between the management of the entities and their shareholders.[84] The principal-agent theory is of particular importance in the context of mergers and acquisitions since it not only provides an explanation for the occurrence of transactions, but it also points out potential problems and their solutions while pursuing transactions.[85]

---

75 See WILLIAMSON (1996), p. 3. This approach can be attributed to COASE (1937). Regarding the governance of transactions as a contracting problem, the core notion of this approach is that the costs of contracting transactions differ depending on their asset specificity, uncertainty, and frequency, see WILLIAMSON (1996), p. 13. Asset specificity refers to the need for making durable investments in order to realize transactions, which may impose contractual problems, as companies need to safeguard specific investments against potential opportunistic behavior.

76 WILLIAMSON (1996), p. 379.

77 See KRÄKEL (1999), p. 8ff.

78 See WIRTZ (2003), p. 26f.

79 See FELLI and ROBERTS (2000).

80 See WIRTZ (2003), p. 54.

81 This approach was mainly developed by JENSEN and MECKLING (1976) and in the current Anglo-American finance literature has become the dominant paradigm of corporate governance research.

82 See ACHLEITNER (2002), p. 49.

83 See KRÄKEL (1999), p. 21.

84 See WIRTZ (2003), p. 29.

85 See WIRTZ (2003), p. 35.

According to the agency theory, the occurrence of M&A activity is viewed as a manifestation of the agency conflict, when the discretionary power resulting from a separation of ownership and control is used by management to engage in acquisitions in order to maximize its own benefits rather than those of the shareholders.[86] Such interests of management could be for example desire for power and prestige, higher compensation, and job security.[87]

In the course of the transaction process, existing information asymmetries between the agent and principal may lead to the problems of adverse selection and moral hazard.[88] Adverse selection refers to a situation before execution of a contract between two parties where ex ante opportunism benefits the agent who hides or gives erroneous information, which may cause the principal, i.e. the acquirer, to select target companies that do not fit the strategic profile.[89] Measures for the acquirer to prevent such negative choices are conducting a thorough due diligence of the target or including preventative sanctions in the acquisition agreement with the seller.[90] Moral hazard is the post-contracting risk that agents, i.e. the acquirer's management, pursue goals that may not coincide with those of the principals, i.e. the acquirer's shareholders.[91] The agency theory suggests solving this problem through monitoring, i.e. the implementation of control systems by the principal, or through realigning the goals and interests of both parties using appropriate incentive mechanisms.[92]

2.3.2.2 Strategic management theories

Within the strategic management literature, the market-based view invokes industry characteristics to explain differences in the profitability of companies by focusing on a company's competitive position in its external product markets.[93] Within this perspective, a company's sources for higher performance are embedded in a market environment that is characterized by (i) the presence of a monopoly or a strong market position, (ii) high barriers to entry for new competitors, and (iii) higher bargaining power within the industry in regards to customers and suppliers.[94] A company's external competitive position may be assessed employing Porter's five forces model.[95] According to PORTER (1985), two strategies that seem to create or sustain superior profitability for companies are low-cost leadership and

---

86 See HUEMER (1990), p. 29; MAGENHEIM (1986), p. 25; KOUTSOYIANNIS (1982), p. 249.
87 See FIRTH (1980), p. 236.
88 See MAS-COLELL ET AL. (1995), p. 477f.
89 See WIRTZ (2003), p. 56.
90 The importance of the due diligence and the drafting of the acquisition agreement are further discussed within the description of a standardized acquisition process in Section 2.5. Within the agency theory, measures by the principals to prevent an adverse selection are referred to as "screening", while measures by the agent are classified as "signaling", see KRÄKEL (1999), p. 28.
91 See ACHLEITNER (2002), p. 51f.
92 See BEA and HAAS (2001), p. 374. The principal's monitoring activities in addition to its screening and the agent's signaling yield the so-called "agency costs", see SPREMANN (1987), p. 8.
93 See BEA and HAAS (2001), p. 25; CAVES and PORTER (1977).
94 See GRANT (1991).
95 See PORTER (1980), p. 3ff.

product differentiation. In the context of mergers and acquisitions, low-cost leadership may be achieved through economies of scale predominantly as a result of a horizontal acquisition of a company producing the same product, while product differentiation may be realized by acquiring a profitable and differentiated target.

In deviation to the outside-in perspective of the market-based view, within the resource-based view a company's sustainable competitive advantages stem from distinctive and comprehensive resources[96] that have to be (i) valuable, (ii) rare, (iii) imperfectly imitable, and (iv) not perfectly substitutable.[97] Accordingly, the resource-based view recommends merger and acquisitions for companies that aim at increasing their economic rent but lack the required resources to implement their strategy.[98] The desired resources may be acquired in transactions of all various strategic directions, hence this perspective offers a broader basis for explaining M&A activity than the more vertical-oriented transaction cost approach or the more horizontal-oriented market-based view.

The theoretical perspective of the resource-based view has been extended recently with the introduction of the capability- and knowledge-based views. The capability-based view does not contribute a company's comparative advantage simply to the possession of unique resources, but to its capability to efficiently use them through innovative configuration and combination of its core competencies[99] in its routines and processes.[100] The knowledge-based view assumes that "... the critical input in production and primary source of value is knowledge".[101] Accordingly, companies may generate higher economic rents as a result of the intransferability of tacit knowledge[102] or through superior knowledge enabling innovation.[103] In light of the difficulties in transferring company-specific capabilities and knowledge, both of these extensions of the resource-based view suggest mergers and acquisitions as a means for companies to gain access to them, though they do not provide an explanation of the strategic direction of transactions.[104]

---

96 According to BARNEY (1991, p. 101), resources are defined as "... all assets, capabilities, organizational processes, firm attributes, information, knowledge, etc. controlled by a firm that enable the firm to conceive of and implement their strategies".

97 See BARNEY (1991), p. 106f; WERNERFELT (1984), p. 172. More recently, HOOPES ET AL. (2003) looked at this perspective as part of broader theory of competitive heterogeneity of companies and claimed that only the criteria value and inimitability are ultimately significant.

98 See WIRTZ (2003), p. 43.

99 The definition of core competencies in this context is not limited only to a company's technological skills, see RASCHE (1994), p. 143ff.

100 See KOGUT and ZANDER (1992); CONNER (1991); PRAHALAD and HAMEL (1990); DEMSETZ (1988).

101 GRANT (1996), p. 112.

102 Tacit knowledge, embodied in individual, group, and organizational routines, is of critical strategic importance since it is both inimitable and appropriable, unlike explicit (or migratory) knowledge. For a further differentiation between tacit and explicit knowledge refer to KOGUT and ZANDER (1992), p. 387ff.

103 See MÜLLER-STEWENS and LECHNER (2001), p. 283; SPENDER (1996), p. 52.

104 See WIRTZ (2003), pp. 46-49.

2.3.2.3 Portfolio theory

Portfolio theory[105] provides a mathematical framework in which investors can minimize their risk by diversifying their investments into holdings with uncorrelated returns.[106] This basic principle of selecting a portfolio by financial investors can be transferred to the context of mergers and acquisitions, given that by acquiring a target with different risks a company may be able to reduce its own unsystematic risk.[107] Accordingly, portfolio theory offers an explanation for the occurrence of predominantly conglomerate transactions.[108] However, the benefits of such a diversification for an acquirer are only aligned with the interests of its shareholders when the individual investor's ability to diversify is comparatively disadvantageous, for example due to differences in tax structures in an cross-border environment.[109]

2.3.3 Motives of the acquiring companies

2.3.3.1 Systematization

The aforementioned economic theories offer general reference points for the occurrence of merger and acquisition activity and serve as a platform to derive specific internal motives for companies to engage in M&A activity. As with the definition and categorization of mergers and acquisitions, the literature on corporate control does not offer a standardized systematization of the broad variety of possible internal motives for companies to pursue transactions. For example, TRAUTWEIN (1990) differentiates amongst the categories efficiency, monopoly, raider valuation, empire-building, process, and disturbance theory. BERKOVITCH and NARAYANAN (1993) group the motives as synergy, agency, and hubris. WIRTZ (2003) and ACHLEITNER (2002) distinguish among strategic, financial, and personnel motives. WESTON ET AL. (2001) offer the motives value increase, hubris, agency, and redistribution.[110] Based on these suggested categories, a possible systematization of endogenous motives for M&A activity can be derived by differentiating shareholder value- and management-related hypotheses (see Figure 2.6).[111] Within the latter, acquisitions can be attributed to management either rationally maximizing its own benefits or acting irrationally.

---

105 This theory was developed by MARKOVITZ (1952).
106 See BREALEY and MYERS (2000), p. 187ff. For a detailed discussion of this theory refer to for example BETSCH ET AL. (2000), p. 55ff.
107 See WIRTZ (2003), p. 56; HUEMER (1990), p. 191.
108 See PAUSENBERGER (1993), c. 4444f.
109 See KIYMAZ and MUKHERJEE (2000), p. 38.
110 Redistribution refers to the redistribution of the value that is generated through the transaction.
111 This categorization is essentially modeled after ZIESCHANG (2000) and KERLER (2000).

Figure 2.6: Systematization of motives for mergers and acquisitions[112]

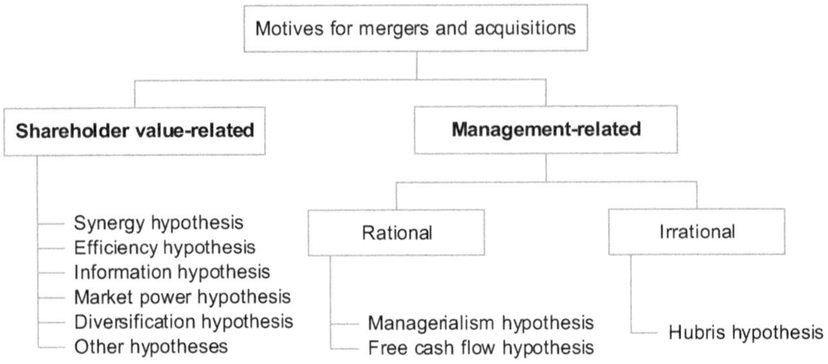

2.3.3.2 Shareholder value-related motives

In the examination of shareholder value-related motives, the literature primarily discusses the synergy, efficiency, information, market power, and diversification hypotheses,[113] of which the synergy hypothesis is the most important and most frequently cited motive, also among practioners.[114]

The synergy hypothesis assumes that companies pursue transactions to create shareholder value by realizing synergy[115] potentials of the combined entities.[116] In a broader definition, synergy potentials imply both cost savings and revenue enhancements that can only be achieved as a result of the combination of two businesses, but not by the individual companies independently.[117] Hence, due to the realization of synergies, the value of the combined entities exceeds the values of each stand-alone company, which ANSOFF (1966) summarized in the formula "2+2=5".[118] Sources of the additional value, or the synergistic

[112] Source: presentation follows KERLER (2000), p. 37.
[113] The term "hypothesis" is used synonymously with "motive theory" and in this context only refers to theories of mergers and acquisitions and not behavioral motives.
[114] See SIROWER (1997), p. 46.
[115] The word synergy is derived from the Greek words "syn" and "ergon", which mean "working together", see GOOLD and CAMPBELL (1998), p. 133; REIßNER (1992), p. 104.
[116] See JENSEN and RUBACK (1983), p. 23f.
[117] See SANDLER (1991), p. 130; LEONTIADES (1986), p. 85; JENSEN and RUBACK (1983, p. 9) offer a more narrow definition of synergies by only referring to cost savings.
[118] See ANSOFF (1966), p. 97. The formula seems to imply that there are only positive synergies, which is not the case. Negative synergies could result for example from costs of the coordination of the synergy management. Whereas positive synergies need to be actively developed as part of the integration phase following the transaction, negative synergies typically occur without further activities by the acquirer. The following discussion is confined to positive synergies.

gains, can be attributed to the exploitation of mainly operational and financial synergies.[119] Operational synergies may arise from economies of scale, production economies of scope, process improvements, transfer of know-how, or the utilization of growth potentials.[120] While economies of scale arise because of indivisibilities and are achieved through an improved utilization of given capacities for one product, economies of scope are achieved through the production of two or more products, either through the common use of inputs or through the repeated use of one input.[121] Accordingly, such synergistic gains are mainly achieved through horizontal acquisitions.[122] Process improvements can be achieved if through an acquisition the internal systems are either more efficiently redesigned or if the better system of the two entities is implemented. Know-how transfer implies that one of the involved companies has achieved for example a higher level of production technology knowledge, which could result in a reduction in production costs of the combined entity.[123] Besides realizing cost benefits, acquisitions may also aim to achieve revenue growth, for example by expanding product lines, entering into new markets, or by obtaining new distribution channels. Financial synergies may result from lower financing costs, for example due to a reduction of the acquiring company's cost of capital through issuing debt at a lower interest rate because of the target company's unused debt capacity.[124]

The efficiency hypothesis[125] assumes that companies do not fully utilize their internal resources due to their inefficient management.[126] Acquirers of such companies believe to better utilize the resources of the target by replacing its management. Improving the efficiency of the target results in lower costs or higher revenues, which increases the shareholder value.[127] Accordingly, acquisitions could be defined as a response to sub-optimal corporate strategies of the target company, which do not yield an optimal return on the employed capital.[128] A particularity exists when the sub-optimal performance can be attributed to management pursuing its own interests, which is discussed in the context of management-related motives in Section 2.3.3.3.

---

119 The literature offers a variety of different categorizations of synergies, as shown by KERLER (2000). TRAUTWEIN (1990, p. 284) for example differentiates between financial, operational, and managerial synergies, while KOGELER (1992, p. 46f) classifies synergies by corporate functions. In practice, the differentiation of synergies by corporate functions, such as distribution, production, administration, and research and development, dominates, see VOGEL (2002), p. 36f.

120 See PAUTLER (2001), p. 2f.; BREALEY and MYERS (2000), p. 943f.

121 See SETH (1990), p. 101; SINGH and MONTGOMERY (1987), p. 379.

122 See ALBRECHT (1994), p. 6.

123 This assumption is based on the theory of the learning curve, as developed by the Boston Consulting Group, see VOGEL (2002), p. 34f.

124 See BREALEY and MEYERS (2000), p. 949f; LUBATKIN and O'NEILL (1987), p. 666; LEWELLEN (1971), p. 533.

125 Another term used in the literature is "improved management hypothesis".

126 See RÖLLER ET AL. (2000), p. 17.

127 See TRAUTWEIN (1990), p. 284.

128 See MALATESTA (1983), p. 157.

In explaining the empirical success of acquisitions, the literature frequently does not differentiate between the efficiency and synergy hypotheses. Any increase of shareholder value as a result of a new and more efficient management is interpreted as a component of synergy gains.[129] However, contrary to synergy gains, the realization of efficiency gains does not require an acquisition and may be achieved by companies on their own.[130]

The information hypothesis attributes acquisition activity to differences in the valuation of a target company that are due to the asymmetry of available information.[131] According to this hypothesis, acquirers believe to have better information about the value of the target company than the rest of the market through non-public (insider) information, which can be obtained for example through an existing business relationship with the target.[132] The acquisition of such a target company creates shareholder value for the acquirer simply through the readjustment of the target's share price to its higher inner value on the basis of the additional non-public information.[133] The information hypothesis is therefore consistent with the efficient capital market theory, since the market price of the target company only reflects all publicly available information.[134] However, empirical studies do not support the validity of this hypothesis.[135] It is further diminished through the hubris hypothesis by ROLL (1986), who comments on the impact of arrogance of the acquirer's management in identifying supposedly undervalued targets.

The market power hypothesis views acquisitions as being executed in order to obtain and expand market power.[136] Market power is defined as "... the ability of a market participant or

129 See for example TRAUTWEIN (1990).

130 See BEITEL (2002), p. 21.

131 See for example TRAUTWEIN (1990); RAVENSCRAFT and SCHERER (1987). Another hypothesis that explains differences in the valuation of a target company is the "Economic Disturbance Theory" by GORT (1969). GORT argues that economic disturbances, which occur for example in the form of technological innovation and the performance of the capital markets, create differences in the valuation of targets since they distort projections for the future performance and therefore increase the volatility of valuation models, see GORT (1969), p. 624 ff.

132 In the context of shareholder value-related motives, this hypothesis does not include arbitrage motives by financial investors who pursue transactions with the sole intention to profit from a higher subsequent selling price for the entire business or for only pieces of it (so-called "asset stripping"), see VOGEL (2002), p. 39f. A special case of the arbitrage motive is the utilization of net operating losses to set off taxable gains from other profitable businesses for taxation purposes, see JENSEN and WERRES (2001), p. 64. However, the utilization of such tax attributes in the United States in connection with an acquisition is strictly limited, see Section 3.4.4.

133 See TRAUTWEIN (1990); RAVENSCRAFT and SCHERER (1987). BÜHNER (1990a, p. 18f.) points out in this context the importance of prior transaction experience of acquirers with regard to identifying undervalued targets.

134 See HAWAWINI and SWARY (1990), p. 27f. FAMA (1970) distinguishes among strong, semi-strong, and low efficiency of capital markets. The assumption of a strong-market efficiency is controversial in the theoretical and empirical research literature, as pointed out for example by OEHLRICH (1999, p. 29).

135 See for example BRADLEY ET AL. (1983). The authors analyzed the performance of shares after an acquirer withdrew from an acquisition offer. If the information hypothesis was valid, the share price should not decline as a result of the withdrawal, since the market has repriced the target on the basis of the additional information available from the offer. However, their findings did not support this theory.

136 See TRAUTWEIN (1990), p. 285ff.

a group of participants to control the price, the quantity or the nature of the products sold, thereby generating extranormal profits".[137] While domestic horizontal transactions offer acquiring companies a vehicle to instantly expand their market power, the same objects can also be achieved in conglomerate acquisitions by

- cross-subsidizing products, i.e. profits from one division are used to support predatory pricing in another,[138]
- simultaneously limiting competition in numerous markets, for example through tacit collusion with competitors with whom the acquirer has multiple market contacts,[139]
- deterring potential entrants from its markets, for example by raising entry barriers to a market,[140] and
- reciprocal buying, i.e. in order to squeeze out smaller competitors companies use corporate diversification to engage in reciprocal buying with other large companies as a result of an open or silent agreement between them.[141]

These various sources of achieving market power are summarized in the literature under the term "collusive synergy".[142] However, both domestic and cross-border transactions are subject to antitrust laws and regulatory approval, therefore this motive is essentially never officially mentioned in surveys on M&A activity.[143]

The diversification hypothesis explains the occurrence of acquisitions either from portfolio theory or the resource-based view.[144] Within portfolio theory, based on the assumption of not perfectly correlated cash flows of the acquirer and the target, diversification lowers the volatility, i.e. risk of future cash flows of the combined entities.[145] The increase in shareholder value may not only be the result of a reduced volatility of profits, but also of a reduced insolvency risk due to the bigger size of the diversified company.[146] In addition, diversification may yield financial synergies[147] and may extend the acquirer's debt

---

137 SETH (1990), p. 101.

138 See TRAUTWEIN (1990), p. 286; LORIE and HALPERN (1970), p. 156.

139 See VILLALONGA (2000), p. 3. EDWARDS (1955) referred to this as the "mutual forbearance theory of conglomerate behavior".

140 See PORTER (1989), p. 610.

141 See MARTIN and SAYRAK (2003), p. 40; LORIE and HALPERN (1970), p. 150.

142 See CHATTERJEE (1986), p. 123.

143 See GLAUM and LINDEMANN (2002), p. 276; KERLER (2000), p. 43. For a discussion of the U.S. regulatory framework see Section 3.7.

144 See for example BÜHNER (1991), p. 5.

145 See STEIN (1992), p. 94.

146 See BEITEL (2002), p. 23.

147 See BÜHNER and SPINDLER (1986), p. 605. LEWELLEN (1971) established the financial theory of corporate diversification (also referred to as "coinsurance hypothesis", see HIGGENS and SCHALL (1975)). An entity's debt capacity is defined as the maximum amount of debt that can be raised at any given interest rate, see WESTON and CHUNG (1983), p. 4.

capacity.[148] However, critics of the diversification motive argue that individual investors may be more efficient in minimizing risk for their portfolio[149] and that the increased complexity of a diversified company yields a discount in its valuation.[150] Another theoretical perspective for explaining diversification is based on the availability of company-specific resources, arguing that shareholder value is created from the transfer of excess capacities in resources and capabilities across industries or countries.[151]

Besides the above motives, companies generally pursue acquisitions to realize their specific strategic goals.[152] Especially in cross-border transactions, access to new geographical markets or technology and immediate market presence are predominant motives.[153] Moreover, there are additional motives that have received only sporadic attention in the literature and therefore are listed only for informational purposes, such as the q-ratio hypothesis,[154] labor hypothesis,[155] tax hypothesis,[156] bondholder hypothesis,[157] raider theory,[158] and defense in a hostile takeover pursuit.[159]

2.3.3.3 Management-related motives

While the underlying goal of the aforementioned motives is the maximization of shareholder value, there are also hypotheses that are based on the agency theory and focus on the interests of the acquirer's management.[160] The two major rational motives linked in the M&A context to this theory are the managerialism hypothesis, which is based on MUELLER (1969), and the free cash flow hypothesis by JENSEN (1986). In contrast, ROLL (1986) attributes acquisition activity to irrational hubris of management.

According to MUELLER (1969), the basic premise of the managerialism hypothesis[161] is that "... the prestige and power which managers can derive from their occupation are directly

148 See MARTIN and SAYRAK (2003), p. 41. Within the Capital Asset Pricing Model, diversification causes a decrease in the unsystematic risk, which in turn results in lower capital cost and therefore in a higher shareholder value, see KERLER (2000), p. 41.
149 See BREALEY and MEYERS (2000), p. 946f.
150 See PORTER (1987), p. 37f.
151 See MARTIN and SAYRAK (2003), p. 40.
152 See ACHLEITNER (2002), pp. 142-144.
153 See PORTER (1989), p. 422; SOUDER and CHAKRABARTI (1984), p. 43.
154 See WESTON ET AL. (2001), p. 143.
155 See WESTON ET AL. (2001), p. 150.
156 See JENSEN and RUBACK (1983), p. 24.
157 See WESTON ET AL. (2001), p. 149.
158 See HOLDERNESS and SHEEHAN (1985), p. 52; BRADLEY (1980), p. 356.
159 See KITCHING (1973), p. 27.
160 See STEGER and KUMMER (2003), p. 6f.; JENSEN and MECKLING (1976), p. 308.
161 Other terms used in the literature for this theory are "empire building theory" (see TRAUTWEIN (1990), p. 287), "managerial welfare hypothesis" (see SCHMIDT and FOWLER (1990), p. 560), and "maximizing management utility" (see FIRTH (1980), p. 236).

related to the size and growth of the company and not to its profitability".[162] In cases where their compensation is linked to the size of the company, managers may seek higher return rates in assets rather than profits.[163] Since the fastest way to achieve external growth is through acquisitions,[164] self-focused management may pursue transactions even if they are not beneficial for the shareholders.[165] In addition, management may also engage in transactions that diversify the business portfolio of their company and thereby reduce the risk of bankruptcy in order to provide enhanced security for their own jobs.[166]

Closely linked to the managerialism hypothesis is the free cash flow hypothesis by JENSEN (1986), who stipulates a correlation between the benefits of management and the availability of internal funds, i.e. free cash flow.[167] The free cash flow hypothesis assumes that management intends to minimize cash distributions to shareholders since such payments reduce the resources it controls and thereby its power. Accordingly, management intends to use available free cash flow, for example for acquisitions.[168] Following this theory, managers in companies with high free cash flow are more likely to engage in transactions, even if the transaction is not creating shareholder value.[169]

The managerialism and free cash flow hypotheses are an outflow of the agency theory, thereby assuming that companies lack an adequate control of their management.[170] These hypotheses do not consider the recently increasing implementation of various internal and external mechanisms that better link the interests of management with the goals of shareholders, for example through compensation that is based on share performance, job competition for executive positions, and the implications of an evolving corporate governance environment.[171]

On the basis of efficient capital markets, ROLL (1986) assumes that the market price of the target company is fair. His hubris hypothesis suggests that acquisitions occur despite the fair

---

162 MUELLER (1969), p. 644.

163 See SETH ET AL. (2000), p. 391.

164 See STEGEMOLLER (2001), p. 2; FIRTH (1980), p. 236.

165 See ANSOFF (1988), p. 98.

166 See AMIHUD and LEV (1981), p. 606. JENSEN and MECKLING (1976, p. 351) classify this diversification motive as a separate expression of the agency theory; a similar conclusion was reached by SAYRAK and MARTIN (2001).

167 See JENSEN (1986), p. 323, who defines free cash flow as cash flow in excess of what is required to fund all projects that have positive net present values (when discounted at the relevant cost of capital).

168 In this aspect this hypothesis differs from the managerialism hypothesis, given that within the latter such funds could also be obtained through external financing, see OEHLRICH (1999), p. 28.

169 See JENSEN (1988), p. 34.

170 See for example MIKKELSON and PARTCH (1997).

171 See SUDARSANAM (1995), p. 19; FAMA (1980), p. 228f. In this context, acquisitions are interpreted as an external means of market control, since in the case of sub-optimal use of the company's resources, current management may fear being substituted through an acquisition, see TRAUTWEIN (1990), p. 285; SCHERER (1988), p. 69f.; JENSEN and RUBACK (1983), p. 29f.; HALPERN (1983), p. 300. This explanation for acquisition activity is closely connected to the aforementioned efficiency hypothesis, but differs with regard to the reason of the target's management inefficiency (i.e. incompetence versus agency conflict).

valuation because managers erroneously believe they are able to identify target companies that are not properly valued by the market.[172] Based on this conviction, managers are willing to pay a premium over the current market price of a target company, which in light of the strong-market efficiency can only be attributed to hubris of the management. "The individual decision makers in the bidding firm are infected by overweening pride and arrogance (hubris) and thus persist in a belief that their own valuation of the target is correct, despite objective information that the targets true economic value is lower".[173] The result of the hubris theory is a significant increase in the market value of the target company and a value reduction for the acquirer.[174] Since it is likely that on average the information asymmetry between a foreign acquirer and a domestic target is greater than in domestic transactions, the hubris hypothesis may be of even higher relevance in the context of cross-border acquisitions.[175]

Overall, acquisition activity might be driven simultaneously by several of the aforementioned exogenous factors and endogenous motives.[176] In addition, the importance of individual motives may change over time,[177] but the creation of shareholder value should be deemed the prevailing goal for pursuing transactions. Hence, management-related motives should rather be used as an explanation why transactions did not create value for acquirer shareholders.[178]

2.3.4 Special considerations for cross-border transactions

According to the theory of foreign direct investment ("FDI"),[179] cross-border acquisitions are motivated by the same strategic considerations and potential benefits that drive other forms of

---

172 See ROLL (1986), p. 212.

173 ROLL (1986), p. 212. In the context of the hubris theory the "winner's curse" phenomenon is frequently cited, which assumes that acquirers engaging in a competitive auction for a target typically overestimate the value of the target and accordingly pay too much, even if there were potential synergy gains; see for example GAUGHAN (1999), p. 160.

174 See ROLL (1986), p. 213. BLACK (1989) gives a similar explanation in his overpayment hypothesis, by postulating that managers overpay for targets because they are overly optimistic and because their interests diverge from those of their shareholders.

175 See SETH ET AL. (2000), p. 391.

176 Several authors highlight this complexity with regard to the motives for acquisitions, for example BÜHNER (1991), p. 5; ROLL (1988), p. 243; RAVENSCRAFT and SCHERER (1987), p. 3. An empirical study of 260 transactions by U.S. Fortune 500 companies in 1999 cites the expansion of the core business, the realization of synergies, the purchase of new technologies, the enhancement of competition, and the realization of tax benefits as the most important motivations for corporate takeovers, see HABECK ET AL. (1999).

177 For example, GRINBLATT and TITMAN (2002) characterize the 1960s and 1970s as a period of conglomerate acquisitions primarily motivated by financial synergies, the 1980s as one of financial acquisitions motivated by potential tax benefits and incentive improvements, and the 1990s as a period in which strategic acquisitions aiming at operating synergies became increasingly important.

178 See BEITEL (2002), p. 30.

179 The literature offers a broad range of theoretical explanations for the occurrence of direct investments in foreign countries. For an overview of the various theories refer to for example DÖRR (2000); GLAUM (1996); ERRAMILLI and D'SOUZA (1993); STEIN (1992); COLBERG (1989). DÖRR (2000, p. 26) groups those theories into the (i) product cycle hypothesis by VERNON (1966), (ii) oligopolistic reaction hypothesis by KNICKERBOCKER (1973), (iii) monopolistic theory by HYMER (1976) and KINDLEBERGER (1969), (iv) internalization hypothesis by WILLIAMSON (1973), which is essentially derived from the transaction cost approach, and the (v) eclectic approach by DUNNING (1977).

entering a foreign geographic market, i.e. greenfield investments, strategic alliances and joint ventures.[180] Such motives are either to exploit the company's competitive advantages in order to take advantage of imperfections and asymmetries in the international factor and capital markets,[181] or to explore necessary strategic resources and knowledge.[182] The traditional FDI theory suggests that cross-border acquisitions allow acquiring companies to obtain monopolistic rents from exploiting their specialized resources, such as technical and managerial know-how.[183] If the market for these specialized resources is inefficient, cross-border acquisitions enable a company to internalize these market imperfections by transferring their valuable assets abroad.[184] Compared to domestic acquisitions, this international use of resources and capabilities generates more synergy gains, resulting in turn in a higher value of the acquirer.

Together with the exploitation of its firm-specific resources, cross-border transactions can be prompted by the desire of the acquirer to diversify internationally. For example, due to non-synchronous business cycles, corporate earnings are likely to be less correlated across countries than within a country, so a company can stabilize its earnings more effectively by acquiring a foreign rather than a domestic target.[185] Cross-border transactions may also be the preferred option to achieve growth if a company reaches its demand capacity in its domestic market or has strict national regulations for domestic acquisitions.[186] Moreover, cross-border acquisitions have been associated with helping acquiring companies overcome traditional trade and investments barriers more quickly than other forms of FDI.[187]

In addition to imperfections in the factor markets, informational asymmetries and structural barriers in the international capital markets can motivate cross-border transactions.[188] By having operations in multiple international locations, an acquirer may be able to raise capital in a low-cost location[189] or to arbitrage institutional restrictions such as tax codes.[190] Since

---

180 See EUN ET AL. (1996), p. 1562. For a discussion of theoretical perspectives on cross-border acquisitions as an entry mode, analyzing country-, firm-, and industry-level factors influencing the choice of a mode of entry, see SHIMIZU ET AL. (2004), p. 319ff. The various forms of FDI can primarily be differentiated by their degree of control, systematic risk, level of resource commitment, and speed of entering the foreign market, with cross-border acquisitions being the main form, see UNCTAD (2000).

181 See HARRIS and RAVENSCRAFT (1991), p. 826.

182 See SETH ET AL. (2000). This stream of research essentially transfers the knowledge-based view to transactions involving foreign countries.

183 EUN ET AL. (1996) and CEBENOYAN ET AL. (1991) provide empirical evidence that for example research and development intensity is related to the observed gains from cross-border acquisitions; CAKICI ET AL. (1996) and HARRIS and RAVENSCRAFT (1991) do not find such a significant relation.

184 See MORCK and YEUNG (1992), p. 41; HARRIS and RAVENSCRAFT (1991), p. 826. This explanation is essentially derived from the transaction cost approach, see DÖRR (2000), pp. 35-40.

185 See EUN ET AL. (1996), p. 1563.

186 See SETH ET AL. (2000), p. 389.

187 See ROOT (1987).

188 See ERRUNZA and SENBET (1981), p. 84.

189 The assumption of an advantage in raising capital implies that capital markets are not perfectly integrated, see BODNAR ET AL. (2002), p. 5.

the net wealth of a cross-border acquirer relative to a domestic acquirer varies with the real exchange rate, international acquirers may also benefit from favorable changes in their currency versus that of their target company.[191]

Finally, international corporate diversification can be attributable to preferences of the shareholders, given that it may provide the benefits of an internationally diversified portfolio that may not be fully realizable or cost-beneficial by the investors on their own.[192] If these investors are willing to pay a premium for shares in cross-border acquirers, this will in turn increase the value of the internationally diversified company compared to that of a domestic one.[193]

The endogenous motives of companies for pursuing transactions are closely correlated to changes in the general conditions of their economic, political, and technological environment.[194] Such changes frequently generate economic booms, which are accompanied by buoyant capital markets and a high level of M&A activity. The following section presents the global and German transaction activity during the period 1990 to 2004 as well as the specific influences of the economic environment during that time.

2.4 Mergers and acquisitions activity in the period 1990 to 2004

2.4.1 Global mergers and acquisitions

2.4.1.1 Volume of transactions

Worldwide M&A activity substantially increased during the 1990s, as illustrated in Figure 2.7. The period including the years from 1993 to 2000 is labeled "the fifth M&A wave" and is characterized by a high number of "mega-deals", i.e. transactions with a volume

---

190 See SCHOLES and WOLFSON (1992). For example, differences in international taxation offer the acquirer the ability to transfer profits within its corporate group to locations where they are tax advantaged, thereby reducing the company's total tax liability and enhancing its cash flow.

191 See KUIPERS ET AL. (2003), p. 13. The authors provide an overview of inconclusive findings in the empirical literature supporting this theory.

192 See KIYMAZ and MUKHERJEE (2000), p. 38.

193 See BODNAR ET AL. (2003), p. 6.

194 See UNCTAD (2000), p. 144f.

of at least $1b.[195] The takeover of *Mannesmann AG* by *Vodafone PLC* in 1999 with a record value of $182b, and the $165b merger of *AOL-Time Warner Inc.* in 2000 were the most noticeable mega-deals during this period.[196] Compared to transactions in the 1980s, the fifth merger wave was characterized by a decline of diversifying transactions, an increased use of shares as the form of payment, and a fairly low number of hostile bids.[197] The M&A activity reached a record regarding the number of transactions in 2000, but regarding the total transaction volume in 1999, in which the total deal volume was almost 10 times higher than in 1991. Industries experiencing the highest level of acquisition activity were the energy, financial services, telecommunications, healthcare, and media sectors.[198]

Figure 2.7: Worldwide M&A activity in the period 1990 to 2004 [199]

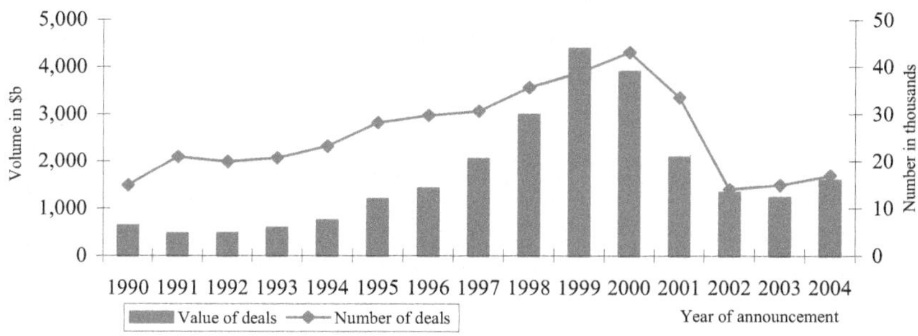

Along with the sharp decline of worldwide stock markets and the burst of the "internet-bubble", compared to 2000 the total volume of announced deals reduced in 2001 by 41

195 See JANSEN (2001), pp. 70-72. Although transactions occur every year, there were significant accumulations of M&A activity in the past, so-called "waves". Over the course of the 20th century five such waves were observed, which differ with regard to the prevailing strategic direction of the transaction and the underlying motives. The first episode of intense M&A activity occurred at the turn of the 20th century in light of the industrial revolution and was marked by the creation of large monopolistic companies (see LAMOUREAUX (1985), Section 1). The second wave occurred between 1916 and 1929 primarily between companies aiming at vertical integration, given that increasing anti-trust regulations impeded horizontal combinations (see KLEINERT and KLODT (2002), p. 29). During the third wave from 1965 to 1969 transactions were mainly motivated by the pursuit to diversify (see BACHMANN (2001), p. 2f.). The fourth merger wave in the late 1980s is widely viewed as a reaction to the creation of conglomerate corporate groups in the previous wave, which appeared to be difficult to effectively manage and which seemed to generate a comparably lower return on investment than companies focusing on their core business (see CARROLL (2002), p. 27; HITT ET AL. (2001), p. 6). As a result, significant restructurings of widely diversified groups occurred, often initiated by corporate raiders through hostile and highly leveraged takeovers (see SCHERER and ROSS (1990), p. 159). In deviation to the first three ones, the fourth wave not only impacted the U.S., but also the European market for corporate control. Each of these waves essentially coincided with a period of buoyant capital markets. An overview of various definitions of prior merger waves is given by KUMMER (2005), pp. 134-145.

196 See KLEINERT and KLODT (2000), pp. 46-50; KUHNER (2000), p. 333.

197 See ANDRADE ET AL. (2001), p. 109.

198 See CARROLL (2002), p. 35f.

199 Source: Thomson Financial Securities Data Company.

percent. In light of the terror attacks on New York and Washington on September 11, 2001, the war in Iraq, the outbreak of SARS, and the accompanying downshift in the global economy, this development continued in 2002 and 2003, in which M&A activity fell to levels not seen since 1997.[200] The decline particularly affected the occurrence of mega-deals, as the use of shares to pay for acquisitions was less advantageous. The level of cash transactions declined as well due to the steep deterioration of corporate earnings and the generally higher level of precaution by companies in approaching transactions.[201] Beginning in 2004, with an overall improved economic environment and increasing M&A activity by private equity companies, the worldwide transaction volume bounced back.[202]

In deviation to previous merger waves, during the 1990s worldwide cross-border M&A activity significantly increased alongside the boom in domestic transactions.[203] The volume of cross-border acquisitions grew in 2000 compared to 1991 from approximately 20 percent to over 30 percent of global M&A volume, rising steadily from about 0.5 percent of world wide gross domestic product in the mid-1980s to over 2 percent in 2000.[204] Cross-border transactions now account for more than 80 percent of all foreign direct investment by industrialized countries.[205] U.S. companies were the most active cross-border acquirers as well as the most predominant cross-border targets.[206] For example, in 1999 foreign acquirers carried out more than a quarter of all transactions in the U.S., compared to only 7 percent in 1997.[207]

The high level of global M&A activity during the period 1990 to 2004 was stimulated by various exogenous influences of the business environment, predominantly changes in the regulatory environment, technological developments, continuous globalization and competition, and increased opportunities and demands of the global capital markets.[208] All of these factors, which are briefly discussed in the following section, led to a decade of relatively high economic growth.

---

200 See WIRTZ (2003), p. 90f.
201 See SIDEL (2002), R10.
202 See KPMG (2004b), noting that acquisitions by private equity firms accounted for 11 percent of global transaction volume in 2004.
203 See BERTRAND ET AL. (2004), p. 3.
204 See UNCTAD (2000), p. 106f.
205 See CONN ET AL. (2005), p. 816.
206 Compared to transactions by European acquirers, the average size of cross-border acquisitions by U.S. acquirers was significantly lower though, due to a higher number of mega-deals involving a U.S. target, such as the $65.6b purchase of *AirTouch Communications* by *Vodafone PLC*; based on data obtained from Thomson Financial Securities Data Company.
207 See UNCTAD (2000), p. 118.
208 See for example ESCHEN (2002), p. 205.

2.4.1.2 Exogenous influences of the business environment

By removing trade restrictions such as compulsory joint venture and non-foreign majority ownership requirements, countries increasingly attracted direct investment.[209] At the same time the international regulatory framework had also been strengthened, mainly through bilateral agreements, such as investment protection guarantees and double taxation treaties.[210] Corresponding with the trade liberalization process, widespread privatization and deregulation programs boosted transaction activity, most notably in the telecommunications, transportation, energy,[211] and financial services industries[212]. Many countries increased the availability of domestic target companies by allowing for private ownership, thereby diluting the concentration of existing industry structures. Facing new competitive pressures at home, previously state-owned companies responded to this changing environment by becoming international acquirers.[213] Deeming deregulation the most dominant factor in explaining the volume of recent merger activities, ANDRADE ET AL. (2001) labeled the 1990s "the decade of deregulation", given that acquisitions in deregulated industries accounted for almost 50 percent of the total transaction volume in the 1990s.[214]

As the costs of technological innovation rose in most industries due to the increased pace of advances of information and communication technologies,[215] companies were prompted to pursue acquisitions as a way of sharing those costs and of accessing new technologies to maintain their competitive advantages.[216] At the same time, an increasingly global technological interrelatedness significantly lowered information-access and communication costs, which allowed management systems to be applied more effectively internationally.[217] In addition to the technology sector, industries mainly affected by the implications of technological progress in the last decade were the financial services[218] and pharmaceutical sectors.[219]

---

209 See CANTWELL and SANTANGELO (2002), p. 411.

210 See UNCTAD (2000), p. 144. In contrast, some countries have implemented additional instruments to more thoroughly screen cross-border M&As for national security considerations. For a discussion of such an instrument in the U.S. environment see Section 3.7.3.

211 For example in the energy sector with the passing of Directive 96/92/EC and Directive 98/30/EC in the EU and the Energy Policy Act in 1992 in the United States, see FREYTAG ET AL. (2005), p. 5.

212 BERGER ET AL. (1999) provide a comprehensive analytic narrative of current research on the consolidation of the financial services industry. For the European banking sector see BEITEL (2002), p. 52f.

213 UNCTAD (2000), p. 152.

214 ANDRADE ET AL. (2001, p. 108) show how transactions in each merger wave strongly clustered by various industries, concluding that a significant portion of M&A activity might be attributable to "industry-level shocks", such as deregulation.

215 See UNCTAD (2000), p. 144f. Examples for those developments are the enhancement of computer technology and the introduction of the Internet.

216 See UNCTAD (2000), p. 145.

217 See ZIESCHANG (2000), p. 29.

218 See BEITEL (2002), p. 50f.

219 For the pharmaceutical industry, acquisitions offered a means to cope with the increasing costs for the research and development of new products, see CANTWELL and SANTANGELO (2002), p. 411.

Deregulation and technological progress also created new opportunities for companies to efficiently access new markets, which precipitated widespread industrial globalization and increasing competition.[220] In such an environment, mergers and acquisitions provided a significant means for achieving synergistic gains or maintaining and expanding market power. As a result, industries such as financial services, automotive, chemicals, and pharmaceuticals had experienced so-called "industry shocks", in which increasing transaction volume provoked a higher industrial concentration.[221]

The buoyant conditions of the global capital markets in the 1990s, with rising share prices and ample liquidity, facilitated M&A activity as well, since they enabled companies to deploy alternative methods of raising capital internationally to finance acquisitions.[222] While bank loans still provided the main funds for transactions, direct financing by issuing common stocks and corporate bonds became increasingly important during this period.[223] As a result of high stock valuations, especially exchange offers contributed to the series of domestic and cross-border mega-deals during the 1990s.[224] Simultaneously, companies were under increased pressure from the capital markets to reduce operating costs and to continuously grow in order to create additional shareholder value.[225] Since opportunities to grow organically in national markets were rather limited, companies increasingly sought to pursue acquisitions in foreign countries.

Another significant exogenous factor contributing to the transaction activity in the 1990s was the availability of the pooling-of-interests method for the accounting of business combinations under accounting principles generally accepted in the United States.[226] However, since 2001 that method is no longer permitted.[227]

---

220 See ANDRADE ET AL. (2001), p. 103f.

221 See HARFORD (2005), p. 559; CANTWELL and SANTANGELO (2002), p. 423; MITCHELL and MULHERIN (1996), p. 196f.

222 See BRUNER (2004a), p. 9f., who labels these conditions as the "hot-market" factor and refers to various research studies that examine a pro-cyclical correlation between high transaction activity and rising share prices.

223 See UNCTAD (2000), p. 108.

224 See BRUNER (2004a), p. 10; SHLEIFER and VISHNY (2003), p. 295f. For example, the $40.5b merger of *Daimler-Benz AG* and *Chrysler Corp.* in 1998, in which the common shareholders of *Chrysler Corp.* received 0.62 and the shareholders of *Daimler-Benz AG* received one new ordinary share of *DaimlerChrysler AG* per share held.

225 See BEITEL (2002), p. 55.

226 See GAUGHAN (1999), p. 52f. This method allowed to the simple addition of both entities, without any effects on taxation and without any resulting goodwill.

227 See FASB Statement of Financial Accounting Standards No. 141.

2.4.2 German mergers and acquisitions

2.4.2.1 Volume of transactions

The total transaction volume by German acquirers, including domestic and cross-border deals, reached its peak in 1999, but with regard to the number of transactions already in 1995 (see Figure 2.8).[228] The worldwide downturn in transaction activity also hit the German market for corporate control, despite structural changes in its economy[229] and a change in taxation for corporate divestitures.[230] The transaction volume decreased in 2001 by 61 percent compared to 2000 and, unlike the worldwide trend, did not rebound in 2004.

Figure 2.8: German M&A activity in the period 1990 to 2004 [231]

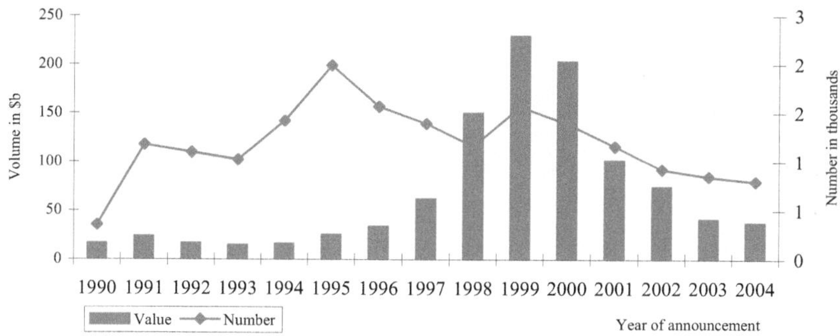

More than two-thirds of all German transactions during the observation period concerned a domestic target company, followed by cross-border acquisitions involving a European target company (see Figure 2.9). The United States was the most important single target country during this period, accounting for four percent of the total number of transactions, but due to a host of large acquisitions, 18 percent of the total transaction volume.[232] After the United Kingdom,[233] Germany was the second largest investor in the United States during the

---

228 While in this period German companies were involved in 20,003 transactions, U.S. companies were involved in 146,740 (based on data obtained from Thomson Financial Securities Data Company).

229 I.e. the unscrambling of the so-called "Germany Inc.", see KLEBNIKOV (2000), p. 162.

230 The German Tax Reduction Act 2001 introduced a number of significant changes into the German tax system including the abolition of corporate tax on capital gains from selling shares of subsidiaries, see EDWARDS ET AL. (2004). In addition, on January 1, 2002 the new German Takeover Law came into effect, which provides more transparency for transactions involving a public target, see GORDON (2002).

231 Source: Thomson Financial Securities Data Company.

232 As pointed out also by GRIESSER and SCHWINGELER (2005), p. 44.

233 The United Kingdom represented also the most significant target country for European cross-border transactions by U.S. companies, mainly as a result of U.S. corporations regarding the United Kingdom with its long history of takeover activity as the best entry for an expansion into Europe, see YATES (2002). German companies accounted for the second highest European M&A activity by U.S. companies, according to data obtained from Thomson Financial Securities Data Company.

1990s.[234] This volume of U.S. transactions reflects the critical importance of the United States for German companies for their strategic goal of becoming a global player.[235] Such a U.S. "imperative"[236] is attributable to the sheer size and strong economic growth of the U.S. economy. The Unites States, currently and at the time the most important consumer market, offers especially large German companies better international growth opportunities than the more mature markets in Europe.[237] Compared to greenfield investments, acquisitions offer a faster means to enter the U.S. market or to enlarge the market presence.[238]

Figure 2.9: German M&A activity in the period 1990 to 2004 by region [239]

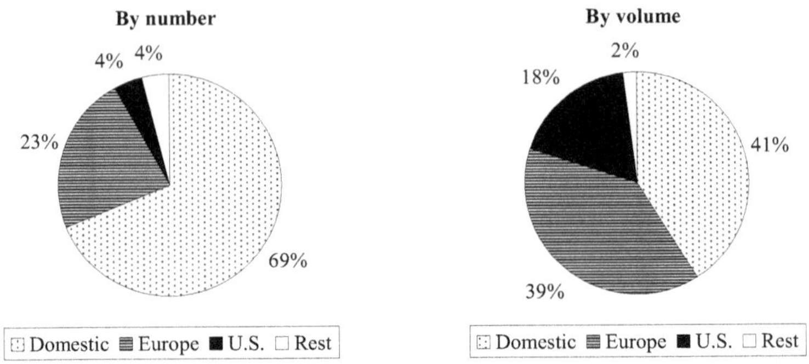

2.4.2.2 Transactions in the United States

According to Thomson Financial Securities Data Company, 737 transactions involving a German acquirer and a U.S. target company occurred in the period 1990 to 2004, with the majority taking place in the years 1998 to 2000 (see Figure 2.10).

The total transaction volume was $154b, although it should be noted that volume data was only available from Thomson Financial Securities Data Company for less than one-third of the U.S. cross-border transactions. German transaction volume reached its peak in the United States alongside the *Daimler-Chrysler* merger in 1998, in which U.S. transactions involving a U.S. target accounted for almost 30% of the total M&A volume of German companies. Analogous to the worldwide M&A activity, most transactions took place in 2000.

234 See HAMILTON and QUINLAN (2005), p. 25.
235 See HAMILTON and QUINLAN (2005), p. 25.
236 WIEANDT and SANTIAGO (2005), p. 86.
237 See GRIESSER and SCHWINGELER (2005), p. 47.
238 See STEINEBACH ET AL. (2005), p. 108.
239 Source: Thomson Financial Securities Data Company.

Figure 2.10: German M&A activity in the United States in the period 1990 to 2004 [240]

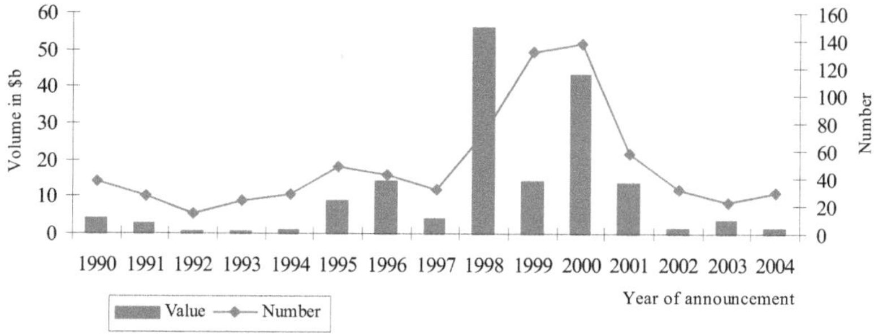

The sharp decrease in worldwide M&A activity also affected the level of U.S. transactions during the period from 2001 to 2003. For example, in 2002 four of the five largest U.S. transactions by German companies did not involve an industrial target, but concerned real estate investments. That development was a reflection of increasing concerns of German companies regarding the implications of the terrorist attacks in 2001, the slow economic growth of the U.S. gross domestic product, and an overall negative bias as a result of presumed failures of prominent transactions such as the *Daimler-Chrysler* merger.[241] In light of a recovered and strong U.S. economy, beginning with the second half of 2004 the number of U.S. cross-border acquisitions by German companies increased again. Recent announcements in 2005, such as of the acquisition of *Reebok Inc.* by *Adidas-Salomon AG*, *Renal Care Group* by *Fresenius Medical Care AG*, and *Genus Inc.* by *Aixtron AG*, confirm this trend.[242]

As a result of numerous mega-deals mainly during the years from 1998 to 2000, U.S. cross-border transactions are marked by a higher average transaction volume compared to German domestic transactions. While domestic transactions yielded an average volume of $30m during that period, U.S. cross-border acquisitions averaged $209m.[243] Table 2.3 displays all German mega-deals in the United States during the period 1990 to 2004.

240 Source: Thomson Financial Securities Data Company.

241 See GRIESSER and SCHWINGELER (2005), p. 46.

242 See DAMS and SEINBEL (2006). GRIESSER and SCHWINGELER (2005, p. 47) cite as another factor stimulating acquisitions of U.S. targets the prospect of favorable returns for acquirers, given that compared to 2000 the Price/Earnings ratio of U.S. Standard & Poor's 500 companies decreased from approximately 26x to around 18x in 2004.

243 Source: Thomson Financial Securities Data Company.

Table 2.3: German mega-deals in the United States from 1990 to 2004 [244]

Year	Target company	Acquiring company	Value $m
1998	*Chrysler Corp.*	*Daimler-Benz AG*	40,466
2000	*VoiceStream Wireless Corp.*	*Deutsche Telekom AG*	29,404
1998	*Bankers Trust New York Corp.*	*Deutsche Bank AG*	9,082
2001	*American Water Works Co Inc*	*RWE AG*	7,726
1995	*Marion Merrell Dow Inc*	*Hoechst AG*	7,265
1996	*National Medical Care Inc*	*Fresenius AG*	4,236
1996	*American Re-Insurance Company*	*Münchener Rückversicherungs AG*	3,968
2000	*American Cyanamid Agri Product*	*BASF AG*	3,900
1990	*Fireman's Fund Insurance Co.*	*Allianz AG*	3,100
2003	*Dial Corp.*	*Henkel KGaA*	2,914
2001	*Zurich Scudder Investments Inc*	*Deutsche Bank AG*	2,500
1999	*Lyondell Chemical-Poly. Business*	*Bayer AG*	2,450
2000	*Nicholas-Applegate Capt Mgmt*	*Allianz AG*	2,220
2000	*Shared Medical Systems*	*Siemens AG*	2,060
1999	*PIMCO Advisors Holdings LP*	*Allianz AG*	1,930
1997	*Westinghouse Power Generation*	*Siemens AG*	1,525
1996	*AlliedSignal Auto-Braking Business*	*Robert Bosch GmbH*	1,500
1998	*Random House Inc.*	*Bertelsmann AG*	1,300
2001	*Sky Chefs Inc.*	*Deutsche Lufthansa AG*	1,300
1996	*Loctite Corp.*	*Henkel KGaA*	1,289
2000	*Wasserstein Perella Group Inc.*	*Dresdner Bank AG*	1,255
2003	*Airborne Inc*	*Deutsche Post AG*	1,200
1998	*Chiron Diagnostics Corp*	*Bayer AG*	1,100
1998	*Dover Corp-Elevator Business*	*ThyssenKrupp AG*	1,100
1999	*Cyprus Amax-US Coal Mining*	*RAG Aktiengesellschaft*	1,100
2000	*Air Express International*	*Deutsche Post AG*	1,100
1999	*Lone Star Industries Inc.*	*Dyckerhoff AG*	1,075
1991	*GTE Electrical Prods-Sylvania*	*Siemens AG*	1,000

The most active acquiring companies during the years from 1990 to 2004 are displayed in Table 2.4. Public companies listed in the prime German stock index DAX30[245] accounted for almost one quarter of all transactions.[246]

[244] Source: Thomson Financial Securities Data Company.
[245] The DAX30 is the stock index on the Frankfurt Stock Exchange that comprises the 30 largest and most liquid shares traded on the exchange.
[246] Source: Thomson Financial Securities Data Company.

Table 2.4: Most active German acquirers of U.S. targets in the period 1990 to 2004[247]

Name of corporation	**Number of transactions**
Siemens AG	20
Bayer AG	15
Bertelsmann AG	11
Robert Bosch GmbH	11
DaimlerChrysler AG	11
Deutsche Bank AG	11
BASF AG	10

The following example transactions illustrate the pressure for German companies to engage in M&A activity in the United States, in light of the increased global competition and deregulation tendencies in various industries:

- As an answer to strategic challenges such as small influence in an increasingly consolidated market, limited growth potential in the mature European markets, and disadvantages in the amortization of research and developments costs due to its small volume base, *Daimler-Benz AG,* at that time only the 15th largest vehicle manufacturer, merged in 1998 with *Chrysler Corp.* to create one of the world's largest automobile manufacturers.[248]
- WIEANDT and SANTIAGO (2005) laid out the challenges *Deutsche Bank* faced within the financial services sector: "It was increasingly apparent that a strong presence in the U.S. was a strategic imperative for global universal banks. By the end of the 1990s, the U.S. market had undergone significant deregulation and liberalization ... Thinking global requires thinking U.S. with North America accounting for about one third of global financial services revenue pools."[249] *Deutsche Bank AG* responded to the increasing global demands by creating a transatlantic platform for its corporate banking and asset management divisions through the acquisitions of *Bankers Trust New York Corp.* in 1998, *National Discount Brokers Group* in 2000, and *Zurich Scudder Investments* in 2001. As a result, businesses in the Americas region accounted in 2004 for more than one-quarter of *Deutsche Bank AG*'s total revenue.[250]
- In another example for transactions in the financial services sector, *Münchner Rückversicherungs AG* acquired *American Re-Insurance Company* in 1996 in order to globally spread the increasing risks facing the reinsurance industry.
- *Siemens AG* spent nearly $12b in the United States on transactions in various sectors during the period from 1990 to 2004, among other reasons to gain leverage against its

247 Source: Thomson Financial Securities Data Company.
248 See GRUBE (2005), p. 59f.
249 WIEANDT and SANTIAGO (2005), p. 86f.
250 See WIEANDT and SANTIAGO (2005), p. 96.

principal competitor *General Electric* in its local U.S. market.[251] The $1.5b acquisition of *Westinghouse Power Generation* in 1998 reflects how deregulation and consolidation created pressure for *Siemens AG* in the utilities industry, as pointed out by LUCKS (2005c): "The U.S. has always been one of the most important regional markets for power plants. Without a significant presence there, no company has a chance of surviving over the long term".[252]

- As a reaction to the worldwide deregulation of national monopolies in the telecommunication industry, *Deutsche Telekom AG* enhanced its global market position in 2001 through the acquisition of *VoiceStream Wireless Corp.* With a total volume of $29.4b, this acquisition marked the second biggest transaction by a German company in the United States.[253]
- The acquisitions of *Marion Merrell* in 1995 by *Hoechst AG* and *Chiron Diagnostics* and *American Cyanamid Agricultural Products* by *Bayer AG* demonstrate how companies in the chemical industry adapted to the challenges brought upon by increasing costs and risks of research and development activities.[254]
- In the consumer industry, the $2.9b acquisition of *Dial Corporation* in 2004 served for *Henkel KGaA* as a platform to establish its personal care business in the United States, which besides aiming at regional diversification was necessary to secure *Henkel KGaA*'s business relationships with major U.S. retail chains. Given its prior limited market share and product breadth, the company deemed its position vulnerable and decided it needed to expand in the United States.[255]
- *Deutsche Post* acquired *Air Express International* in 2000 for $1.1b in order to become a major player in the world's biggest logistics market, which was necessary for offering its customers a "complete one-stop-shopping solution".[256]
- *Bertelsmann AG* entered the publishing market in the United States already in the 1980s through its acquisitions of *Bantam Books* and *Doubleday*. The 1998 acquisition of the premier consumer-book publisher in the United States, *Random House Inc.*, instantly made *Bertelsmann AG* the worldwide biggest publisher of English-language books.[257] This meant that the United States now accounts for more than a third of *Bertelsmann*'s revenue.[258]

---

[251] See NOLAN (2005), p. 137.
[252] LUCKS (2005c), p. 146.
[253] Prior to this takeover, *Deutsche Telekom AG* entered into an alliance with *France Telekom* in order to acquire *Sprint Corp.*, but that transaction fell through.
[254] See KLEINWORT (2000), p. 3; TZERMIAS (1995), p. 27.
[255] See STEINEBACH ET AL. (2005), p. 97.
[256] ZUMWINCKEL (2005), p. 172.
[257] See STRUNCK (2003), p. 238.
[258] See STURM (1999), p. 28.

With more than 80 percent, the vast majority of U.S. transactions involved private target companies. Only two transactions were structured as a direct merger between the German acquiring company and the U.S. target,[259] which can be attributed either to a general reluctance of U.S. sellers' to exchange their shares for those of a foreign company,[260] or to the fairly low number of German companies that are listed or willing to be listed on a U.S. stock exchange.[261] Hostile takeovers occurred during the period 1990 to 2004 only in two cases, i.e. the acquisition of the remaining 62 percent interest that it did not already own in *Loctite Corp.* by *Henkel KGaA* in 1997 for a total of \$1.3b,[262] and the acquisition of *Detection Systems Inc.* by *Robert Bosch GmbH* in 2001 for a total value of \$117.5m.[263]

Following the analysis of general endogenous motives and specific exogenous factors stimulating domestic and cross-border M&A activity in the observation period, the goal of the next section is to present the various phases of a standardized acquisition process.

2.5 Phases of the mergers and acquisitions process

2.5.1 Structure of a standardized acquisition process

From the perspective of the acquiring company, the literature offers various structures of a typical acquisition process that differ with regard to the number of individual phases and their denomination. The most common approach is to divide the process of managing a friendly transaction[264] into the three phases (i) strategic analysis and conception, (ii) acquisition structuring and management, and (iii) post-closing integration.[265] This standardized structure as shown in Table 2.5 is adopted for the purpose of this study. Since certain steps and activities of these interdependent phases overlap with no explicit beginning or ending, this structure does not necessarily render the chronological order of the process.[266]

Starting point of the acquisition process is formulating a stringent corporate strategy. If achieving the strategic goals requires external growth, an acquisition strategy is developed to lay out the framework for the transaction and to give the required criteria for screening

---

259 These are the *Daimler-Chrysler* merger in 1998 and the *CE Computer Equipment AG-Treev Inc.* merger in 2001. The mechanics of the *Daimler-Chrysler* merger are discussed in more detail in Section 3.2.3.4.

260 See CONN ET AL. (2005), p. 823.

261 An overview of German companies listed on a U.S. stock exchange as of December 31, 2004, is given in Section 3.2.3.4.

262 See ALTHAUS (1996), p. 27.

263 Source Thomson Financial Securities Data Company. In the same period, *BERU AG* withdrew its unsolicited bid to acquire all the outstanding common stock of *IMPCO Technologies Inc.*, via a tender offer for \$14 in cash per share, or a total value of \$124.7m.

264 For a hostile transaction or in an auction the transaction process is often shaped by external advisors, e.g. investment banks, which might alter the presented structure, see PICOT (2002), p. 25.

265 See RICHTER (2005), p. 202ff.; WIRTZ (2003), p. 107; VOGEL (2002), p. 113; JANSEN (2001), p. 164. The following presentation excludes a discussion of the interaction of communication and culture during those stages, which is given for example by BERK (1996).

266 See VOGEL (2002), p. 113.

potential target companies. During the acquisition structuring and management phase, the value analysis of the target, i.e. the due diligence and the pricing, is conducted simultaneously with the negotiation and documentation of the acquisition. The integration phase begins upon closing the transaction and includes the implementation of integration measures and a post-acquisition controlling, i.e. the assessment whether the strategic and operational goals of the transaction were achieved.

Table 2.5: Structure of a standardized acquisition process[267]

Phase	Strategic analysis and conception	Acquisition structuring and management	Post-closing integration
Main focus	• Determination of the acquisition concept	• Execution and consummation of the transaction	• Implementation of integration measures
Steps and activities	• Formulation of corporate and business-unit strategy • Identification of strategic gaps • Determination of growth strategy through acquisitions and definition of acquisition objectives • Preparation of target profile, screening, and selection the acquisition	• Pre-signing - Confidentiality agreement - Letter of intent - Due diligence - Memorandum of understanding - Initial negotiations • Pricing: Valuation of target and assessment of financing options • Signing and Closing - Draft of acquisition agreement - Assessment of antitrust considerations and securities laws - Final offer - Negotiation of details (warranties, indemnifications etc.) - Signing and Closing	• Integration conception: analysis and planning of integration potential • Implementation of organizational, strategic, administrative, operative, and cultural integration measures • Integration controlling (post-acquisition audit)

Following is a brief discussion of the various steps and activities of these phases. With regard to this study's goal to analyze the specific considerations for the acquisition structuring and management phase and their potential implications for the success of a U.S. transaction by a foreign acquirer, the strategic analysis and conception and the post-closing integration phases are only briefly introduced.

267 Source: presentation follows JANSEN (2001), p. 164.

2.5.2 Strategic analysis and conception phase

The strategic analysis and conception phase begins with the development of the corporate strategy, which follows the formulation of the company's overall vision and business goals and typically includes an extensive assessment of its external corporate environment, resources, and competitive position.[268] The analysis of the company's business environment is followed by an analysis of its internal strengths, weaknesses, opportunities, and threats,[269] which may reveal a strategic gap that prevents the company from realizing its pre-defined business goals.[270] Hence, the main focus of the strategic analysis and conception phase is to determine whether amongst a range of possible alternatives, an external growth through an acquisition is the most suitable one to fill such gaps.[271] Compared to internal measures, external acquisitions typically offer a faster vehicle to achieve strategic growth goals.[272] The determination of an external growth strategy provides the framework for formulating the objectives for the acquisition, which serve as a basis for the determination of profiling and screening criteria for potential targets (so-called "qualifying criteria").[273] The screening process begins with the compilation of a broad range of potential candidates (so-called "long list") which seem to generally suit the acquirer's acquisition strategy.[274] Based on available information about the potential targets and frequently with the help of external advisors, the list is then subsequently reduced to a "short list" that includes only one or two targets that appear to fit best from a strategic,[275] organizational,[276] financial, and cultural[277] perspective to the acquirer's strategy.[278] Due to confidentiality reasons, an adviser often makes the initial contact with the potential target. If the potential target is interested in the transaction, both parties enter into the acquisition structuring and management phase.[279]

---

268 See WIRTZ (2003), p. 108; CULLINAN and HOLLAND (2002), p. 17f.; KERLER (2000), p. 235; GOMEZ and WEBER (1989), p. 40; MÖLLER (1983), p. 130.

269 See BRUNER (2004a), p. 123. There are numerous tools to conduct such an analysis, for example via the growth-share matrix by the Boston Consulting Group, the Porter Model, and the learning curve. For a discussion of these measures refer to for example BRUNER (2004a), p. 130f.; STORCK (1993), p. 71ff.

270 See PAUSENBERGER (1989), p. 621; LUTZ (1984), p. 121.

271 See HOHNHAUS (2004), p. 53; WIRTZ (2003), p. 108. Other alternatives besides the "buy" decision for a company are to "make" the desired resources or products on its own or to enter into a strategic cooperation with a partner, see for example KOLBE (1993), p. 189. Possible criteria to choose among these alternatives are for example time, costs, and operational and integration risks, see GOMEZ and WEBER (1989), p. 15.

272 See GOMEZ and WEBER (1989), p. 15.

273 See KRÜGER and MÜLLER-STEWENS (1994), p. 80; REIßNER (1992), p. 152.

274 See SANDLER (1991), p. 186. Possible risks and errors in screening potential targets may be that acquisitions are pursued although they should have been rejected earlier (so-called "α-error"), or that potential targets are eliminated although they would have met the acquirer's strategic goals (so-called "β-error"), see BERENS ET AL. (2005), p. 54.

275 Strategic fit is defined as "... the degree to which the target firm augments or complements the parent's strategy and thus makes identifiable contributions to the financial and nonfinancial goals of the parent", JEMISON and SITKIN (1986), p. 146f.

276 "Organization fit is defined as the match between administrative practices, cultural practices, and personnel characteristics of the target and parent firms and may directly affect how the firms can be integrated with respect to day-to-day operations", JEMISON and SITKIN (1986), p. 147.

277 See WEBER ET AL. (1996), p. 1215f.; NAHAVANDI and MALEKZADEH (1988), p. 79f.

278 See WIRTZ (2003), p. 172.; JUNG (1993), p. 163.

279 See HOHNHAUS (2004), p. 59.

2.5.3 Acquisition structuring and management phase

The acquisition structuring and management phase, or acquisition execution phase, comprises the span after the initial contact with the target to the closing and consummation of the deal, i.e. the actual "deal making". It primarily involves the three steps (i) pre-signing, (ii) valuation, and (iii) signing and closing, with especially the valuation overlapping with the other steps of this phase.[280] The course of the negotiations as well as scope and content of the documentation typically vary between transactions.

2.5.3.1 Pre-signing

The main purpose of the pre-signing phase is for the acquirer and the target to obtain more information from each other in order to reduce the information asymmetry between them. At the same time, potential ranges for the purchase price are assessed and broad representations and warranties are laid out.[281] The pre-signing phase comprises generally signing of a confidentiality agreement and a letter of intent, conducting a due diligence, and quite often the preparation of a memorandum of understanding.

Especially in cases where the acquirer initiates the transaction, the seller is typically only willing to provide the acquirer with more sensitive information about the target company after the acquirer executes a confidentiality agreement. Such an agreement, which is also referred to as a "non-disclosure agreement", is intended to protect the information exchanged during the negotiations and in the course of a due diligence. Confidentiality provisions are often incorporated into a letter of intent ("LOI").[282] The LOI suggests the principal terms of the transaction and usually sets forth at a minimum key provisions regarding

- the form of the acquisition, the preliminary purchase price or the method for determining it, and the form and terms of payment,
- other general transaction features, such as tax and accounting considerations,
- the extent to which the seller is obligated to give the acquiring company comprehensive access to its business for the purpose of conducting a due diligence, and
- an agreement on a payment if the transaction is not consummated (so-called "break-up fee").[283]

---

280 See MIDDELMANN and HELMES (2005), p. 655.
281 See JANSEN (2001), pp. 179-188.
282 See REED and LAJOUX (1999), p. 447.
283 See GOMEZ and WEBER (1989), p. 70.

The LOI is usually executed after the acquirer has completed its basic assessment of the target company, i.e. the due diligence.[284] The term "due diligence" originates from U.S. securities law[285] and, in the context of acquisitions, denotes the systematic and detailed analysis of the target company.[286] The due diligence represents the cornerstone of the acquisition management phase.[287] Its main focuses are to (i) verify the potential of realizing the company's strategic goals with the target, (ii) identify and evaluate potential risks and weaknesses of the target, so-called "deal breakers",[288] (iii) obtain information needed for the structuring of the transaction and the preparation of the definitive acquisition agreement, especially with regard to its representations and warranties, and (iv) gather information for the valuation and subsequent price negotiations.[289] The due diligence efforts typically include a presentation by the target's management, the review of information provided in a "data room", question and answer sessions, and visits to the target's operations sites.[290] Besides financial aspects, due diligence encompasses the legal, tax, environmental, human resources, marketing (or commercial), organizational and information technology, and cultural aspects of the target company. Table 2.6 displays the main goals and focus areas of these due diligence subjects, which are mainly interdependent.[291]

The main conclusions as well as open issues from the financial, legal, and tax due diligence are often summarized in a memorandum of understanding. It is essentially similar in structure to the LOI and serves as a basis for drafting the definitive acquisition agreement.[292]

---

284 See REED and LAJOUX (1999), p. 352. The author notes that the LOI is typically executed before the acquirer carries out a substantial review of the target, thereby reducing the likelihood of incurring material expenses before both parties have reached an agreement in principle as to the basic terms of the transaction.

285 Under the Securities Act of 1933 and the Securities Exchange Act of 1934, underwriters and other professionals can be held liable for the failure to disclose risks, which a "duly diligent" researcher should have been able to uncover, see BRUNER (2004a), p. 208f.; PICOT (2002), p. 269f. A similar codification within German law is not given. MIDDELMANN and HELMES (2005, p. 657) point out that compared to Germany, within the U.S. corporate governance framework decisions by the management of a company are more transparent. For a detailed discussion of the origin of the term "due diligence" refer to BERENS and STRAUCH (2005), pp. 6-10.

286 The literature offers various definitions for the term due diligence in the context of acquisitions, an overview is given for example by KOCH and WEGMANN (2002) and SCOTT (2001).

287 See MIDDELMANN and HELMES (2005), p. 656.

288 In their empirical study, BERENS and STRAUCH (2002, p. 52) concluded that 44.6 percent of acquiring companies listed the identification of risk as the main goal of the due diligence.

289 See LUCKS and MECKL (2002), p. 163.

290 See SELLMANN and MAIER (2005), p. 199.

291 For more information about individual subjects of due diligence refer to for example BERENS ET AL. (2005); LAJOUX and NESVOLD (2004); ROSENBLOOM (2002).

292 For a description of the content of a memorandum of understanding refer to for example JANSEN (2001), p. 185f; JUNG (1993), p. 357ff. Some authors do not differentiate between the letter of intent and the memorandum of understanding, for example HACKETT and CRAIG (1999), p. 1.

Table 2.6: Subjects of due diligence[293]

Subject	Goal	Main focus areas
Financial and accounting	Analysis of current financial situation and future earnings projections	• Accounting systems and organization • Adequacy of accounting procedures • Compliance with generally accepted accounting principles • Identification of extraordinary and unusual influences on results in the past • Viability of projected future cash flows, synergy potentials, and capital expenditures
Legal	Assessment of the legal status and condition of the target	• Proper legal standing • Compliance with laws and regulations • Ownership of assets and exposure to associated liabilities • Actual or pending litigation
Tax	Analysis of the target's compliance with tax laws and regulations	• Potential tax liabilities of the target • Identification of alternative ways of doing business that might reduce taxes • Planning a tax beneficial transaction structure
Environmental	Assessment of potential risks	• Compliance with laws and regulations • Exposure to environmental liabilities • Inefficiencies in recycling or the disposal of wastes
Human resources	Assessment of potential risks and human capital	• Exposure to workforce problems, especially union issues • Inefficiencies in compensation and benefits • Exposure to benefits claims • Adequacy of talent and leadership
Marketing (Commercial)	Assessment of competitive market position and future growth potential of the target's products	• Strength of brand or franchise • Strength of marketing and sales organization • Competitive marketing and sales advantages versus competitors • Potential revenue enhancing synergies • Outlook for future performance, including verification of assumptions for projected future growth
Organization and information technology	Assessment of adequacy of organizational and IT structure and resources	• Organization of the enterprise • Adequacy of management information systems • Effectiveness of the target's IT • IT compatibility between target and acquirer • Plan for the post-merger integration of IT
Cultural and ethics	Analysis of cultural and corporate identity	• Compliance with existing policies and laws • Assessment of the management style • Management hierarchy and levels

293 Source: own presentation following VOGEL (2002), pp. 164-171.

2.5.3.2 Valuation

Following the due diligence, the acquirer determines its maximum purchase price for the target and enters into price negotiations with the sellers.[294] The choice of the valuation method and its underlying assumptions is a controversial subject not only between the acquirer and target, but also within the finance literature.[295] Figure 2.11 provides an overview of available valuation methods, distinguishing between assets- or enterprise-oriented approaches.[296]

Figure 2.11: Overview of valuation methods[297]

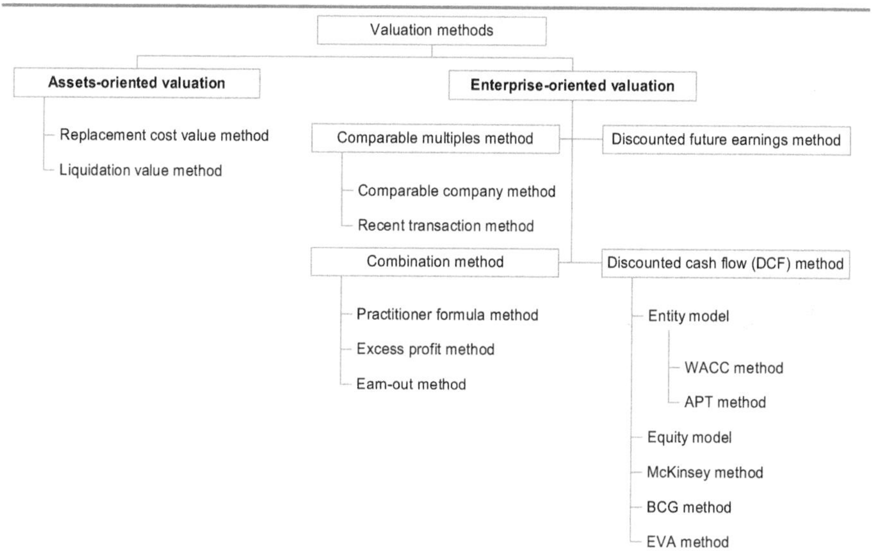

The assets-oriented approach values the target as the sum of its individual net assets, either under the assumption of a going-concern at their replacement cost[298] or at their liquidation values.[299] This approach does not consider the future earnings potential of the target, as well as certain off-balance sheet items such as human capital, image, brand, and other intangible

[294] See HÖLTERS (1992), p. 30.
[295] See TISCHENDORF (2000), p. 10.
[296] For a detailed overview of various valuation methods refer to RICHTER (2005); BRUNER (2004a); DRUKARCYZK (2003); JANSEN (2001); COPELAND ET AL. (2000). Another method not included in Figure 2.11 is the use of a real options analysis, see ERNST ET AL. (2004).
[297] Source: presentation follows JANSEN (2001), p. 194.
[298] See MOXTER (1991), p. 41f.
[299] See BORN (2003), p. 154.

assets.[300] Despite these omissions, practitioners use this method since the liquidation value generally provides the minimum price for the company.[301]

Among the enterprise-oriented valuations, the comparable multiples, discounted future earnings, and weighted-average-capital-cost-based discounted cash flow methods are most frequently used amongst practitioners. The comparable multiples method calculates the target's value as the product of (i) either a revenue- or profit-based reference figure of the target and (ii) a respective multiple that is either derived from peer companies or comparable prior transactions.[302] Unlike the previous approach, the discounted future earnings and discounted cash flow methods aim to calculate a fundamental valuation of the target.[303] The discounted future earnings method uses accounting-based projections and a risk-adjusted rate in the calculation of the present value of the target's future earnings.[304] In contrast, the discounted cash flow method focuses on the projection of future free cash flows and predominantly uses a weighted-average-capital-cost-based discount rate to derive the target's enterprise value.[305] The free cash flow is defined as "the total after-tax cash flow generated by the company that is available to all providers of the company's capital, both creditors and shareholders",[306] and is typically derived from an operating perspective from the company's earnings before interest and tax ("EBIT").[307] Based on the company's capital structure, the weighted-average-capital-costs ("WACC") are determined as a blend of the required rate of returns on its debt and equity,[308] with the latter being derived using the Capital Asset Pricing

---

300 PEEMÖLLER (2001), p. 80f. For a further discussion see JUNG (1993), p. 180ff.

301 See VOGEL (2002), p. 175; SERFLING and PAPE (1995), p. 816.

302 See BRUNER (2004a), p. 258f. The assumption is that these multiples reflect the general outlook for the target's industry or group of firms with similar quantitative and qualitative characteristics. A problem of applying the multiples method is the selection of the appropriate peer group, especially if the target is diversified, see KERLER (2000), p. 204. If the peer companies or previous transactions were overvalued, so will be the target, as it was for example the case for transactions with internet-based targets in the late 1990s, see WIRTZ (2003), p. 209.

303 See BUCHNER (1995), p. 408ff.

304 See HELBLING (1993), p. 102f.; FISCHER (1989), p. 93. The definition of earnings and how they are derived from the financial accounting of a company is subject to extensive and controversial discussion in the literature, see for example SCHULTZE (2001), p. 329ff.; HENSELMANN (1999), p. 78ff.; HERING (1999), p. 103ff.

305 See COPELAND ET AL. (2000), p. 201. VOGEL (2002, p. 183) attributes the increased use of this method in Germany not only to the influence of U.S. investment banks, but also to the incorporation of this method in "S1 Standard for valuation within M&A transactions" of the German Institute for Auditors.

306 COPELAND ET AL. (2000), p. 167. According to this definition, the free cash flow is before financing and therefore is not affected by the company's financial structure, even though the financial structure may affect the company's weighted-average-capital cost and therefore its value.

307 See for example BALLWIESER (1993), p. 164.

308 WACC for the target is computed as: $WACC = i_d(1\text{-}t)W_d + K_eW_e$, with i_d = internal rate of return on target's new debt post-closing; K_e = current cost of target's equity; W_d, W_e = debt and equity as percentages of the target's market value capital structure post-closing; t = marginal tax rate of the target, see BRUNER (2004a), p. 264; for a detailed discussion see RICHTER (2005), p. 55ff.; BAETGE ET AL. (2001), p. 275ff.; HACHMEISTER (1999), p. 94ff.; KNÜSEL (1994), p. 105ff.

Model ("CAPM").[309] The need to use CAPM theory implies that the discounted cash flow method typically is more complex in its application than the aforementioned valuation methods.[310]

The valuation of the target company is accompanied with an assessment of internal and external financing options[311] and is followed by the negotiation phase, which ends with the final determination of the purchase price. The purchase price may be subject to post-closing adjustments, for example based on the future performance of the target.[312]

2.5.3.3 Signing and closing

After all regulatory and anti-trust requirements[313] are fulfilled, both parties finalize their negotiations by signing the definitive acquisition agreement.[314] In contrast to the letter of intent, the acquisition agreement is legally binding upon signing.[315] In addition to the negotiated terms of the transaction structure, it typically contains the following:[316]

- In the representations and warranties section,[317] the involved parties provide assertions with respect to their legal and financial condition as of the signing date.[318] Additional disclosures about the target company include material aspects of its financial statements, assets, taxes, leases and other contracts, employee matters, environmental protection, product liability, and litigation.[319]

---

309 See for example COPELAND ET AL. (2000), p. 214. Within the CAPM, K_e is calculated as: $K_e = R_f + \beta(R_m - R_f)$, with R_f= risk-free rate of return; β = systematic risk of a company's common shares; R_m-R_f= market risk premium for common shares, see BRUNER (2004a), p. 265; other methods are the dividend growth model and the risk component approach, see JANSEN (2001), p. 209. Surveys of practioners found that the CAPM is the predominant method used for estimating equity capital costs, see GRAHAM and HARVEY (2001); BRUNER ET AL. (1998).

310 For an extensive discussion of the applicability of the CAPM for valuing companies see WIRTZ (2003), p. 213ff.; SCHULTZE (2001), p. 165ff.; HERING (1999), p. 119ff.; HÖLSCHER (1998), p. 130ff.; BÖCKING and NOWAK (1998), p. 125ff.

311 For a detailed discussion of various forms of financing of companies see for example PERRIDON and STEINER (2004).

312 Such provisions are referred to as "earn out provisions", see REED and LAJOUX (1999), p. 117. The purchase price may also be adjusted based on the target's net equity or working capital at the closing date as confirmed by external auditors, see MORRIS (2000), p. 229ff.

313 For a discussion of German law requirements, see VOGEL (2002), p. 45ff. The U.S. regulatory framework is discussed in Section 3.7.

314 See REED and LAJOUX (1999), p. 450; MORGAN LEWIS & BOCKIUS (1996), p. 52.

315 See TANKERSLEY (1999), p. 22.

316 See HALL (2001), p. 4; MORGAN LEWIS & BOCKIUS (1996), p. 52.

317 Some practioners use both terms interchangeably.

318 See TANKERSLEY (1999), p. 21.

319 See ERNST & YOUNG (1994), p. 125ff. In order to narrow the scope of the disclosures, the representations are usually framed by the phrases "ordinary course of business" and "best of knowledge", see MORGAN LEWIS & BOCKIUS (1996), p. 52.

- The covenants concern each party's conduct with regard to the consummation of the transaction, employee related matters, and the target's business during the period between the signing and the closing.[320]
- Under the conditions to closing, the acquiring company must complete the transaction only if all of the representations and warranties are continuously accurate on the closing date and if none of the covenants is breached.[321]
- The indemnification provisions outline the post-closing liabilities and legal procedures arising from non-compliance with representations and warranties or breach of covenants.[322] This section also sets forth a limited duration of the indemnity terms.[323]

In addition to the definitive acquisition agreement, both parties often enter into a number of ancillary agreements, especially in the context of an asset purchase. Examples of such agreements include an obligation for the seller not to compete for a certain period of time,[324] employment contracts with key personnel of the target,[325] and service contracts, for example in case the acquirer intends to use the seller's IT resources post-closing for the target's business.

With a typical time lag of several weeks following the signing of the acquisition agreement, the transaction is consummated with the closing, i.e. the actual transfer of ownership and control rights as well as profit rights from the target shareholders to the acquirer.[326] The next step is to integrate the target into the acquirer's group, which is the focus of the post-closing integration phase.

2.5.4 Post-closing integration phase

The integration phase essentially comprises the definition of the integration concept, the prioritization and implementation of integration measures, and the post-acquisition controlling.[327] Within the conception of the integration, which typically begins during the acquisition structuring and management phase, goals, intended degree, and measures are determined and the team responsible is selected.[328] This step is followed by the actual implementation of the specified integration measures, which generally concern strategic (i.e. the consolidation of corporate strategies, transfer of strategic resources and know-how),

320 See HALL (2001), p. 6; REED and LAJOUX (1999), p. 467.
321 See ERNST & YOUNG (1994), p. 131; MORGAN LEWIS & BOCKIUS (1996), p. 53.
322 See BENDANIEL and ROSENBLOOM (1998), p. 43.
323 See MORGAN LEWIS & BOCKIUS (1996), p. 54.
324 See TANKERSLEY (1999), p. 26.
325 See REED and LAJOUX (1999), p. 492f.
326 See KERLER (2000), p. 242; BENDANIEL and ROSENBLOOM (1998), p. 55f.
327 See for example WIRTZ (2003), p. 110ff. For a detailed discussion of the integration process refer to for example CHAPMAN ET AL. (1998); GOMEZ and WEBER (1989).
328 See BERENS ET AL. (2005), p. 61.

personnel (i.e. motivating management and workforce of the target), structural (i.e. eliminating divergent or redundant organization and IT structures), and corporate culture aspects.[329] The acquisition process typically concludes with an assessment of whether the goals for the acquisition were achieved or not.

2.5.5 Special considerations for cross-border transactions

The suggested structure of the standardized acquisition process remains essentially unchanged in a cross-border transaction, but the legal, tax, labor, and cultural differences to the acquirer's home country add more complexity and risks to the acquisition process. Overall, cross-border transactions bear a higher risk of greater information asymmetry between the acquirer and the seller. As a result, external consultants, such as investment banks etc., more frequently assist acquirers in cross-border transactions.[330] The following is a brief discussion of the various implications of differentiating aspects on each phase of the cross-border transaction process.[331]

2.5.5.1 Strategic analysis and conception phase

While analyzing the strategic goals of the transaction, the acquirer needs to evaluate whether entering a foreign market suits its growth strategy and whether it has adequate qualitative and quantitative resources for entering it. The strategic analysis includes a check of whether acquiring an existing company is a more beneficial means to enter the foreign market than starting its own investment or forming a joint venture with a local company. Compared to domestic transactions, specific risks in this context are a false assessment of its own competitiveness in a foreign environment, an overestimation of the growth potential, or the generally more limited availability of information.[332]

With regard to the screening of potential targets, the assessment of the compatibility of the cultural fit of the target, for example its leadership styles or hierarchy orientation, requires special attention. Following the preparation of the short list, the initial contact typically poses an additional challenge, given that the local habits, perceptions, and negotiation styles have to be respected. These aspects are also relevant for the subsequent acquisition structuring and management phase.

---

329 See VOGEL (2002), p. 254ff.

330 See ROSENBLOOM (2002b), p. 4f.

331 The discussion in Section 2.5.5 essentially follows LUCKS and MECKL (2002) and BENDANIEL and ROSENBLOOM (1998).

332 See LUCKS (2005b), p. 11.

2.5.5.2 Acquisition structuring and management phase

Due to the inherent complexity, only a minor fraction of the total number of cross-border transactions are structured as direct mergers between the ultimate acquiring company and the foreign target company.[333] In addition, unsolicited bids are fairly unusual as well.[334] The various forms of documentation for the transaction, i.e. LOI, confidentiality agreement, and definitive acquisition agreement, are subject to the local legal framework. The due diligence is generally more challenging, given that the acquirer has to familiarize itself with a different institutional environment. The financial due diligence is more complicated as a result of disparities in national accounting standards. A typical example for differences in legal frameworks are more stringent consumer protection laws regarding default products in the United States compared to those in Europe.[335] Differences in the taxability of the various transaction structures are most important for the tax due diligence, while specific laws governing the compensation and social welfare of employees as well as their termination, particularly in case of a unionized workforce, need to be considered during the human resources due diligence. In addition, requirements for the remediation of contaminated industrial sites may vary significantly between countries. Overall, insufficient knowledge of the particular circumstances in the target's business environment may lead to overlooking significant potential risks that are not sufficiently addressed in the acquisition agreement.

Cross-border specific aspects to be considered for the valuation of the target are relatively limited, given that the discounted cash flow method is internationally the most accepted and widespread methodology. Hence, the main implication for a cross-border transaction is not necessarily the choice of the appropriate valuation method, but the specification of the appropriate input data for the model.

For obtaining regulatory approval of the transaction, not only the local authorities of the acquirer, but also those of the target's country need to be informed and their specific requirements have to be observed.

2.5.5.3 Post-closing integration phase

The implementation of human resources integration measures frequently creates problems for a foreign acquirer in a cross-border transaction. Such problems may result from (i) defining the appropriate management style and degree of integration into the acquirer's decision making process, since imposing decisions centrally made by the acquirer's management may

---

333 See UNCTAD (2000), p. 103.

334 According to UNCATD (2000, p. 103), for example in 1999 out of 6,200 cross-border transactions only ten were hostile. A prominent hostile takeover was the *Vodafone-Mannesmann* transaction.

335 See LUCKS and MECKL (2002), p. 258.

alienate and demotivate the target's workforce, most notably its executives, (ii) determining the number and positions of employees to be transferred from the acquirer into the target without creating the impression of an "invasion" while maintaining sufficient control of the new business, and (iii) equating the compensation and incentive systems, especially for upper management, and thereby securing that key personnel remain with the target. Overall, the implementation of human resource measures contains the risk of being too fast or inconsiderate of the target's local socio-cultural environment.

2.6 Summary

This chapter provided an overview of the theoretical and institutional framework of mergers and acquisitions for the purpose of this study. The term "mergers and acquisitions" was defined, different criteria for categorizing transactions were introduced, and a perspective for measuring transaction success was given, i.e. value creation for shareholders of acquiring companies. Following the discussion of relevant economic theories and various theories explaining shareholder- and management-related motives for companies to pursue transactions, the recent U.S. cross-border M&A activity by German acquirers was described, including an overview of various exogenous factors stimulating global M&A activity. This chapter concluded with a systematization of a standardized acquisition process and a general discussion of special considerations for the strategic analysis and conception, acquisition structuring and management, and the post-closing integration phase of a cross-border transaction. The following chapter addresses specific issues for the acquisition structuring and management phase in case of a cross-border transaction involving a target company in the United States.

3 Special considerations for structuring and managing a cross-border acquisition of a U.S. target company

3.1 Introduction

The purpose of this chapter is to provide an overview of specific considerations for the transaction structuring and management phase when acquiring a U.S. target company. As mentioned earlier, the main concerns and risks for a foreign acquirer for the structure and management of a cross-border transaction result from the impact of the local institutional peculiarities of the target's country. This presentation of U.S. specific considerations begins with laying out the possible structures for the U.S. transaction, which is focused on the implications of the U.S. securities laws applicable to the acquisition of a public target company (Section 3.2). Following is a discussion about conducting a due diligence for a U.S. target, with an emphasis on the U.S. accounting and legal environment (Section 3.3). Also of particular interest for a foreign acquirer are tax consequences of alternative acquisition structures (Section 3.4), various aspects for the valuation (Section 3.5), and the principal documentation (Section 3.6) of the U.S. transaction. After a brief description of the U.S. regulatory framework of antitrust laws (Section 3.7), a summary of the main implications for the acquisition structuring and management phase concludes this chapter.

It should be noted that the following sections describe the current status of legal regulations applicable to U.S. transactions. Any significant changes of respective laws during the observation period of this study, i.e. the years from 1990 to 2004, are highlighted.

3.2 Structure of the transaction

3.2.1 Overview

When a foreign company decides to pursue an acquisition in the United States, it must consider certain implications with regard to its structure, the status of the target, the identity of the acquisition vehicle, and the form of payment.[1]

The range of structures available in a cross-border acquisition of a U.S. target is equivalent to those in a domestic one: a purchase of the target's assets, a purchase of the target's shares, or a merger with the target. As seen in Section 2.4.2.2, a direct merger of a German ultimate acquiring company with a U.S. target is rather uncommon, instead the acquirer typically sets up a subsidiary as an acquisition vehicle and then either merges that target into the subsidiary (so-called "forward subsidiary merger") or that subsidiary into the target (so-called "reverse

---

[1] See for example DICKEY (2000), p. 288f.

subsidiary merger").[2] In case the target is a public company listed on a U.S. stock exchange, the acquirer needs to consider the requirements of the local securities laws. Compared to acquisitions of a private target, the applicability of such laws adds complexity to the transaction process and depends on whether the transaction is paid for with cash or shares. The choice of the form of payment also impacts the taxation of the transaction.[3] For example, using shares allows for a tax-free treatment under the U.S. Internal Revenue Code ("IRC"), though it is rather uncommon and usually limited to those companies whose shares are already traded on a U.S. stock exchange.[4] Figure 3.1 exhibits the various forms of structuring a U.S. transaction.

Figure 3.1: Predominant U.S. transaction structures[5]

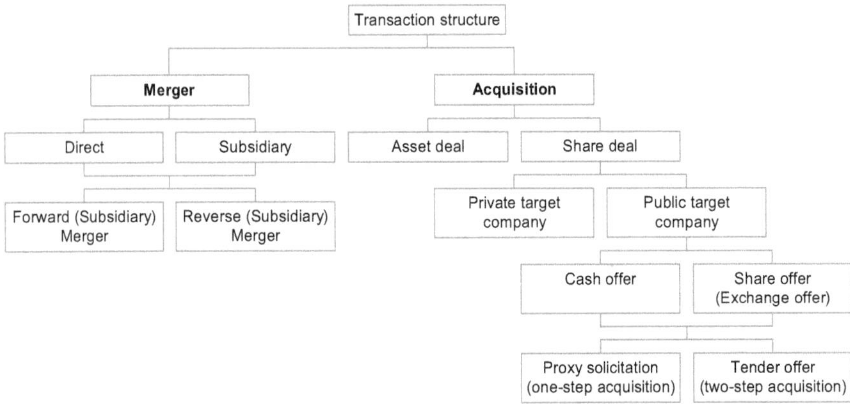

[2] See LAJOUX and NESVOLD (2004), p. 19. In the *Daimler-Chrysler* case, the transaction was structured as a "merger of equals", resulting in the creation of a new parent company with two newly formed subsidiaries. Each of the constituent corporations then merged with one of the subsidiaries with the effect that each of the constituent corporations became a subsidiary of the new parent and the outstanding shares of each of the constituent corporations were converted into shares of the new parent.

[3] The impact of taxes on acquisitions has been subject to extensive empirical research in the literature, concluding that the tax structure and the tax attributes of the target influence the purchase price that acquirers are willing to pay; see for example AYERS ET AL. (2004); ERICKSON and WANG (2000); WEAVER (2000); PLUMMER and ROBINSON (1990); HAYN (1989).

[4] Some German acquirers listed themselves on a U.S. stock exchange in order to pursue a merger with a U.S. public company, for example *Aixtron AG* in its acquisition of *Genus, Inc.* in March 2005. A listing of those German companies that were listed in the United States as of December 31, 2004, is provided in Section 3.2.3.4.

[5] Source: own presentation.

The acquirer must also decide on the identity of the acquisition vehicle, whether it will be the foreign acquiring company itself or a U.S. subsidiary that either already exists or that is specifically created for the transaction.[6] The choice may depend on whether and where debt financing will be raised for the purchase or, in the case of an exchange offer, whether target shareholders will accept shares of the acquiring company.[7] In case an existing subsidiary is not used, an acquirer may choose among a variety of U.S. corporate vehicles, for example C- or S-Corporations,[8] general or limited partnerships, or limited liability companies ("LLC").[9] These forms of business entities are formed under applicable U.S. state laws, rather than under federal laws.[10] Besides taxation, these acquisition vehicles mainly differ with regard to their limitation of legal liability, capitalization requirements, and management and control organization, as shown in Table 3.1.

Table 3.1: Form of a U.S. acquisition vehicle[11]

	Acquisition vehicle			
	C-Corporation	**S-Corporation**	**Partnership**	**LLC**
Type of owners permitted	No restrictions	Only U.S. citizens or resident aliens	No restrictions	No restrictions
Number of owners	At least one	No more than 100	At least two	At least one *
Minimum capital investment	None *	None *	None	None *
Liability	Limited to the investment	Limited to the investment	Unlimited for general partner, limited to the investment for other partner	Limited to the investment
Taxation of operations	Double tax: for the corporation on income, for the shareholders on distributions	Single tax on income flow-through to shareholders	Single tax on income flow-through to shareholders	Single tax on income flow-through to shareholders
Minimum number and nationality of directors	One natural person of any nationality *	One natural person of any nationality *	Typically the general partner	One natural person or body corporate of any nationality *

* refers to requirements in the states of Delaware and New York.

6 See BENDANIEL and ROSENBLOOM (1998), p. 36.

7 CONN ET AL. (2005) point out that in cross-border transactions the sellers are usually unwilling to receive shares of a foreign company. In addition, only a few German companies are listed on a U.S. stock exchange, as shown in Section 3.2.3.4.

8 A definition of these two types of U.S. corporations is given in Section 3.4.2.1.

9 Other forms include joint ventures, trusts, or sole proprietorships. For further information refer to for example LAJOUX and NESVOLD (2004), p. 263f. DASILVA (2005) notes that until recently, most companies in the U.S. were organized as corporations, but that currently LLCs are nearly as common.

10 Regardless of the location of the headquarter, most acquisition vehicles are incorporated in the states of Delaware or New York, given their well-developed, but flexible corporate statutes, see ZINN (2004).

11 Source: own presentation.

3.2.2 Acquisition of a private company

In case the U.S. target is a private company, the acquisition can be structured as a merger, asset, or share deal (as shown previously in Figure 3.1). While the same advantages and disadvantages that were laid out in Table 2.1 apply, specific attention in a U.S. asset deal should be paid to liabilities.[12] In this case the acquirer is not subject to liabilities of the target, regardless whether disclosed, undisclosed, or contingent, unless expressly stated in the asset purchase agreement. However, there are several exceptions to this general rule:[13]

- In some states, a purchase of all (or substantially all) of a company's assets means the acquiring company, as a mere continuation of the predecessor, assumes all of the target's liabilities.[14] In determining whether the acquirer is considered a continuation of the target, U.S. courts weigh a number of factors, such as retention of the same management and employees, use of the same production facilities, manufacturing of the same products, and selling to the same customers.[15] This concept of "successor liability" does not apply though to target companies incorporated in Delaware.[16]
- In some jurisdictions (for example California) the U.S. courts increasingly require the buyer of a manufacturing business to automatically assume the tort liabilities for faulty products manufactured by the target prior to the acquisition.[17]
- When acquiring bulk business, the acquirer can be held responsible for certain liabilities of the seller as a result of the bulk sales law.[18] The requirements of this law to notify each creditor of the seller are deemed inconvenient and are often ignored;[19] instead, an acquirer typically relies on the seller's indemnifications against any creditors' claims.[20]
- The acquirer cannot usually terminate an agreement with the unionized employees, a so-called "collective bargaining contract", when it keeps the target's employees.[21]

In addition to liability issues, there are also U.S. tax implications to be considered in an asset deal, which are discussed in Section 3.4.2. Certain states, for example New Jersey, require

---

12 See LAJOUX and NESVOLD (2004), p. 13.

13 See REED and LAJOUX (1999), p. 257ff.

14 In such instance the transaction is regarded as a de facto merger, see LAJOUX and NESVOLD (2004), p. 13.

15 See FROMM ET AL. (1997), p. 443, who note that some courts have pursued a more narrow definition of the successor liability exception in the past, which allowed some responsible parties to avoid liabilities. As a result, courts have expanded the general rule for liability responsibility.

16 See LAJOUX and NESVOLD (2004), p. 13.

17 This obligation comes under the "continuity of product line" rule, see LAJOUX and ELSON (2000), p. 133f.

18 These provisions are codified in Article VI of the U.S. Uniform Commercial Code. The bulk sales law is applicable in all jurisdictions in the United States except Louisiana, and is subject to variations among states.

19 See HALL (2001), p. 3. Sections 6-104, 6-105, and 6-107 of the bulk sales law require the buyer of a substantial part of the material, supplies, merchandise, or other inventory of a seller whose main business is bulk sales to give at least 10 days advance notice of the transaction to each creditor of the seller. The notice must identify the seller and the acquirer and state whether or not the liabilities of the seller will be paid as they fall due.

20 See GRAFER and BALDASERO (1994), p. 334.

21 Issues in connection with the unionization of the target's workforce are discussed in Section 3.3.5.2.

their approval of the transferability of existing state environmental permits and licenses from the target to the acquirer before the transaction is closed.[22] Finally, under some jurisdictions, for example in Delaware, a sale of all (or substantially all) the assets of a company requires the approval of the majority of the shareholders.[23]

In a share acquisition, the acquirer typically assumes the rights and liabilities of the target. Special attention is directed to the increasing prevalence of so-called "change of control clauses" in various contracts in the United States, which allow for a termination right in case of a change of ownership. Such provisions are typically part of contracts with insurances, banks, suppliers, and licensees.[24]

3.2.3 Acquisition of a public company

3.2.3.1 Type of transaction

The acquisition of a publicly held U.S. company is subject to regulations under federal securities laws and rules promulgated hereunder by the Securities and Exchange Commission ("SEC"). The basic securities laws that govern the acquisition of a U.S. public company are the Securities Act of 1933 ("Securities Act") and the Securities Exchange Act of 1934 ("Exchange Act"), as amended. These Acts contain procedural and disclosure requirements for the transaction, including filing requirements upon the purchase of five percent or more of the common stock of a U.S. public company. For target companies not listed on the New York or American Stock Exchange or the NASDAQ national market, state securities laws also apply, so-called "blue sky" laws.[25] In connection with acquisitions, state laws primarily contain antitakeover statutes for hostile bids, by either limiting the transfer of voting rights regardless of the actual amount of acquired shares,[26] or by limiting an acquirer's ability to conduct certain actions after the closing of a transaction.[27] In case the proposed transaction requires a vote of the target's shareholders, the acquisition process must comply with U.S. state corporate laws, for example the Delaware General Corporation Law ("DGCL").[28] The target company must also consider such state corporate laws, since these laws create fiduciary responsibilities for the board of directors that restrict its ability to favor or reject an offer.[29]

---

22 See BENDANIEL and ROSENBLOOM (1998), p. 45.
23 See LAJOUX and NESVOLD (2004), p. 15.
24 See RUEGGER (1999), p. 10.
25 See LAJOUX and ELSON (2000), p. 200.
26 For example in the state of Indiana.
27 For example the state of Delaware, which in case an acquirer purchased more than 15 percent but less than 85 percent of the shares of a target in a hostile takeover, limits the acquirer's ability to merge with the target or sell substantial assets unless the target's board of directors or remaining shareholders approve such transactions, see ROSENGREN (1988), pp. 71-73.
28 See LAJOUX and NESVOLD (2004), p. 11.
29 In the case of *Revlon Inc.* versus *MacAndrews*, a U.S. court described the role of the target's board of directors as that of a price-oriented "neutral auctioneer", see LAJOUX and ELSON (2000), p. 205. Since then, the target's board's obligations are also known as the "Revlon duties".

Similar to transactions involving private companies, the acquisition of a U.S. public company may be made in consideration for cash or shares of the acquirer, and may be accomplished either through a "proxy solicitation" or a "tender offer".[30] In a proxy solicitation, which does not exist under German law, the foreign acquirer typically forms a U.S. acquisition vehicle that merges with or into the target company upon approval of target's shareholders (so-called "one-step acquisition").[31] To effect this approval, federal securities laws require the target company to solicit proxies from its shareholders and to vote on the proxies at the shareholders' meeting called for the purpose of the acquisition. The required percentage of the shareholder approval follows the target's articles of incorporation and applicable state corporate laws. For example, in the states of Delaware and New York, a simple majority of the voting power of the common stock is sufficient.[32]

In a tender offer an acquiring company offers the target's shareholders to purchase their shares. Since generally not all shares are tendered, the initial offer is typically followed in a second step by a mandatory merger that converts all shares into cash (so-called "two-step acquisition").[33] Often, the tender offer is conditioned upon enough shares being tendered to ensure that the merger will not require the approval of the target's remaining shareholders (so-called "short-form merger").[34] Even though the tender offer is made directly to the shareholders, the acquirer typically seeks approval from the target's board and enters into an

---

30 See BRUNER (2004a), p. 725ff; REED and LAJOUX (1999), p. 723ff.

31 See BREALEY and MYERS (2000), p. 956f. A proxy is the right to vote someone else's share, hence this type of transaction is also referred to as a "proxy fight".

32 DGCL § 251. In New York, businesses incorporated before February 22, 1998, require an approval of two-thirds of the voting shares, while for companies incorporated after that date a simple majority is sufficient, according to New York Business Commercial Law ("BCL") §§ 614(b) and 708.

33 See LAJOUX and NESVOLD (2004), p. 21. Structuring the acquisition as a two-step transaction impacts its financing possibilities in light of the margin rules by the Federal Reserve Bank. In case of tender offers, these rules generally prohibit lenders from making loans that are directly or indirectly secured by "margin stock" if the loans exceeds 50 percent of the value of the collateral. An exception to this rule is provided when the acquisition agreement is signed prior to the closing of the tender offer, see REED and LAJOUX (1999), p. 773.

34 A variation is the use of a "two-tier tender offer". A "front loaded" two-tier tender offer is a tender offer that gives a certain price to shareholders who tender their share before the acquirer's interest in the company reaches a certain level (for example 51 percent, which would give the acquirer control of the company). All other shares will thereafter be tendered at a lower price. This tender offer coupled with the announcement of the intention of carrying through a "freeze-out merger" (also referred to as "squeeze-out") afterwards is meant to coerce the shareholders into selling their shares without reflection of the fairness of the price, since they otherwise risk losing potentially even more money on the subsequent sale of their shares, see REED and LAJOUX (1999), p. 727. For example the acquisitions of *Acuson Corp.* by *Siemens AG* and *National Discount Brokers* by *Deutsche Bank AG* were pursued in such a manner. However, numerous states have implemented freeze-out statutes containing fair price provisions and a minimum waiting period for completing the second-step merger of up to five years following the tender offer. DGCL freeze-out statutes suspend any merger and forced sell out of the remaining minority shareholders for three years unless the target's board approves it or the acquirer obtained 85 percent of the target's shares in its initial tender offer, see REED and LAJOUX (1999), p. 792.

acquisition agreement before the commencement of the offer in order to protect the transaction from competing offers.[35]

Compared to a proxy solicitation, a tender offer is more beneficial in limiting the acquirer's exposure to competing offers.[36] While in a proxy solicitation the designated time period to gain control over a target is typically a minimum of 45 to 60 days after the required proxy materials are submitted to the SEC, a tender offer can be completed as early as 20 business days from the commencement date. In case the acquirer cannot purchase a sufficient majority of shares to effect a short-form merger, a disadvantage of tender offers may be the impact of dissenter's appraisal rights under applicable state laws, which could result in additional expenses and a delay of the consummation of the second-step merger.[37] Additional expenses compared to proxy solicitations could also result from the requirement for interim financing at the conclusion of the initial tender offer.[38]

An exchange offer may also be structured as either a one-step or two-step transaction, though as mentioned earlier in the context of cross-border transactions such structures are rather infrequent.[39] Two-step exchange offers were previously uncommon in the United States, since the registration requirements under the Securities Act associated with the issuance of securities significantly reduced the above mentioned timing advantage of the two-step acquisition.[40] In 2000, the SEC adopted rules that extended the timing advantages of cash tender offers to share tender offers.[41] The following sections present the applicable securities laws for these types of acquisitions in more detail.

3.2.3.2 Securities laws applicable to a cash tender offer

Tender offers as well as reporting requirements on "beneficial ownership"[42] of five percent or more of the voting shares of a public company are regulated in the United States by the Williams Act. This Act, which was enacted in 1968 as an amendment to the Exchange Act, contains the legal requirements for the disclosure and process of a takeover attempt of a

---

35 The acquirer will be subject to competing offers until the offer is successfully concluded. An example of this exposure for the acquirer is the unsuccessful attempt of *SAP AG* to acquire *Retek Inc.* in 2005. After making the initial offer, *SAP AG* was finally outbid by *Oracle*, see RHODE (2005), p. 8.

36 See LAJOUX and NESVOLD (2004), p. 76f.

37 See REED and LAJOUX (1999), p. 727f.; SHAPIRO and STRAUSS (1987), p. 8f.; shareholders who dissent from the transaction are entitled to be paid the "fair value" of their shares in the target as of the merger date.

38 See REED and LAJOUX (1999), p. 727.

39 In the years from 1990 to 2004 six U.S. transactions by German acquirers were structured as an exchange offer.

40 See REED and LAJOUX (1999), p. 727. Under the previous rules, an exchange offer did not commence until a registration statement was filed and became effective. A cash tender offer commenced as soon as a tender offer schedule was filed and the information was disseminated to the shareholders.

41 This is "Regulation of Takeovers and Security Holder Communications, Release No. 33-7760, 34-42055; 1C-24107".

42 As defined in Section 13(d) of the Williams Act.

public target company, but purposefully does not offer a legal definition of a tender offer in order to allow for flexible interpretations in accordance with the intended purposes of the regulations.[43] Flexible criteria allowing for determining when a takeover bid must be considered a tender offer were subsequently developed as a result of various court rulings, which set forth the characteristics constituting a tender offer by naming an eight-factor test:[44]

(i) Active and widespread solicitation of public shareholders for the shares of an issuer.

(ii) Solicitation made for the substantial percentage of an issuer's shares.

(iii) Offer to purchase made at a premium over the prevailing market price.

(iv) Terms of the offer are firm rather than negotiated.

(v) Offer contingent on the tender of a fixed number of shares, often subject to a fixed maximum number to be purchased.

(vi) Offer open only a limited period of time.

(vii) Offeree subject to pressure to sell his shares.

(viii) Public announcements of a purchasing program concerning the target company precede or accompany rapid accumulation of larger amounts of the target company's securities.

The first public announcement of a proposed tender offer does not automatically commence a tender offer,[45] though it triggers restrictions on purchasing shares of the target outside the proposed tender offer.[46] The offer only commences when the acquirer first sends or gives the target shareholders the means to tender their shares, either by (i) providing the target

---

[43] See GAUGHAN (1999), p. 62; ARANOW ET AL. (1977), p. 1. In Germany comparable regulations were not promulgated until 2002.

[44] See GAUGHAN (1999), p. 74. The eight-factor test was developed in the *Wellman* versus *Dickinson* case, see SODERQUIST (1987), p. 236. In 1979 the SEC proposed the following definition of a tender offer: "The term 'tender offer' includes a 'request or invitation for tenders' and means one or more offers to purchase or solicitations of offers to sell securities of a single class, whether or not all or any portion of the securities sought are purchased, which (i) during any 45-day period are directed to more than 10 persons and seek the acquisition of more than 5 percent of the class of securities, except that offers by a broker (and its customer) or by a dealer made on a national securities exchange at the then current market or made in the over-the-counter market at the then current market shall be excluded if in connection with such offers neither the person making the offers nor such broker or dealer solicits or arranges for the solicitation of any order to sell such securities and such broker or dealer performs only the customary functions of a broker or dealer and receives no more that the broker's usual and customary commission or the dealer's usual and customary mark-up; or (ii) are not otherwise a tender offer under [clause (i)] of this section, but which (A) are disseminated in a widespread manner, (B) provide for a price which represents a premium in excess of the greater of 5 percent of or $2 above the current market price and (C) do not provide for a meaningful opportunity to negotiate the price and terms", see SEC (1979). This suggestion never became effective as a rule though.

[45] As required by Rule 14d-2(b)(2), which also applies to all related subsequent communication, such an initial announcement must be filed on or before the date of first use with the SEC. Written communications must be filed under cover of Schedule TO, which has a check box indicating that these are pre-commencement communications.

[46] Rule 14e-5. Section 14(e) generally prescribes means to prevent fraudulent or manipulative practices in connection with tender offers. For example, Rule 14e-8 prohibits acquiring companies from announcing an offer (i) without an intent to commence the offer within a reasonable time and to complete the offer, (ii) with the intent to manipulate the price of the bidder or the target's shares, and (iii) without a reasonable belief that a person will have the means to purchase the shares sought.

shareholders with a transmittal form to use to tender shares or by (ii) publishing an advertisement that advises the shareholders how to tender their shares or how to contact the acquirer for more information.[47] At that time, the acquirer must file with the SEC and simultaneously disseminate to the target company the tender offer statement ("Schedule TO"), which must comply with Regulation M-A.[48] Item 1001 of Regulation M-A requires a "plain English" summary term sheet that highlights the material features of the proposed transaction. The shareholders of the target must receive two documents, the "offer to purchase" and the related "letter of transmittal". The offer to purchase outlines the key terms of the proposed transaction and must include for example all material events leading to the public announcement of the acquisition[49] and any proposed plans of the acquiring company with regard to a reorganization and restructuring of the target or a change in the its current management.[50] In order to accept the offer and to tender their shares, the shareholders of the target need to send back the letter of transmittal.[51]

Upon its commencement, a tender offer must remain open for at least 20 business days (Rule 14e-1(a)). If during this period the acquirer announces an increase in the percentage of the shares being sought or the price offered, based on Rule 14e-1(b) the offer must remain open for at least another ten business days. The initial offering may be expanded for a minimum of three business days and up to a maximum of 20 business days if certain conditions are met.[52] In addition to these time requirements, the acquirer must also consider the following procedural rules:

- Rules 14d-10(a)(1) and (2) require that the terms of the offer, including the price paid per share, must be equal for all shareholders of the target (so-called "all holder rule").

---

47 Rules 14d-2 and 14d-4(a)(2). Typically, a summary advertisement is published in the financial pages of The Wall Street Journal. Another form of commencement is by means of a long-form publication, as specified in Rule 14d-4(a)(1).

48 Rule 14d-3(a)(2). Regulation M-A contains the centralized disclosure requirements for Schedule TO in cash and share tender offers, as well as in any subsequent second-step mergers (so-called "going private transactions"). As a result, in the case of a two-step acquisition one filing satisfies the disclosure requirement for both steps of the transaction (Schedule TO has boxes on the cover to check in order to indicate whether the filing is a tender offer and/or a going private transaction).

49 For example, meetings and contacts between the acquiring company and the target in which significant issues of the proposed transaction were discussed.

50 See JARRELL and BRADLEY (1980), p. 374f.

51 See LAJOUX and ELSON (2000), p. 202.

52 According to Rule 14d-11 those criteria are: (i) the offer is for all outstanding shares of the class sought, (ii) the initial offering period remains open for at least 20 business days, (iii) all conditions of the offer are deemed satisfied or waived by the acquirer on or before the close of the initial offering period, (iv) the acquirer accepts and promptly pays for all shares tendered during the initial offering period on the closing of the initial offering period, (v) the acquirer announces the approximate number and percentage of outstanding securities that were deposited by the close of the initial offering period no later than 9:00 a.m. Eastern time on the next business day after the scheduled expiration date of the initial offering period, and (vi) the acquirer immediately accepts and promptly pays for all shares as they are tendered in the subsequent offering period. Any extension of the subsequent offering period must be made in accordance with Rule 14e-1(d).

- Each shareholder must receive the highest price offer according to Rule 14d-10. As a result, if the tender price is increased at any time during the offering period, the higher price must be paid to all tendering shareholders (so-called “best price rule”).
- If less than all of the tendered shares are to be acquired, the acquirer must purchase the shares tendered on a pro rata basis from all tendering holders (Rule 14d-8).
- During the time from the first public announcement of the offer until the expiration of the initial offering period, the acquiring company is not permitted to directly or indirectly purchase shares of the target (Rule 14e-5). However, this prohibition does not apply to a subsequent offering period, if the price paid per purchased share is of the same amount as in the tender offer.
- The target shareholders may withdraw tendered shares at any time during the initial, but not the subsequent offering period (Rule 14d-7(a)), or at any time 60 days after the commencement of the tender offer, if the acquirer has not purchased those shares by then (Rule 14d-5).

Within ten business days after the commencement of the offer, the board of directors of the target company must respond to it by filing with the SEC Schedule 14D-9, which analogous to Schedule TO must comply with the disclosure requirements of Regulation M-A (Rule 14e-2(a)). Schedule 14D-9 must contain a statement from the board of directors expressing either (i) no opinion on the offer, (ii) a recommendation to accept or refuse it, or (iii) its inability to take a position. In a friendly transaction, the board’s position is usually negotiated with the acquirer in advance, so that Schedule 14D-9 is typically filed and disseminated simultaneously with Schedule TO at the commencement of the offer.[53]

Upon completion of the tender offer, the acquiring company must pay for all tendered shares, publish a press release discussing the results of the offer, and file a final amendment to Schedule TO with the SEC according to Rule 14e-1(c). In case the number of shares tendered does not allow for a short-form merger, the second step must take the form of a “long-form merger”, i.e. the target shareholders approve the merger either by written consent or in an extraordinary shareholders’ meeting, for which the proxy requirements of Section 14(a) of the Exchange Act must be met.[54]

3.2.3.3 Securities laws applicable to a proxy solicitation

In case the desired transaction requires a vote by the target shareholders, the acquirer has to provide them with a proxy statement filed under Schedule 14A (Rule 14a-3). Schedule 14A is

---

[53] In case there is a material change to the information provided in Schedule 14D-9, the target company must “promptly” file an amendment, according to Rule 14d-3.

[54] See SCHENCK ET AL. (2005), p. 42; HUTTER and LAWRENCE (1999), p. 121.

intended to give the target shareholders the information necessary to enable them to make an informed decision on whether to vote for the proposed transaction or not. It generally includes a summary of the main features of the proposed acquisition, a discussion of the motives for pursuing it, a description of any major differences in the shareholders' rights as a result of the proposed acquisition, an explanation of financial accounting and federal income tax consequences, and a statement on the status of the regulatory approval process.

In deviation to a tender offer, the minimum time period required for a proxy solicitation is not regulated by federal securities laws, but is governed by applicable state corporate laws.[55] These laws generally require the company to send to its shareholders a respective notice at least ten, but not more than 60 calendar days before the planned day of a shareholder meeting.[56] The minimum period to ensure that the target shareholders receive the proxy materials and have sufficient time to review them and to submit their proxy is typically 20 days.[57] No less than ten calendar days before the proxy statement is mailed though, it must be filed with the SEC in at least preliminary form.[58] Typically, the shareholders do not receive the proxy statement until the SEC has completed its mandatory review, which on average takes from ten to 30 days.[59] The requirement of filing Schedule 14A with the SEC is the main reason that, compared to a proxy solicitation, an acquisition may be achieved more quickly through a tender offer.

3.2.3.4 Securities laws applicable to an exchange offer

In an exchange offer, the rules relating to a tender offer or a proxy solicitation generally apply as well.[60] In addition, the shares used by the acquirer to pay for the transaction have to be effectively registered pursuant to the filing requirements of the Securities Act. However, effectiveness of the registration is not mandatory for the commencement of an exchange offer. An exchange offer is permitted to commence as early as the filing of the registration

---

55 See SHIELDS (1994), p. 326.

56 For example pursuant to DGCL §213(a).

57 See GAUGHAN (1999), p. 276.

58 Rule 14a-6(a). The filing must be made electronically, with an exemption for foreign private issuers that according to Rule 3a-12-3 are not required to file the annual SEC disclosures electronically.

59 See LAJOUX and NESVOLD (2004), p. 77.

60 For example the *Daimler-Chrysler* merger was effected in two stages, beginning with a voluntary exchange offer by *DaimlerChrysler*, the acquisition vehicle, for *Daimler-Benz* shares. For the pooling-of-interests method of accounting to be available, 90 percent of the shares had to be tendered, while in order to make the transaction tax neutral for the *Chrysler* shareholders, 75 percent of all outstanding stock had to be rendered. At the consummation of the transaction, a total of 98.2 percent of all shares were tendered. A reverse triangular merger of a newly incorporated Delaware corporation with and into *Chrysler* followed. Finally, contributions in kind of the *Daimler-Benz* and *Chrysler* shares into *DaimlerChrysler* and two increases in the share capital of *DaimlerChrysler* completed the transaction, making the two original companies subsidiaries of *DaimlerChrysler*. The final stage involved the merger of *Daimler-Benz* with and into *DaimlerChrysler*, leaving *Chrysler* as a subsidiary, see REUTER and THOMA (1999).

statement.[61] The filing of the registration statement must be accompanied with a tender offer statement as well as with a preliminary prospectus that provides the shareholders with all information necessary to enable them to make an informed decision on the proposed transaction.[62] An early commencement also requires the dissemination of the preliminary prospectus and a related letter of transmittal to the target shareholders. In case material changes to the initial offer are proposed, the acquirer must provide the target shareholders with a supplement to the preliminary prospectus. In this case, in deviation to the rules for cash tender offers, the offer must remain open for at least

- five business days, if the material changes do not concern the share price offered,
- ten business days, if the material changes concern the share price offered, the number of shares sought, or other similarly significant terms of the proposed acquisition, and
- 20 business days, if the initial preliminary prospectus was materially deficient.[63]

Any shares tendered cannot be exchanged until after the registration statement becomes effective and the minimum tender offer period of 20 business days has expired.

In order to effectively register shares in the United States in connection with an exchange offer, a foreign company needs to file Forms F-4 and F-6.[64] Form F-4 requires the foreign acquirer to disclose the terms and risk factors of the proposed acquisition, certain information about its financial condition, and all material contracts with the target. Form F-6 contains financial statements of the foreign company that are either initially prepared in accordance with U.S. GAAP or reconciled from the respective locally adopted accounting principles to U.S. GAAP.[65] Form F-6 must also include a section summarizing the differences between the rights of the target shareholders under its charter, by-laws and applicable state laws, and the rights of the acquirer shareholders.

A foreign company typically does not register ordinary shares in the United States, but American Depositary Receipts ("ADR").[66] Resembling a stock certificate, an ADR is a U.S. dollar denominated negotiable instrument that represents ownership in one or several American Depository Shares ("ADS").[67] An ADS is a U.S. dollar denominated form of

---

61 Or on a later date selected by the acquirer up to the date of effectiveness, according to Rules 162, 13e-4(e)(2), and 14d-4(b).

62 The preliminary prospectus must be prepared under Rule 425.

63 Rule 14d-4(d).

64 Compared to Forms S-4 and S-6 for a domestic U.S. company.

65 RUEGGER (1999, p. 7) points out that the time-consuming preparation of such a conversion of the financial statements could be quite disadvantageous for the acquiring company if it is competing with a public U.S. company to acquire the U.S. target. In addition, once a foreign company is a reporting company under the Exchange Act, it is required to comply with SEC reporting requirements on an on-going basis, which in light of the Sarbanes-Oxley provisions could prove costly and extensive, see NOCERA (2005).

66 An exception is *DaimlerChrysler*, which has registered ordinary shares on the New York Stock Exchange.

67 See ROSEN and SEIFERT (1998), p. 5. In practice, the terms ADR and ADS are often used interchangeably. For a further discussion of ADRs refer to for example GREENE ET AL. (1998).

equity ownership in a foreign company, representing its shares held on deposit by a custodian bank in the foreign company's home country. Accordingly, an ADR carries the corporate and economic rights of the foreign shares, subject to the terms specified on the ADR certificate, but it is priced and its dividends are paid in U.S. dollars. The deposit agreement with the U.S. depository bank creates a sponsored ADR program, which can generally be grouped into four categories.[68] The first two categories, unsponsored and sponsored level-I ADRs, are traded in the over-the-counter market and cannot be effectively registered. In this case, companies usually obtain an exemption from disclosure rules.[69] In the third category of sponsored level-II ADRs, a foreign company registers its shares on a U.S. exchange without making a public offering in the United States. Only companies in the fourth category with sponsored level-III ADRs register their shares on a U.S. exchange through a public offering. For the purpose of filing with the SEC the mandatory annual Form 20-F and semiannual Form 6-K, companies in categories three and four are required to submit financial statements that are directly prepared in compliance with or reconciled to U.S. GAAP.

ADRs gained increased acceptance among German companies in the late 1990s, especially in light of an increased volume of exchange offers and as a result of the availability of a tax-free-treatment of an exchange offer in the United States.[70] Those German companies that had registered ordinary shares or ADRs in the United States as of December 31, 2004 are displayed in Table 3.2, with the respective ticker-symbol shown in parentheses.[71]

Table 3.2: German companies with registered ordinary shares and ADRs in the United States

Registered ADRs by German companies as of December 31, 2004	
• *Allianz AG* (AZ)	• *Fresenius Medical Care AG* (FMS)
• *Altana AG* (AAA)	• *GPC Biotech AG* (GPCB)
• *BASF AG* (BF)	• *Hannover Rückversicherungs AG* (HVRRY)[72]
• *Bayer AG* (BAY)	• *Infineon Technologies AG* (IFX)
• *DaimlerChrysler AG* (DCX)	• *Pfeiffer Vacuum Technology AG* (PV)
• *Deutsche Bank AG* (DB)	• *QIAGEN N.V.* (QGEN)
• *Deutsche Telekom AG* (DT)	• *SAP AG* (SAP)
• *Dialog Semiconductor GmbH* (DLGS)	• *Schering AG* (SHR)
• *E.ON AG* (EON)	• *SGL Carbon* (SGL)
• *Epcos AG* (EPC)	• *Siemens AG* (SI)

68 See COYLE (1995), p. 71f. Unsponsored ADRs are initiated by a U.S. depository bank without an agreement with the underlying foreign company, see FROST and KINNEY (1996), p. 67f.

69 Exchange Act Section 12g3-2(b).

70 See RUEGGER (1999). The implications of the various forms of acquisition with regard to their taxation in the United States are discussed in Section 3.4.

71 Recently, *Sirona Dental Systems GmbH* announced on September 26, 2005 that it agreed to merge with *Schick Technologies* and will trade as *Sirona Dental Systems* on the NASDAQ, see KIRCHHOFF (2005).

72 The shares of *Hannover Rückversicherungs AG* are the only ones of Table 3.2 that are listed within the Level I-ADR program.

Table 3.3 summarizes the main procedural and disclosure requirements for the various types of acquisitions of a public U.S. company.

Table 3.3: Securities laws applicable to acquisitions of public U.S. targets[73]

	Type of transaction		
	Cash tender offer	**Proxy solicitation**	**Exchange offer**
Main applicable rules	• Exchange Act Rules 14a-12, 14d-2(b), 14d-9, 14d-100, 14e-1(a), 14e-5, 14e-8 • Regulation M-A	• Exchange Act Rules 14a-6(b), 14a-9, 14a-12 • Securities Act Rule 425 (in case of a share offer)	• Exchange Act Rules 14a-12, 14d-2(b), 14d-9 • Securities Act Rules 135, 165, 166, 425
Commencement / Duration	• Offer commences when the acquirer first sends or gives the target shareholders the means to tender securities • Offer must remain open for at least 20 business days	• Minimum proxy solicitation period is governed by applicable state corporate laws, which usually require that notice of a meeting is sent out at least 10 days, but not more than 60 days before the meeting	• Offer commences as early as the filing of a registration statement, or on a later date selected by the acquirer (but before effectiveness of the registration) • Early commencement requires dissemination of a preliminary prospectus to the target shareholders
Required filings by the acquirer	• Schedule TO • Summary term sheet according to Regulation M-A	• Cash offer: definitive proxy statement filed under Schedule 14A • Share offer: registration statement filed under Rule 425	• Preliminary prospectus filed under Rule 425 • "Plain English" summary according to Item 3 of Form F-4
Required filings by the target	• Schedule 14D-9 • Recommendation statement no later than 10 business days after the commencement, filed under Schedule 14D-9	• Schedule 14A	• Schedule 14D-9 • Recommendation statement no later than 10 business days after the commencement in a proxy solicitation
Communication / Other procedural requirements	• Communications must be filed on the date of first use, generally under cover of Schedule TO • Restrictions on purchasing shares outside the tender offer	• Communications must be filed on the date of first use, generally under cover of the proxy statement cover sheet	• Communications must be filed under Rule 425 beginning with the first public announcement

73 Source: own presentation.

3.2.3.5 Protective measures for the target in a hostile offer

Primarily as a result of a wave of hostile takeovers in the 1980s attempted by investors known as "corporate raiders", a variety of protective measures were developed to offer a U.S. public company protection in case of an unsolicited bid.[74] Although during the recent merger wave the frequency of hostile takeovers significantly decreased,[75] the potential implications from existing protective measures still need to be considered, given that the acquisition of a U.S. public company is often negotiated against the backdrop of a hostile takeover possibility.[76]

The protective measures available to a U.S. public company can generally be distinguished into corporate charter and by-law provisions, defensive payments, defensive sales, and other defenses.[77] Table 3.4 highlights the main implications of various alternatives of these measures, which differ with regard to their efficiency, costs, and timing, i.e. whether they are implemented before or after the offer was made.

Table 3.4: Protective measures for a U.S. company in a hostile offer[78]

Corporate charter and by-law provisions	• Supermajority voting provision Requires more than a simple majority of its shareholders to approve a business combination (both friendly and hostile) unless an "escape clause" is added to the charter, which overrides the supermajority provisions in case the company's board approves the proposed transaction.[79] • Staggered board Only a specified number of directors – typically one-third of the entire board – is elected at each annual meeting for a three-year term, thereby preventing an acquirer to gain immediate control of the company's board.[80] • Fair price amendment The transaction does not need to be approved by a specified supermajority if the bidder offers the minority shareholders a fair price, i.e. a price that at least equals the highest price paid to shareholders before the merger.[81]

74 See GAUGHAN (1999), p. 243.

75 As mentioned in Section 2.4.2.2, only two U.S. targets were acquired by German companies in a hostile transaction during the past decade.

76 See GORDON (2002), p. 2. For example *RWE* in its acquisition of *American Water Works* ("*AWW*"), in which *AWW* amended its poison pill to exempt *RWE* from all provisions of the rights agreement. In addition, COMMENT and SCHWERT (1995) showed higher takeover premiums for firms with anti-takeover provisions in place.

77 See for example RUBACK (1987).

78 Source: own presentation.

79 See JARRELL and POULSEN (1987), p. 129-132; LINN and MCCONNELL (1983), p. 365.

80 See REED and LAJOUX (1999), p. 785. However, the staggered board defense can be an ineffective measure since the hostile acquirer can amend the charter of the target upon gaining substantial control of the company, see POUND (1987), p. 353. For empirical studies on the impact of staggered board provisions on share prices, refer to BHAGAT and BLACK (1999); GARVEY and HANKA (1999).

81 See REED and LAJOUX (1999), p. 784. As such, the fair price amendment is not a means to prevent an unsolicited bid, but it provides a protection for the offered share price.

Table 3.4 (cont.): Protective measures for a U.S. company in a hostile offer

	• Poison pills Seek to make hostile acquisitions prohibitively expensive by either diluting the acquirer's interest in the target company or by offering the target shareholders a right to buy shares in the acquiring company at bargain prices upon consummation of the merger of both entities.[82] The most common variations of this measure are a "flip-in", "flip-over", and a "back-end" plan.[83]
Defensive payments	• Golden parachutes Employment agreements with executives that provide for large severance payments in the event of a "change in control".[84] • Greenmail If an investor has accumulated stock of the target without the intention of obtaining control of the target but with the sole purpose of reselling those shares at a premium, it might be possible for the target to repurchase those shares at a special offering price, so-called "greenmail".[85]
Defensive sales	• Crown jewels Selling particularly attractive assets to a third party and therefore making the target company less attractive. • White knight Takeover of the target company by a more favorable acquirer.[86] • White squire Selling a substantial block of the target's shares to a friendly investor that is not deemed being a takeover threat while simultaneously entering into a standstill agreement.[87]
Other defenses	• Corporate restructuring Recapitalization through the use of an employee stock ownership plan or a self-tender.[88] • "Pac-Man" defense Making a counteroffer for the shares of the hostile acquirer, thereby conceding that the transaction as such is desirable but preventing the loss of control over the company.[89]

82 See CAYTAS and MAHARI (1988), p. 242; DAWSON ET AL. (1987), p. 423ff. Several studies have examined the impact of poison pill provisions on stock price reactions in the context of an announced transaction, for example by COMMENT and SCHWERT (1995); HUANG and WALKING (1987); BRADLEY ET AL. (1982).

83 See REED and LAJOUX (1999), p. 780f.

84 See WHITE (1994), p. 439f.; MERKT (1991), p. 633. In comparison to other defense measures, the effectiveness of golden parachutes is doubtful, considering their relatively low value in relation to the total price of a transaction, see RIFKIND (1998), p. 108. For empirical studies on the impact of golden parachute provisions on share prices refer to SCHNITZER (1995); BORN and TRAHAN (1993).

85 See PELTZER (1986), p. 292f. Given that this form of intended repurchase of shares is discriminatory to other shareholders, it is a very ineffective and therefore a broadly unused takeover defense, see MIKKELSON and RUBACK (1986).

86 See BANERJEE and OWERS (1992), p.48ff.

87 See REED and LAJOUX (1999), p. 787.

88 See BRUNER (2004a), p. 847f.

89 See MERKT (1991), p. 640f.

Protective measures are generally not sufficient in preventing a hostile acquisition, but they prevent management from entrenching itself and give the target company to some extent negotiating leverage to maximize the premium offered to its shareholders.[90] The implementation of such measures requires a company's board of directors to consider its fiduciary duties with regard to the interests of its shareholders, i.e. it must pay attention to aspects such as the present and future impact of the measures on the company's share price and its ability to pursue a friendly business combination.[91] For example, the requirement of offering a fairness opinion in a proposed offer restricts the board's ability to quickly react to an acquisition attempt.[92] Moreover, the adoption of some protective measures requires the approval of the company's shareholders.

3.3 Due diligence for the transaction

3.3.1 Overview

In the United States conducting a transactional due diligence is usually an integral part of the acquisition process, due to the potential legal liability triggered by the "caveat emptor" (buyer beware) principle.[93] As defined in Section 2.5.3.1, the main purpose of due diligence is to evaluate the target company's business and financial position and to identify any legal risks and impediments to completion of the proposed transaction. The extent of the due diligence procedures will generally be determined by such features as the status[94] and size[95] of the target, the complexity of its business, the proposed transaction structure, and the time available to the closing.[96] As mentioned earlier, in the context of a cross-border transaction additional complexity to the due diligence process might result from the particularities of the U.S. business environment.[97] Respective concerns for a foreign acquirer predominantly cited in the literature focus on financial accounting, legal, taxation, environmental, and human

90 See MARGOTTA (1988).

91 See REED and LAJOUX (1999), p. 775.

92 See LAJOUX and ELSON (2000), p. 213. This requirement results from the "business judgement rule", under which directors will not face liabilities for their actions on behalf of the corporation when they act in good faith and have no personal interest in the transaction, see ANGERER and WINCKLER (2005), p. 288.

93 See TIGGES (2005), p. 95. In comparison, FLEISCHER and KÖRBER (2001) point out that in Germany the seller is essentially liable for any undisclosed or unnoted deficiencies of the target company.

94 In case the target is a public company, access to documentation within the due diligence is generally restricted to public and fairly limited information, as noted by MIDDELMANN and HELMES (2005), p. 658.

95 MIDDELMANN and HELMES (2005, p. 658) point out that in the United States mid- and small-sized companies are typically characterized by a high degree of pragmatism; accordingly these authors suggest foreign acquirers to exercise judgment while determining the scope of desired due diligence, i.e. to refrain from the fairly complex approach generally seen in transactions involving large targets.

96 As a result of their empirical study on the use of due diligence in transactions, MARTEN and KÖHLER (1999) concluded that in Germany due diligence has also become more widespread. According to these authors, financial due diligence was mostly conducted (94 percent), followed by tax due diligence (78 percent); environmental due diligence (47 percent) and insurance due diligence (49 percent) were not performed as frequently.

97 See ROSENBLOOM (2002a), p. 1ff.

resources aspects.[98] These areas were also expressed in a survey of chief financial officers of German acquirers of U.S. targets, in which the executives were asked to provide their perspective on which concerns mainly apply to a due diligence for an acquisition in the United States (see Table 3.5).[99]

Table 3.5: Importance* of subjects of due diligence for a U.S. target

Rank	Subject	Mean	Mode	Skew	Relative frequency°
1	Legal	1.4	1	0.24	100%
2	Tax	1.5	2	-0.15	91%
3	Financial	1.6	1	0.69	100%
4	Cultural	1.8	1	0.99	17%
5	Environmental	2.1	2	0.53	48%
6	Human resources	2.3	2	0.44	57%
7	Marketing	2.5	2	1.32	43%
8	Organization & IT	2.5	3	-0.15	52%

* importance is measured using the following scale: 1=very high; 2=high; 3=low; 4=very low; 5=n/a;

° relative frequency refers to how many German acquirers conducted a due diligence in the respective subject for their acquisition of a U.S. target company.

There are numerous sources publicly available for a foreign acquirer to obtain information about a potential U.S. target company, such as "The Directory of Corporate Affiliations", "Factiva", "Hoover's Online", "Bloomberg", "Lexis-Nexis", and "InfoUSA".[100] In case the target is a public company, various SEC filings can be obtained,[101] most importantly the company's annual financial statements in Form 10-K and the quarterly financial statements in Form 10-Q, which are not required to be audited, as well as any proxy materials.[102] Since due diligence is widely accepted in the U.S. corporate business environment, target companies in the United States generally display a high level of readiness to supply potential acquirers with answers to detailed information requests.

3.3.2 Financial and accounting due diligence

3.3.2.1 Overview

The review of the financial and accounting data of a target company in order to determine its current and future earnings and financial position is frequently considered in the literature

98 See Section 2.5.5.2.

99 A detailed description of this survey is given in Section 5.2.2.

100 See BRUNER (2004a), p. 192f.

101 An overview of all relevant SEC-filings can be obtained via the SEC web page at www.gov/info/egdar/forms/edgform.htm.

102 See ERNST & YOUNG (1994), p. 59. All SEC filings can be downloaded from the Electronic Data Gathering, Analysis, and Retrieval System ("EDGAR") database of the SEC, which can be accessed via its web page at www.sec.gov/info.edgar.

and amongst practitioners as being the most important aspect of due diligence.[103] While the future earnings potential of the target is assessed based on its past performance and projections for the future, the analysis of the financial position aims at identifying liquidity and financing potentials of the target as well as risks that are not sufficiently reflected in its balance sheet, such as over-valuation of assets and under-valuation or non-recognition of liabilities.[104] In light of a contemplated transaction, the accounting procedures of a target company may be aggressive in order to enhance its financial position and to maximize its earnings.[105]

Since the general approach to the controlling based internal reporting of companies has become more standardized in the past, specific U.S. considerations for a foreign acquirer primarily address the target's external financial reporting under accounting principles generally accepted in the United States ("U.S. GAAP").[106] U.S. GAAP are promulgated by the Financial Accounting Standards Board ("FASB") and comprise Statements of Financial Accounting Standards ("SFAS"), FASB Interpretations ("FIN"), Emerging Issues Task Force Issues ("EITF"), and Accounting Research Bulletins ("ARB"). In light of the "decision usefulness" principle, the main goal of financial reporting under U.S. GAAP is to offer relevant and reliable information for investors.[107]

The adoption of GAAP is only compulsory for U.S. companies in case their financial statements are audited, which is legally required only for public U.S. companies.[108] However, certain contractual agreements between creditors and other parties, for example loan agreements with banks or leasing contracts, may also require private U.S. companies to have their financial statements audited.[109] Financial statements in the United States must be prepared on a consolidated basis[110] and generally are not linked to federal tax regulations.[111]

---

103 See LAJOUX and ELSON (2000), p. 69.

104 See NIELAND (2001), pp. 74-87.

105 See DIAZ (2002), p. 101; such accounting is also referred to as "window dressing".

106 See MIDDELMANN and HELMES (2005), p. 666.

107 See KPMG (2003), pp. 15-18.

108 See KPMG (2003), p. 2.

109 See FISCHER ET AL. (2001), p. 2864.

110 ARB No. 51; SFAS No. 94. There is no requirement for consolidated financial statements at a level other than that of the ultimate parent company of the corporate group.

111 See BORN (2005), p. 452f. There is one exception for the determination of costs for inventories, for which the last-in-first-out cost flow assumption is only permitted for the computation if it is also applied for the financial statements (Section 472(c) of the Internal Revenue Code). An indirect influence of the tax law on financial accounting results from the fact that small companies try to achieve conformity between the accounting systems in order to minimize their costs for the preparation of financial and taxation statements; therefore those small and medium-sized firms, which are not required to have an annual audit, usually base their accounting on the common tax law, see FISCHER ET AL. (2001), p. 2883.

3.3.2.2 Financial position of the target company

The analysis of the financial position of the target company is focused on the applied accounting principles, which a foreign acquirer typically compares to its own standards, which in case of a German company are either German GAAP or International Financial Reporting Standards ("IFRS").[112] The following discussion of financial accounting aspects under U.S. GAAP is not meant to be comprehensive; it rather highlights the material differences between accounting standards that need to be considered by a foreign acquirer in assessing a U.S. target company's financial statements.[113] Such issues typically concern the accounting for (i) goodwill, (ii) impairment of property, plant, and equipment, (iii) inventory, (iv) provisions, and especially (v) pension and health care retirement benefits.[114]

Since 2002, business combinations must be accounted for under SFAS 141 using the purchase method. The allocation of purchase price frequently results in the recognition of other intangible assets apart from goodwill, for example for patents, customer lists, trademarks, and other internally generated intangibles that have not been recorded previously.[115] Under German GAAP such intangibles are typically included as part of goodwill.[116] The importance of the allocation of purchase price to intangible assets was further enhanced with the introduction of SFAS 142, which in deviation to German GAAP requires that goodwill as well as other intangible assets with an infinite useful life no longer be amortized. Goodwill must be tested annually for impairment at the reporting unit level, using a two-step approach (SFAS 142.19-22).[117] The first step is to compare the carrying value of the reporting unit with its fair value, which is generally determined as the net present value of discounted cash flows. If the fair value is less than the carrying amount, goodwill is deemed impaired and the second step of the test must be performed. In this step, an implied value of goodwill is determined by allocating the fair value of the reporting unit to the assets and liabilities in a manner similar to a purchase price allocation in a business combination. Only if its carrying value exceeds its implied value, is goodwill impaired. Compared to German GAAP and IFRS, this two-step approach frequently results in no or less impairment losses for goodwill.

Whenever events or changes in circumstances suggest that the carrying value of non-current assets, for example property, plant, and equipment, is not recoverable, SFAS 144 requires an impairment test by comparing the carrying amount of the asset to the undiscounted cash

---

[112] See BREBECK and BREDY (1999), p. 221ff.
[113] For a detailed discussion of U.S. GAAP refer to for example KPMG (2003).
[114] See MIDDELMANN and HELMES (2005), pp. 667-669.
[115] See ZELGER (2005), pp. 96-98.
[116] See for example HAYN and WALDERSEE (2004), pp. 240-246.
[117] A reporting unit is an operating segment as defined in SFAS 131, or, in certain circumstances, one level below an operating segment (SFAS 142.30). As such, compared to the definition of a cash generating unit under IAS 38.6, a reporting unit may be broader in scope.

flows generated from it. Only in cases where those undiscounted cash flows are not sufficient, is the asset written down to its fair value, which is determined either as the net present value of the projected cash flows or as a quoted market value (SFAS 144.22-23). Accordingly, the use of discounted cash flows under German GAAP and IFRS for impairment testing purposes may yield in an impairment loss that under U.S. GAAP would not be required.[118] As a result, property, plant, and equipment may be overstated under U.S. GAAP.

Inventories are either valued at acquisition or production cost, which according to ARB No. 43 include an appropriate portion of direct materials, direct labor, and indirect production cost, both fixed and variable. SFAS 151 requires that abnormal amounts of idle facility expense, freight, handling costs, and wasted materials be recognized as current-period charges,[119] and that the allocation of fixed production overheads be based on the normal capacity of the production facilities. In deviation to German GAAP, there are generally no options for including certain cost components in production costs. In addition, certain capitalizable costs under German GAAP, for example costs for voluntary social benefits (including pensions and health care), must not be included in the valuation of inventory under U.S. GAAP. Hence, depending on a company's accounting policy, production cost may be lower or higher under German GAAP compared to the U.S. GAAP requirements. Production cost may be determined using a variety of methods, including the last-in and first-out ("Lifo") assumption.[120] Under IFRS (IAS 2), Lifo is not permitted.

SFAS 5.7 requires recognition of a provision if it is probable that a liability had been incurred on the balance sheet date and if its amount can be measured reliably. The "probable" criterion is stricter than under German GAAP and IFRS.[121] In addition, when only a range can be estimated, then the minimum amount of that range of possible losses (which could be zero) is recorded as a provision.[122] Under the guidance of the prudence principle within German GAAP, such provisions are typically recorded at the higher end of the range, while under IFRS (IAS 37) the midpoint is frequently used.[123] Overall, certain obligations for which an adverse outcome is not deemed likely on the balance sheet date, for example for pending legal claims, are not accounted for under U.S. GAAP or are recorded at an amount which may be substantially lower than under German GAAP or IFRS.

Benefit plans offered by a U.S. company raise many challenging issues for a foreign acquirer. In the United States, a benefit plan is generally defined as an arrangement through which

---

118 See HACHMEISTER (2005), p. 209.
119 SFAS 151 amended the previous guidance of ARB No. 43, Section 4, and was effective beginning in 2005.
120 As long as this method is also used for tax purposes, according to Internal Revenue Code Section 472.
121 See HAYN and WALDERSEE (2004), p. 178f.
122 See KPMG (2002b), p. 60.
123 See BORN (2005), p. 781.

benefits are to be provided to all or a selected group of employees.[124] Main benefit plans for employees typically cover pensions and health care, in addition there are frequently separate compensation arrangements with the executives.[125] Pension plans are classified as "nonqualified" and "qualified", depending on whether they meet certain federal regulations, mainly the Employee Retirement Security Act of 1974 ("ERISA"),[126] as well as federal income tax requirements to allow for tax-favorable treatment.[127] Qualified pension plans are further categorized as "defined contribution" or "defined benefit" plans.[128] In a defined contribution plan the employer agrees to contribute to an external pension fund a certain amount each year based on a fixed formula, accordingly the employer's contribution is defined.[129] Defined contribution plans usually take the form of the so-called "401(k) plan", which allows for a tax-beneficial deferral of salary under the requirements of Section 401(k) of the Internal Revenue Code ("IRC"). In a defined benefit plan the total value of benefits that the employee is entitled to at the time of retirement is based on the employee's years of service and compensation. Unlike in Germany,[130] in the United States pension liabilities are generally funded through external funds, which in turn invest the contributions in shares and/or fixed income.[131] Nonpension benefit plans are typically not funded, since contributions beyond those required to pay for current benefits are not deductible for tax purposes.[132] Key concerns for a foreign acquirer typically center around defined benefit plans and the measurement of related liabilities and expenses in the financial statements.

U.S. GAAP accounting requirements for defined benefit plans are given by SFAS 87, 88, 106, 112, and 132, which differ significantly from German GAAP and may also yield different results than IFRS. Under SFAS 87, the recognition of a benefit liability and the measurement of net periodic pension cost are based on the computation of the projected benefit obligation ("PBO"), which is the actuarial present value of all vested and non-vested benefits of the plan participants. Compared to the computation under German GAAP, which

---

124 See KIESO and WEYGANDT (1998), p. 1092f.

125 See REED and LAJOUX (1999), p. 388.

126 Section 302 of ERISA provides extensive federal regulations for fringe benefits such as pension and heath care plans. These provisions mandate numerous pension plan requirements, including vesting, participation, funding, and disclosure policies. In addition, ERISA created the Pension Benefit Guaranty Corporation, which guarantees a pension benefit in cases where pension plans have insufficient funds. ERISA does not cover other post-retirement benefits.

127 See REED and LAJOUX (1999), p. 402. Qualified plans are covered in Internal Revenue Code Sections 401-416. For example, Section 412 permits tax deductibility of an employer's contributions to the pension fund and tax-free treatment of earnings from fund assets in case of a qualified plan.

128 See KIESO and WEYGANDT (1998), p. 1094. In this context, the term "defined" is used synonymously with the term "qualified".

129 See KIESO and WEYGANDT (1998), p. 1094.

130 WALDENMAIER ET AL. (2005) note that the outsourcing of pension financing by implementing Contractual Trust Arrangements becomes increasingly more popular in Germany.

131 See FISCHER ET AL. (2001), p. 2943. The allocation of the pension assets among various asset classes is usually restricted by state law requirements. Usually, plan assets may not be withdrawn by a company, unless they exceed the pension liability upon termination of a plan.

132 See COMISKEY and MULFORD (2000), p. 535.

typically follows tax rules, the PBO is generally higher, since it includes future salary increases as well as biometric mortality tables.[133] Analogous to the expected compensation increases, for computing the present value of health care benefits, anticipated future cost trends need to be considered. Such rates are affected by a variety of company or industry-specific factors, for example, composition and location of the workforce, and frequently range between 6.5 percent to 10 percent.[134]

In case of an underfunded status of a benefit plan, i.e. an excess of the PBO over the plan assets, a provision must be recognized in the balance sheet, which unlike under German GAAP rarely equals the underfunding.[135] This is principally due to the deferrals of actuarial gains and losses, i.e. changes in the PBO on the balance sheet date are not recognized as they occur, but systematically and gradually over subsequent years.[136] The feature of deferral not only impacts the valuation of the PBO, but also of the plan assets, since in the measurement of the net pension cost for the period credit is taken for the expected and not the actual return on plan assets. The deferral of the differences between expected and actual returns as well as of effects from changes in the actuarial assumptions (for example the discount rate) reduces the volatility of periodic net benefits cost. However, as a result of the deferral, on a going concern basis, the defined benefit plans of a U.S. company are typically underfunded in its balance sheet.[137] In addition, due to the external funding, in times of declining capital markets the gap between the PBO and the plan assets may substantially increase, thereby creating an additional financial burden.[138]

Table 3.6 provides a summary of the main U.S. GAAP issues and their differences to German GAAP and IFRS.

---

133 Under German GAAP, mortality tables provided by Heubeck are typically applied.

134 See COMISKEY and MULFORD (2000), p. 531.

135 In case of a surplus, an asset must be recorded, the so-called "net periodic pension cost". However, the FASB is currently working on a joint project with the International Accounting Standards Board, which is expected to conclude by the end of 2006, on a statement that would require employer sponsors of defined benefit plans to reflect the plan's funded status as a liability or an asset on the balance sheet.

136 A recognition of such deferred, so-called "unrecognized", items through the income statement is only required if they exceed 10 percent of the higher of the PBO or plan assets (SFAS 87.32).

137 SFAS 87.36 requires recognition of a liability that is sufficient from a liquidation standpoint, the so-called "additional minimum liability" ("AML"). The AML is calculated as the pension obligation that excludes future salary increases (the so-called "accumulated benefit obligation", which approximates the pension obligation to be satisfied in case of a termination of the plan) minus the fair value of the plan assets minus existing pension provisions. The recognition of the AML does not affect the income statement, since it is directly booked in equity with an offset through other comprehensive income (in case of any unrecognized prior service costs, the additional minimum pension liability is reduced by recognizing an intangible asset). IFRS do not provide similar rules.

138 In light of increasing funding gaps, U.S. companies are increasingly freezing their defined benefit plans recently, such as *IBM Corp.*, see BUCHTER (2006), p. 4.

Table 3.6: Major differences between U.S. GAAP, German GAAP, and IFRS[139]

	Accounting standards		
Subject	**U.S. GAAP**	**German GAAP**	**IFRS**
Goodwill			
• Amortization	Not amortized	Amortized generally over the useful life	Not amortized
• Impairment	Two-step test for reporting units: 1. Carrying amount > fair value 2. Carrying amount > implied fair value	No specific guidance	Single-step test for cash-generating units: Carrying amount > recoverable amount
	Allocation of loss first to other assets, then to goodwill	No specific guidance	Allocation of loss first to goodwill, then to other assets
Other intangibles			
• R&D costs	Expensed as incurred	Expensed as incurred	Research costs are expensed, development costs are capitalized under stringent criteria
Non-current assets			
• Borrowing cost	Must be capitalized if criteria for qualifying asset are met	Capitalization is prohibited with regard to acquisition cost	Capitalization is permitted, but not required
• Useful lives	Not predefined	Usually follows tax rules	Not predefined
• Impairment (assets in use)	Carrying amount > undiscounted cash flows	Carrying amount > attributable value	Carrying amount > recoverable amount
	Write down to the higher of quoted market values or discounted cash flows	Write down only if attributable value is permanently lower than carrying amount	Write down to the higher of net selling price or discounted cash flows
	Reversal prohibited	Reversal permitted	Reversal permitted
Inventories			
• Cost components	No valuation options; capitalization of interests prohibited	Options for including certain costs; capitalization of interests permitted	No valuation options; capitalization of interests permitted
• Cost formula	Lifo permitted	Lifo permitted	Lifo prohibited

139 Source: own presentation.

Table 3.6 (cont.): Major differences between U.S. GAAP, German GAAP, and IFRS

	Accounting standards		
Subject	**U.S. GAAP**	**German GAAP**	**IFRS**
Provisions			
• Recognition	"Probable" (i.e. > 70 percent likelihood)	Similar to IFRS, but also permits provisions without external obligation	"More likely than not" (i.e. >50 percent likelihood)
• Measurement	Minimum of a given range with equally probable outcome	Usually higher point of a range due to prudence principle	Midpoint of a given range with equally probable outcome
• Restructuring	Recognition solely based on commitment prohibited	General recognition criteria for provisions apply	Recognition when the entity is "demonstrably committed"
• One-time termination benefits	Recognized over the future service period in case employees are required to render services beyond the notification period	One-time benefits are fully recognized on the balance sheet date	One-time benefits are fully recognized on the balance sheet date
Retirement benefits			
• Determination of pension expense	Projected unit credit actuarial method	No specific guidance, follows tax rules	Similar to U.S. GAAP
• Additional minimum liability	If ABO > plan assets + accrued pension cost	Not required	Not required
• Prepaid pension cost	No restrictions for recognition	No specific guidance	Asset ceiling test-limitations
• Recognition of actuarial gains / losses	Recognized over expected remaining working lives or life expectancy, at a minimum amount exceeding corridor[140] must be recognized	No deferral permitted, gains / losses are recognized immediately	Similar to U.S. GAAP, but IFRS also permits full recognition directly in equity
• Expected return on plan assets	Measurement may be based on calculation that recognizes value over a period of up to five years	Due to the realization principle only realized gains are included in measurement	"Smoothing" as under U.S. GAAP is not permitted
• Prior / past service cost	Amortized over the average future service lives	Immediately expensed	Immediately expensed if fully vested
• Curtailment / Settlement gains	Recognition only to the extent that they exceed unrecognized actuarial losses, but not until the event causing the curtailment has occurred	Immediately recognized	Proportionate recognition
• Multi-employer plans	Defined contribution plan accounting	No specific guidance	Defined benefit plan accounting

140 The corridor rule requires that actuarial gains and losses are amortized through the income statement when at the beginning of the period they exceed the higher of 10 percent of plan assets or the PBO (SFAS 87).

3.3.2.3 Earnings situation of the target company

In addition to analyzing the target's financial position, the financial due diligence aims at identifying its sustainable earnings, which requires elimination of non-recurring and extraordinary income and expenses from the target's net income as shown in its statement of operations.[141] The U.S. GAAP requirements for presenting the statement of operations are less detailed compared to German GAAP, accordingly its structure may vary significantly between U.S. companies.[142] Under U.S. GAAP the statement of operations may take on a single-step or multi-step format.[143] The single-step format involves limited subtotals and basically provides a summary listing of all revenues and expenses. The multi-step format is used most frequently and provides subtotals for gross profit (i.e. revenues minus cost of goods sold), operating income (i.e. gross profit minus operating expenses such as selling, general, and administrative expenses), and other income and expenses. As a result, unlike in a single-step format, the development of the operating income category requires U.S. companies to separate operating and non-operating items.[144]

U.S. GAAP do not strictly define operating income, and thereby allow certain flexibility by classifying items within the income statement either into or out of the scope of operating income, or moving expenses from costs of goods sold to the selling, general, and administrative expense category. For example, while shipping and handling costs must be recognized as revenue based on EITF 00-10, there is no requirement to classify the associated costs as costs of goods sold and thereby to include them in gross profit. In addition, certain nonrecurring items such as restructuring, asset impairment, environmental, and litigation settlement charges can be classified within or outside of operating income and may be combined with recurring items such as foreign currency transaction gains in "other income and expenses". In order for nonrecurring items to be presented as extraordinary, they must also be deemed unusual, which, contrary to German GAAP, is rarely the case.[145] Beyond extraordinary items, special income statement categories are provided for discontinued operations and the cumulative effects of accounting changes, for which specific rules limit flexibility in determining the classification.[146] Another aspect to be considered is that the interest costs in connection with the calculation of defined benefit plans are included per SFAS 87 and SFAS 106 in the net period costs and therefore are part of operating income.

141 See PACK (2002), p. 280; NIELAND (2001), p. 83.
142 See KPMG (2003), p. 133.
143 See KPMG (2003), p. 133f.
144 See MULFORD and COMISKEY (2002), p. 280f.
145 See MULFORD and COMISKEY (2002), p. 283.
146 The presentation of discontinued operations is guided by SFAS 144.43. The disclosure of cumulative effects of accounting changes and errors follows Accounting Principles Board No. 20.

There is no U.S. GAAP standard dealing generally with the recognition of revenue.[147] Specific guidance is given though for advertising barter transactions (EITF 99-17), software revenue (Statements of Positions 97-2 and 98-9), and long-term construction-type contracts. If certain criteria are met, revenues from construction contracts generally are recognized using the percentage-of-completion method, which under German GAAP is permitted only in exceptional circumstances.[148]

Of particular consideration with regard to preparing the business plan for the U.S. target company is the impact of anticipated fluctuations in the USD/EUR exchange rate, since it will impact the projections for the sales of the foreign acquirer's group, the amount of dividends and profits, and perhaps the financing of the transaction.[149]

3.3.2.4 Impact of the Sarbanes-Oxley Act

As a result of the introduction of the Sarbanes-Oxley Act[150] with its Section 404 ("SOX 404"), a public company in the United States is required since the beginning of 2005[151] to include in its quarterly and annual filings with the SEC a report on the effectiveness of its internal control system[152] for financial reporting. Such reports must be audited and certified by independent auditors. As a result of SOX 404, numerous U.S. public companies reorganized their internal financial reporting structures in order to achieve the required level of reliability, verifiability, and transparency. Although the Sarbanes-Oxley Act does not apply directly to merger and acquisition activity, it is expected to especially impact the way in which public companies approach transactions.[153] In case a foreign company that is also listed on a U.S. stock exchange acquires a relatively large target, it needs to ensure that the target's internal control system is sufficiently in compliance with the SOX 404 requirements. As a result, acquirers are more cautious and perform more due diligence.[154] Acquisition agreements might include additional warranties by the sellers that the target company was in compliance with SOX 404 in the past. In addition, the requirements of

---

147 The SEC has stated its view on revenue recognition in SAB 101.

148 These criteria require that estimates of revenues, costs to complete, and the extent of progress towards completion be reasonably reliable (ARB 45). In case these requirements are not met, the completed contract method should be used.

149 See MIDDELMANN and HELMES (2005), p. 682.

150 This act was effective as of June 30, 2002, and brought extensive changes in corporate governance and disclosure of companies that file registration statements under the Securities Act or Exchange Act.

151 For small-sized and foreign companies, the provisions of SOX 404 apply for financial years beginning January 2006.

152 The internal controls for financial reporting are defined as a system of processes ensuring that (i) the company maintains sufficient documentation about its transactions that enable it to compile financial statements that are in compliance with GAAP, (ii) revenue and expenses are only recorded in accordance with the policies set by the company's management, and (iii) each material transaction involving the acquisition, use, or sale of assets that is not in compliance with the company's internal policies and guidelines is detected, see RIPIN and GEYRHALTER (2005), p. 301.

153 See ANGERER and WINCKLER (2005), p. 287.

154 See FOLEY & LARDNER (2005).

SOX 404 may warrant a higher reliability of the internal control systems for the financial reporting of U.S. companies, which may facilitate a more efficient and effective financial due diligence for potential acquirers.[155] Due to the perception of a widening difference in scrutiny between audits of public and private companies as a result of SOX 404, cautious acquirers may perform more intense accounting due diligence for private target companies.[156]

3.3.3 Legal due diligence

Legal due diligence for a U.S. target is typically focused on an assessment of the (i) proper legal standing, (ii) compliance with laws and governmental regulations, (iii) ownership of assets and exposure to associated liabilities, and (iv) actual or pending litigation of the target company.[157]

Legal due diligence begins with an analysis of the corporate organization in order to ensure a proper legal standing of the target company as a counterparty in the transaction. The legal framework for the foundation and status of companies is given through the applicable corporate laws of the state in which the company is chartered, which particularly in case of a public company is frequently the state of Delaware as a result of its specialized, wide-ranging, and corporation-friendly case law.[158] The inquiries include a review of the incorporation and registration documentation, as well as the target's bylaws, major agreements with shareholders, and significant contracts with third parties.[159] Of particular interest in this context is whether certain provisions in the target's bylaws impact or burden the transfer of ownership in that company, for example as a result of poison pills or specific approval requirements by the target's board of directors.

Operating a business in the United States requires compliance with numerous federal, state, and local laws and regulations, for example regarding environmental protection, labor and employment, and consumer protection. Non-compliance with such statutes could result in potentially significant liabilities for the acquirer.

The foreign acquirer intends to ensure that those assets that are part of the transaction are actually owned by the target and therefore are available for the realization of the planned strategic goals and business objectives of the transaction. Ownership of assets is primarily

155 Such a higher reliability may be attributable to the expectation that failure of a company to assess or correct a weak control environment could jeopardize the credibility of its management and could negatively impact its share price, see ANGERER and WINCKLER (2005), p. 287.

156 See STERN (2004).

157 See for example BRUNER (2004a), p. 216.

158 See MIDDELMANN and HELMES (2005), p. 675

159 See MIDDELMANN and HELMES (2005), p. 675. The review of existing contractual relationships for a U.S. company essentially follows the general approach of any legal due diligence, as described for example by FRITSCHE and GRIESE (2005).

evaluated by inspecting titles and deeds for tangible assets, and the sufficiency of the documentation for patents and licenses for intangible assets, such as intellectual property ("IP"),[160] and trademark and copyrights.[161] In addition, the acquirer makes certain that no claims exist with regard to the proper title or patent of an asset, such as infringement of IP licenses.[162]

In the United States, involvement in litigation through single claims or class action lawsuits may cause significant legal defense expenses as well as substantial compensatory damage and punitive damage payments, while the latter frequently exceed the actual damage by multiples.[163] Hence, a foreign acquirer typically directs its analysis at an evaluation of the potential for adverse judgments in ongoing or pending litigation. Litigation can result from various areas, but particular attention is generally paid to the following:

- Environmental matters, which are discussed in detail in Section 3.3.5.
- Employee matters, which for example result from workers compensation in the case of accidents, employment termination, discrimination of minorities, or sexual harassment claims. Extensive statutory laws and regulations require a U.S. company to have a system in place to prevent such cases. However, a foreign acquirer typically seeks to ensure the compliance of the target's policies and investigates whether any discrimination-related claims occurred in the past since additional claims may follow.[164] Section 3.3.6 provides a more detailed analysis of human resources considerations for the due diligence inquiries.
- Material business risks issues, predominantly with regard to product liability in light of a tendency of U.S. juries to award substantial compensatory and punitive damages for personal injuries caused by defective products.[165] There is no single product liability law in the United States, rather a patchwork of federal[166] and state statutes. Based on those statutes, a party named in a product liability suit may include the (i) manufacturer of the parts that make up the product, the (ii) assembler of the product, the (iii) wholesaler of the

---

160 In case intellectual property is part of a separate entity of the seller's corporate group, a so-called "IP holding", this entity is usually either part of the transaction or the respective patents are transferred from this entity to the target; see also Section 3.4.1.

161 In the United States, federal copyright filings are made with the U.S. Copyright Office and filings for patents and trademarks are made with the U.S. Patent and Trademark Office. Under the "work made for hire" doctrine, an employer will be deemed the owner of an employee's work created within the tasks of his employment. However, in 1989 the Supreme Court narrowed the definition of "employee" by excluding independent consultants, who retain ownership rights in a work until those rights are specifically transferred. Accordingly, if applicable, an acquirer needs to inquire whether the target enacted appropriate agreements. For further information on conducting due diligence inquiries for the target's intellectual property, see AGRAWAL and MAEBIUS (2004), p. 1ff. BEEZY and PECOT (2004, p. 14ff.) provide comprehensive information with regard to due diligence inquiries for trademark and copyright issues.

162 See DE ANDINO ET AL. (2004), p. 1ff.

163 See RESNICOW and RATHKOPF (2002), p. 184f.

164 See MIDDELMANN and HELMES (2005), p. 680.

165 See LAJOUX and ELSON (2000), pp. 306-311. The authors provide a detailed overview of U.S. consumer protection on the basis of product liability, food and drug, and consumer liability laws.

166 Within the U.S. Uniform Commercial Code.

product, and the (iv) retailer of the product.[167] For the foreign acquirer, a key element in this context is the analysis of the sufficiency of the target's quality management and control and its level of insurance.[168] U.S. companies are frequently self-insured with regard to product liability claims, i.e. they recognize an accrual in their balance sheet within the provisions of SFAS 5.[169] External insurance for product claims is also available, but usually only at high costs of up to three percent of annual revenue.[170] Other areas of evaluating the target's insurance program include the coverage of its directors' and officers', property damage, business interruption, and its umbrella liability.[171]

3.3.4 Tax due diligence

The tax due diligence is typically focused on assessing potential tax liabilities of the target company arising from non-compliance with tax laws and regulations.[172] For a U.S. target this exposure may arise from

- omitted or incorrect filing of federal and state tax returns,[173]
- non-payment of all tax obligations, including income, sales, and payroll taxes,
- inappropriate allocation of income amongst the states in which the company conducts its business,[174]
- inappropriate intra-group transfer pricing and insufficient documentation thereof,[175] and

---

167 See LAJOUX and ELSON (2000), p. 306.

168 See BRUNER (2004a), p. 218.

169 In addition to product liability claims, U.S. companies are typically self-insured also for workers compensation issues, see MIDDELMANN and HELMES (2005), p. 676. TANKERSLEY (1999, p. 42) notes: "While workers compensation has become notoriously expensive in recent years, the alternative can be far more expensive. Juries have become so oriented to the injured employee's interest that the average judgment awarded in all employment related cases exceeds $500,000."

170 See MIDDELMANN and HELMES (2005), p. 676.

171 TANKERSLEY (1999, p. 41f.) provides a detailed description of various forms of insurance typically considered by a U.S. company.

172 See PICOT (2002), p. 291.

173 MIDDELMANN and HELMES (2005, p. 670) note that in the United States deadlines for filing federal and state tax returns are generally more often observed than in Germany. In addition, even little business activity in a state may require the filing of an income tax return in that state. Non- or erroneous filing of a tax return may lead to substantial fines for companies.

174 Income is typically allocated through application of a specific key, such as revenue, salaries, or assets. Generally, neither the state of incorporation of the acquisition vehicle nor the location of its headquarters determines the taxability of the acquired business under state statutes. State taxes, which are deductible for federal tax purposes, are imposed by the states based on a concept called "nexus", which governs taxation for those companies with "sufficient contact" with the respective state, see BOSSART (2002), p. 225. The definition of sufficient contact varies from state to state, but generally requires fairly minimal activity, such as maintaining a sales office, see MIDDELMANN and HELMES (2005), p. 671.

175 See BRUNER (2004a), p. 231. Permitted methods of determining transfer prices under the IRC are comparable uncontrolled price, resale price, cost plus, profit split, transactional net margin, and global formulary apportionment, see MIDDELMANN and HELMES (2005), p. 674f. As required by Section 482 IRC, transactions between related parties must be carried out "at arm's length".

- omitted bulk-sales notification in connection with an asset deal.[176] In such instances the acquirer may be responsible for state taxes due by the target company that result from activities prior to the closing.

A review of available prior years' tax returns and information on the date and the results of a recent audit by the Internal Revenue Service ("IRS")[177] or other tax authorities may provide an indication for any potential tax liabilities.

Another main focus of the tax due diligence is the planning of a tax beneficial form of the acquisition, comprising the (i) taxability of the transaction for the acquirer, target, and its shareholders, the (ii) ability of the acquirer to utilize the target's tax attributes, the (iii) deductibility of interests incurred for debt in connection with the transaction, and (iv) post-merger tax optimization opportunities. These aspects are discussed in detail in Section 3.4.

3.3.5 Environmental due diligence

In light of rigorous regulatory requirements and the potentially significant expenses for companies of complying herewith in the United States, assessing environmental liabilities is a crucial step in the process of acquiring a U.S. company, especially if the target is in the manufacturing industry. Environmental due diligence is not only important to identify potential liabilities due to the cash outflows associated with environmental compliance, it may also impact the valuation of the target.[178]

Environmental restrictions and liabilities are imposed upon U.S. companies by federal, state, and local statutes and regulations, whereby the Comprehensive Environmental Response, Compensation, and Liability Act ("CERCLA"), with its onerous provisions for joint, several, and retroactive liabilities, gives rise to the most significant environmental exposure.[179] In addition to the Superfund Amendments and Reauthorization Act ("SARA"),[180] this statute governs the remedy and clean-up of hazardous waste and contaminants and imposes liabilities for damages arising from contamination, regardless of whether a waste disposal activity was conducted legally prior to the enactment of the law.[181] Both CERCLA and SARA are collectively referred to as the "Superfund Act", accordingly a waste site deemed

---

176 See MIDDELMANN and HELMES (2005), p. 672.
177 See BRUNER (2004a), p. 231.
178 See MIDDELMANN and HELMES (2005), p. 677.
179 See THELEN REID & PRIEST (2004), p. 85; MORIYAMA (1994), p. 354.
180 42 U.S.C. § 9601 (1994). SARA provides an acquirer with a highly conditional innocent defense ("safe-harbor") on the basis of appropriate due diligence prior to the closing of a transaction; such a safe-harbor only applies though to CERCLA, and not to liabilities imposed by comparable state regulations.
181 42 U.S.C. §§ 9601-9675 (1994).

severely contaminated under this statute is referred to as a "superfund site".[182] Additional environmental requirements are contained in the Resource Conservation and Recovery Act ("RCRA"),[183] Emergency Planning and Community Right-to-Know Act ("EPCRA"),[184] Toxic Substances Control Act ("TSCA"),[185] Clean Water Act ("CWA"),[186] and the Clean Air Act ("CAA").[187]

The Environmental Protection Agency ("EPA"), the federal government agency primarily responsible for enforcing environmental requirements,[188] has extended the responsibility for violations of environmental requirements beyond those parties who caused or who were directly involved in activities causing a violation.[189] Therefore, any of the CERCLA statute parties potentially liable for the clean-up of hazardous waste sites include (i) current owners or operators of a facility where hazardous wastes were released or disposed, (ii) prior owners or operators of a facility at the time of disposal of hazardous wastes, (iii) those who generated or arranged for disposal of hazardous wastes at a facility, and (iv) transporters of hazardous wastes.[190] Because of the retroactive liability, a responsible party may not have caused the contamination but merely inherited a past problem through an acquisition.[191]

As a result, if a property containing hazardous wastes is part of the acquisition, the foreign acquirer may be subject to significant environmental liabilities, regardless whether owned or leased by the target and also regardless whether such wastes are currently generated or not.[192] In addition, the liability may be extended regardless whether the transaction was structured as a share or asset deal. Under U.S. state corporate law the acquirer in a share deal essentially becomes the successor of the target and as such becomes liable for remediation costs for its

---

182 The term "superfund" stems from the fund that the U.S. Congress established to clean up abandoned hazardous sites, see FROMM ET AL. (1997), p. 430.

183 42 U.S.C. §§ 6901-6992k (1994). This statute imposes requirements on the generation, storage, transportation, treatment, and disposal of hazardous waste, and principally applies to active facilities.

184 40 U.S.C. §§ 350-372 (1994). This statute establishes requirements for governmental authorities and industries for emergency planning and "Community Right-to-Know" reporting on hazardous and toxic materials.

185 15 U.S.C. §§ 2601-2629 (1994). This statute regulates the manufacturing and disposal of asbestos-containing materials and sets forth numerous requirements for the manufacturing of other chemicals.

186 33 U.S.C. §§ 1251-1387 (1994). This statute requires obtaining wastewater and stormwater permits for the discharge of pollutants into the waters of the United States.

187 42 U.S.C. §§ 7401-7671q (1994). This statute sets forth air quality standards and governs emissions of pollutants into the air by requiring compliance with regulations through obtaining permits.

188 The EPA often delegates its enforcement obligations to authorized state environmental agencies, see BRUNER (2004a), p. 219.

189 See THELEN REID & PRIEST (2004), p. 86.

190 See FROMM ET AL. (1997), p. 431.

191 See MORIYAMA (1994), p. 354.

192 See MIDDELMANN and HELMES (2005), p. 678. Information about prior notifications of contaminations by the EPA can be obtained from its web page (http://www.epa.gov). Other sources of information are the Emergency Response and Remedial Investigation System ("ERRIS") list and the Environmental Compliance History Online ("ECHO") list.

on-site as well as off-site[193] wastes.[194] An acquirer in an asset deal is generally only liable to the extent explicitly stated in the acquisition agreement. However, as mentioned earlier, under the "substantial continuity of enterprise" approach, the acquirer in an asset deal may also be liable.[195] The EPA policy on successor liability essentially follows the aforementioned general criteria[196] and may require an acquirer found liable under CERCLA to fund the entire cost of remediation of a target's own and off-site locations.[197]

Accordingly, as part of its due diligence procedures, a foreign acquirer typically inquires about notices from the EPA identifying the target as a "potentially responsible party under CERCLA", including the determination of the amount the target company has been requested to contribute toward remediation of a hazardous site.[198] The evaluation of potential on-site hazardous wastes is often conducted through a phased approach, beginning with a "Phase I" environmental site assessment for any real estate properties owned and leased by the target.[199] A Phase I audit is generally not very expensive and involves investigation of prior uses of the facilities and physical inspection of the properties with regard to signs of contamination.[200] A subsequent "Phase II" or "Phase III" audit typically includes soil borings and substantial water and air tests.

In addition to the federal regulations, each state has implemented its own environmental laws, which are generally at least as restrictive as the federal set of laws. Some states (for example Indiana and Michigan) require in cases where ownership in a property is transferred that the local authorities are informed about prior contaminations on that site, while the New Jersey Environmental Cleanup Responsibility Act ("ECRA"), which is perceived as being the most restrictive anticontamination law in the country,[201] requires a mandatory environmental assessment before an acquisition is consummated. Any identified material contamination must be remediated to the satisfaction of the state authorities before the closing of the deal. In addition, several states (for example New Jersey and Connecticut) have implemented so-called "super-lien" laws, which enable the state authority to place a priority lien on any

---

193 These can be properties not owned by the company or locations to which it has shipped hazardous substances. It is important to note that the safe-harbor provisions of SARA are not extended to claims related to off-site disposal activities.

194 See FROMM ET AL. (1997), p. 430.

195 See MORGAN LEWIS & BOCKIUS (1996), p. 165.

196 See Section 3.2.2.

197 See EPA (1984), p. 2.

198 See FROMM ET AL. (1997), p. 446. Information could for example be obtained from the EPA web page.

199 See MORRISS and JOLIN (2004), p. 7. Although in the United States the terms "Phase I" and "Phase II" environmental site assessments ("ESA") are commonly used, they generally refer solely to the investigation of conditions on the property for sale and the potential of those conditions to create liability for remediation costs. When acquiring an ongoing industrial operation, a full environmental compliance audit is typically conducted. The American Society for Testing and Materials developed guidelines for an ESA and environmental compliance audit, which may assist in determining a "superfund" liability, see MORRISS and JOLIN (2004).

200 See TANKERSLEY (1999), p. 41.

201 See MORIYAMA (1994), p. 354.

property on which it has had to spend its own funds for remediation.[202] State laws and the resulting requirements and standards are of particular importance in case of a Phase II investigation of properties.[203]

Both parties of the transaction typically allocate environmental liabilities between each other by drafting respective representations and warranties and indemnification provisions in the acquisition agreement.[204] These provisions usually cover environmental liabilities arising from on-site or off-site pollution and all actions causing pollution, whether or not such actions when taken were in violation of any law.[205] The second point is essential, since under the Superfund Act a company's liability may reach back to actions taken before the passing of current environmental requirements, for example when the shipment of wastes by unlicensed carriers to unlicensed disposal sides was legal.[206] Due to their potentially extensive scope, indemnifications given by the seller for environmental claims are usually unlimited in amount and time.

3.3.6 Human resources due diligence

As discussed in Section 2.5.3.1, principal concerns for a foreign acquirer in conducting a human resources due diligence center around compensation and benefit plans for the target's executives and employees as well as on the protection of the target's employees with regard to planned post-closing reductions of the workforce, especially when acquiring a unionized target company.

3.3.6.1 Compensation and benefit plans

The treatment of the executive compensation agreements is a sensitive issue in a cross-border acquisition, as a result of certain specialties of U.S. compensation systems, such as the existence of golden parachutes, extensive severance arrangements, change of control provisions, and stock options and phantom stock plans, and due to the fact that compensation levels for a U.S. management typically exceed those of similarly sized German companies.[207]

---

202 See MORIYAMA (1994), p. 355. As a result of this potential super-lien, commercial lenders are encouraged to require prospective borrowers to investigate a property thoroughly before loans for a transaction are approved.

203 See MIDDELMANN and HELMES (2005), p. 677. The authors note that currently 40 states have promulgated specific standards for contaminations of industrial sites.

204 Section 107(e) of CERCLA explicitly recognizes the validity of provisions in the acquisition agreement that allocate liability for environmental claims between both parties.

205 See LAJOUX and ELSON (2000), p. 321f.

206 Due to the potentially substantial legal and consulting fees typically incurred during an investigation period, from the perspective of a foreign acquirer it may be beneficial to define the "trigger" for such claims at the point in time when a contamination is discovered and not when an actual claim is filed by a governmental agency, see MORIYAMA (1994), p. 360f.

207 See MIDDELMANN and HELMES (2005), p. 678f.

Usually the consummation of an acquisition requires entering into new employment contracts with the target's key management. Retention bonus programs that depend upon the executive's years of post-closing employment are commonly used when the U.S. target is a public company and its stock, and therefore its associated stock option programs, cease to exist.[208]

Of particular importance for an acquirer are liabilities resulting from underfunded defined benefit plans.[209] Underfunding can imply (i) in a worst case of assuming termination of the plan upon acquisition that the fund's assets are not sufficient to cover the pension liabilities or (ii) in a more typical situation that the assets are at least equivalent to the liabilities, but not sufficient on an ongoing basis. Only in the latter case can the plan be transferred without immediate adverse financial consequences for the acquirer, though the plan's future funding requirements may still represent a significant long-term liability for the acquirer.[210] If the target company's plan is overfunded, the acquirer may be able to either recover this asset in the future by reducing its funding requirements, or by taking a reversion of the surplus upon termination of the plan.[211] However, both options are subject to the strict limitations imposed by the Consolidated Omnibus Budget Reconciliation Act ("COBRA") of 1985.[212] Besides the assessment of potential liabilities from underfunded pension plans,[213] the due diligence focuses on health care plans, mainly due to the increasing health care expenses for retirees in the United States.[214]

In case of a unionized workforce, the employer and other unionized employers often jointly sponsor a multiemployer pension plan.[215] In such a case, the transaction structure generates different implications for the acquirer.[216] While in a share deal a withdrawal liability is transferred to the acquirer in case the acquirer ceases contributions to the plan,[217] in an asset

208 See MIDDELMANN and HELMES (2005), p. 679. For a detailed analysis of the impact of employee stock option plans on an acquisition refer to GAUGHAN (1999), p. 372ff. Private companies in the United States frequently offer so-called "phantom stock" plans. Prior to 2005, stock option plans were not treated under SFAS 123 as an expense of the company.

209 Defined contribution plans cannot be underfunded by definition and therefore do not represent a similar potential financial risk for the acquirer.

210 See REED and LAJOUX (1999), p. 417.

211 See REED and LAJOUX (1999), p. 418f.

212 For example, COBRA precludes termination and reversion of a plan unless it is new or has permitted a reversion for at least five years.

213 See MORGAN LEWIS & BOCKIUS (1996), p. 184. For example the acquisition of *Cyprus Amex-US Coal Mining* by *RAG Aktiengesellschaft* in 1999 resulted in a legal suit by *RAG* for reimbursement of approximately $35m in underfunded assumed retirement obligations, see WIDENER UNIVERSITY SCHOOL OF LAW (1999).

214 For example, *Delphi Automotive Systems International, Inc.* cited the drastic increase in the expenses for its health care obligations as a major reason for its bankruptcy filing, see MEIER (2005), p. 21.

215 See KIESO and WEYGANDT (1998), p. 1123.

216 See LAJOUX and NESVOLD (2004), p. 105.

217 ERISA § 4201; 29 U.S.C. §1381.

deal the withdrawal liability remains with the seller, unless special agreements are made that meet certain statutory exceptions.[218]

Nonqualified plans are typically set up for senior executives of a company and often provide for a deferral of compensation through a so-called "rabbi trust" vehicle.[219] Responsibility for continued funding of benefit plans subsequent to an acquisition may not only exist in a share deal, but also in an asset deal, given that the seller of a target company generally prefers the acquirer to continue the existing pension plans, due to the high costs and extensive administrational efforts associated with a termination of pension plans.[220]

3.3.6.2 Employee protection

In the 1990s, employees or their unions filed over half of all lawsuits targeting U.S. corporations.[221] Accordingly, a primary human resources concern for a foreign acquirer relates to potential liabilities resulting from U.S. employment laws, which literally consist of thousands of federal and state statutes, regulations, and juridical decisions.[222] Employment related lawsuits usually cite federal or state laws setting standards for equal opportunity or employment reduction.[223] In the context of employee protection, typical issues encountered by a foreign acquirer of a U.S. target relate to a planned reduction of the target's workforce and the presence of a labor union.[224]

U.S. employees have principally no right to review, approve, or even be consulted about an acquisition and its potential implications such as a reduction of the workforce.[225] U.S. companies are essentially free to reduce their workforce, as long as in doing so they comply with applicable laws, most notably the equal opportunity law prohibiting discrimination.[226] As a result of this law, the selective termination of even a relatively small number of the target's employees, as opposed to for example the elimination of entire departments subsequent to an acquisition, may give rise to discrimination litigation assuming that (i) the acquirer's individual hiring decisions were based on "protected" characteristics, such as

---

218 These exceptions are defined in ERISA § 4204; 29 U.S.C. § 1384.

219 See BAKER (1993), p. 75ff. The author provides an overview of regulatory aspects of such nonqualified benefits in connection with an acquisition. The term "rabbi trust" results from an IRS letter ruling that confirmed to a synagogue tax deferral for a rabbi who was the beneficiary of a trust established to pay him retirement benefits. Such plans are often referred to in the United States as Supplemental Executive Retirement Plans ("SERP").

220 See BENDANIEL and ROSENBLOOM (1998), p. 47. A termination is typically only available if the acquirer is willing to offer essentially comparable benefits through its own plan.

221 See LAJOUX and ELSON (2000), p. 335.

222 See TURCON (1994).

223 See LAJOUX and ELSON (2000), p. 336.

224 See MORGAN LEWIS & BOCKIUS (1996), p. 179.

225 See BENDANIEL and ROSENBLOOM (1998), p. 46.

226 See LAJOUX and ELSON (2000), p. 348.

gender, race or national origin, or that (ii) the selection criteria used had an adverse impact upon those in a protected group.[227]

Under the federal Worker Adjustment Retraining and Notification Act of 1988 ("WARN"), covered employers, i.e. companies having 100 or more employees, must give 60 days advance written notice to employees who will lose their employment for reasons including an acquisition.[228] The obligation to give notice is generally triggered only when 50 or more employees at a single site of employment are laid off within a 30-day period (or in some circumstances a 90-day period).[229] There are no statutes requiring retention of the target's employees or special severance payments upon termination of employment as a result of an acquisition.[230] However, in light of this absence of specific statutory requirements, many U.S. companies have adopted provisions in the individual employment contracts providing for some form of severance pay.[231]

In addition to severance, the termination of the target's employees may also trigger obligations with regard to the full vesting of pension benefits in some instances and the continuous payments of health care benefits for up to 18 months under COBRA.[232] Even in the absence of any employee termination, the mere change in control of the target company may result in golden parachute obligations for its management or the accelerated vesting of stock-based compensation programs.[233]

In case the target's workforce is unionized, specific notification and termination procedures typically apply.[234] Most U.S. companies operating in a private sector are subject to the National Labor Relations Act of 1935 ("NLRA"),[235] which protects the right of employees to bargain collectively with the employer through representatives of their choice, i.e. a union.[236]

Typically, such "collective bargaining agreements" require employers to give sufficient notice of major changes such as an acquisition, thereby enabling the employees (or unions respectively) to bargain effectively about the impact of the anticipated change.[237] Collective bargaining agreements also govern the post-closing compensation of the unionized

---

227 See MORGAN LEWIS & BOCKIUS (1996), p. 187.
228 29 U.S.C. §§ 2101-2109.
229 See U.S. DEPARTMENT OF LABOR (2003).
230 See THELEN REID & PRIEST (2004), p. 96.
231 See BENDANIEL and ROSENBLOOM (1998), p. 46.
232 ERISA § 603.
233 See MORGAN LEWIS & BOCKIUS (1996), p. 185. The authors point out that in an asset deal, an employment termination has technically occurred even for those employees who continue with the acquirer, which might be sufficient to trigger the aforementioned obligations.
234 See LIEBERMANN and MOSS (2001), p. 117.
235 29 U.S.C. §§ 151-169.
236 See THELEN REID & PRIEST (2004), p. 97.
237 See LAJOUX and NESVOLD (2003), p. 106f.

employees and usually also prohibit the acquirers from arbitrarily laying off employees.[238] MIDDELMANN and HELMES (2005, p. 685) point out that foreign acquirers frequently do not sufficiently consider the impact of existing union relationships, since it significantly reduces the flexibility for implementing cost saving measures via a reduction of the workforce in the post-closing implementation phase. In a share deal, the acquirer will be required to recognize the union and assume the collective bargaining agreement. As mentioned in Section 2.2.2, in an asset deal the foreign acquirer will generally be bound only if the collective bargaining agreement is expressly assumed as stated in the acquisition agreement.[239]

3.4 Tax planning for the transaction

3.4.1 Overview

The U.S. tax system generally comprises federal, state, and local income taxes. Since in the context of cross-border acquisitions state and local taxes are generally of minor importance, this discussion of tax planning aspects is confined to the implications of federal income tax.[240] The primary sources for federal income tax laws are the statutes of the Internal Revenue Code of 1986, as amended. Specific guidance for applying the IRC to mergers and acquisitions is mainly provided by the federal tax authority, the Internal Revenue Service, in revenue or private letter rulings, or by the U.S. Department of the Treasury in interpretive or legislative regulations.[241] For federal tax purposes, taxable income is currently taxed at a progressive rate of up to 35 percent, while state tax rates may vary between zero[242] and up to ten percent,[243] given that each state is autonomous in setting its respective tax rate.

The principal considerations from a taxation perspective for planning a U.S. acquisition concern the transformation of the purchase price into future amortization and depreciation expense, the ability to use tax attributes of the target company, and the deductibility of interest expense incurred for financing the transaction. In the United States, the taxability of a transaction is directly linked to whether cash, shares, debt instruments, or a combination

238 See LAJOUX and NESVOLD (2003), p. 105.

239 See BENDANIEL and ROSENBLOOM (1998), p. 46. As mentioned before, the concept of successor liability in certain states may also impose employee-related obligations to the acquirer in an asset deal.

240 From a state tax perspective, one relevant aspect for an acquirer may be the differing tax rates and definitions of taxable income in some states. For example, income from licenses is taxed differently in various states, which under certain circumstances offers the opportunity for a corporate group to concentrate its intellectual property in an IP holding that is incorporated in a state that does not tax income from IP license payments. The IP license payments by the affiliates of the group to the IP holding may be tax deductible though. A similar structure could be set up also for intercompany interest, see MIDDELMANN and HELMES (2005), p. 673f.

241 For further information see PRATT and KULSRUD (2003), p. 2ff.

242 For example in the states of Delaware, Nevada, Washington, Florida, and Texas.

243 For example in the state of New York the rate is 8.75 percent.

thereof is used as the form of payment to the target shareholders.[244] The main prerequisite for tax-free treatment is to pay the seller at least partially with shares.[245]

The choice of the transaction structure that from a tax perspective is most favorable for the foreign acquirer may not be optimal for the seller, given that the acquirer prefers a form that reduces the after-tax cost of the acquisition, whereas the sellers aim to maximize their after-tax proceeds from the sale.[246] For the acquirer, the decision to either purchase individual assets or shares of the target determines the (i) post-closing tax basis[247] of the acquired business and thereby the future deductions for amortization and depreciation expense and the (ii) ability to utilize the target's tax attributes. For the seller this decision may not only affect the amount but also the timing and character (i.e. ordinary or capital income) of their taxable gain from the transaction.

3.4.2 Taxable transaction

3.4.2.1 Asset deal

In a taxable asset deal most acquired assets are assigned a new tax basis. Pursuant to IRC Section[248] 1060 the total purchase price[249] must be allocated among the acquired assets by grouping each acquired asset with its fair market value to one of the seven classes shown in Table 3.7. Within this "residual approach", any excess of the total purchase price over the fair market value of the assets is deemed goodwill.[250] Similar to purchased intangible assets, goodwill is amortizable over 15 years for tax purposes.[251]

---

244 See DICKEY (2000), p. 288 ff.

245 See HERZIG (2004), p. 134. Another aspect to be considered by a foreign acquirer is the choice of the acquisition vehicle. For example, in case the target is a group including non-U.S. subsidiaries, the acquisition of those foreign entities through a non-U.S. acquisition vehicle may permit the avoidance of withholding taxes on dividend payments in the future, see MIDDELMANN and HELMES (2005), p. 674f.

246 See JUNG (1993), p. 154.

247 A taxpayer's basis in an asset represents the extent to which the asset may be depreciated or amortized and thereby may generate non-cash deductions of taxable income.

248 Unless otherwise indicated, all section references contained herein are to the Internal Revenue Code of 1986, as amended, or to the Treasury regulations promulgated hereunder.

249 The total purchase price comprises the amount paid to shareholders, assumed liabilities, and incurred transaction expenses. In case the payment of the purchase price is deferred in fixed installments, these payments need to be included in the basis of the acquired assets at their principal amount, despite the fact that for the seller the installment sales method might result in a deferral of taxable gain recognition. If a portion of the purchase price is contingent upon certain future events, according to Treasury Regulation § 1.1060-1T(f) the acquirer cannot include those contingent amounts in the allocation.

250 See DICKEY (2000), p. 292.

251 Prior to the Omnibus Budget Reconciliation Act (Tax Reform Act) of 1993 goodwill was not amortizable in the United States. By generally requiring an amortization period of 15 years for intangible assets, this treatment is less favorable for the amortization of covenants not to compete, which generally are enforceable only for periods of five years or less, see AYERS ET AL. (2000, p. 34f.). These rules are similar to the treatment of an asset deal under the German Tax Code (§ 7 Abs. 1 S. 3 EStG).

Table 3.7: Tax asset classes for purchase price allocation[252]

Class	Description
I	Cash and cash equivalents
II	Readily marketable securities, foreign currency, and certificates of deposit
III	Accounts receivable and assets that are marked-to-market annually for federal income tax purposes as well as selected debt instruments
IV	Assets held for sale, including inventory
V	All tangible assets not included in classes I-IV
VI	Intangible assets as defined in Section 197, such as patents, customer lists, workforce, franchises, licenses, and covenants not to compete, but excluding goodwill
VII	Any remaining purchase price, i.e. goodwill

In case the target's tax basis of depreciable and amortizable assets is lower than the fair value, the purchase price allocation will result in a so-called "stepped-up" tax basis. Due to the higher deduction for amortization and deprecation expense, such a step-up provides the acquirer with the benefit of future tax savings. The target company on the other hand will realize a gain in this instance that is subject to either capital gain or ordinary income taxes.[253] In case the target company is a C-Corporation[254] that is liquidated subsequent to the sale of its assets, the target shareholders are additionally taxed on their investment gain, i.e. the difference between the amount of cash received and the tax basis in their sold shares. As a result, a taxable asset deal creates a double taxation for the seller, which under the current IRC may only be mitigated if the seller is either an S-Corporation[255] or a subsidiary of another corporation that owns at least 80 percent of the target's shares.[256]

The purchase price allocation is usually agreed by the parties and is either included in the asset acquisition agreement or is completed as a post-closing item.[257] According to Section 1060(a), any written consent on the allocation is binding on both parties. Although the IRS generally respects the allocation, it may require changes upon its audit.

252 Source: own presentation following Treasury Regulations §§ 1.338-6, 1.338-7.

253 Depending on the allocation of the purchase price in accordance with Section 1060. In effect, the target company is taxed as if it had sold each asset separately.

254 The IRC labels a regular corporation as a C-Corporation and defines it as any corporation that is not an S-Corporation.

255 An S-Corporation is a regular corporation that elects to be taxed pursuant to subsection S of the IRC, which under certain restrictions permit it not to be treated and therefore be taxed as a separate taxpayer. Instead, the earnings of this corporation are taxed directly to the shareholders, whether or not they are distributed. Pursuant to Section 1361(b), the main requirements for eligibility of an S-Corporation tax treatment are that it (i) may not have more than 100 shareholders, whereby each shareholder must be a resident individual (hence no shareholder can be a corporation, a partnership or a nonresident alien individual), (ii) only has one class of common, but no preferred stock, and (iii) is not a member of an affiliated group.

256 Sections 332 and 337.

257 Each party has to file in Form 8594 ("Asset Acquisition Statement under Section 1060") the purchase price allocation together with the tax return in the year of acquisition.

3.4.2.2 Share deal

In deviation to an asset deal, to the extent that the purchase price exceeds the tax basis in their shares, the target shareholders are taxed in a share deal at the capital gains tax rate rather than the generally higher ordinary income tax rate.[258] In addition, the target retains its tax attributes, such as tax elections, carryforwards of net operating losses, and credits.[259] Since there is no step-up, i.e. no change in the tax basis of its assets and liabilities, the target company itself is not taxed in a share deal. As a result, contrary to an asset deal, in a share deal tax-deductible goodwill is not recognized. However, an exemption is provided under Section 338, which allows structuring a share deal in a manner that combines the respective taxation benefits of both an asset and a share deal.

Depending on the corporate identity of the target, Section 338 provides for two alternative structures. If the target is a C-Corporation, the Section 338(g) election is available, while Section 338(h)(10) election is available if the target is either a subchapter S-Corporation, a subsidiary in a U.S. affiliated group,[260] or a member of a U.S. consolidated group.[261] These two elections allow a share deal to be treated for tax purposes as though the assets of the target company were acquired, thereby enabling the acquirer to obtain a stepped-up basis for the target's assets.[262] In the Section 338(g) election, this deemed asset sale is achieved in four steps (see also Figure 3.2):[263]

(i) The acquirer purchases at least 80 percent of the target's shares within a 12-month window.

(ii) It is assumed that the target company sells its assets to a hypothetical intermediary target company at fair market value and subsequently liquidates.

(iii) This hypothetical intermediary target company takes an aggregate basis in the "old" target company's assets equal to the purchase price that the acquirer paid for the target's shares; identical to a regular asset deal, the allocation of the purchase price requires the application of the residual approach.[264]

(iv) The acquirer "purchases" the shares of this hypothetical intermediary target.

---

[258] See DICKEY (2000), p. 295f. The Jobs and Growth Tax Relief Reconciliation Act of 2003 established a maximum tax rate of 15 percent on net long-term capital gains of individuals and replaces the prior maximum capital gains rate of 20 percent (effective through December 31, 2008). In case the consideration received is comprised of debt or installment payments, under Section 483 shareholders may defer the recognition of the gain until principal payments are received.

[259] Although subject to certain limitations, as shown in Section 3.4.4.

[260] An "affiliated group" is broadly defined in Section 1504(a) as a group of U.S. corporations all of which are at least 80 percent owned by a common parent company, which is also a U.S. corporation.

[261] See DICKEY (2000), p. 296f.

[262] See DICKEY (2000), pp. 296-298.

[263] See LAJOUX and NESVOLD (2004), p. 153f.

[264] Since 2003, the IRS requires a Form 8883, "Asset Allocation Statement under Section 338", in which information about transactions involving a deemed asset sale under Section 338 are reported.

Figure 3.2: IRC Section 338(g) election[265]

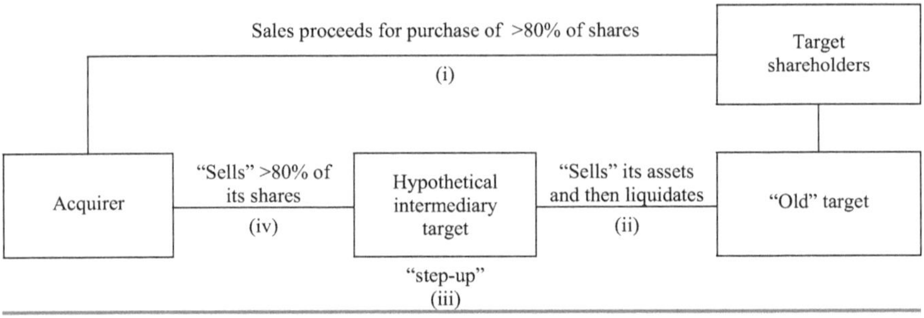

The election is irrevocable and has to be made no later than the 15th day of the ninth month beginning after the month in which the acquisition date occurs. It has no impact on the target shareholders, since they are still treated for tax purposes as having sold their shares. The target company is treated as being liquidated after having sold its assets to a hypothetical intermediary company at fair value. The liability for the taxes on the gain arising from this deemed asset sale is borne by the acquirer, since the target has become a subsidiary of the acquiring company.[266] As a result, a Section 338(g) election yields in a double taxation: the target shareholders are taxed on their share sale and the acquiring company is taxed on the deemed sale of the assets of the target company.

The applicability of this election is not restricted in the case of a cross-border transaction. It is typically used when the target company has net operating loss or tax credit carryforwards available, since these may offset the gain resulting from the deemed asset sale. However, since the deemed liquidation of the "old" target occurs subsequent to the deemed asset sale, any net operating loss or tax credit carryforwards exceeding the gain from the deemed asset sale are forfeited. In addition, that gain may not be offset against any carryforwards of tax attributes of the acquirer, since the respective gain is triggered on the "old" target's final tax return.[267]

The double taxation of the Section 338(g) election may be avoided in a Section 338(h)(10) election. In this case, the transaction is only taxed once on the level of the "old" target's parent, which is treated as having sold not the shares, but the net assets of the target and of

265 Source: presentation follows LAJOUX and NESVOLD (2004), p. 157.
266 This shifting of tax obligations is usually factored into the final purchase price, see BRUNER (2004a), p. 553.
267 The federal income tax liability of the target is to be included in a special one-day tax return filed by the acquiring company as the new owner of target, according to Section 338 (h)(9).

having subsequently distributed those sales proceeds tax free in a Section 332 liquidation of the target (see Figure 3.3).[268]

Figure 3.3: IRC Section 338(h)(10) election[269]

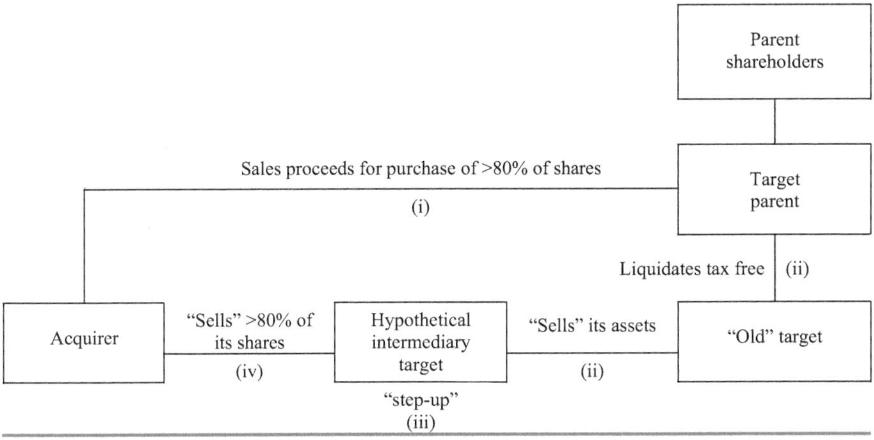

Accordingly, in deviation to the Section 338(g) election, the gain from the deemed asset sale to the hypothetical intermediary target is included in the consolidated tax return of the target's parent, which may be able to offset it with any operating losses from its other subsidiaries.[270] For the seller this election, which has to be made jointly by both parties,[271] is generally only beneficial when the unrealized appreciation in its shares exceed that in the target's net assets. Since this is rarely the case, a Section 338(h)(10) election typically requires the acquirer to compensate the seller for its tax disadvantage, thereby resulting in a higher purchase price.[272] Due to the stepped-up basis of the target's assets, the acquiring

[268] A perquisite for this election is that the parent owns at least 80 percent of the target's shares. The IRC permits this transaction form because the parties could achieve the same result if the target sells its assets in a regular asset deal and then liquidates tax-free under Section 332.

[269] Source: presentation follows LAJOUX and NESVOLD (2004), p. 158.

[270] In case the divesting parent has capital loss carryforwards, the incremental taxes on a share deal without the Section 338(h)(10) election would be relatively lower than those from a sale with that election. This is due to the divesting parent offsetting its capital gain from the sale of the shares with its capital loss while that loss cannot offset the portion of the gain on a deemed asset sale that is recaptured deprecation, i.e. ordinary income. Similarly, carryforwards of net operating losses reduce the tax cost of a Section 338(h)(10) election for the divesting parent, see ERICKSON and WANG (2000), p. 67f.

[271] As a result of this prerequisite, the Section 338(h)(10) election essentially is not applicable in acquisitions of public target companies.

[272] See ERICKSON and WANG (2000), p. 64f. The authors analyze the manner in which tax-based transaction structures influence the acquisition price of corporate subsidiaries. They compare various proxies for the premium paid in taxable subsidiary share acquisitions in which an IRC Section 338(h)(10) election was made to premiums in transactions completed in the absence of the election. Other studies that analyzed the effect of taxes on corporate valuation and corporate restructuring transactions are by AYERS ET AL. (2000); HAND and SKANTZ (1999); MAYDEW ET AL. (1999); ALFORD and BERGER (1998); AUERBACH and REISHUS (1988).

company derives its tax benefit from this election over time from higher amortization and depreciation expenses. Therefore, from the acquirer's perspective the use of this election may only be beneficial when the present value of the future tax savings exceeds the additional premium it may incur to compensate the seller for its higher tax cost. Besides the avoidance of double taxation, another benefit of the Section 338(h)(10) election is that, unlike in a Section 338(g) election, any unused carryforwards of tax attributes are preserved for future use. Another difference is that only in a Section 338(h)(10) election is the acquirer liable for the target's pre-acquisition taxes.

A share deal is often combined in a two-step acquisition with a statutory merger of the acquisition vehicle and the target. A forward subsidiary merger, i.e. the merger of the target into the acquisition vehicle, is treated for federal tax purposes as if the target sold its assets and distributed the sales proceeds to its shareholders in a liquidation.[273] A reverse merger, i.e. the merger of the acquisition vehicle into the target, is treated for tax purposes like a regular share deal, often in combination with a Section 338 election.

3.4.2.3 Comparison of taxable transaction structures

From a pure tax perspective, the acquirer typically favors to structure the transaction as an asset deal, since the stepped-up basis of the acquirer assets reduces its future tax burden. The present value of this future tax benefit is typically lower than the immediate[274] tax liability for the target and its shareholders in this case.[275] Hence, most taxable acquisitions are usually structured in the United States as a share deal, in which the seller is only subject to a single level of capital gains tax. The survey of German acquirers of U.S. target companies confirmed this conclusion, since asset deals accounted for less than one third of the transactions evaluated in the survey.[276] However, an asset deal may be favorable for both parties if (i) the target company is an S- or C-Corporation with sufficient carryforwards of net operating losses to offset the taxable gain from the transaction, or if (ii) the target company is an at least 80 percent owned subsidiary of another corporation, since a subsequent liquidation of the target would be tax-free, therefore resulting in only one level of tax. If the realized gain from the asset sale exceeds the taxable income the shareholders would realize in case of a share deal, the acquirer may compensate the seller for the increased tax burden by paying a higher purchase price, as long as the tax benefit from the asset step-up to the acquirer would

---

273 IRS Revenue Ruling 69-6, 1969-1 C.B. 104.

274 The seller may be able under certain circumstances to defer all or part of the gain by deferring receipt of payment and reporting the transaction as an installment sale, regardless of whether the transaction is structured as an asset or share deal.

275 IRS Revenue Ruling 69-6, 1969-1 C.B. 104.

276 The executives were asked to provide their assessment of which concerns specifically apply to the management of an acquisition involving a target company in the United States. For a detailed discussion of the scope of this survey refer to Sections 5.2.2 and 5.4.4.3.

justify it.[277] Another aspect to be considered in this connection is the joint election under Section 338(h)(10), in case both parties prefer an asset acquisition but need to enter into a share acquisition agreement for various, predominantly legal reasons.[278]

Table 3.8 summarizes the U.S. tax consequences of an asset and share deal for the acquirer, the target, and the target shareholders.

Table 3.8: Tax implications of asset and share deals[279]

	Tax structure		
Criteria	**Taxable asset deal**	**Taxable share deal**	**Taxable share deal + § 338(h)(10) election**
Consequences for the acquirer			
• Taxation of the transaction	No	No	Yes
• Tax rate	n/a	n/a	Ordinary income
• Tax basis in target's assets	Stepped-up	Historical basis is carried over	Stepped-up
• Tax basis in target's shares	n/a	Purchase price	Purchase price
Consequences for the target			
• Taxation of the transaction	Yes	No	Yes
• Tax rate	Ordinary income / Capital gain	n/a	Ordinary income
• Target's tax attributes (NOL)	Remain with seller, may be used to offset gain from the sale	Remain with target, annual limitation	Remain with seller, may be used to offset gain from the sale
Consequences for target shareholders			
• Taxation of the transaction	Yes, in case target is liquidated	Yes	Yes
• Computation of gain	Liquidation proceeds less basis in target's shares	Purchase price less basis in target's shares	Purchase price less basis in target's shares
• Tax rate	Capital gain	Capital gain	Capital gain

277 AYERS ET AL. (2004) concluded in their empirical study of the impact of the tax structure on the purchase price that shareholders are compensated for the costs of accelerating capital gains taxes that otherwise could have been deferred in certain transaction structures. They find a positive association between acquisition premiums for taxable acquisitions and shareholder capital gains taxes for individual investors, thereby concluding that target shareholders require compensation for the incremental costs associated with accelerating capital gains taxes.

278 Within the survey sample, approximately 10 percent of the evaluated transactions were structured using the joint election of Section 338(h)(10) (it should be noted though that not all executives answered the question of which tax structure was employed in case of a share deal).

279 Source: own presentation.

3.4.3 Tax-free transaction

Under certain circumstances, a U.S. acquisition may qualify as a "reorganization" that is accorded tax-free treatment for the target shareholders. Section 368 sets forth the provisions for tax-free acquisitions, with the main prerequisite being that the target shareholders receive shares in the acquiring company as the principal and sometimes only form of consideration for the transaction. In this case the shareholders are treated as having exchanged their old shares for similar ones, hence no capital gain is recognized.[280] In addition to the conditions of Section 368(a)(1), other judicially created requirements that need to apply to a tax-free treatment are the (i) existence of a business purpose other than pure tax avoidance,[281] (ii) continuity of shareholder interest,[282] and (iii) continuity of the target's "historic" business or the continuous use of a substantial portion of the target's "historic" assets.[283] The three most common forms of tax-free transactions are type "A"-, "B"-, and "C"- reorganizations. A type A-reorganization consists of a statutory merger of two or more companies, a type B-reorganization involves a stock-for-stock exchange, and a type C-reorganization involves the exchange of stock for assets.[284]

A type A-reorganization is defined as a statutory merger either in form of a forward or reverse subsidiary merger.[285] Although it may be the most favorable tax-free structure in a domestic transaction, it is currently not applicable to a cross-border acquisition, since the IRS took the position that when the acquirer is not subject to the corporate law of any state, a merger under state law and therefore a tax-free A-reorganization cannot occur.[286] The only exception may be if the acquirer offers the target shareholders shares in its U.S. acquisition vehicle, but this may not be feasible or desirable for reasons other than taxes.

In order to qualify as a type B-reorganization, the acquirer needs to purchase at least 80 percent of the target's shares solely in exchange for its own shares.[287] Any related

---

280 See BREALEY and MYERS (2000), p. 959.

281 Common business purposes include cost savings, economies of scale, and expansion into new markets.

282 Evidenced by the target shareholders receiving at least 50 percent of the transaction consideration as the acquiring company's shares.

283 For a detailed description of these requirements refer to for example BRUNER (2004a), pp. 554-558.

284 Other types of tax-free transactions contained in Section 368 are the forward triangular merger (so-called type "D"-reorganization, in which the acquirer must purchase substantially all of the assets, thereby not permitting the disposal of unwanted assets) and the reverse triangular merger (so-called type "E"-reorganization).

285 Section 368(a)(l)(A). The transaction will be tax-free for the target shareholders only in case it is entirely paid for with shares.

286 However, in 2005 the IRS proposed amendments to Section 368 that would allow such reorganizations also in the case of cross-border transactions, see NEW YORK STATE BAR ASSOCIATION (2005), p. 2.

287 Section 368(a)(l)(B). In the context of a cross-border transaction, the target shareholders owning more than 5 percent of the acquirer's shares after the transaction must enter into a written agreement with the IRS in which they agree to be taxed on the difference between the fair market value of the received shares and the tax basis of the transferred shares of the target in the event the acquirer disposes of the target within a period of five years after the acquisition date, see ABAHOONIE and BRENNER (1994), p. 222.

transactions with the target shareholders involving cash disqualify the tax-free treatment.[288] Similar to a type A-reorganization, this structure may also not be acceptable for a foreign acquirer.

A type C-reorganization involves the acquisition of substantially all of the target's assets, i.e. 90 percent of the net or 70 percent of the total assets (valued at fair market value), solely in exchange for shares.[289] The target company is subsequently liquidated and the shares in the acquiring company received in exchange for its assets are distributed to the target shareholders.[290] In case the acquirer is a foreign company, a C-reorganization is only available if the acquirer intends to use the purchased assets in the conduct of business outside the United States and if at least 80 percent of target's shares are owned by no more than five U.S. corporations.[291]

3.4.4 Other considerations

In addition to the primary question of which form the acquisition should take, other main tax implications for a foreign acquirer concern any limitations on the use of the target's tax attributes and the deductibility of acquisition indebtedness-related interests.

A significant difference between taxable asset and share deals is the acquirer's ability to utilize the tax attributes of the target subsequent to the transaction, predominantly its carryforwards of net operating losses ("NOL") and credits. A NOL stems from an excess of tax deductions over taxable income and may be carried forward, i.e. used to offset taxable income in the future, for federal tax purposes up to 20 years.[292] Tax credits may result from unused capital losses, excess foreign tax credits, or investment credits.

The tax attributes of a target may only be retained by the acquirer in a share deal that results in a substantial change in ownership.[293] However, the acquirer's annual use of carryforwards is limited to an amount equal to the fair market value of the target company[294] multiplied by a

---

288 See DICKEY (2000), p. 301f.

289 Section 368(a)(1)(C).

290 See DICKEY (2000), p. 301f; GAUGHAN (1999), p. 594.

291 See LAJOUX and NESVOLD (2004), p. 189ff.

292 Sections 172 and 1082. These sections also permit a carryback up to three years in certain very limited situations. Each state has its own regulations for carryforwards of NOLs that do not necessarily match the federal regulations.

293 For tax purposes a substantial change in ownership generally occurs when one or more major shareholders have increased their ownership of the target company's shares by more than 50 percentage points over a three-year period. A sale of a parent company will generally also constitute a change in ownership of its subsidiaries. Generally, all carryforwards are completely disallowed if the business of the target company is discontinued during the first two years following the change in ownership.

294 The fair market value is typically established by the price paid for the shares and may be reduced by contributions to the target's capital within a two-year period prior to the ownership change.

long-term tax-exempt interest rate[295] established by the IRS.[296] In addition, NOL carryforwards of the acquired company may only be used to offset its own future taxable income, and not that of other businesses included in the acquirer's consolidated tax return.[297]

Interest expenses for debt incurred in connection with an acquisition are generally tax-deductible in the United States.[298] However, for foreign acquirers the deductibility is limited in case of so-called "disqualified interest".[299] Disqualified interest is defined as interest paid by a U.S. corporation either to a non-U.S. related party, or to a third party on loans guaranteed[300] by a non-U.S. related party, when that non-U.S. related party is not subject to taxation in the United States due to applicable tax treaties.[301] If the non-U.S. related party receives interest payments from its U.S. subsidiary free of U.S. withholding tax and if the debt-to-equity ratio of the U.S. subsidiary exceeds 1.5 to 1, the deductibility of such disqualified interest is limited to the extent of the company's "excess interest expense" for the year. Such excess interest expense equals the excess of the company's total interest obligations over 50 percent of its "adjusted taxable income".[302] Any excess interest limitation amount may be carried forward for three years, while any disqualified interest may be carried forward indefinitely (Section 163(j)). These so-called "earnings stripping" provisions were essentially designed to prevent foreign acquirers from avoiding U.S. taxes by financing their acquisition of a U.S. company with a disproportionately high amount of debt (so-called "thin capitalization"), with the effect that profits are being stripped off in the form of deductible interest rather than as dividends out of after-tax income.[303] Accordingly, the tax planning of

---

295 The interest rate is derived from long-term tax-exempt interest rates paid on U.S. bonds and is lower than commercial interest rates, see ZINN (2004).

296 Section 382. The intention of the Section 382 limitation is to prevent investors from simply acquiring companies with NOLs, merging them with their own profitable businesses, and thereby using the NOLs to shield taxable income (so-called "trafficking"). Under this limitation, investors may only earn a "tax-free" return on their investment equal to the tax-exempt rate, i.e. equal to an investment in municipal bonds. In addition to Section 382, corporate tax attributes may also be limited by Sections 269, 381, and 384 and additional provisions applicable for consolidated returns, see DICKEY (2000), p. 308f.

297 Section 384.

298 Section 163(a). In case the target company is to be included in a consolidated tax return of the acquirer, for federal tax purposes the group is treated as a single taxpayer. However, for state tax purposes such a consolidation does not apply in this case, i.e. the interest payments of the acquiring parent do not reduce the state income tax liability of the target company, see ZINN (2004).

299 Section 163(j). Another limitation on interest deductibility is imposed by Section 279, which also applies to domestic companies. Under the applicable criteria of these provisions, interest in excess of $5m annually may not be deductible.

300 The term "guarantee" is defined rather broadly and comprises essentially any type of assurance that another party's debt will be paid, for example by means of a comfort letter.

301 For German lending companies, pursuant to Article 11 paragraph 1 of the "Convention between the Federal Republic of Germany and the United States of America for the Avoidance of Double Taxation and the Prevention of Fiscal Evasion with Respect to Taxes on Income and Capital and to certain other Taxes" as of August 29th, 1989, interest income is exempt from U.S. taxes, i.e. it is deemed disqualified interest under Section 163(j).

302 The adjusted taxable income is the taxable income computed without regard to deductions for net interest expense, net operating losses, depreciation, and amortization.

303 See ZEHETMEIER-MÜLLER and DOERR (2005), pp. 335-339.

the transaction typically includes the determination of an appropriate post-closing level of equity of the target company.[304]

3.5 Valuation of the target company

3.5.1 Overview

In general, there are no conceptual differences between the applied methods for valuing a target company in Germany and the United States.[305] The standard approach for determining the target's value is to discount its free cash flows using a weighted-average-capital-cost based discount rate, as shown in the responses of the surveyed German acquirers of U.S. targets (see Table 3.9).[306]

Table 3.9: Method applied for determining the value of a U.S. target company

	Status of the target	
Applied valuation method	**Private**	**Public**
Discounted cash flows	50%	59%
Comparable multiples	22%	35%
Discounted earnings	17%	0%
Asset-based	6%	0%
Combination methods / Other	6%	6%

Additionally, the application of the DCF method dominates in legally motivated valuations in Germany.[307] Due to the strong focus on capital market information and the absence of applicable requirements in the United States,[308] a U.S. target's board of directors typically benchmarks a DCF valuation against comparable market multiples when obtaining a fairness opinion in order to fulfill its fiduciaries duties when facing a takeover bid. SCHENCK ET AL. (2005) note that despite similar underlying fundamentals, the perceived relevance and actual

---

304 See MIDDELMANN and HELMES (2005), p. 673.

305 See JAENSCH (1992), p. 377.

306 See Section 5.2.2 for a detailed description of this survey. The widespread use of the DCF method in Germany can be attributed to the increasing internationalization of M&A activity during the fifth merger wave, which was accompanied by the increasing influence of U.S. investment banks, and to a stronger focus on a shareholder value-orientation of companies, see TIMMRECK (2004), p. 61; VOGEL (2002), p. 183; JANSEN (2001), p. 207.

307 For example for a squeeze-out according to AktG Section 327(a) or for mergers according to UmwG Section 60, for which strict requirements promulgated in IDW S1 and IDW ES1 (2004) by the German Institute of Chartered Accountants require the use of the DCF method; the results obtained from a DCF valuation need to be benchmarked against the actual share price, according to a ruling of the Federal Constitution Court, see BÖGLE and BÄTZ (2005), p. 346f.

308 In contrast to Germany, there is no institution in the United States that issues generally accepted principles and recommendations for the application of valuation methods. The American Institute of Certified Public Accountants issued in 2005 the Exposure Draft "Proposed Statement on Standards for Valuation Services: Valuation of a Business, Business Ownership Interest, Security, or Intangible Asset", which sets forth the use of income, asset-based, and market approaches, without specifying the determination of the various input parameters, see BÖGLE and BÄTZ (2005), p. 348.

valuation level of the applied multiples are different compared to a German environment, which might complicate the negotiation process.[309]

3.5.2 Application of the comparable multiples method

Due to the large number of public companies in the United States, compared to Germany there is a broader availability of trading and transaction multiples for peer companies, which creates stronger expectations among U.S. investors with regard to the average price premium in an acquisition.[310] On average, the pricing levels for U.S. public companies are higher than those of their German peers.[311] In addition, while in Germany applying the comparable multiples method is based typically on EBITDA, in the United States Price/Earnings ratios are widely used in the financial community.[312] From the perspective of a foreign acquirer, both effects yield tendentiously higher purchase premiums for a U.S. acquisition, particularly in the case of an exchange offer.[313] Based on an analysis of the employed multiples in two samples of domestic and U.S. cross-border transactions by identical German acquirers during the period from 1990 to 2004, Table 3.10 shows that the U.S. transactions were relatively more expensive.[314]

Contradicting these observed multiples, the majority of the surveyed executives stated that they do not believe that the premiums in cross-border transactions exceed those of domestic ones, as displayed in Figure 3.4.

---

309 See SCHENCK ET AL. (2005), pp. 36-41.

310 See JAENSCH (1992), p. 387.

311 See SCHENCK ET AL. (2005), p. 36. The authors demonstrate the different valuation levels with the example of *Continental AG*, which traded in mid-2005 at an enterprise value/EBITDA multiple of around 4.9x and a Price/Earnings ratio of 10.9x, compared to median EBITDA multiples and Price/Earnings ratios of U.S. automotive suppliers of 6.3x and 13.5x, respectively.

312 See SCHENCK ET AL. (2005), p. 33; JAENSCH (1992), p. 387. Regardless of the chosen valuation metrics, BRUNER (2004a, p. 259) lists as potential problems of employing the multiples approach the (i) definition of an appropriate peer group, the (ii) dependence on accounting data, and the (iii) non-consideration of potential changes in future capital expenditures and investments in working capital. To alleviate the first problem, RICHTER (2005) for example suggests compilation of the target's peer group based on the use of value drivers (such as expected growth rate, reinvestment rate, and leverage ratio) instead of a Standard Industry Classification code identity.

313 See SCHENCK ET AL. (2005), p. 41. This effect is further implicated by differences between U.S. GAAP and German GAAP regarding the determination of the net earnings of a company. SCHENCK ET AL. (2005) note as another challenge to be considered in this context the possibility that the domestic capital market will not assign the higher value of the target to the combined post-closing value, which could have a negative impact on the acquirer's share price; accordingly, the authors conclude that "...in many cases the capital market may hinder rather than facilitate an M&A transaction if the parties proposing a transaction on the one hand and the investors on the other disagree with the pricing levels generated by the markets", SCHENCK ET AL. (2005), p. 41.

314 For a description of the composition of these samples refer to Sections 5.2.1.1 and 5.6.1.

Table 3.10: Transaction multiples paid by German acquirers[315]

	Transaction volume /		
	Sales	**EBITDA**	**Net income**
German domestic acquisitions			
Average	1.25	6.07	27.39
Median	0.69	5.16	23.48
(Sample size)	(18)	(8)	(10)
U.S. cross-border acquisitions			
Average	4.35	9.64	31.25
Median	1.28	10.05	20.07
(Sample size)	(31)	(17)	(21)

Figure 3.4: Differences in premiums between domestic and cross-border transactions

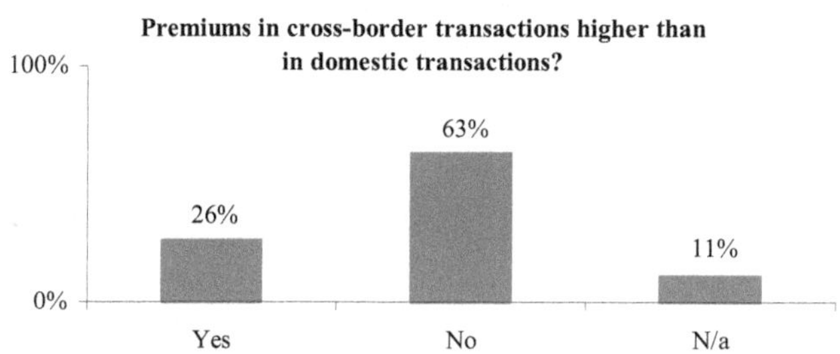

3.5.3 Application of the discounted cash flow method

When applying the DCF method, the previously mentioned differences between U.S. and German accounting principles are not relevant for a foreign acquirer,[316] although the assessment of the target's earnings situation requires familiarity with U.S. GAAP and, if necessary, elimination of one-time issues distorting the quality of earnings, since free cash flow is typically derived from an operating perspective from the target's EBIT.[317] For the projection of free cash flows a foreign acquirer needs to consider in particular the impact of the (i) anticipated payouts for litigation, product liability, and environmental protection claims, the (ii) potentially limited use of tax attributes and tax planning strategies (for example transfer pricing and royalties arrangements), the (iii) effects of foreign currency exchange rate fluctuations, and the (iv) ongoing external funding requirements for pension and other post-employment benefits.[318]

315 Source: Thomson Financial Securities Data Company.

316 See BRUNER (2004a), p. 354.

317 See NIEWANDT and SEIBERT (2004), p. 21ff.

318 See BRUNER (2004a), pp. 348-389; COPELAND ET AL. (2000), pp. 353-372; JAENSCH (1992), p. 383f.

In contrast to the majority of German companies, the external funding of pension obligations in the United States does not directly influence the determination of the U.S. target's capital structure and therefore of its WACC.[319] When using the CAPM to calculate a U.S. target's cost of equity, the required risk-free rate of return frequently reflects the yield curve of 20-year U.S. treasury bonds,[320] while the market risk premium is historically estimated to be between 5 and 6 percent for U.S. companies.[321] In addition, the WACC need to be adjusted for the tax shield, i.e. the deductibility of interest expenses for tax purposes.[322]

Within the surveyed German executives, the majority of the companies did not discount the projected free cash flows using the estimated cost of capital of the U.S. target, but instead employed its own cost of capital (see Table 3.11). Apparently, those companies assumed an associated inherent risk for the foreign target similar to their own overall risk.[323]

Table 3.11: Applied WACC-rate for transactions in the survey

Determination of WACC	Frequency
Acquirer	79%
Target	17%
Other (i.e. country specific)	4%

Overall, despite formal similarity of the adopted valuation methods, due to disparate preferences of investors in light of not yet fully integrated global capital markets, the level of applied interest rates and market multiples and therefore the valuation of the target can significantly vary for German companies when pursuing a domestic or a U.S. cross-border transaction.[324]

319 See RICHTER (2002), p. 321; DRUKARCYZK (2001), p. 272; however, German companies increasingly tend to outsource their pension obligations through the implementation of Contractual Trust Arrangements, as noted in Section 3.3.2.2.

320 See BÖGLE and BÄTZ (2005), p. 353.

321 See WIRTZ (2003), p. 219; BRUNER ET AL. (1998), p. 20f. These input parameters are usually obtained from the "Cost of Capital Yearbook", which is compiled annually by Ibbotson Associates, Chicago, or the annual Mergerstat Review, see BÖGLE and BÄTZ (2005), p. 349; the systematic risk β of a U.S. public company is computed for example by BARRA.

322 See DRUKARCYZK (2001), p. 176ff.

323 See RAPPAPORT (1994), p. 165.

324 See SCHENCK ET AL. (2005), p. 43; BRUNER (2004a), p. 360. For a discussion of the presumed degree of segmentation of international financial markets refer to for example BEKAERT and HARVEY (1995).

3.6 Principal documentation of the transaction

3.6.1 Acquisition of a private company

For the acquisition of a private U.S. company the seller and foreign acquirer customarily enter into a letter of intent.[325] Although a standard LOI provides that it does not create a binding obligation to conclude the transaction and that either party may terminate negotiations at any time,[326] in the United States it typically includes provisions intended to be binding with regard to confidentiality, "no-shop" agreements,[327] the bearing of expenses, and "break-up" fees. Such intended degree of contractual obligation is either established by using specific precautionary language[328] or by dividing the document into binding and non-binding sections.[329] Additionally, the execution of a U.S. LOI often imposes upon both parties an implied moral commitment to continue negotiations in good faith in accordance with the outlined terms of the letter.[330] Accordingly, absent a material change in the facts and circumstances surrounding the transaction, in a U.S. transaction there are rarely differences between the substantial terms of the acquisition set fourth in the LOI and the acquisition agreement.[331]

The drafting of the acquisition agreement is not strictly governed by U.S law of contract, but it typically emphasizes the following sections:[332]

- Representations covering employee benefit plans and their funding and compliance with ERISA often run several pages. A typical representation for environmental matters states that the seller is in compliance with all terms in all environmental laws and permits and that there have been no reportable conditions of discharging or releasing of hazardous substances that would give rise to environmental liabilities in the future. Other significant provisions focus on product liability and litigation issues and will generally state that there are no claims pending against the target company beyond those specifically identified in the acquisition agreement.

---

325 See BRUNER (2004a), p. 767f.

326 See HOLZAPFEL and PÖLLATH (2000), p. 14; REED and LAJOUX (1999), p. 447f.

327 With a no-shop agreement the seller agrees to exclusivity of the negotiations and to cease active discussions with other potential acquirers for a certain period of time.

328 For example "except for the provisions of paragraphs …, and this sentence, however, nothing herein shall constitute a legally binding agreement of purchase and seller", see HACKETT and CRAIG (1999), p. 7.

329 See STELLINGWERF and MANTESE (2000), p. 2f. The magnitude of problems that can arise when there is confusion as to the binding or non-binding nature of the letter of intent is highlighted in the *Texaco* versus *Pennzoil* decision, in which a U.S. court awarded *Pennzoil* damages of over $10b after *Getty Oil* walked away from a letter of intent that included the phrase that is was "subject to execution of definitive merger agreement", see TANKERSLEY (1999), p. 4.

330 See REED and LAJOUX (1999), p. 447.

331 See SELLMANN and MAIER (2005), p. 201.

332 See HALL (2001), p. 4; ERNST & YOUNG (1994), p. 125ff. In order to narrow the scope of the disclosures, the representations are usually framed by the phrases "ordinary course of business" and "best of knowledge", see MORGAN LEWIS & BOCKIUS (1996), p. 52.

- The most important condition to closing the transaction is the absence of a "material adverse change" in the target's legal and financial position between signing and closing. This provision is commonly known as the "MAC clause" and allows for a considerable number of extraordinary circumstances to arise between signing and closing that enable the acquiring company to terminate the transaction in case they have a material effect on the value and future prospects of the target's business.[333] Depending on how this clause is phrased, such effects may involve industry-wide changes or company-specific problems.[334] As a result of this clause, due diligence is typically performed up to the closing.[335] Other common closing conditions refer to the compliance with U.S. antitrust laws, receipt of third-party consents, settlement of litigation, signing of employment or non-compete agreements by key personnel, and results of environmental studies.[336]
- The acquisition agreement usually outlines the procedural aspects of indemnity claims and the rights of the parties to take part in remedial action.[337] Although under U.S. case law[338] the parties have a right to collect damages in the event of breach of a representation or warranty or non-compliance with a covenant, such indemnification provisions are necessary since those rights do not always provide the extent of recovery the parties may feel entitled to. The typical time limitation for representations is at least one complete financial year following the transaction. For some items the limitation may be longer, for example for environmental issues and employee benefits, or may be governed by the statute of limitation applicable to actions of breach of contract, for example for tax and product liability matters.[339] A time limitation generally does not apply to non-compliance with a covenant.[340] The indemnification section frequently also defines a monetary threshold for individual claims (so-called "basket") and an aggregate monetary limitation for all claims (so-called "cap").[341] Basket amounts usually range from 1 to 2 percent of the purchase price, while a cap is often set at an amount equal to half of the purchase price or less.[342] Representations for environmental liabilities are usually not subject to a monetary threshold.

---

333 See REED and LAJOUX (1999), p. 469. For example, if material litigation arises between the signing of the acquisition agreement and the closing of the transaction, no breach of the litigation representation as a result of the post-signing event would exist. However, under the so-called "bring-down condition" the acquirer may terminate the acquisition agreement, since the value or viability of the target has changed compared to the situation at the signing of the acquisition agreement.

334 A recent example of such changes was cited by *Johnson & Johnson* in its proposed acquisition of the *Guidant Corporation*, see CLEIS (2005), p. 23.

335 See REED and LAJOUX (1999), p. 472.

336 See ERNST & YOUNG (1994), p. 132.

337 See BENDANIEL and ROSENBLOOM (1998), p. 43.

338 The U.S. legal system is generally characterized as a federal and state case law system (also referred to as "common law"), which is principally based on court rulings, see BURNHAM (1999), p. 38ff.

339 See MORGAN LEWIS & BOCKIUS (1996), p. 54.

340 See MORGAN LEWIS & BOCKIUS (1996), p. 54.

341 See HALL (2001), p. 6.

342 See REED and LAJOUX (1999), p. 476; TANKERSLEY (1999), p. 22f.

3.6.2 Acquisition of a public company

Contrary to private transactions, in an acquisition of a U.S. public company a letter of intent is usually not prepared in order to avoid public disclosure of the proposed deal under SEC filing requirements before a definitive acquisition agreement is negotiated.[343] The acquisition agreement essentially includes the same sections as in a private acquisition, but some components may be significantly different.[344] For example, provisions governing the mechanics of the transaction are usually more extensive, given that for public transactions issues such as competing offers and exemption from existing defense measures may need to be addressed.[345] The most common contractual mechanism for an acquirer to protect the transaction from competing bids and to provide for compensation from the target in case the transaction is abandoned in favor of a competing bid are break-up fees, also referred to as "bust-up" fees. At a minimum, these fees are designed to cover the acquirer's expenses incurred before the target abandoned the transaction.[346] More often, bust-up fee provisions include an additional compensation for lost time and opportunity, usually 1 to 3 percent of the transaction value to the shareholders.[347] Other protective mechanisms are "asset lock-up" provisions, i.e. the target grants the acquirer the right to purchase a number of its most significant assets, and "no-shop" provisions, which prevent the target company from soliciting other offers or encouraging negotiations with other potential acquirers.[348]

Indemnities against breaches of representations and warranties are of lesser importance in a public transaction, given that there is no private seller who can provide them. Accordingly, while the significance of individual representations and warranties is diminished, greater emphasis is placed in this case on the determination of the purchase price and the treatment of postsigning covenants.[349] However, in light of a U.S. board of director's fiduciary duties to maximize the benefits for the target shareholders, most U.S. acquisition agreements include a "fiduciary out clause", which gives the board of directors in the event of a more favorable offer the ability to withdraw its approval of the transaction or to terminate the agreement even if it has been signed already.[350] If that fiduciary duty under applicable state corporate laws is

---

343 See BENDANIEL and ROSENBLOOM (1998), p. 41.

344 See RUEGGER (1999), p. 8.

345 This is exemplified by the unsuccessful takeover bid of *SAP AG* for *Retek Inc.* in March 2005. After a bidding contest against *Oracle*, *SAP AG* had to withdraw from its intention, even though an acquisition agreement with the target was signed, see LAUBE and OTTOMEIER (2005), p. 1.

346 See REED and LAJOUX (1999), p. 760.

347 For example, in the acquisition of *AWW* by *RWE AG* this fee was set at 3 percent; *SAP AG* received a termination fee payment of $25m for the aforementioned unsuccessful acquisition attempt for *Retek Inc.* The size of break-up fees must be negotiated to a level where it would withstand juridical scrutiny, see ROBERTS and BOONE (1998), p. 3.

348 See REED and LAJOUX (1999), p. 761. Other preclosing deal protections are voting agreements and cross-option agreements, see LAJOUX and NESVOLD (2004), p. 59f.

349 See LAJOUX and NESVOLD (2004), p. 58.

350 This obligation stems from the earlier mentioned "Revlon duties" (see Section 3.2.3.5).

not fulfilled,[351] the acquisition may be enjoined, thus denying the acquirer to be reimbursed for expenses it incurred in pursuing the transaction. Accordingly, not only the target but also the foreign acquirer needs to make sure that the target's board fulfills its fiduciary duties.[352]

Another difference to acquisitions of private targets is the absence of purchase price adjustment provisions in the acquisition agreement, i.e. the shareholders of a public target do not make certain guarantees with regard to the net equity value of the target at the closing of the transaction. In addition, public transactions do not entitle the selling shareholders to additional considerations if the target company meets certain financial milestones. Such "earnout" provisions are frequently included in private transactions, especially when the foreign acquirer and the seller disagree on the projected future financial performance of the target's business.[353]

3.7 U.S. antitrust laws and regulatory pre-acquisition review requirements

3.7.1 Overview

In the United States M&A activity may be restricted by federal and state antitrust laws. The two main federal laws governing antitrust considerations for acquisitions[354] are the Sherman Antitrust Act of 1890 and the Clayton Act of 1914. While Section 2 of the Sherman Act contains rather general language outlawing monopolies, Section 7 of the Clayton specifically prohibits acquisitions that would substantially lessen competition or tend to create a monopoly in any line of commerce or in any section of the United States.[355] These laws apply to all industries, but acquisitions in highly regulated industries, such as the banking, insurance, power generation and utility services, and communications sectors, or particularly sensitive industries, such as the defense, broadcasting and telecommunications, domestic air and marine transportation, and fishing sectors, must be approved by specific federal agencies

---

351 Most of the legal cases dealing with the fiduciary duty of directors in connection with a proposed acquisition involve companies incorporated in Delaware, given that more than 50 percent of all public U.S. companies are incorporated in Delaware, more than ten times as many as the second largest concentration of incorporated companies, i.e. the state of New York, see KUIPERS ET AL. (2003), p. 9. Accordingly, such cases have been decided by Delaware courts under the provisions of the DGCL. In transactions involving the corporate law of states other than Delaware, practitioners and courts frequently look to Delaware for guidance, see, RUEGGER (1999).

352 See ROBERTS and BOONE (1998), p. 5.

353 See LAJOUX and NESVOLD (2004), p. 64. The authors cite in this context the occurrence of the "hockey-stick" phenomena, meaning a projected sharp increase in the target's performance in the immediate future years.

354 In this case the term "acquisitions" comprises mergers, share deals, asset deals, and the formation of joint ventures.

355 See ERNST & YOUNG (1994), p. 171. Section 7 of the Clayton Act was amended in 1950 by the Celler-Kefauver Act to extend the antitrust provisions to transactions structured as asset deals as well as vertical acquisitions.

applying individually adapted statutes, for example the Federal Communications Commission for transactions in the media industry.[356]

The Department of Justice ("DOJ") and the Federal Trade Commission ("FTC") enforce federal antitrust laws[357] and have jointly published an updated consolidated set of merger guidelines.[358] These guidelines provide the framework for defining the relevant product and geographic market of the acquirer's and target's combined businesses as well as the criteria for measuring concentration and competitive effects of a proposed transaction.[359] In addition to federal laws, some states promulgated their own antitrust laws, which are fairly similar to the federal requirements.[360]

3.7.2 Hart-Scott-Rodino filing process

The Clayton Act was amended in 1976 by adding in Section 7A the Hart-Scott-Rodino Antitrust Improvements Act, commonly known as the Hart-Scott-Rodino ("HSR") Act, which grants the FTC and DOJ the right of refusal of a transaction.[361] In case certain jurisdictional thresholds are met, the HSR Act requires an advance filing of a premerger notification and report form with the Premerger Notification Office of the FTC.[362] The HSR filing form concerns information about the contemplated transaction and requires a description of the parties, current financial information, and a breakdown of revenues according to industry codes and copies of existing written agreements between both parties.[363] As a summary of the principal terms of a transaction, the letter of intent is usually sufficient documentation for the purposes of these pre-acquisition review requirements. The information provided is used by the authorities to assess whether the proposed transaction would have any anticompetitive impacts on the market.

---

356 For further information on the specific federal laws restricting foreign ownership in those industries refer to THELEN REID & PRIEST (2004), p. 44ff.

357 See BREALEY and MYERS (2000), p. 956; HAY and NYDAM (1989), p. 232. For further information on the respective policies and activities of the DOJ and FTC refer to their official web pages, www.usdoj.gov/atr/overview.html and www.ftc.gov.

358 See HAY and NYDAM (1989), pp. 236-245. These guidelines in their latest version from 1992 can be found on the DOJ web page: www.usdoj.gov/atr/public/guidelines/horiz_book/hmg1.html for horizontal mergers, www.usdoj.gov/atr/public/guidelines/ 2614.htm for non-horizontal mergers.

359 The agencies apply a five-step process to assessing whether a transaction will create market power, see BRUNER (2004a), p. 752; THOMPSON (2001), p. 477f.

360 Accordingly, a further discussion of such laws is omitted.

361 15 U.S.C. Section 18a, title II of the original law.

362 KING & SPALDING (2000) provide a detailed discussion of these statutory filing requirements.

363 See LOY (1985), p. 322. The pre-merger notification form can be found at http://www.ftc.gov/bc/hsr/hsr.htm. The applicable industry codes are obtained from the North American Industry Classification System.

The pre-merger notification is only required when the (i) transaction involves a target that participates in business activities in the United States, the (ii) transaction volume exceeds a certain limit (so-called "size of transaction test"), and (iii) for transactions valued at less than $212.3m, the size of the any of the involved entities exceeds a certain threshold (so-called "size of person test"). According to current levels of the size of transaction test, a HSR filing form is required when the acquisition results in the transfer of voting securities and/or assets of the target in excess of $53.1m.[364] In addition to these initial minimum thresholds, the HSR Act also introduced four subsequent reporting thresholds: (i) more than $53.1m but less than $106.2m, (ii) more than $106.2m but less than $530.7m, (iii) in excess of $530.7m, and (iv) 25 percent of the voting securities of the target if greater than $1.061b or 50 percent of the voting securities of the target if greater than $53.1m. In essence, an acquirer that is subject to any one of these jurisdictional thresholds may give notice of an intention to acquire more shares up to one of the higher regulatory thresholds, and then may make additional acquisitions up to that level for a period of five years without any additional pre-merger notification requirement. No notice is required of an acquisition by a party that already owns 50 percent or more of the acquired entity. Under the size of person test, acquisitions valued between $53.1m and $212.3m are reportable if the annual net sales or total assets of either the acquirer (including its ultimate parent) or the target are at least $106.2m for one and $10.7m for the other. Regardless of the size of the parties, transactions valued in excess of $212.3m are reportable.

There are several exceptions to these requirements that apply specifically for foreign acquiring companies. If the transaction is valued at less than $15.93m or concerns less than 50 percent of the voting shares, a foreign acquirer is exempt from the HSR filing. In case a foreign acquirer intends to purchase more than 50 percent of the voting shares of a target company in which sales or assets do not exceed $26.55m or $15.93m, respectively, a filing is also not required.[365]

The filing requires payment of a fee, which varies with the size of the transaction based on a three-tier structure.[366] Until the fee is paid and the notification form is filed, the pre-acquisition notification filing is deemed incomplete.

---

364 HSR Act Section 801.1. The jurisdictional thresholds of the HSR Act were amended in 2000, requiring annual indexing of the thresholds based on changes in U.S. gross national product for each fiscal year beginning after September 30, 2004. Accordingly, the applicability requirements will continue to change each year going forward. For 2005, the FTC increased this threshold from $50m to $53.1m.

365 See COOLEY and GODWARD (2001).

366 $45,000 fee for transactions valued at less than $100m; $125,000 fee for transactions valued between $100m and $500m; $280,000 for transactions in excess of $500m. As with the jurisdictional thresholds for the size of the transaction and size of the person test, these fees and the associated size limits are adjusted each fiscal year to account for changes in the Gross National Product during the previous year.

Upon complete filing, the transaction may only be consummated after a mandatory waiting period of 30 days for exchange offers and 15 days for cash tender offers.[367] If the transaction raises antitrust concerns, the FTC or DOJ may formally request additional information ("second request") from the acquirer or target before the end of the initial waiting period.[368] As a result, a second waiting period from the date of "substantial" compliance by the acquiring company with the second request of 20 days for an exchange offer and ten days for a cash tender offer begins.[369] As part of this second step review, the federal authorities require more information regarding the potential competitive situation following the acquisition and a prognosis of the post-closing market share and key players, which the DOJ uses to measure the change in the market structure by applying the Herfindahl-Hirschman Index.[370]

3.7.3 Exon-Florio process

While the HSR act applies to domestic and cross-border transactions, only foreign acquirers must also consider the potential implications of Section 721 of the Defense Production Act, commonly known as the Exon-Florio statute.[371] Certain cross-border acquisitions of U.S. companies are subject to a federal review in order to investigate and assess their impact on the national security in the United States. The Exon-Florio statute gives the President of the United States authorization to suspend or block any foreign acquisition that is deemed to impair national security. Neither the statute nor the regulations provide a definition of the term "national security", thereby allowing for a case-by-case determination and a broad interpretation without sole limitation to the defense industry.[372]

Under this statute, a foreign acquiring company can submit a voluntary formal notification to the Committee on Foreign Investment in the United States ("CFIUS"). The notification triggers a thorough review to determine whether national security considerations require

[367] According to Sections 7A (b)(1)(B) and 7A(e)(2) of the Clayton Act. In case of an acquisition of a public target company, the waiting period commences with the filing by the target, which is required within 15 days (for non-cash public offers) or ten days (for cash tender offers) following the notification by the potential acquirer about its intentions.

[368] See JOHNSON (2001), p. 3.

[369] Such a request for additional information was for example imposed on the proposed acquisition of the *Renal Care Group* by *Fresenius Medical Care*, see FRESENIUS MEDICAL CARE (2005).

[370] See MIDDELMANN and HELMES (2005), p. 684.

[371] 50 U.S.C. § 2170; 31 C.F.R. § 800.101-702. The Exon-Florio statute was implemented in 1988 by the Committee on Foreign Investment in the United States.

[372] See KAYE and SCHOLER (2002). The act cites the following factors that may be considered within this review: (i) domestic production capacity needed for defense, (ii) capabilities and resources needed for defense, (iii) control of industries and commercial activity needed for national security, (iv) impact of the deal on sales of military goods, equipment, or technology to any country, and (v) impact on U.S. technological leadership in areas affecting national security, see BRUNER (2004a), p. 755.

undertaking a full-scale investigation of the notified transaction.[373] Such an investigation must commence no later than 30 days after receipt of a notice and must be completed within 45 days. It culminates in a recommendation to the U.S. President to either block the acquisition or not. The President must take action within 15 days of receipt of that recommendation. The notification to the CFIUS is voluntary, though in a post-September 11 environment it is expected that the federal government may put a stronger emphasis on the Exon-Florio provision.[374]

3.8 Conclusions and implications

The discussion of specific aspects for structuring and managing a cross-border acquisition of a U.S. target showed that many issues must be considered in order to address potential risks resulting from differences in the institutional environment between the United States and Germany that might negatively affect the success of the transaction.

A primary concern in a U.S. cross-border transaction is to avoid inadvertently assuming the target's liabilities caused by specific rules, regulations, and practices, which an acquiring company from a foreign jurisdiction might not be accustomed to. Such liabilities typically result from pending or potentially forthcoming litigation or product liability claims, environmental matters, underfunded retirement and post-employment benefits plans, and employee discrimination and workers compensation claims. The nature and extent of existing and potential liabilities must be assessed during the due diligence process, which in the United States even for smaller sized companies has become quite standardized.[375] In addition to differences in the legal framework, the identification of potential transaction risks and the evaluation of the U.S. target company may be hampered for a foreign acquirer by its unfamiliarity with U.S. accounting standards, especially regarding the recognition of goodwill, the potential impairment of fixed assets, the valuation of inventory, the recognition and measurement of provisions, and the accounting for retirement benefits. In this context the nonexistence of audited financial statements for smaller private companies or corporate divisions in the case of a carve-out could further enhance potential problems.[376]

---

373 It should be noted that those transactions for which an Exon-Florio notice was not filed remain open indefinitely to federal scrutiny.

374 See MARCHICK ET AL. (2005). However, since passing the Exon-Florio statute, according to the General Accounting Office of the United States as of December 31, 2004, only one transaction has been blocked by the U.S. President, which was a proposed acquisition of an aircraft parts manufacturer by a Chinese government-owned company.

375 See SCHMIDT, V. (2005), p. 224, who notes that, unlike in Europe, in the United States the content of the information memorandum and the preparation of the data room consistently meet certain minimum quality standards.

376 Since in the United States financial statements have to be prepared on a consolidated basis with no legal requirements for separate statements for subgroups or separate legal entities, in case of a carve-out the valuation of the U.S. target is largely based on internal management accounts, especially in non-auction transactions, see KASCHKE and PHILIPP (2005), p. 118; SELLMANN and MAIER (2005), p. 200.

The only transaction structure permitting the acquirer to avoid assuming the target's disclosed and undisclosed liabilities is an asset deal, though subject to certain exceptions under the bulk transfer laws or multi-employer collective bargaining agreements.[377] In case the U.S. cross-border transaction is structured as a share deal, the responsibility for liabilities can be shifted to the seller by providing for appropriate representations and warranties and indemnification provisions in the acquisition agreement. In light of the drafting flexibility implied by U.S. law, the acquirer, who is typically responsible for preparing the initial draft of the acquisition agreement in the United States, can calibrate these provisions to the target's particular business. The representations and warranties section is usually quite extensive, especially for acquisitions of a private target company, and includes detailed disclosure schedules attached to the agreement.[378] The indemnification provisions are usually also tailored to the particular business by including a specific dollar limit, time limitations and "baskets" for filing claims, and post-closing dispute resolution mechanisms.[379] Hence, although structure and size of the individual transaction define its complexity and length, a U.S. acquisition agreement with its annexed schedules and exhibits often exceeds the width of the phonebook of a decently sized U.S city. In contrast, German acquirers are used to a concise listing of more general principals implicit in a larger body of applicable German statutory law.[380]

Regarding the tax implications, the acquirer needs to consider whether the transaction is immediately taxable for the target shareholders and whether it has an effect on the target's tax attributes. While sellers in the United States typically seek to avoid a double layer of tax at the company and shareholder level and aim to secure lower capital gains rates versus ordinary income rates on the sale proceeds by entering into a share deal, the acquirer is mainly interested in benefiting from higher depreciation deductions for the acquired assets by pursuing an asset deal. A vehicle to overcome these conflicting tax objectives between both parties is the joint election under Section 338(h)(10), which allows a share deal to be treated for federal tax purposes as an asset deal. Another tax aspect to be considered by the acquirer is the payment of transfer taxes, which especially in an asset deal could be substantial.[381]

---

377 In this regard, compared to the strict limitations of § 613a of the German Commercial Code, an asset deal in the United States offers more flexibility to renegotiate existing collective bargaining, see SELLMANN and MAIER (2005), p. 206.

378 See HALL (2001), p. 5; WHITE (2001), p. 3. In this context SELLMANN and MAIER (2005, p. 204) point out that the application of either Delaware or New York corporate law would be beneficial for a foreign acquirer, since only these statutes offer a sufficiently reliable legal basis in the case of any potential post-merger disputes.

379 See SCHMIDT, V. (2005), p. 224; the author points out that unlike in Europe, such items are common practice in the United States and typically do not need to be negotiated. In this context WHITE (2001, p. 4) notes that acquirers often overlook the collectibility of indemnification claims, for example by not including the ability to adjust the purchase price post-closing through means of installment payments.

380 See SELLMANN and MAIER (2005), p. 205. The authors point out that another difference between U.S. and German acquisition agreements is the definition of a retroactive effective date regarding the transfer of the commercial risk and rewards, which is fairly unusual in the United States.

381 See HALL (2001), p. 2.

A tax-free treatment of a cross-border transaction in the United States requires at least a partial use of shares as the form of payment. However, the use of shares is limited for a foreign acquirer and represents a major obstacle in structuring a U.S. cross-border transaction as an exchange offer.[382] Given that target shareholders are usually very reluctant to receive shares of a foreign company, an exchange offer involving a public U.S. target essentially requires a secondary listing of the acquirer's shares in the United States.[383] However, adopting SEC filing and U.S. GAAP accounting requirements, including the onerous reporting and certification obligations of the Sarbanes-Oxley Act, results in substantial complexity and costs for foreign companies.[384] In addition, most German companies have experienced very low acceptance of their ADRs by U.S. investors,[385] resulting in a median split between the shares traded in Germany and the United States of 93 percent to 7 percent.[386] As a consequence, foreign acquirers using shares to pay for the cross-border transaction could face substantial flow-back issues, which could cause significant price pressure on the acquirer's shares in its home market.[387] The use of shares is further complicated by on average higher market valuation levels and a stronger emphasis on relevant transaction multiples such as Price/Earnings ratios in the United States, which not only complicate the negotiation process for a foreign acquirer, but they could also make the U.S. cross-border acquisition more expensive than a domestic transaction. Overall, the potential disadvantages of a secondary listing seem to outweigh the potential benefit of having an increased ability to pursue external growth by using shares as an acquisition currency.[388] Accordingly, only a very limited number of German companies used shares to pay for a U.S. acquisition.[389]

---

382 See GRIESSER and SCHWINGELER, (2005), p. 50.

383 For example, *Aixtron AG* completed a listing on the NASDAQ in March 2005 with sponsored Level II-ADRs to pursue its exchange offer for *Genus, Inc*.

384 See RIPIN and GEYRHALTER (2005), p. 302. The complexity of a transaction further increases in case the acquirer needs to obtain shareholder approval for the planned increased in share capital to finance the transaction, see SCHENCK ET AL. (2005), p. 43.

385 See GRIESSER and SCHWINGELER (2005), p. 50, who cite as one explanation for low acceptance of foreign shares the trading boundaries or "index-tracking" of institutional investors in the Unites States.

386 See SCHENCK ET AL. (2005), p. 33f. For example, for *Deutsche Telekom AG*, as one of the few German acquirers that used shares as a form of payment in a U.S. acquisition, the trading split was 97 percent to 3 percent in 2005.

387 See SCHENCK ET AL. (2005), p. 33f. MITCHELL ET AL. (2004) list arbitrage positions by short-sellers as another factor causing price pressure on the acquirer's shares in an exchange offer.

388 See SCHENCK ET AL. (2005), p. 32f. As a result of these negative factors, some German companies with a dual listing, such as *Siemens AG*, were rumored to consider a delisting in the United States, see LANDLER (2004), p. C1. In fact, following its NASDAQ listing in early 2000 for the purpose of being able to pursue exchange offers, *LION bioscience AG* delisted from the NASDAQ on December 22, 2004, citing benefits being outweighed by expenses, see REICHE (2005).

389 Some examples are the *Daimler-Chrysler* merger, the *Telekom-Voicestream* acquisition, and a few transactions by relatively small new economy companies during the years of the internet bubble, i.e. the *GemStone Systems Inc.* and *Blaze Software Inc.* acquisitions by *Brokat Infosystems AG* and the merger of *C.E. Computer Equipment* AG with *Treev Inc.*

In case an acquisition of a public company is paid for with cash, it can be structured as a tender offer or proxy solicitation. A tender offer may not be the most beneficial form if not enough shareholders tender their shares to achieve a short-form reverse triangular merger. A proxy solicitation may provide a more satisfactory transaction structure since a one-step merger of the target with the acquisition vehicle can be realized upon sufficient shareholder approval, forcing all shareholders, including dissenting ones, to deliver their shares under the terms of the acquisition agreement. For example, following its experience with the hostile takeover of the remaining shares it did not receive in a tender offer for *Loctite Corp.* in 1996, *Henkel KGaA* decided to structure its acquisition of *Dial Corp.* in 2004 as a proxy solicitation.[390] However, a proxy solicitation takes longer than a tender offer and thereby exposes the acquirer for a longer period to competing bids by other parties.[391] In order to mitigate such a risk, no-shop and break-up fee provisions are typically incorporated in either the letter of intent[392] or the acquisition agreement.[393] Compared to exchange offers, which frequently require at least three to six months,[394] tender offers and proxy solicitations require a shorter period of two to four months to close the transaction following the signing of the acquisition agreement.[395]

Besides the existence of protective defensive mechanisms in the target's corporate charter, pursuing a public acquisition also requires the consideration of fiduciary duties imposed on the board of directors of the target company by state laws, since these duties restrict the directors' ability to favor one acquirer over another. In order to contain the high risk of litigation by shareholders in case of any violations of such duties, the target's directors must act in the best interest of the shareholders. For example, offers made by the acquirer to the target's executives for post-closing employment would create a conflict of interest and violate the business judgment rule.[396] A means for the directors to demonstrate that they exercised due care is to obtain a fairness opinion, i.e. an independent third party assessment of the target's fair market value that typically employs market-based valuations such as transaction

---

390 See STEINEBACH ET AL. (2005), p. 103.

391 For example, the *Henkel-Dial* transaction was announced on December 14, 2003, and closed on March 29, 2004, two days subsequent to the shareholders' approval. In comparison, following the due diligence based on publicly available data about the target, the acquisition agreement was agreed upon between these two parties in just four weeks, see STEINEBACH ET AL. (2005), p. 102.

392 As mentioned earlier, signing a LOI generally requires a filing with the SEC, therefore making the proposed transaction public. Instead, in such instances both parties could agree on a term sheet, either verbally or by conduct. However, SELLMANN and MAIER (2005, p. 201) observed that the reluctance of U.S. public companies to execute a LOI has lessened recently, due to an announcement from the SEC that there is no obligation to make public the signing of a LOI as long as it is ensured that commercial terms are still preliminary and that only aspects such as the confidentiality agreement are binding.

393 This was the case for the above cited *Henkel-Dial* acquisition, see STEINEBACH ET AL. (2005), p. 103.

394 For example the *Daimler-Chrysler* merger took six months to close following its announcement.

395 See SCHENCK ET AL. (2005), p. 42f. For example, the *RWE-AWW* transaction closed three months after its announcement, while *Hochtief AG*'s tender offer for *Turner Corp.* in 1999 required less than two months to close.

396 See KASCHKE and PHILIPP (2005), p. 116.

multiples.[397] In this context, the aforementioned differences between a U.S. and German market valuation need to be considered, which could result in a relatively higher purchase price.

Finally, each U.S. cross-border transaction, regardless of the status of the target, gives rise to regulatory approval requirements, ranging from complex and time-consuming filings under the HSR Act to substantive consents by the DOJ and FTC.[398] For example, due to the ongoing regulatory review, the proposed acquisition of the *Renal Care Group* by *Fresenius Medical Care* was not expected to close until ten months after its announcement in May 2005.[399]

Besides the more technical aspects regarding the acquisition structuring and management phase, the process of a U.S. cross-border transaction is also impacted by the realization and consideration of so-called "soft factors". Such soft factors comprise differences in leadership styles,[400] country and corporate culture,[401] work habits,[402] and communication styles,[403] which frequently create disparate expectations between the German acquirers and the U.S. target.[404] PALAZZO ET AL. (2005) summarized these differences in soft factors as the clash between "German Gründlichkeit" and "US pragmatism".[405]

The identified main "hard" issues as well as the soft factors are mirrored in the concerns cited by executives in the survey of German acquirers of U.S. target companies in the period 1990 to 2004.[406] Table 3.12 concludes the discussion of Chapter 3 by displaying these U.S. specific concerns.

---

397 See ANGERER and WINCKLER (2005), p. 288; SCHENCK ET AL. (2005), p. 37.
398 SURA (2005, p. 389) points out that in contrast to the approach taken by the European Commission and the German Federal Cartel Office, the U.S. agencies are not as receptive to objections by actual and potential competitors.
399 See FRESENIUS MEDICAL CARE (2006).
400 See MATTHIESSEN ET AL. (2005).
401 See GRUBE (2005), p. 66; JESUTHASAN and UDER (2005), p. 179; VERY and SCHWEIGER (2001), p. 19f. For a detailed comparison of corporate cultures between both countries refer to SCHMIDT (2001).
402 See KREUZ and ROTHENBÜCHER (2005), p. 165, who for example note different levels of formalism.
403 See GEISER and JUCHEM (2005), p. 411. SCHMIDT, P. (2005, p. 429) states that the communication styles "are almost diametrically opposed" and notes as an example that Germans are more direct in expressing criticism, while Americans are more direct in expressing compliments.
404 See SCHWEIGER (2005), p. 357.
405 See PALAZZO ET AL. (2005), p. 439f.
406 A detailed description of this survey is given in Section 5.2.2.

Table 3.12: Specific concerns for U.S acquisitions cited by German acquirers

Specific concerns for U.S. acquisitions cited by German acquirers

Aspects of transaction structuring and management

- "In case of public company: legal side of acquisition process"
- "Most of publicly listed companies have very effective defense measures (poison pills) available, so to convince the management of the target company in a friendly approach is key to success"
- "Underfunding of pension liabilities"
- "Corporate governance and control issues"
- "Open litigation issues"
- "Power of unions if job relocation is necessary"
- "Bonus scheme"
- "Have advisors and own people on site and make them meet management beforehand"
- "Regulatory issues (industry specific), Human Resources"
- "Regulatory environment"

Soft factors

- "Different understanding in leading"
- "Partly different management culture"
- "Loyalty and quality of management"
- "Staff loyalty"

Against this backdrop, the further analysis aims at assessing how German companies have actually succeeded in avoiding the potential pitfalls in structuring and managing their acquisition of a U.S. target company. The analysis focuses on transactions in the period from 1990 to 2004, during which from a legal perspective essentially similar conditions for the acquisition management phase applied to all transactions, except for the introduction of new federal rules on corporate governance through the Sarbanes-Oxley Act in 2002. The empirical part of this study begins in Chapter 4 with a review of existing prior research on the success of cross-border transactions and its determinants.

4 Prior research on the success of cross-border acquisitions and its determinants

4.1 Introduction

The purpose of this chapter is to provide a concise overview of the results of previous research on the success of cross-border mergers and acquisitions. The review of prior studies focuses on the methodologies used for measuring success (Section 4.3) and the accumulated evidence (i) proving if and to what extent transactions were successful (Section 4.4) and (ii) suggesting which characteristics of the acquiring and target companies and the transaction structures make it more likely that a particular transaction will be successful (Section 4.5). A condensing of the empirical results into testable hypotheses with regard to the goal of this study to analyze the success and its determinants of U.S. acquisitions by German companies will conclude this review (Section 4.6).

4.2 Selection of prior research

There is a significant body of literature analyzing the success of M&A activity.[1] As defined in Section 2.2.3, for the purpose of this study success is predominantly assessed from the perspective of the shareholders of acquiring companies. Accordingly, the review of the existing research is primarily focused on studies measuring the implications of transactions on acquirer shareholder wealth.

The review is further confined to studies analyzing acquisitions during the fifth merger wave, since potential differences in the legal, corporate governance, institutional, or economic environment may distort the generalization and relevance of the findings from research of transactions during earlier merger waves.[2] In light of the U.S. cross-border focus of this study, the review is also limited to acquisitions in which either a U.S. target was acquired or the acquiring company, based in the U.S. or in Europe, engaged in a cross-border transaction. Especially comparing domestic to cross-border transactions of U.S. targets may provide an indication into whether systematic differences exist, i.e. whether there are any U.S. specific aspects that determine the success of a transaction for a foreign acquirer.

---

1 As the number of empirical studies seems to be correlated with the volume of local M&A activity, the vast majority of research is focused on transactions involving a company in the United States. The dominance of U.S. based literature may also be attributable to the depth of the U.S. capital market with its widespread availability of public information about transactions. Beginning in the late 1990s, studies analyzing transactions by European acquirers as well as cross-border acquisitions became more common.

2 See Section 2.4.1.1 for an overview of the different motives underlying each merger wave. In addition to changing motives, other effects such as amendments in the U.S. regulatory framework with the introduction of the Williams Act or the IRC, most notably in 1986, make an intertemporal comparison of the observed results more difficult.

The predominant general methodologies for measuring success are capital market based event studies, financial statements based studies, and surveys of executives.[3] The general mechanics and limitations of these methods are discussed in Section 4.3 before the results of prior research are presented. Other methods for measuring success comprise the analysis of the quota of subsequent divestitures of acquired companies, the analysis of the impact of the transaction on the market position of the combined companies, and clinical studies of the structure and management of individual acquisitions. However, as a result of their limited dissemination in the empirical literature these alternative methodologies are not further reviewed in this study.[4]

Overall, 47 studies are included in this review of prior empirical research, of which 32 are capital market based event studies, three are financial statements based studies, and 12 are surveys of executives or alternative studies by consulting firms. Table 4.1 displays the reviewed studies. Besides the applied methodology and their geographic focus, these studies differ with regard to the business sector, selection of the sample transactions, and timeframe for which success was analyzed.

Event studies that are frequently cited in the literature in connection with cross-border acquisitions of U.S. targets before the fifth merger wave are those by KIYMAZ and MUKHERJEE (2000), CAKICI ET AL. (1996), EUN ET AL. (1996), MATHUR ET AL. (1994), SERVAES and ZENNER (1994), PETTWAY ET AL. (1993), and KANG (1993).[5] Shareholder wealth creation by U.S. companies in cross-border acquisitions before the 1990s were for example analyzed by ECKBO and THORBURN (2000), MARKIDES and OYON (1998), YOOK and MCCABE (1996), DATTA and PUIA (1995), MARKIDES and ITTNER (1994), MORCK and YEUNG (1992), and DOUKAS and TRAVLOS (1988).[6]

---

3 See BRUNER (2004a), p. 33f.; STORCK (1993), p. 139; BÜHNER (1990a), p. 30f.

4 For a detailed discussion of these methodologies refer to for example BRUNER (2004a) and KERLER (2000).

5 Overall, the results of these studies, which primarily analyze acquisitions in the 1980s, are inconclusive. While EUN ET AL. (1996), KANG (1993) and PETTWAY ET AL. (1993) found significant positive cumulative abnormal returns for Japanese and CAKICI ET AL. (1996) for other foreign acquirers, EUN ET AL. (1996) and MATHUR ET AL. (1994) observed for acquirers of other countries, especially in the United Kingdom, significantly negative cumulative abnormal returns. German acquirers were explicitly listed only in the studies by CAKICI ET AL. (1996) and MATHUR ET AL. (1994), which both report insignificant negative cumulative abnormal returns.

6 For U.S. acquirers in cross-border transactions the empirical results are also mixed, though with a generally more positive overall bias. Three studies report significant positive cumulative abnormal returns (MARKIDES and OYON (1998), MARKIDES and ITTNER (1994), and MORCK and YEUNG (1992)), while other studies computed shareholder losses, which only in the study by DATTA and PUIA (1995) were significant. In addition, the study by CAKICI ET AL. (1996) also examined cross-border acquisitions of U.S. acquirers, noting significant negative returns.

Table 4.1: Overview of reviewed empirical studies of transaction success

Authors	Year	Authors	Year
Capital market based event studies			
TOYNE and TRIPP	1998	RAU and RODGERS	2002
ALLEN ET AL.	2000	BHARADWAJ and SHIVDASANI	2003
CLARK ET AL.	2000	CORNETT ET AL.	2003
CORHAY and RAD	2000	DELONG	2003
DÖRR	2000	ALLEN ET AL.	2004
MULHERIN and BOONE	2000	BEITEL	2004
RAU	2000	BEITEL ET AL.	2004
WALKER	2000	BRADLEY and SUNDARAM	2004
ANDRADE ET AL.	2001	CAMPA and HERNANDO	2004
BLACK ET AL.	2001	GOERGEN and RENNEBOOG	2004
DELONG	2001	LOWINSKI ET AL.	2004
HOUSTON ET AL.	2001	MOELLER ET AL.	2004
SAUNDERS and SRINIVASAN	2001	BRUNER	2005
CHOI AND TSAI	2002	CONN ET AL.	2005
FAN and GOYAL	2002	GREGORY and MCCORRISTON	2005
FULLER ET AL.	2002	MOELLER and SCHLINGEMANN	2005
Financial statements based studies			
GHOSH	2001	GUGLER ET AL.	2003
HERON and LIE	2002		
Survey of executives and other studies by consulting firms			
MERCER CONSULTING[7]	1995	MERCER CONSULTING	2001
A.T. KEARNEY[8]	1999	BOSTON CONSULTING GROUP ("BCG")	2002
KPMG	1999	KPMG	2002
PRICEWATERHOUSECOOPERS ("PWC")	2000	BCG[9]	2004
KPMG	2001	KPMG	2004
MCKINSEY & CO.	2001	KPMG[10]	2005

Acquisitions by German companies prior to the 1990s were analyzed by ECKARDT (1999), BÖHMER and LÖFFLER (1997), GERKE ET AL. (1995), GRANDJEAN (1992), and BÜHNER (1990a).[11]

---

7 See ZWEIG (1995).
8 See HABECK ET AL. (1999).
9 See HENRY and JESPERSEN (2002).
10 See ECKER and HECKEMUELLER (2005).
11 BÜHNER (1990a) examined the performance of German acquirers' shares from a long-term perspective, observing negative cumulative abnormal returns during the first months after the announcement of the transaction, but significantly positive cumulative abnormal returns two years subsequent to the announcement.

The number of financial statements based performance studies covering transactions in the 1990s is fairly limited.[12] With regard to German acquirers, ALBRECHT (1994), BÜHNER (1990a), and MÖLLER (1983) conducted such studies; since their focus was on transactions prior to the 1990s they are not included in this review.[13] Analogously, a survey of executives of German acquiring companies by BAMBERGER (1994) for transactions between 1980 and 1991 is excluded from the review scope as well.[14]

4.3 Methodologies for measuring success

4.3.1 Capital market based event studies

4.3.1.1 Mechanics of the methodology

FAMA ET AL. (1969) introduced the methodology of capital market oriented event studies, which was subsequently further developed mainly by BROWN and WARNER (1980, 1985) and DODD and WARNER (1983). Event studies measure the success of transactions from the perspective of the shareholder value by analyzing the unexpected, or "abnormal" returns to the shareholders either in the period immediately surrounding the public announcement of a transaction or in a subsequent longer timeframe. This approach is regarded as being a future-oriented measure of success of acquisitions, since it is based on the central assumption that share prices reflect the present value of all expected future cash flows to the shareholders.[15] Since the share price can change with the occurrence of unanticipated events, such as an acquisition, event studies yield insights into abnormal returns to the shareholders of the acquirer, the target company, or a combination of both.

The mechanics of an event study essentially comprise four steps: (i) defining the day on which the acquisition was announced and the time window for which the share price reactions are measured, the so-called "event window", (ii) estimating expected returns of the share during the event window assuming that the announcement of the transaction had not occurred, (iii) computing the abnormal returns of a share, i.e. the difference between the

12 BRUNER (2005) and MUELLER (1997) provide an overview of the results of financial statements based studies covering transactions before the 1990s.

13 Based on an analysis of the impact of 692 domestic and cross-border transactions by German companies between 1985 and 1989 on the return on assets, ALBRECHT (1994) observed a significant correlation between the change in profitability and the relative size of the acquisition and the quality of the management. The studies by BÜHNER (1990a) and MÖLLER (1983) covered the periods 1973 to 1985 and 1967 to 1981, respectively, and drew different conclusions. While MÖLLER (1983) classified only conglomerate transactions as unsuccessful, BÜHNER (1990a) concluded that all types of acquisitions yielded a negative impact on profitability of the combined entities. DÖRR (2000) provides a summary of these studies.

14 BAMBERGER (1994) surveyed the success of 397 transactions by German companies, of which nearly two-thirds were deemed a success. A differentiation between domestic and cross-border transactions did not yield significant results.

15 See BRUNER (2004a), p. 33f.

actual and the expected return, and (iv) measuring the statistical significance of the abnormal returns.[16]

- Step (i) Definition of the announcement day and the event window

The announcement date of an acquisition is the day the public is first informed of the transaction.[17] However, it is possible that information may have leaked to some market participants prior to the initial announcement, resulting in trading activities that impact the share price. Most researchers have addressed this potential influence on the share price by including a period of several days or weeks before the announcement day in the event window.[18] Other studies analyze the share price reaction over a time horizon of up to several years subsequent to the announcement, assuming that new information pertinent to the first announcement may become available to the shareholders or due to the occurrence of certain events subsequent to the acquisition, such as the arrival of a second bidder or regulatory objections.[19] The use of such long-run studies and their analytical techniques are controversial in the finance literature given that for periods beyond a few months it is difficult to solely attribute abnormal share returns to the acquisition rather than to other activities of the acquirer.[20] Since the main focus of this review of the empirical research is on short-run event studies, a discussion of the mechanics of such long-run studies is omitted.[21]

Overall, the research literature is divided with regard to the appropriate determination of the event window, though the majority of the reviewed studies computed cumulative abnormal returns for the period from one trading day before until one trading day after the announcement, i. e. the [-1,1] interval.[22] In order to account for early share price reactions induced by the anticipation of the stock market of an upcoming announcement before and potentially slow information processing after the event, cumulative abnormal returns are frequently also calculated for intervals such as [-2,2], [-5,5], [-10,10], and [-20,20].[23]

---

16 See for example BEITEL (2004), p. 79; BHAGAT and ROMANO (2001), p. 5; DÖRR (2000), p 65f.

17 See DODD and WARNER (1983), p. 408.

18 See WESTON ET AL. (2001), p. 171f.

19 AGRAWAL and JAFFE (2000) provide a review of 22 empirical studies on long-run wealth effects of acquisitions, whereby the majority of the reviewed studies examine transactions prior to the 1990s.

20 See PAUTLER (2001), p. 13. A summary of the implications of various methodologies for conducting long-term event studies is given for example in MITCHELL and STAFFORD (2000), LYON ET AL. (1999), FAMA (1998), and KOTHARI and WARNER (1997). FAMA (1998, p. 304) for example concludes that his survey of the long-run performance literature might be nothing more than chance results.

21 Long-run studies of cross-border acquisitions of public targets were conducted for example by ANDRE ET AL. (2004), AW and CHATTERJEE (2004), DANBOLT (1995), and CONN and CONNELL (1990). Studies by CONN ET AL. (2005), GREGORY and MCCORRISTON (2005), ECKBO and THORBURN (2000), and BÜHNER (1991) examined cross-border acquisitions of both public and private targets. These studies report negative wealth effects, although only the results by CONN ET AL. (2005) are statistically significant. AW and CHATTERJEE (2004) and ECKBO and THORBURN (2000) directly compare cross-border with domestic acquisitions, and in deviation to CONN ET AL. (2005) find that in cross-border acquisitions returns are lower, though not significantly so.

22 See Table 4.2. in Section 4.3.1.2.

23 See for example LOWINSKI ET AL. (2004), p. 322.

- Step (ii) Estimating the expected returns of the share during the event window assuming that the announcement of the transaction had not occurred

The finance literature developed several basic models for calculating the expected return of a share during an event window assuming that the announcement of the transaction had not occurred. These models can be broadly categorized into statistical and economic models, as shown in Figure 4.1. Statistical models are derived from specific economic theories of asset price formation[24] and can be differentiated into the market model (also referred to as the "market and risk adjusted model")[25] and the group of adjusted analytical models.[26] Economic models apply either the Capital Asset Pricing Model or Arbitrage Pricing Theory.[27]

Figure 4.1: Basic analytical models for estimating the expected return of a share[28]

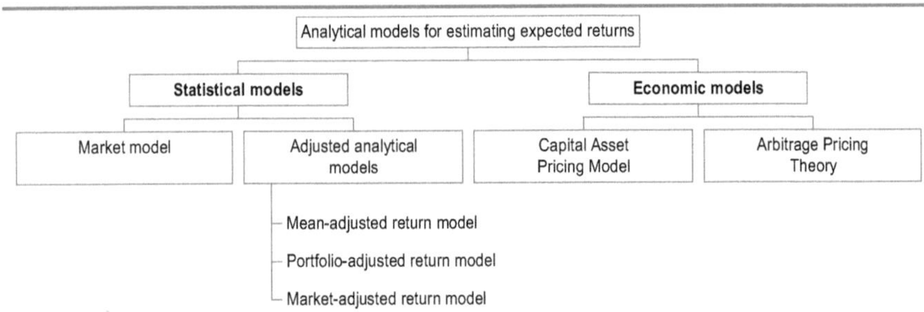

Almost all of the observed event studies use a statistical model; the CAPM model is only employed by CAMPA and HERNANDO (2004).[29] While the vast majority of the studies apply the market model, seven authors compute the expected share price based on the market-adjusted return model.[30] For three studies no information with regard to the applied model was provided.[31] Four studies use various measures for computing beta simultaneously, but with the exception of CLARK ET AL. (2000), all conclude that their results are not influenced by the choice of estimation technique.[32]

24 See BHAGAT and ROMANO (2001), p. 8f.
25 See BROWN and WARNER (1980), p. 208.
26 See CHATTERJEE and KUENZI (2001), p. 17f.
27 See BHAGAT and ROMANO (2001), p. 8.
28 Source: own presentation.
29 None of the reviewed studies employed Arbitrage Pricing Theory.
30 These are the studies by BRUNER (2005), CONN ET AL. (2005), MOELLER and SCHLINGEMANN (2005), BRADLEY and SUNDARAM (2004), DELONG (2003), FULLER ET AL. (2002), and WALKER (2000).
31 These are the studies by ANDRADE ET AL. (2001), DELONG (2001), and HOUSTON ET AL. (2001).
32 GREGORY and MCCORRISTON (2005), MOELLER and SCHLINGEMANN (2005), and CLARK ET AL. (2000) employ the market and market-adjusted return model, whereby the last study observed considerably higher and more significant abnormal returns for the market-adjusted return model. GOERGEN and RENNEBOOG (2004) use six methods: (i) the market model with a 195 day estimation period ending 6 months prior to the event date, (ii) the market model with a 195 day estimation period ending 1 month prior to the event date, (iii) Datastream beta corrected for mean reversion, (iv) Merrill Lynch method-adjusted betas, (v) betas corrected for reversion to the mean according to Vasicek's technique, and (vi) Dimension-betas.

The market model assumes a linear relationship between the return of share *i* and the return of a market portfolio *m*.[33] The return of a share *i* is calculated using the following equation:[34]

$$R_{it} = \alpha_i + \beta_i R_{mt} + \varepsilon_{it}, \qquad (1)$$

where:

R_{it} : return of a share *i* on event day *t*

α_i : intercept term

β_i : slope coefficient associated with the return of the market portfolio *m*

R_{mt} : return of the market portfolio on event day *t*

ε_{it} : error term

The slope coefficient β_i is the systematic risk component of the return of share *i* and measures the sensitivity of the share return with regard to the performance of the overall stock market. The intercept term α_i and the error term ε_{it} are the unsystematic risk components and are independent from the market performance. They reflect the impact of company-specific information on the share price.[35] The parameters α_i and β_i are estimated by an ordinary least squares ("OLS") regression using historical share and market returns of a estimation period preceding the event.[36] Within the observed studies, this estimation period varies from 60 days (TOYNE and TRIPP (1998)) to 280 days (BEITEL (2004)), whereby most studies use a full year, i.e. approximately 252 trading days.[37] Assuming $E(\varepsilon_{it}) = 0$,[38] the expected daily return $E(R_{it})$ of a share *i* is calculated as

$$E(R_{it}) = \alpha_i + \beta_i R_{mt} \qquad (2)$$

This basic form of the market model can be adjusted by including an industry-specific market index[39] or by computing logarithmic expected returns, though comparisons between the results of the market model and its logarithmic alteration have not shown statistically significant differences.[40]

---

33 See BROWN and WARNER (1980), p. 208. The market model can be attributed to the work of SHARPE (1963) and within the basic analytical models is most preferable, according to a study by CABLE and HOLLAND (1999).

34 See CHATTERJEE and KUENZI (2001), p. 17.

35 See COPELAND ET AL. (2000), p. 223f.

36 See WESTON ET AL. (2001), p. 172.

37 The length of the estimation period of each study is displayed in Table 4.2 in Section 4.3.1.2.

38 See WESTON ET AL. (2001), p. 172.

39 With $R_{it} = \alpha_i + \beta_i R_{mt} + \gamma_i R_{Indt} + \varepsilon_{it}$, where γ_i is the slope coefficient associated with the return of a industry-specific market portfolio and R_{Indt} is the return of the industry-specific market portfolio on the event day *t*, see FRANKS ET AL. (1977), p. 1522; HALPERN (1973), p. 565.

40 See FAMA ET AL. (1969), p. 4.

Within the group of the adjusted analytical models the abnormal return of a share *i* can be computed as the difference between the actual return R_i and either

- the mean of past returns of the share *i*, the so-called "mean-adjusted return model",
- the return of a risk-similar portfolio, the so-called "portfolio-adjusted return model", or
- the return of the market portfolio, the so-called "market-adjusted return model".

In the mean-adjusted return model the expected return of a share *i* is calculated as the average return of the share over the estimation period [τ_1, τ_2] of *k* days:[41]

$$E(R_{it}) = \overline{R}_i = \frac{\sum_{\tau=\tau_1}^{\tau_2} R_{i\tau}}{k}, \tag{3}$$

where:

$\overline{R}_i$: average return of share *i* over the estimation period [τ_1, τ_2]

R_τ : return of share *i* on day τ

k : number of days in the estimation period

τ_1 : first day in the estimation period ; τ_2 : last day in the estimation period

Within the portfolio-adjusted return model, the shares of all public companies are allocated into similar sized portfolios, based on the value of their systematic risk β_i.[42] The returns of the shares in the analyzed sample are then adjusted by the return of that portfolio with a corresponding systematic risk.

The market-adjusted return model is a special variation of the market model, assuming that β_i equals 1 and α_i equals 0.[43] Accordingly, the expected return is estimated as

$$E(R_{it}) = R_{mt}. \tag{4}$$

Within the economic models, the share return applying the CAPM is calculated as[44]

$$R_{it} = R_{ft} + \beta_i (R_{mt} - R_{ft}) + \varepsilon_{it}, \text{ with } \quad \beta_i = \frac{\operatorname{cov}(R_i, R_m)}{\sigma^2_{R_m}}, \tag{5}$$

where:

R_{ft} : risk-free rate

$\operatorname{cov}(R_i, R_m)$: covariance between the returns of share *i* and the market portfolio *m*

$\sigma^2_{R_m}$: variance of the returns of the market portfolio *m*

41 This model was not used in the surveyed studies. It was adopted first by MASULIS (1980) and applied in studies for example by DRAPER and PAUDYAL (1999) and LAHEY and CONN (1990).

42 See for example ASQUITH (1983), p. 51f.

43 See CHATTERJEE and KUENZI (2001), p. 18.

44 For a detailed discussion refer to for example KERLER (2000), pp. 92-96.

By extrapolating the values of the regression analysis in determining the cost of equity, the CAPM assumes constant conditions. Hence it does not consider that the change of owners of the target company may significantly impact the risk situation of the company.[45] In absence of coherent theories on how to modify β_i in case of an acquisition and in light of the criticism in the literature of the CAPM's restrictive assumptions,[46] ROLL and ROSS (1980) recommend to use of Arbitrage Pricing Theory ("APT") instead.[47]

- Step (iii) Computing the abnormal return

The abnormal return ("AR") of a share *i* for the event day *t* reflects the estimated impact of the event on the share price. AR is calculated by subtracting the estimated return from the actual return, i.e. the change of the closing price of the share on an event day compared to the previous day, typically while considering dividend payments:[48]

$$AR_{it} = R_{it} - E(R_{it}), \tag{6}$$

where:

AR_{it} : abnormal return of the share *i* on event day *t*

R_{it} : actual return of the share *i* on event day *t*

The average abnormal return ("$\overline{AR}_t$") of event day *t* and the cumulative average abnormal return ("CAR_T")[49] for the event window $[t_1, t_2]$ are calculated as follows:

$$\overline{AR}_t = \frac{1}{n}\sum_{i=1}^{n} AR_{it}, \quad (7); \qquad CAR_T = \sum_{t=t_1}^{t_2} \overline{AR}_t \tag{8}$$

where:

$\overline{AR}_t$: average abnormal return of all shares in the sample on event day *t*

n : numbers of transactions in the sample

CAR_T : cumulative abnormal return for the event window T, with $T = [t_1, t_2]$

t_1 : first day of the event window; t_2 : last day of the event window

---

45 See MANDELKER (1974), p. 303ff., who conducts an empirical study proving that betas of merged companies change subsequent to the transaction.

46 See for example the discussion in KERLER (2000), pp. 92-95.

47 Within the APT, expected returns are computed as follows:
$R_{it} = \delta_0 + \delta_{i1}F_{1t} + \delta_{i2}F_{2t} + ... + \delta_{in}F_{nt} + \varepsilon_{it}$, where F1, F2,...,Fn are the returns of the n factors that generate returns, and $\delta_{i1}, \delta_{i2}, ..., \delta_{in}$ are the factor loadings, see BHAGAT and ROMANO (2001), p. 8.

48 In case of uncertainty whether the public announcement was made before or after the trade closing on the stock market, the returns from the following day are sometimes included, see PETERSON (1989), p. 50.

49 From hereon the terms "cumulative abnormal return(s)" or "CARs" are used synonymously to imply the cumulative average abnormal returns in an event window for a sample of transactions.

CAR_T reflects the shareholder value created or destroyed through the acquisitions in the event window.[50] Arguing that percentage based returns do not sufficiently capture the actual change in shareholder wealth, some authors have also estimated dollar abnormal returns[51] or value-weighted abnormal returns.[52]

- Step (iv) Measuring the statistical significance of the abnormal returns

In the final step the statistical significance of the daily average and cumulative abnormal returns needs to be assessed. In order to test the null hypothesis that the average abnormal returns for the day t are equal to zero, i.e. the acquisition has no impact on shareholder value, a test statistic proposed by DODD and WARNER (1983) is predominantly used.[53] Within this test statistic, instead of raw abnormal returns, average standardized abnormal returns ("$\overline{SAR_t}$") are employed, calculated as follows:[54]

$$\overline{SAR_t} = \frac{1}{n}\sum_{i=1}^{n}\frac{AR_{it}}{\hat{s}_{it}}, \qquad \text{with} \quad \hat{s}_{it} = s_i \sqrt{1 + \frac{1}{L} + \frac{\left(R_{mt} - \overline{R}_m\right)^2}{\sum_{\tau=\tau_1}^{\tau_2}\left(R_{m\tau} - \overline{R}_m\right)^2}} \tag{9}$$

where:

$\overline{SAR_t}$	: average standardized abnormal return on event day t
s_i	: standard deviation of share i's abnormal returns during the estimation period
L	: number of days of the estimation period
R_{mt}	: return of the market index for event day t,
$\overline{R}_m$	: average return of the market index during the estimation period
$R_{m\tau}$	: return of the market index on day τ of the estimation period

The test statistics for the average abnormal return on day t and cumulative abnormal return for the event window T are calculated as shown in equations (10) and (11):[55]

50 It should be pointed out that the observed abnormal returns for each day within the event window are simply added rather than multiplied, as it is customary in the finance literature. For a critique of this arithmetic method refer to for example DISSANAIKE (1994).

51 For example in the study by BRUNER (2005).

52 For example MOELLER ET AL. (2004). For value-weighted returns the dollar abnormal returns across the samples are divided by the aggregate market capitalization of acquirers.

53 Not all reviewed studies provide information regarding which test statistics were employed to measure significance.

54 See DODD and WARNER (1983), p. 436f. Using standardized (cumulative) abnormal returns yields a test statistic that tends to follow a t-distribution more closely than raw (cumulative) abnormal returns.

55 DODD and WARNER (1983) point out that if most CARs are positive and the sample includes a few extreme genitive outliers with large standard deviations, the CARs and test statistic may have opposite signs.

$$Z_{AR_t} = (\sqrt{n})\,\overline{SAR}_t \quad (10); \qquad Z_{CAR_T} = \sqrt{\frac{n}{(t_2 - t_1 + 1)}} \sum_{t=t_1}^{t_2} \overline{SAR}_t \quad (11)$$

where:

Z_{AR_t}	: test statistic for average abnormal return for event day t
Z_{CAR_T}	: test statistic for cumulative abnormal return for event window T
$t_2 - t_1 + 1$	: number of days in the event window T

Assuming that the abnormal returns are normally distributed,[56] the shares' residuals are not cross-sectionally correlated,[57] and the event-induced variance is insignificant, these test statistics follow the standard normal distribution N(0,1).

4.3.1.2 Variations of the input parameters in prior research

Besides the choice of the basic statistical model to use for computing estimated share returns, the observed event studies exhibit a broad variety of different input parameters, i.e. the industry and nationality of the acquirer and target companies, the observation period, and the size of the transaction sample. Table 4.2 displays the input parameter for each event study.

While the majority of the reviewed event studies selected transactions including either all or only non-financial business sectors, six studies solely measure cumulative abnormal returns for acquisitions in the financial services industry.[58] 20 studies report abnormal returns for U.S. acquirers in domestic transactions, of which three studies also report results for cross-border transactions.[59] Cumulative abnormal returns for German acquirers in domestic acquisitions are only reported by BEITEL (2004). Within the studies of cross-border transactions, four authors analyze the wealth effects for U.S. acquirers, three for German acquirers. Eight studies assess the share price reactions for acquiring companies of other European countries, of which two specifically report results for the acquisition of U.S. targets.

---

[56] Due to the Central Limit Theorem, the distribution of the sample mean returns converges to normal as the number of shares increases. BROWN and WARNER (1985) show that for sample sizes exceeding 50, the mean abnormal returns appear close to normal. In order to test whether the average abnormal returns are normally distributed, a Kolmogorov-Smirnov test can be performed, see BROWN and WARNER (1980), p. 219.

[57] Cross-sectional correlation might occur if the shares' residuals have a common event date. MACKINLAY (1997) and BROWN and WARNER (1985) show that the power of the test statistics improves as the number of transactions in the sample increases and as the number of days in the event window decreases. For a further discussion of assumptions required for the significance test refer to CHATTERJEE and KUENZI (2001), p. 20f. and DODD (1980), p. 111f.

[58] These are the studies by BEITEL ET AL. (2004), CORNETT ET AL. (2003), DELONG (2003), DELONG (2001), HOUSTON ET AL. (2001), and TOYNE and TRIPP (1998). For a comprehensive overview of the existing literature concerning bank acquisitions and their empirical success refer to BEITEL and SCHIERECK (2001).

[59] I.e. the studies by MOELLER and SCHLINGEMANN (2005), FULLER ET AL. (2002), and ALLEN ET AL. (2000).

Table 4.2: Variations of the input parameters in the reviewed studies

Authors	Year	Industry sector	Acquirer nation	Target nation	Observation period from	Observation period to	Sample size	Analytical model*	Estimation period	Cross-sectional analysis
TOYNE and TRIPP	1998	Financial	U.S.	U.S.	1991	1995	68	MM	60	No
ALLEN ET AL.	2000	All	U.S. & Foreign	U.S.	1995	1998	229	MM	190	Yes
CLARK ET AL.	2000	Industrial	Foreign	U.K	1985	1997	730	MM **	220	No
CORHAY and RAD	2000	Industrial	Dutch	Foreign	1990	1996	111	MM	200	Yes
DÖRR	2000	All	German	Europe	1990	1996	120	MM	n/a	Yes
MULHERIN and BOONE	2000	All	U.S.	U.S.	1990	1999	281	MM	n/a	No
RAU	2000	Industrial	U.S.	U.S.	1980	1994	857	MM	255	Yes
WALKER	2000	Industrial	U.S.	U.S.	1980	1996	278	MA	-	Yes
ANDRADE ET AL.	2001	All	U.S.	U.S.	1990	1998	1,864	n/a	n/a	No
BLACK ET AL.	2001	All	U.S.	Foreign	1985	1995	316	MM	n/a	No
DELONG	2001	Financial	U.S.	U.S.	1998	1995	280	n/a	250	Yes
HOUSTON ET AL.	2001	Financial	U.S.	U.S.	1991	1996	37	n/a	n/a	Yes
SAUNDERS and SRINIVASAN	2001	All	U.S.	U.S.	1985	1998	564	MM	240	Yes
CHOI and TSAI	2002	All	U.S.	Foreign	1992	2000	369	MM	200	Yes
FAN and GOYAL	2002	Industry	U.S.	U.S.	1991	1996	514	MM	255	Yes
FULLER ET AL.	2002	Industry	U.S.	U.S.	1990	2000	3,135	MA	-	Yes

*MM: Market model; MA: Market adjusted return-model; CAPM: Capital Asset Pricing Model. n/a: Information is not available. -: Data is not necessary. ** denotes use of alternative methods to compute the expected return.

Table 4.2 (cont.): Variations of the input parameters in the reviewed studies

Authors	Year	Industry sector	Acquirer nation	Target nation	Observation period from	Observation period to	Sample size	Analytical model*	Estimation period	Cross-sectional analysis
RAU and RODGERS	2002	All	U.S.	U.S.	1980	1994	218	MM	255	Yes
BHARADWAJ and SHIVDASANI	2003	Industrial	U.S.	U.S.	1990	1996	115	MM	150	Yes
CORNETT ET AL.	2003	Financial	U.S.	U.S.	1988	1995	423	MM	120	Yes
DELONG	2003	Financial	U.S. & Foreign	U.S. & Foreign	1988	1999	438	MA	-	Yes
ALLEN ET AL.	2004	Industrial	U.S.	U.S.	1995	2000	495	MM	190	Yes
BEITEL	2004	Industrial	German	German & Foreign	1995	2001	287	MM	280	Yes
BEITEL ET AL.	2004	Financial	European	Foreign	1985	2000	98	MM	252	Yes
BRADLEY and SUNDARAM	2004	All	U.S.	U.S.	1990	2000	12,476	MA	-	Yes
CAMPA and HERNANDO	2004	All	European	European	1998	2000	262	CAPM	150	Yes
GOERGEN and RENNEBORG	2004	All	European	European	1993	2000	158	MM **	195	Yes
LOWINSKI ET AL.	2004	All	Swiss	Swiss & Foreign	1990	2001	114	MM	245	Yes
MOELLER ET AL.	2004	All	U.S.	U.S.	1980	2001	12,023	MM	200	Yes
BRUNER	2005	All	U.S.	U.S	1985	2000	2,805	MA	-	Yes
CONN ET AL.	2005	All	U.K.	Foreign	1984	1998	3,186	MA	-	Yes
GREGORY and MCCORRISTON	2005	All	U.K.	Foreign	1985	1994	343	MM **	250	Yes
MOELLER and SCHLINGEMANN	2005	All	U.S.	Foreign	1991	1995	281	MA **	-	Yes

* MM: Market model; MA: Market adjusted return-model; CAPM: Capital Asset Pricing Model. n/a: Information is not available. -: Data is not necessary. ** denotes use of alternative methods to compute the expected return.

As mentioned earlier, only those studies were selected that observed the acquirer's shareholders wealth effects for transactions during the fifth merger wave. However, 13 studies also included transactions during the 1980s in their sample, and not all of them split their findings by the different time periods. The size of the analyzed samples ranges from a few dozen (for example HOUSTON ET AL. (2001) and DELONG (2001)) to over ten thousand transactions (BRADLEY and SUNDARAM (2004) and MOELLER ET AL. (2004)). Excluding these extreme values, the average sample size is 274, with a median of 278.

Finally, most studies not only reviewed the overall success of transactions, but also aimed to identify its underlying determinants using certain features of the transaction, such as hostility of the bid, number of bidders, method of payment, and status of the target. The significance of the impact of those determinants was measured in univariate and/or cross-sectional analyses.

4.3.1.3 Evaluation of the methodology

Event studies are currently the most widespread and accepted methodology for measuring the implications of acquisitions from the perspective of the shareholders of the involved entities. Their dominance can be attributed to various attractive features:[60]

- They focus on capital market data, thereby providing a direct measure of the value created through the transaction for the shareholders.
- Capital market data is publicly available, which permits empirical studies on large samples of public acquirers and targets.
- The approach is future-oriented, since it uses expectations of future cash flows.
- The methodology is relatively easy to implement, given that the only data necessary are the names of the publicly traded firms, event dates, and share prices.
- Since abnormal returns are calculated, the data is not subject to industry sensitivity, thereby enabling a broad cross-section of transactions to be evaluated.
- Using share prices avoids the data contamination problems inherent in financial statements based measures.[61]

As a result of various assumptions and issues inherent in the design of this methodology, the meaningfulness of the obtained results from event studies may be limited though: [62]

---

[60] See BEITEL (2002), p. 90f.; MCWILLIAMS and SIEGEL (1997), p. 626. BROMILEY ET AL. (1988) provide a critique of the event study method as a tool for measuring the impact of strategic decisions.

[61] See Section 4.3.2.3.

[62] HIETALA ET AL. (2002) raise fundamental objections to the interpretation of abnormal returns. Arguing that the announcement of a transaction reveals information about the potential synergy gains and the stand-alone and combined valuation of both entities, the authors note that a separation of such effects is impossible. Accordingly, they conclude that the meaningfulness of abnormal returns may be distorted.

- The central prerequisite for using this method is the existence of a (semi-) efficient capital market, i.e. the assumption that all publicly available information and future expectations are completely reflected in the share price without any bias.[63] However, short-run market inefficiencies could induce over- or under-reaction of the share prices to the announcement of acquisitions.[64] In addition, share prices incorporate any financially relevant information that is revealed to shareholders, such as the future market positioning of the company, efficiency and revenue increases, and profit growth potential.[65] As a result of these broad factors influencing the share price, the computed results of the event study may not solely reflect the impact of the announced transaction.[66]
- This method essentially assumes that the capital market does not have information of the transaction prior to its initial public announcement. However, it is possible that the transaction has been anticipated or that information is leaked to the market in advance of the formal announcement, which is difficult to precisely determine. The approach taken in the research of extending the announcement period has the problem of increasing the noise-to-signal ratio as well, which makes it more difficult to reliably measure the specific impact of the acquisition on the share price.[67] In addition, the greater the time gap between the day of the acquisition's announcement and the ending day of the analyzed event window, the more unsuitable the applied parameters of the market model become.[68]
- The model assumes that there are no confounding effects from other events that are not linked to the analyzed transaction.[69] If other financially relevant events occur during the event window, such as the announcement of dividends or a change in key executives, it is difficult to isolate the impact of one particular event. Another limitation in measuring the particular impact from one transaction may occur in case the acquiring company announces the transaction as part of a previously communicated external growth strategy. In such a case part of the share price reaction may have been triggered already at the initial public announcement of that strategy.[70]
- The validity of the computed results of event studies may be restricted by the fact that the statistical model is testing several hypotheses simultaneously; not only hypotheses on the underlying goal of the study of measuring the success of acquisitions are tested, but also on the applied model to determine the abnormal return of the share, the choice of the

---

63 See FAMA (1970), p. 383. The efficient markets hypothesis is frequently addressed in the economics and finance literature, as summarized for example in DÖRR (2000), pp. 88-91.

64 FAMA has recently conceded that share prices could become "somewhat irrational", see HILSENRATH (2004), A1.

65 GRINBLATT and TITMAN (2002, p. 708) further note that "the stock returns of the bidder at the time of the announcement of the bid may tell us more about how the market is reassessing the bidder's business than it does about the value of the acquisition".

66 See SHLEIFER and VISHNY (1991), p. 54f.; TRAUTWEIN (1990), p. 293.

67 See HARRISON ET AL. (2005), p. 6f.

68 See RHOADES (1994), p. 6.; BROWN and WARNER (1980), p. 206.

69 See MÖLLER (1985), p. 510. A study by AKTAS ET AL. (2004) shows how the existence of firm-specific events during the estimation period can cause distortions of the results of an event study.

70 See BRUNER (2004a), p. 35.

event window, and the test for statistical significance. If the abnormal return is statistically insignificant, this does not necessarily indicate a lack of reaction of the capital market towards the acquisition; it may also be the consequence of a false analytical model or the faulty adaptation of a statistical testing method.[71]

- The instability of the systematic risk component β_i of a share *i* over a longer time period and its changes due to events such as an acquisition are frequently discussed problems in the literature.[72]
- The assumption of a linear relationship between the systematic risk and the share return has not been conclusively substantiated.[73]
- A distorting influence especially in a short event window may be caused by trading driven by speculation and merger-arbitrage short-selling.[74]
- Capital market based event studies only analyze the success of transactions by public companies, which in light of the respective capital market structure of a country limits the size of the sample. For example, in Germany only approximately 1,300 out of 2.5m companies are publicly traded.[75]
- Empirical studies found evidence that smaller companies generally yield better results with regard to their risk-adjusted returns than the overall capital market. This so-called "small firm-effect", which cannot be isolated, may attribute to the measured abnormal returns.[76]
- Shares of small companies frequently show only a very limited trading volume over time, so that for example only call-bid spreads are available. This may result in the problem of non-synchronized trading while applying the market model. In such instances the share return and the performance of the market portfolio are measured over a different time frame, leading to distorted and inconsistent estimates of the parameter of the market model based on the OLS-regression.[77] Such distortion may be the result of autocorrelation of the share returns.[78]
- As pointed out before, in case the CAPM is used, its underlying assumptions are subject to fundamental criticism.

71 See APENBRINK (1993), p. 105 ff.; BOWMAN (1983), p. 577f.

72 See CHATTERJEE and LUBATKIN (1990), p. 266; CONN (1985), p. 47f.; MALATESTA (1983), p. 178. Several older studies have tested significant changes of the systematic risk with mixed results, for example LAHEY and CONN (1990), SHRIEVES and LUBATKIN (1990), CHOI and PHILIPPATOS (1983), FIRTH (1980), and HAUGEN and LANGENSTIEG (1975).

73 As for example pointed out by FAMA and FRENCH (1992).

74 See RHOADES (1994), p. 7. The study by MITCHELL ET AL. (2004) argues that as much as 50 percent of the price movement in an acquirer's shares on the announcement day is not attributable to the market perception of the transaction but rather reflects short-term technical effects as a result of merger-arbitrage short-selling.

75 See VOGEL (2002), p. 289.

76 See SCHIERECK and WEBER (2000), p. 293.

77 See BROWN and WARNER (1985), p. 5.

78 See BROWN and WARNER (1985), p. 19. However, these authors conclude that those distortions are only minimal and occur rarely.

4.3.2 Financial statements based studies

4.3.2.1 Mechanics of the methodology

Financial statements based studies generally examine the financial performance of the acquiring or combined entities before and subsequent to the acquisition using external accounting data. The goal of such studies is to determine whether the financial or earnings position of the companies have changed as a result of the transaction.

Transaction success is measured applying either standard methods for valuating companies[79] or various comparative financial ratios in a before-and-after or comparative object analysis.[80] Financial ratios focusing on the earnings position may be absolute measures, such as EBIT and EBITDA, or relative measures, such as return on investment ("ROI").[81] Other key performance indicators measure the levels of revenue and cash flows of the companies.[82]

Whether a transaction is considered a financial success depends on the benchmark that is chosen for the comparison of the financial ratio. Standard benchmarks are for example (i) a set of matched companies in the same industry and of the same size in order to determine whether the acquirer outperformed its non-acquiring peers,[83] (ii) budgeted numbers for future periods in order to determine whether the projections at the time of the acquisition were achieved post-closing,[84] and (iii) the pre-acquisition performance in order to determine whether the earnings situation has improved after the consummation of the transaction.[85]

4.3.2.2 Variations of the input parameters in prior research

All three financial statements based studies focus on U.S. acquirers, while only the research by GUGLER ET AL. (2003) examines differences between domestic and cross-border transactions by also including non-U.S. acquirers. Besides transactions during the fifth merger wave, all studies analyze the success of acquisitions in the 1980s as well, without explicitly differentiating the findings between both time periods. Analogous to the reviewed event studies, the sample sizes are relatively high, varying from 315 to 2,753 transactions. Table 4.3 summarizes the individual input parameters for the three performance studies.

---

79 See Section 2.5.3.2.

80 See VOGEL (2002), pp. 277-280; BÜHNER (1990a), p. 84f.

81 For a discussion of various financial ratios see ALBRECHT (1994), pp. 58-60. COCHRAN and WOOD (1984) point out that there is no consensus on an appropriate measure of financial performance.

82 HEALY ET AL. (1992) for example argue that post-acquisition operating cash flows are an appropriate indicator to measure post-acquisition performance, while claiming that event studies cannot identify the real economic value gains of a transaction.

83 See PAUTLER (2003), p. 5. For a discussion of situations in which matched sets of firms may provide the best benchmark refer to GHOSH (2001), p. 177.

84 See VOGEL (2002), p. 277.

85 See ALBRECHT (1994), p. 61.

Table 4.3: Variations of the input parameters in the reviewed studies

Authors	Year	Geographical focus	Observation period from	to	Sample size	Financial ratio
GHOSH	2001	U.S. domestic	1981	1995	315	Cash-flow
HERON and LIE	2002	U.S. domestic	1985	1997	859	Operating income scaled by sales
GUGLER ET AL.	2003	U.S. & Foreign	1981	1999	2,753	Net profit, sales volume

Based on the suggestion that comparisons with industry-median companies will most likely lead to biased results when pre-event size and performance vary between sample and industry-median companies, GHOSH (2001) evaluates the performance of U.S. acquirers against a set of matched control companies that is based on pre-acquisition performance and size of the merging entities.[86] This approach follows the general prescriptions offered by BARBER and LYON (1996), arguing that acquiring companies undertake acquisitions following a period of superior performance and that they are generally larger than industry-median companies. HERON and LIE (2002) examined the post-merger changes in operating performance compared to an industry-adjusted performance metric and, similar to GHOSH (2001), to a control group of companies with similar pre-transaction performances. GUGLER ET AL. (2003) analyzed the impact of transactions on profitability and sales of acquiring companies by comparing the performance of the merging companies with a control group of industry-median non-merging companies.[87]

4.3.2.3 Evaluation of the methodology

Accounting based measures are generally considered to be credible, given that financial statements are typically audited and used by investors in judging corporate performance. However, the meaningfulness of the results obtained from these studies are subject to the following limitations:[88]

- The reliability of the underlying financial statements as a basis for comparing financial ratios is frequently questioned in the literature, due to existing alternative treatments when applying accounting principles such as U.S. GAAP, IFRS, or German GAAP.[89] To

[86] Previous research studies predominantly observed post-acquisition improvements in operating performance when comparing the merged companies with a sample of industry-median firms, see for example DALEY ET AL. (1997); KANG and SHIVDASANI (1997); HEALEY ET AL. (1992).

[87] The authors essentially follow the approach of prior accounting studies by HEALY ET AL. (1992), RAVENSCRAFT and SCHERER (1987), and MUELLER (1980).

[88] See NUPPONEN (1995), p. 37; ALBRECHT (1994), pp. 69-73; GERPOTT (1993), pp. 194-196; MÖLLER (1983), pp. 52-57. However, PERIN (1996, p. 54) concluded that the results of accounting studies and event studies yield correlated results.

[89] For a discussion of major differences between these accounting standards refer to Section 3.3.2.1.

some extent, such choices enable management to deliberately influence the published financial earnings of their companies.[90]

- Accounting measures only reflect the past performance of a company, not the expectations for its future profitability.[91]
- The difficulty in isolating the impact of a transaction on the financial ratios from other internal efforts, such as other acquisitions, restructuring programs, or from external factors of the business environment is difficult, especially if the transaction occurred some years ago.[92]
- Financial ratios do not reflect the companies' risk profile, i.e. changes in an acquirer's risk situation for example through increased indebtedness or incurred costs of equity are not considered.[93]
- The acquirer's financial earnings position may not be significantly impacted if the target company is only of a small size.[94]
- Frequently the target is fully absorbed into the corporate group of the acquirer. As a result, a comparison of past and current financial ratios of the target's performance may be distorted.[95]
- Using the company's pre-acquisition performance as a benchmark is frequently subject to criticism, as noted by FAIRBURN and KAY (1989): "The proper comparison is, of course not with the pre-merger performance of the merging firms but rather with what the post-merger performance would have been if the merger had not occurred."[96]

Due to these potential limitations, financial statements based studies, which were predominantly applied in research during the 1980s, are not as widespread any longer. Accordingly, for the purpose of this review, only three studies were identified that met the general selection criteria.

---

90 See for example COENENBERG (2000), p. 878f.; ALBRECHT (1994), p. 71; KIRCHNER (1991), p. 92f., SETH (1990), p. 99; RAPPAPORT (1981), p. 139f. These authors argue that accounting data is generally distorted and therefore may not be used for academic research.

91 See ALBRECHT (1994), p. 73.

92 See CANTWELL and SANTANGELO (2002), p. 405. The problem of potentially confounding events also applies to event studies.

93 See GOMEZ and GANZ (1992); p. 45; JOHNSON and NATARAJAN (1985); p. 53; RAPPAPORT (1981), p. 140.

94 See BAMBERGER (1994), p. 113f.; KIRCHNER (1991), p. 92f. As mentioned before, this issue may also impact the credibility of long-term event studies.

95 See MÖLLER (1983), p. 52f.

96 FAIRBURN and KAY (1989), p. 23.

4.3.3 Surveys of executives

4.3.3.1 Mechanics of the methodology

In a survey of executives, those people directly involved in a transaction are asked to offer their subjective assessment of the success of acquisitions.[97] The goal of such surveys is to yield generalizations from data that considers the specific internal conditions of the transaction and its underlying business objectives.[98] Surveys are generally conducted by business consulting firms,[99] while comprehensive scholarly studies of executives' perception of success are relatively seldom. The assessments are provided by means of scaled answers in a standardized written questionnaire or through confidential personal or telephone interviews with executives who are knowledgeable about a transaction.[100] The questions put to the executives typically include the objective of the acquisition, the type of expected synergies, characteristics and problems of the transaction process, and the post-closing performance relative to planned expectations.[101] Surveys frequently differ with regard to their dimension for measuring success, which may range from the achievement of the original goals of a transaction to, in rare cases, the changes in the share price of the company.[102]

4.3.3.2 Variations of the input parameters in prior research

Unlike the event and financial performance studies, a significant fraction of approximately 60 percent of the reviewed studies by consulting firms covered cross-border transactions (see Table 4.4). Of those seven studies, six conducted a survey of executives, while the study by A.T. KEARNEY (1999) only applied a quantitative success measure to cross-border transactions. The survey by MERCER CONSULTING (2001) specifically analyzed transatlantic transactions, but did not explicitly report results for German acquiring companies.

The studies by KPMG (2004a, 2001, 1999), PWC (2000), and MERCER CONSULTING (2001) combined their surveys with a quantitative share performance analysis. Six studies measured success strictly on a quantitative basis. With the exception of MCKINSEY & CO. (2001), these studies used share price performance over a long-term period as the success measure. The applied methodology of the alternative success measures is often described rather casually. For example, KPMG (2001) notes that "for each deal a relative measure of change in equity price was taken pre-deal and again approximately one year afterwards. This result was then compared with the overall trend in the relevant industry segment, in order to assess which

---

97 See CORDING ET AL. (2002), p. 36.; BÜHNER (1990a), p. 98.
98 See MÖLLER (1983), p. 52. Hence, such data is typically considered being broader than any available external information.
99 Marketing firms conducted most of the interviews for the consultants.
100 See VOGEL (2002), p. 288f.
101 See BRUNER (2004a), pp. 57-60.
102 See PAUTLER (2003), p. 3.

benchmark rating was most appropriate".[103] In their 2002 study, KPMG compared the share price performance of acquirers over a two-year period to an expected return using CAPM. MERCER CONSULTING (2001) compared the share price performance of the acquiring companies over the two years subsequent to the announcement of the transaction to an industry-specific S&P index benchmark, while the 1995 study by MERCER CONSULTING as well as the 2002 BCG study compare the total return to acquirer shareholders three months prior to a transaction to the return up to three years after its closing.[104] In their 2004 study, BCG examined the ten-year total shareholder return as the benchmark performance measure, splitting their sample of U.S. acquirers into companies with highly acquisitive, mixed, and organic growth strategies.[105] A similar approach was taken by KPMG in their 2005 study. The analysis by MCKINSEY & CO. (2001) compared the three year post-merger revenue growth of acquirers to industry benchmarks.

Table 4.4: Variations of the input parameters in the reviewed studies

Consulting firm	Year	Geographical focus	Observation period from	to	Sample Size	Method
MERCER	1995	U.S. domestic	1990	1995	150	Share performance
A.T. KEARNEY	1999	Cross-border	1993	1996	115	Share performance
KPMG	1999	Cross-border	1996	1997	107	Survey/Share performance
PWC	2000	U.S. domestic	1999	1999	125	Survey/Share performance
KPMG	2001	Cross-border	1997	1999	118	Survey/Share performance
MERCER	2001	Transatlantic	1994	1999	152	Survey/Share performance
MCKINSEY & CO.	2001	U.S. domestic	1995	1996	160	Growth rates analysis
BCG	2002	U.S. domestic	1995	2001	302	Share performance
KPMG	2002	German domestic and cross-border	1998	2001	154	Share performance
BCG	2004	U.S. acquirers	1993	2002	700	Share performance
KPMG	2004	Cross-border	2000	2001	122	Survey/Share performance
KPMG	2005	German cross-border	2000	2005	22	Survey

Similar to event and accounting studies, surveys of executives tend to focus on larger[106] acquisitions by U.S. companies and none of the surveys was limited to only one specific

[103] KPMG (2001), p. 10.
[104] In both cases the minimum transaction volume in the surveyed sample was $500m.
[105] As such, the methodology of this study differs from the others since it does not focus on the short-term performance of individual transactions but rather on the long-term performance of individual companies categorized by their degree of acquisition activity, see BCG (2004), p. 11.
[106] Not all studies provide information with regard to the size of the included transactions.

business sector. The 2002 and 2005 studies by KPMG examined the success of German acquiring companies, while the latter study specifically surveyed executives of mid-cap companies. With 22 questionnaires this study represents the smallest sample size, which compares to an average size of 186 transactions and a median of 138. As with the majority of event studies, most of the reviewed studies not only measured the average success of transactions but also aimed to identify determinants of transaction success.

4.3.3.3 Evaluation of the methodology

Using executives' opinions as a benchmark for measuring success has the benefit of including only internally available information in the measurement.[107] In contrast to capital market oriented studies, such surveys are not limited to public transactions and also offer the opportunity to measure success from various perspectives, depending on which parties are included in the survey. Besides executives, a survey for example may include employees as well as external specialists that were involved in the transaction.[108]

The main prerequisite for the meaningfulness of the results of self-reporting surveys is the open-mindedness and critical faculty of the executives.[109] Since such requirements are typically only met in case of acquisitions which from the perspective of both the executives and the public are viewed as successful, the internal and external validity of these surveys is frequently questioned:[110] The internal validity of a survey may be distorted by the tendency of executives to present those transactions they were involved with in a better light than they actually are in order to retrospectively justify them. External validity of surveys may be limited through the tendency of executives not to reply to surveys if they deem their transaction unsuccessful.[111] Overall, the subjective assessment of executives may lead to overestimation of transaction success.[112]

---

107 See BAMBERGER (1994), p. 120f.

108 See GERPOTT (1993), p. 210; KIRCHNER (1991), p. 98f.

109 See VOGEL (2002), p. 289.

110 For example, PAUTLER (2003, p. 4) states: "One can readily ask whether these surveys ... provide a valid test, because one can hardly expect the executives involved in the deal and responsible for its success to be unbiased evaluators of the deal." For a critical discussion of qualitative data based measurements of transaction success refer to for example PERIN (1996), p. 55f.; KÜBLER (1994), p. 51f.; GERPOTT (1993), pp. 211-213.

111 See ALBRECHT (1994), p. 193; GERPOTT (1993), p. 213. In addition to the time aspect of completing a questionnaire, these potential problems may explain the on average usually low participation rates of approximately 15 percent. Moreover, non-successful deals may not be represented proportionally.

112 See KERLER (2000), p. 130f. Some older studies found a significant correlation of subjective success measures with quantitative methodologies, see GERPOTT (1993), p. 211. DATTA (1991, p. 288) concludes that this methodology "...is likely to provide a picture of performance which is much closer to reality". JANSEN and KÖRNER (2000) and PERIN (1996) observed contradicting results though.

As pointed out in the discussion of potential implications stemming from agency conflicts,[113] the assessment by executives may also be significantly detached from that of shareholders and hence may not be aligned to the goal of shareholder value creation.[114] In addition, the measures of success frequently vary between surveys, accordingly a comparison of individual studies may yield limited evidence with regard to generalized statements on the success of transactions. Finally, a reliable interpretation of a survey's results requires the ability to replicate it in order to evaluate whether its questions were framed in a way to avoid coaching the respondent to give a desired answer and whether the survey probes the respondent's factual knowledge of actual transactions.[115] None of the reviewed studies by business consulting firms provided the applied questionnaire though.[116]

4.3.4 Comparison of the methodologies

While all of the three main methodologies for measuring success exhibit general problems with regard to defining the observation period for which success is measured, they each have certain individual strengths and weaknesses, as summarized in Table 4.5.

From the perspective of the shareholders of the acquiring companies, only capital market based event studies offer a direct and objective measure of the wealth effects. Unlike in a survey of executives, the applied measure is not simultaneously influenced by other groups and their interests. Additionally, only event studies provide a future oriented measurement, while financial statement based studies and surveys focus on the realized success in the past.

Since the main perspective of this study is that of shareholders of German acquiring companies, success of U.S. cross-border transactions will be analyzed using event study methodology. In order to yield additional observations, the event study will be complemented by a survey of executives of those German companies that were involved in cross-border acquisitions of U.S. targets. The findings of these studies are presented in Chapter 5, following the review of the results of the prior empirical research.

---

113 See Section 2.3.2.1.

114 See KERLER (2000), p. 130.

115 See BRUNER (2004a), p. 60.

116 PAUTLER (2003, p. 3) points out this weakness by providing an example: "For example, if a respondent were asked whether a merger fully attained all its goals, the likely answer would be 'no' simply because the question asked about full attainment rather than general success. Because survey results are likely to have been highly dependent on how the survey's questions were worded, a reader of the results cannot effectively evaluate the answers without knowledge of the survey instrument itself." The absence of a detailed description of the methodology might be explained by the consulting firm's desire to protect client confidentiality and propriety information.

Table 4.5: Comparison of main methodologies for measuring transaction success[117]

	Methodology for measuring success		
	Capital market based event study	**Financial statements based study**	**Survey of executives**
Focus of the approach	• Market expectations of future cash flows in order to determine shareholder value creation	• Financial ratios derived from accounting data in order to measure improvements in financial results	• Subjective assessment of success by those executives that were involved in the transaction
Strengths	• Direct measure of value creation for investors • Unbiased rational expectations of future cash flows, since share prices reflect the present value of expected future cash flows • Possibility to eliminate some extraneous factors • Use of public data	• Credibility, since financial statements are typically audited and used by investors in judging corporate performance; accordingly, they serve as an indirect measure of economic value creation • Permit a multi-year perspective reflecting belief that it may take years before merger benefits are fully realized	• Yields insights into transactions that may not be known in the capital market • Benefits from the intimate familiarity of the executives with the transaction • Recognizes the complexity and multi-dimensional nature of measuring success of transactions
Weaknesses	• Requires significant assumptions about the functioning of capital markets: efficiency, rationality, and absence of restrictions on arbitrage • Assumes that market participants are able to quickly and accurately predict the impact of the transaction • Factors other than the transaction may be impacting the returns	• Only reflects the past • Great latitude in financial reporting, i.e. differences among companies in accounting policies add noise and differences in accounting standards make cross-border comparisons difficult • No adjustment for changing risk profiles • Factors other than the transaction may be impacting the results	• Self-reporting bias: recall of historical results can be slanted to present results in the best light • Gives the perspectives of managers whose interests may not be aligned with those of shareholders • Typically surveys have a low rate of participation, making them vulnerable to criticism of generalizability

[117] Source: presentation follows BRUNER (2004a), p. 35; CORDING ET AL. (2002), p. 35.

4.4 Overall success of analyzed transactions

4.4.1 Capital market based event studies

4.4.1.1 Cumulative abnormal returns to target shareholders

Of the 32 reviewed event studies, ten report cumulative abnormal returns to shareholders of target companies. All studies found those to be significantly positive, which in light of the premiums typically paid in transactions is not surprising.[118] The observed cumulative abnormal returns range from 2.97 percent (ALLEN ET AL. (2000))[119] to 24.60 percent (HOUSTON ET AL. (2001)).[120] Despite variations in the applied event window, all studies also detect positive cumulative abnormal returns in the days before the announcement date, suggesting that the capital market anticipated information on the transaction.[121]

Only the studies by CAMPA and HERNANDO (2004) and GOERGEN and RENNEBOOG (2004) provide cumulative abnormal returns to target shareholders in cross-border transactions, while the latter found that those were higher than in domestic acquisitions.[122] Similar observations of relatively higher premiums in cross-border transactions involving a U.S. target are also reported in studies by INKPEN ET AL. (2000) and HARRIS and RAVENSCRAFT (1991).[123] These authors suggest that such higher premiums may be explained by overly aggressive bidding by foreign acquirers in light of their strong desire to expand into the U.S. market. ECKBO and THORBURN (2000) interpret the difference in premiums between domestic and cross-border transactions as a required compensation to the shareholders of a U.S. target company for incurring worse corporate governance as a result of selling to a foreign company.[124]

---

118 A summary of CARs for target shareholders in older domestic studies is provided by BRUNER (2004a), while CHENG and CHAN (1995), CEBENOYAN ET AL. (1991), and HARRIS and RAVENSCRAFT (1991) review such returns in older cross-border transactions.

119 Unlike other studies, this study as well as the one by ALLEN ET AL. (2004) report standardized CARs.

120 The following CARs were observed in the other studies: GOERGEN and RENNEBOOG (2004) 12.96 percent; CAMPA and HERNANDO (2004) 3.93 percent; ALLEN ET AL. (2004) 3.38 percent; BEITEL ET AL. (2004) 12.39 percent; ANDRADE ET AL. (2001) 15.9 percent; DELONG (2001) 16.61 percent; MULHERIN and BOONE (2000) 21.2 percent; TOYNE and TRIPP (1998) 10.97 percent. Most of these studies measured the CAR for the [-1,1] event window.

121 See for example CAMPA and HERNANDO (2004), p. 50.

122 See GOERGEN and RENNEBOOG (2004), p. 24.

123 INKPEN ET AL. (2000) examined 11,639 transactions of U.S. technology companies, of which 446 involved an European acquirer, while HARRIS and RAVENSCRAFT (1991) examined 1,273 acquisitions of U.S. companies in the period 1970 to 1987, of which 159 involved a foreign acquirer. They found that the premiums paid by the European acquirers were about three times higher than those of U.S. acquiring companies.

124 In contrast, DEWENTER (1995) did not find a significant premium difference, noting that foreign acquirers pay a higher premium in case of hostile transactions, but also pay less when there are other bidders for the target. He concluded that the reaction of the capital market to the acquirer's nationality is closely tied to the transaction's characteristics.

4.4.1.2 Cumulative abnormal returns to acquirer shareholders in domestic transactions

Compared to target shareholders, the wealth implications for shareholders of acquiring companies in domestic transactions are much less certain, as displayed in Table 4.6.[125] Overall, the evidence is almost evenly distributed between studies reporting significant[126] positive and negative cumulative abnormal returns.

Table 4.6: Cumulative abnormal returns in domestic transactions

Authors	Year	Size		Event window	CAR	Significance
Panel A: U.S. acquirers						
TOYNE and TRIPP	1998	68		[-1,0]	-2.24	***
ALLEN ET AL.	2000	194	a	[-1,1]	-0.16	-
		34	b	[-1,1]	-0.62	*
MULHERIN and BOONE	2000	281		[-1,1]	-0.37	-
RAU	2000	857		[-1,1]	0.37	*
WALKER	2000	278		[-2,2]	-0.84	*
ANDRADE ET AL.	2001	1,864		[-1,1]	-1.00	-
DELONG	2001	280		[-10,1]	-1.68	***
HOUSTON ET AL.	2001	37		[-4,1]	-2.61	*
SAUNDERS and SRINIVASAN	2001	564		[-5,5]	-0.82	-
FAN and GOYAL	2002	514		[-1,1]	0.24	***
FULLER ET AL.	2002	3,135		[-2,2]	1.77	***
RAU and RODGERS	2002	218		[-1,1]	-0.74	-
BHARADWAJ and SHIVDASANI	2003	115		[-1,1]	1.45	***
CORNETT ET AL.	2003	423		[-1,1]	-0.74	**
DELONG	2003	397		[-10,1]	-2.10	***
ALLEN ET AL.	2004	495		[-1,1]	-0.31	***
BRADLEY and SUNDARAM	2004	12,476		[-2,2]	1.45	***
MOELLER ET AL.	2004	12,023		[-1,1]	1.10	***
BRUNER	2005	2,805		[-5,5]	-0.51	***
MOELLER and SCHLINGEMANN	2005	2,832		[-1,1]	1.49	***
Panel B: German acquirers						
BEITEL	2004	47	c	[-1,1]	2.54	-
		22	d	[-1,1]	2.44	-

a: banking sector; b: non-financial sector; c: non-inclusion of external financial advisors; d: inclusion of external financial advisors; *, **, *** denote significance at the 10%, 5%, and 1% level, respectively.

Of the 20 studies calculating wealth effects for shareholders of U.S. domestic acquiring companies, nine report significant negative cumulative abnormal returns, which vary from -0.31 percent (ALLEN ET AL. (2004)) to -2.61 percent (HOUSTON ET AL. (2001)). Some of

[125] For an overview of studies analyzing abnormal returns for U.S. domestic acquirers prior to 1990 refer to for example BRUNER (2004a); ANDRADE ET AL. (2001); AGRAWAL and JAFFE (2000); DATTA ET AL. (1992); JARRELL and POULSEN (1989); JARRELL ET AL. (1988); ROLL (1988); JENSEN and RUBACK (1983).

[126] Significance refers to the results of the test statistics, not to the economic impact.

these studies observe that the combined net economic gain for the shareholders of the acquirer and the target is only barely positive, thereby concluding that the synergistic benefits of a transaction usually appear to accrue to the shareholders of the target company, given that the average target company is usually significantly smaller than the average acquirer.[127] Notably, more than half of these nine studies solely analyze transactions in the financial services industry.[128] Seven studies observed significant positive shareholder gains, among them those three with the largest sample size (BRADLEY and SUNDARAM (2004), MOELLER ET AL. (2004), and FULLER ET AL. (2002)). On average, the positive cumulative abnormal returns were slightly lower in absolute value than the negative ones, with a range from 0.24 percent (FAN and GOYAL (2002)) to 1.77 percent (FULLER ET AL. (2002)). The remaining five studies all observed negative, but insignificant cumulative abnormal returns. BRUNER (2004a) for example deems abnormal returns to acquirer shareholders that do not significantly deviate from zero a success, since such a "break even" means that those acquirers earn their required return.[129]

The study by BEITEL (2004) is the only one in this review analyzing domestic transactions by German acquirers during the fifth merger wave. For his two subsamples of transactions that are either carried out in-house or assisted by external financial advisors, i.e. investment banks, the author observes positive cumulative abnormal returns of approximately 2.5 percent, though not statistically significant.[130] Compared to the average size of the U.S. studies, BEITEL's sample size is relatively small though.

4.4.1.3 Cumulative abnormal returns to acquirer shareholders in cross-border transactions

The results for the shareholder wealth effects in cross-border transactions are not as mixed, as shown in Table 4.7. All six studies reporting significant cumulative abnormal returns conclude that acquirers in cross-border transactions experience wealth gains, which vary from 0.25 percent (CORHAY and RAD (2000)) to 1.50 percent (BLACK ET AL. (2001)).[131] These significant positive cumulative abnormal returns are observed regardless of the nationality of the acquirer, with two studies each relating to U.S. and U.K. acquirers, one to Swiss, and one to European acquirers. With the exception of the study of bank transactions by BEITEL ET AL.

---

[127] Such combined positive returns are reported in the studies by ANDRADE ET AL. (2001), DELONG (2001), HOUSTON ET AL. (2001), MULHERIN and BOONE (2000), and TOYNE and TRIPP (1998).

[128] These are the studies by CORNETT ET AL. (2003), DELONG (2003), DELONG (2001), HOUSTON ET AL. (2001), and TOYNE and TRIPP (1998).

[129] See BRUNER (2004a), p. 31.

[130] These findings are in line with the study by GERKE ET AL. (1995), which also reported insignificant CARs around the announcement of 105 transactions by German acquirers during the period 1987 to 1992.

[131] These findings are in line with older studies by CAKICI ET AL. (1996), DOUKAS (1995), and MARKIDES and ITTNER (1994). On the other hand, EUN ET AL. (1996), SERVAES and ZENNER (1996), DANBOLT (1995), DATTA and PUIA (1995), and MATHUR ET AL. (1994) found no significant or negative CARs.

(2004), all other remaining studies report positive shareholder wealth gains as well, though not significant. The studies by GREGORY and MCCORRISTON (2005) and CORHAY and RAD (2000) provide shareholder wealth effects for a subsample of cross-border acquisitions of U.S. targets by U.K. or Dutch acquirers, respectively, though also in these cases no significant results were found.[132]

Table 4.7: Cumulative abnormal returns in cross-border transactions

Authors	Year	Size		Event window	CAR	Significance
Panel A: U.S. acquirers						
BLACK ET AL.	2001	316		[-5,5]	1.50	***
CHOI and TSAI	2002	369		[-1,1]	0.83	***
CAMPA and HERNANDO	2004	80		[-1,1]	0.05	-
MOELLER and SCHLINGEMANN	2005	281		[-1,1]	0.15	-
Panel B: German acquirers						
CLARK ET AL.	2000	61		[-1,1]	0.16	-
DÖRR	2000	120				-
BEITEL	2004	98	a	[-1,1]	0.89	-
		120	b	[-1,1]	0.87	-
Panel C: European acquirers						
CLARK ET AL.	2000	730		[-1,1]	0.29	-
CORHAY and RAD	2000	111		[1,5]	0.25	**
-thereof U.S. targets		17		[1,5]	0.14	-
DELONG	2003	41		[-10,1]	0.17	-
BEITEL ET AL.	2004	98		[-1,1]	-0.01	-
GOERGEN and RENNEBORG	2004	158		[-2,2]	1.18	***
LOWINSKI ET AL.	2004	91		[-1,1]	1.26	**
CONN ET AL.	2005	1,134		[-1,1]	0.33	**
GREGORY and MCCORRISTON	2005	343		[-3,1]	0.00	-
-thereof U.S. targets		206		[-3,1]	0.00	-

a: non-inclusion of financial advisor; b: inclusion of financial advisor; **, *** denote significance at the 5% and 1% level, respectively.

Insignificant results were also computed in all three studies reporting cumulative abnormal returns for German acquirers in cross-border transactions: CLARK ET AL. (2000) focused only on German acquisitions in the United Kingdom, while DÖRR (2000) analyzed transactions involving European targets. Only BEITEL (2004) included a broader worldwide scope of target companies in his sample.

132 Several older studies computed significant positive wealth affects for shareholders of foreign acquirers of U.S. targets, for example for Japanese acquirers (CAKICI ET AL. (1996), KANG (1993), and PETTWAY ET AL. (1993)). Significant negative CARs are reported for example by EUN ET AL. (1996) and MATHUR ET AL. (1994). Insignificant results are reported by DATTA and PUIA (1995). Of those studies, CAKICI ET AL. (1996) and MATHUR ET AL. (1994) provide data for German acquirers, which in both cases with a small sample size of three and 14, respectively, are insignificantly negative.

Seven studies evaluated whether there are systematic differences between the cumulative abnormal returns for acquirer shareholders in domestic compared to cross-border transactions. For their sample of European transactions, CAMPA and HERNANDO (2004) concluded that shareholders obtain lower benefits in cross-border transactions, "i.e. acquiring firms are to some extent penalized for engaging in a cross-border merger".[133] Similar conclusions were reached by MOELLER and SCHLINGEMANN (2005) and FULLER ET AL. (2002)[134] for U.S. acquirers,[135] by CONN ET AL. (2005) for U.K. acquirers, and by BEITEL ET AL. (2004) for German acquirers of banks.[136] Only LOWINSKI ET AL. (2004) found higher cumulative abnormal returns in their univariate analysis of transactions by Swiss acquirers, though that difference was not significant.[137] According to these studies, cross-border transactions do not seem to have additional benefits that yield higher shareholder wealth gains for acquirer shareholders than domestic transactions.

4.4.2 Financial statements based studies

The empirical results of financial statements based studies are not conclusive, as shown in Table 4.8. While GHOSH (2001) did not find any evidence that operating cash flow performance improved subsequent to an acquisition, HERON and LIE (2002) observed that acquiring companies exhibited operating performance levels in excess of their respective industries and significantly outperform control firms with similar pre-merger operating performance. The results of the study by GUGLER ET AL. (2003) also show that acquisitions on average significantly increase profitability, while simultaneously the authors found post-merger sales levels of the combined entities to be reduced compared to the benchmark group. For example for transactions by U.S. companies, which represent a substantial fraction of the entire sample in this study, GUGLER ET AL. (2003) found that transactions increased profits by 8.1 percent and decreased sales by 14.8 percent five years after the transaction. The results for acquirers of other countries exhibited similar patterns. The study also tested for differences in the effects of cross-border mergers that were related to the country of origin of either the acquiring or target company, but did not find any significant differences. By separating the observations into those transactions that increased profits and those that reduced them and by then examining the patterns of post-transaction sales changes, GUGLER

---

133 CAMPA and HERNANDO (2004), p. 68.

134 FULLER ET AL. (2002) only measured the impact of cross-border compared to domestic transactions through the use of a respective dummy variable in a cross-sectional regression analysis. In contrast, ALLEN ET AL. (2000) did not observe a significant correlation in their cross-sectional analysis.

135 The authors concluded that acquirers in cross-border transactions yield shareholder returns that are approximately one hundred basis points less than those for domestic acquirers. Significant differences between domestic and cross-border U.S. acquirers were also observed by ALLEN ET AL. (2004) in their cross-sectional analyses of determinants of transaction success.

136 Older studies by CHATTERJEE and AW (2000) and ECKBO and THORBURN (2000) also showed that acquirers of U.K. and Canadian targets, respectively, underperformed compared to their domestic peers.

137 The authors observed the same findings in a cross-sectional regression analysis.

ET AL. (2003) tried to determine the effects of mergers on efficiency and market power.[138] Their results suggest that the largest proportion of transactions in their sample decreased profits and efficiency, with only a fourth of all transactions enhancing profits by either having increased market power or efficiency.

Table 4.8: Results of studies of financial statements data

Authors	Year	Results
GHOSH	2001	• Operating cash flow performance did not improve subsequent to an acquisition • Post-acquisition returns on assets was similar to those of a matched control sample of non-acquiring companies
HERON and LIE	2002	• Post-acquisition levels of operating performance significantly exceeded those of non-acquiring control firms • Acquiring companies significantly outperformed non-acquiring firms
GUGLER ET AL.	2003	• Acquisitions resulted on average in significant increases of profitability, but simultaneously resulted in reduced sales of the combined entities • No significant differences between domestic and cross-border transactions

4.4.3 Surveys of executives and other studies by consulting firms

The results of the surveys of executives are unanimous, given that in all six surveys the majority of the transactions were deemed a success, with success rates ranging from slightly more than 50 percent (MERCER CONSULTING (2001)) to 82 percent (KPMG (1999)), as shown in Table 4.9.

The results from the consultants' quantitative analyses are not as conclusive. Those four studies conducting simultaneously a survey and a share price analysis reported a considerable gap between executives' perception of transactions success and the measured share performance. Interestingly, in the three consecutive studies of cross-border transactions by KPMG (2004a, 2001, 1999), the observed success rate of the surveys decreased from 82 percent in 1999 to 65 percent in 2004, while the assessed shareholder value-enhancing transactions steadily increased from 17 percent to 34 percent. Apparently, the observed gap narrowed, letting KPMG to conclude that the practices of transaction process management are evolving such as to increase the likelihood of success.[139] As an explanation for the observed gap, KPMG cited the objectives of executives, which in only 23 percent of all cases were aligned to the goal of shareholder value maximization.[140]

138 GUGLER ET AL. (2003) found that 56.7 percent of all transactions achieved higher profits than initially projected, but almost the same fraction of transactions resulted in lower than projected sales after five years. Thus, using profitability as the measure of success would lead one to conclude that the average transaction was a success, while using sales one would reach the opposite conclusion.

139 See KPMG (2004a), p. 2.

140 See KPMG (2001), p. 6. 29 percent of the executives referred to increases in market shares and 28 percent to expansion into new geographic markets. Similar objectives were noted in the survey by PWC (2000).

Table 4.9: Results of studies by consulting firms

Consulting firm	Year	Survey results	Quantitative study results
Studies including a survey of executives			
KPMG	1999	• 82 percent of transactions were deemed successful	• 17 percent of the transactions added, 30 percent did not change, and 53 percent reduced shareholder value
PWC	2000	• Majority achieved their market penetration objectives • Only minority reached their cost-cutting objectives	-
KPMG	2001	• 75 percent of transactions were deemed successful	• 30 percent of the transactions added, 39 percent did not change, and 31 percent reduced shareholder value
MERCER CONSULTING	2001	• More than half of transatlantic mergers were deemed successful	• Slightly more than half of the acquirers outperformed their industry benchmarks
KPMG	2004	• 65 percent of transactions were deemed successful	• 34 percent of the transactions added, 34 percent did not change, and 32 percent reduced shareholder value
KPMG	2005	• Majority of acquisitions were deemed successful	-
Studies not including a survey of executives			
MERCER CONSULTING	1995	--	• 17 percent added, 33 percent did not change, 20 percent reduced some, and 30 percent substantially eroded shareholder value
A.T. KEARNEY	1999	--	• 58 percent of acquisitions reduced shareholder value
MCKINSEY & CO.	2001	--	• 42 percent of acquiring companies had lower revenue growth than the industry benchmarks for the three years following the transaction • 40 percent of transactions failed to capture cost synergies
KPMG	2002	--	• 62 percent of transactions failed in enhancing shareholder value • Highest success rates were observed in the materials, utility, and automotive sectors
BCG	2002	--	• 61 percent of transactions reduced shareholder value one year after the closing
BCG	2004	--	• Highly acquisitive companies achieve higher total shareholder returns than non-acquisitive companies

-: a quantitative analysis was not part of the study; --: a survey was not part of the study.

Share performances diametrically opposing the survey results were also reported by BCG (2002) and MERCER CONSULTING (1995) for large U.S. transactions. MERCER CONSULTING (1995) observed that non-acquiring U.S. companies outperformed their acquiring peers in the first half of the 1990s. These results were validated in the study by BCG (2002) for similar transactions in the second half of the 1990s.[141] As an example of failure, BCG (2002) listed the *Daimler-Chrysler* merger, based on a post-closing underperformance of the stock of the combined entity by 30 percent compared to the S&P's index of automotive stocks. In contrast, A.T. KEARNEY (1999) noted as a successful U.S. transaction by a German company the acquisition of *Spiegel Inc.* by *Otto GmbH & CoKG* in 1982.[142] Contrary to their earlier studies, MERCER CONSULTING (2001) and BCG (2004) also observed on average successful transactions by U.S. acquirers. In their 2001 study, MERCER CONSULTING computed that slightly more than half of the acquirers in its sample outperformed their industry-specific benchmark over the two years subsequent to the transaction. Using a different methodology for measuring success compared to their 2002 study, BCG concluded in a more recent study that U.S. companies with a highly acquisitive strategy achieved higher total shareholder returns than those with an organic growth strategy. Applying a comparable method, KPMG (2005) reported similar results for its sample of mid-size German acquirers in cross-border transactions.[143]

The only study assessing success using a quantitative measure other than share performance also came to the conclusion that the majority of acquisitions are not successful. MCKINSEY & CO. (2001) observed that the majority of acquiring companies as well as targets experienced growth rates post-closing that underperform the industry average.[144]

Only one of the observed studies by consulting firms specifically examined differences in the success between domestic and cross-border transactions. Contrary to the findings in the event study literature, in their 2002 analysis of acquisitions by German companies, KPMG did not note any significant differences.

---

141 PAUTLER (2003, p. 19) points out that both studies may not have been done in a similar manner, so that the comparison over time may be distorted.

142 It should be noted that *Otto GmbH & CoKG* is not a public company, accordingly the conclusion by A.T KEARNEY (1999) was based on measures other than share performance.

143 KPMG (2005) points out that compared to large companies, as a result of their predominantly private ownership, mid-size companies have the advantage of not having to focus on short-term improvements of their financial ratios, but are able to better prioritize strategic motives while pursuing cross-border transactions.

144 A decline of revenue growth for both the target and the acquiring company was also reported in another study by BCG, see VINER ET AL. (2000).

4.5 Determinants of transaction success

4.5.1 Overview

Following this description of the observed overall success is a review of the findings in the empirical research with regard to which factors drove the direction and degree of the success of a transaction. The majority of the reviewed studies provide a univariate analysis of various subsamples of the examined transactions that is frequently accompanied by a cross-sectional regression analysis in order to measure the statistical significance of the simultaneous impact of numerous determinants of transaction success. Determinants of transaction success comprise (i) endogenous factors that can be directly or indirectly influenced by the management of the involved entities and (ii) exogenous factors that can only be observed by the entities before entering into the transaction.[145]

Endogenous determinants can generally be distinguished into ex ante features of the acquiring and target company and characteristics of the transaction structuring and management phase.[146] The analyzed determinants are manifold, ranging for example from the acquirer's absolute size,[147] financial condition,[148] and transaction experience,[149] and the target's industry sector[150] and status,[151] to the choice of form of payment,[152] inclusion of external advisors in the transaction management,[153] and the degree of post-merger integration of the target.[154]

The majority of the examined determinants are not necessarily unique to cross-border transactions. Additionally, numerous studies examine exogenous forces of the economic environment on the success of transactions, such as the relative strength of a country's economic growth[155] and capital markets,[156] and in connection with cross-border acquisitions, the strength of foreign currency exchange rates.[157] Although the factors are out of the control of the acquirer's management, they drive acquisition activity[158] and are likely to influence transaction success. Accordingly, such determinants are included in this review as well.

---

145 See BEITEL (2002), p. 130.
146 See for example MOELLER ET AL. (2005), p. 208; BEITEL (2002), p. 131.
147 See for example CONN ET AL. (2005), p. 858.
148 See for example CHOI and TSAI (2002), p. 25.
149 See for example BRADLEY and SUNDARAM (2004), p. 19.
150 See for example CAMPA and HERNANDO (2004), p. 68f.
151 See for example FULLER ET AL. (2002), p. 1779.
152 See for example LOWINSKI ET AL. (2004), p. 326f.
153 See for example ALLEN ET AL. (2000), p. 24f.
154 See for example MERCER CONSULTING (2001).
155 See for example DÖRR (2000), p. 185.
156 See for example BRUNER (2005), p. 19.
157 See for example GREGORY and MCCORRISTON (2005), p. 120.
158 See Section 2.4.1.2.

Table 4.10 provides a categorical overview of those determinants included in the review of prior empirical research. The observed directional correlations of those determinants with transaction success serve as a basis to derive testable hypotheses for the goal of this study to identify which characteristics had a significant impact on the success of the U.S. cross-border transactions by German companies.

Table 4.10: Overview of reviewed determinants of transaction success

Determinants of transaction success	
Characteristics of the acquiring company	
• Size	• Transaction experience
• Financial condition (level of excess cash)	• International exposure
• Valuation ratio (market-to-book ratio)	• Ownership structure
• Pre-transaction participation in the target	
Characteristics of the target company	
• Industry sector (regulated versus non-regulated)	• Relative size to the acquirer
• Status (private versus public)	• Financial condition pre-merger
Characteristics of the transaction structuring and management	
• Strategic direction	• Participation of multiple bidders
• Form of payment (cash versus shares)	• Attitude of the offer
• Acquisition structure (asset versus share deal)	• Retention of the target's key employees
• Form of acquisition for public targets	• Post-closing integration process
• Use of external advisors	
Influences of the economic environment	
• Economic growth	• Foreign currency exchange rates
• Capital markets	

4.5.2 Characteristics of acquiring companies

Three studies examined the influence of the size of the acquirer, without drawing conclusive results. While MOELLER ET AL. (2004) found that the cumulative abnormal returns for smaller acquiring companies were higher than those for larger acquirers, DÖRR (2000) observed an opposite effect, which he attributed to the ability of larger companies to dedicate more resources to the transaction management and post-merger integration process.[159] CONN ET AL. (2005) did not observe a statistically significant correlation.

In light of JENSEN's free cash flow theory,[160] five studies have linked the financial condition of an acquiring company, approximated by its debt ratio and level of free cash flow, to

159 A positive influence was also measured in older studies of cross-border transactions by KANG (1993) and MORCK and YEUNG (1991).

160 See Section 2.3.3.3.

transaction success, arguing that acquiring companies with excess cash flow could potentially be prone to use their resources for managerial empire building and to invest in targets without positive net present value, thereby destroying shareholder value. Accordingly, a high debt ratio was expected to have a positive impact on cumulative abnormal returns, since "debt reduces the agency costs of free cash flow by reducing the cash flow available for spending at the discretion of managers."[161] However, the research findings were mixed, with observations of positive,[162] negative,[163] and insignificant correlations.[164]

CONN ET AL. (2005), MOELLER and SCHLINGEMANN (2005), and KPMG (2002) showed that the pre-merger valuation ratio of an acquirer, i.e. its market-to-book value ("MTBV"), and the measured cumulative abnormal returns to its shareholders in a transaction are negatively correlated.[165] Companies with a relatively high MTBV, so-called "glamour acquirers", generated lower shareholder wealth than acquirers with a relatively low MTBV, so-called "value acquirers".[166] The underperformance of such glamour acquirers is contributed to investors reconsidering the high stand-alone valuation of the acquirer[167] and to increased managerial discretion as a result of a high share valuation that may promote value destroying empire building.[168]

The study by MOELLER ET AL. (2004) assessed that a pre-merger participation of the acquirer in the target company (so-called "toehold stake") was positively correlated with cumulative abnormal returns. The impact of this determinant might be explained by better access to information about the target for performing due diligence and with an improved bargaining advantage to the acquirer as a result of its toehold stake.[169]

Assuming that pursuing multiple transactions yields a learning curve for companies with regard to their ability to better screen potential targets, to improve its acquisition management

161 JENSEN (1986), p. 324.
162 See CHOI and TSAI (2002), p. 25; RAU and RODGERS (2002), p. 16. In an older study, DOUKAS (1995) found that positive abnormal returns for acquiring companies in cross-border transactions are consistent with the free cash flow hypothesis.
163 See DÖRR (2000), p. 184.
164 See MOELLER and SCHLINGEMANN (2005), p. 549; MOELLER ET AL. (2004), p. 216.
165 A similar conclusion was reached in an older study by RAU and VERMAELEN (1998).
166 BHARADWAJ and SHIVDASANI (2003) did not find a significant relation.
167 As suggested by JOVANOVIC and BRAGUINSKY (2004), such a revaluation may stem from investors reassessing the future cash flows of the acquirer on a stand-alone basis and concluding that the transaction signals a lack of internal growth opportunities (the so-called "growth opportunities signaling hypothesis"). TRAVLOS (1987) points out that those glamour acquirers offering shares as the form of payment signal that their shares are overvalued (the so-called "equity signaling hypothesis").
168 See BRADLEY and SUNDARAM (2004), p. 9. In addition, SHLEIFER and VISHNY (2003) argue that companies use their overvalued shares for acquisitions to take advantage of a window of opportunity offered by temporary market inefficiency. By their argument, the inevitable value loss resulting from the acquisition is less than what would have transpired had the company omitted the transaction, as the capital market would eventually correct any overvaluation in time.
169 See KALE ET AL. (1998), p. 24.

process, and to more efficiently execute a post-merger integration program, frequent acquirers were expected to generate higher shareholder wealth.[170] On the other hand, frequent transactions may also lead to overtaxing the acquirer's management and therefore deficiencies especially in the post-merger integration of the target company.[171] Ten studies provide evidence for both arguments. For example, MOELLER ET AL. (2004) concluded that especially unsuccessful large transactions were pursued by serial acquirers who were previously successful in their acquisition activity. The authors assumed that investors deemed the acquirer's strategy of external growth no longer sustainable and therefore in contrast to previous transactions not value creating. FULLER ET AL. (2002) also found that subsequent transactions by frequent acquirers resulted in lower wealth effects than the first acquisition, arguing that after making several transactions, acquiring companies either create less synergy gains or negotiate less efficiently. The studies by the consulting firms KPMG (2005),[172] BCG (2004), MCKINSEY & CO. (2001), A.T. KEARNEY (1999), and MERCER CONSULTING (1995) posit a positive correlation, while BEITEL ET AL. (2004) and BRADLEY and SUNDARAM (2004) did not detect any significant influence.

Some studies examined whether the experience of acquirers in foreign countries, especially in the country of the target company, had a significant influence on the wealth creation in cross-border transactions. While CHOI and TSAI (2002) and CORHAY and RAD (2000) found that the capital markets attached less value to a cross-border acquisition when the acquirer was highly active in the international environment,[173] the study by DÖRR (2000) did not indicate the existence of such a negative correlation.[174]

The ownership structure of the acquiring company was found to be positively related to wealth creation for shareholders, given that equity ownership by the management of the acquirer provides a mechanism for better aligning the interests of shareholders and management and thereby reducing negative implications from potential agency conflicts.[175]

170 See BAMBERGER (1994), p. 223f. A prerequisite for this conclusion is that the acquisition experiences are homogenous, see SINGH and ZOLLO (1998), p. 30. When the previous acquisition experiences are heterogeneous, a study by HALEBLIAN and FINKELSTEIN (1999) suggests an inverted U-shape relationship between acquisition experience and acquisition success.

171 See KUSEWITT (1985), p. 159. In addition, the CARs could be lower if investors already expected the acquisition as part of the company's external growth program, as mentioned earlier.

172 In contrast, KPMG observed a negative correlation in their 2004, 2001, and 1999 studies.

173 The authors argue that less prior foreign involvement indicates room for improvement through new foreign acquisitions, see CHOI and TSAI (2002), p. 19. Similar findings were also reported in older studies by CAKICI ET AL. (1996) and DOUKAS (1995). ZAHEER (1995) stresses the "liability of foreignness" for acquirers with no prior experience as a negative determinant for transaction success.

174 The author attributes his observations to the availability of external consultants that compensate for the lack of international exposure, see DÖRR (2000), p. 183. CAKICI ET AL. (1996) report a similar conclusion.

175 See for example CORNETT ET AL. (2003), p. 124. The authors observed that the alignment was not as effective in conglomerate transactions as it was in focusing transactions.

In addition, similar results may be achieved through concentrated ownership, which allows for a stronger monitoring of decisions of the company's management.[176]

4.5.3 Characteristics of target companies

CAMPA and HERNANDO (2004) noted that acquisitions of target companies in regulated industries[177] yielded relatively lower cumulative abnormal returns, arguing that the existence of a strong regulatory framework creates a difficult environment that hampers the potential success of transactions. The authors further observed that this negative correlation applied especially to acquisitions in the financial services sector by a foreign company, thereby concluding that these adverse conditions are more relevant in cross-border transactions. The previously noted negative cumulative abnormal returns in the majority of event studies solely analyzing bank mergers corroborate these findings.[178] Similar underperformance of transactions involving targets in regulated industries was shown in the study by GOERGEN and RENNEBOOG (2004), though their findings apply mainly to the energy sector.[179]

Comparing acquisitions of public and private target companies, the results of the majority of empirical research suggest that abnormal returns to acquirer shareholders in private transactions significantly exceed those obtained in takeovers of public targets. Shareholder wealth gains in public acquisitions were only observed when the transaction was paid for in cash, while exchange offers on average generated significant negative cumulative abnormal returns.[180] These observed variations are attributed to various qualitative differences in the process of acquiring a public or private target. One difference is that private companies, including subsidiaries of public groups,[181] cannot be sold as easily as publicly traded firms. This lack of marketability offers the acquirer a bargaining advantage and allows it to capture a "liquidity discount" when acquiring a privately-held target.[182] This favorable impact of the liquidity effect on the purchase price might be enhanced by the lower probability of the

---

176 See CARLINE ET AL. (2004), p. 7.

177 In absence of a standard definition of what may be considered a regulated industry, CAMPA and HERNANDO (2004) consider the utilities, communication, transportation, and financial services sectors as regulated industries. In their sample, these industries correspond to the following 2-digit Standard Industry Classification codes: 10, 13, 33, 40, 44, 45, 48, 49, 60, 61, 80, see CAMPA and HERNANDO (2004), p. 69. The Standard Industry Classification Code is a system by the U.S. Department of Commerce that organizes all industry types in the United States by classifying each company according to its primary activity, which is signified by a four-digit code.

178 See Section 4.4.1.2.

179 See GOERGEN and RENNEBOOG (2004), p. 29.

180 As shown in the studies by MOELLER and SCHLINGEMANN (2005), BRADLEY and SUNDARAM (2004), MOELLER ET AL. (2004), and FULLER ET AL. (2002). These findings were more differentiated than those of older studies, which generally concluded that acquisitions of public targets seem to yield negative returns.

181 MOELLER and SCHLINGEMANN (2005), MOELLER ET AL. (2004), and FULLER ET AL. (2002) concluded that the acquisitions of subsidiaries of public companies also outperform those of public targets. CONN ET AL. (2005) did not observe a significant difference.

182 See FULLER ET AL. (2002), p. 1784.

emergence of competitive bidding in private transactions.[183] CONN ET AL. (2005, p. 822) point out another aspect of the different bargaining situation, in that potential acquirers of a private target can end the negotiations with the sellers without the loss of face that may occur in a public transaction, especially in case of a hostile takeover attempt. Accordingly, the authors argue that the lack of publicity may decrease the likelihood of hubris-motivated transactions. Another explanation for the presumed discount in private transactions points to information asymmetries, which typically pose a bigger challenge in private transactions.[184] Additionally, private companies generally exhibit a concentrated ownership, which leads to less agency conflicts during the transaction process.[185]

The empirical evidence on the impact of the relative size of the target company compared to the acquirer is not conclusive.[186] While some studies did not observe any significant influence,[187] FULLER ET AL. (2002) found that cumulative abnormal returns were more positive the greater the relative size of private target companies, but more negative the greater the relative size of public targets.[188] Evidence supporting the authors' findings for private companies was provided in the studies by MOELLER and SCHLINGEMANN (2005), CAMPA and HERNANDO (2004), LOWINSKI ET AL. (2004), MOELLER ET AL. (2004), DELONG (2001), and WALKER (2000). Higher success rates for acquisitions of relatively small target companies were noted by DELONG (2003), ALLEN ET AL. (2000), and A.T. KEARNEY (1999). The mixed findings in the studies reflect the potentially bidirectional influence of the size of a transaction on its success. On the one hand acquiring a large target typically implies higher complexity, which may add more difficulties and inefficiencies to the post-merger integration process.[189] ALLEN ET AL. (2005) posit that "integration of larger targets into the acquiring firm is likely to generate agency cost reductions in value".[190] In addition, a relatively large size of the target usually reduces the power asymmetries between the entities with regard to

---

183 See BRADLEY and SUNDARAM (2004), p. 23. While sales of public targets are typically more auction-like in nature and require full disclosure to the SEC, private targets are generally sold in limited auctions or in a negotiated transaction with a small number of interested acquirers, see FULLER ET AL. (2002), p. 1784. BRADLEY and SUNDARAM (2004, p. 23) assume that "it is possible that the auction mechanism for non-public companies somehow works to the advantage of the bidder, and is inefficient for the seller".

184 See BRADLEY and SUNDARAM (2004), p. 8. The authors linked the greater information asymmetries to the liquidity discount by arguing that an acquirer of a private target would seek a discount to compensate for a potential "lemon" problem.

185 See CONN ET AL. (2005), p. 822f.

186 Relative size is usually measured as the market capitalization of the target or the transaction volume divided by the market capitalization of the acquirer, see for example FAN and GOYAL (2002), p. 33.

187 As shown in the studies by CONN ET AL. (2005), GOERGEN and RENNEBOOG (2004), BHARADWAJ and SHIVDASANI (2003), FAN and GOYAL (2002), KPMG (2002a), MERCER CONSULTING (2001), and CORHAY and RAD (2000).

188 BRADLEY and SUNDARAM (2004) made the same observations for their sample of public targets acquired in an exchange offer.

189 See CARLINE ET AL. (2004), p. 14. Such inefficiencies may result from internal power struggles over capital allocation or a broader span of control and coordination issues.

190 ALLEN ET AL. (2004), p. 205.

negotiations over both price and conduct of due diligence.[191] On the other hand, larger targets are deemed to offer more potential for producing synergistic gains for the combined entity, especially in case of so-called "mergers of equals". Accordingly, FULLER ET AL. (2002) were not able to provide a clear explanation for the observed discrepancy in their results, except for the aforementioned liquidity effect observed in connection with the method of payment.

Other positive success determinants cited in the empirical studies with regard to the characteristics of the target company are relatively poor pre-merger performance,[192] high intensity of research and development activities,[193] cultural fit with the acquiring company,[194] and the state of incorporation.[195]

4.5.4 Characteristics of transaction structuring and management

The prevailing view in 19 studies analyzing the impact of the strategic direction of the transaction, i.e. the business sector relatedness[196] of both entities, on the success suggests that diversification destroys shareholder value.[197] Only the study by CORHAY and RAD (2000) observed opposing results, while GOERGEN and RENNEBOOG (2004), LOWINSKI ET AL. (2004), and FULLER ET AL. (2002) did not find a significant correlation.[198] Apparently, the potential for synergistic gains and market power in focusing transactions seems to outweigh the benefits from the diversification effect.[199] The value reducing effect in diversifying

---

191 See BRADLEY and SUNDARAM (2004), p. 8. The authors also noted that smaller transactions are less likely to be motivated by hubris and "empire-building" ambitions.

192 As shown for example by ALLEN ET AL. (2004), BEITEL ET AL. (2004), BRADLEY and SUNDARAM (2004), and RAU and RODGERS (2002). These findings suggest that the capital market expects the transaction to enhance the performance of the target (thereby confirming the validity of the efficiency hypothesis discussed in Section 2.3.3.2) and to realize growth opportunities. As a proxy for the growth potential, several studies employed "Tobin's q", which measures the ratio of the market price to the book value of a company, see ALLEN ET AL. (2004), p. 206.

193 As shown for example by GREGORY and MCCORRISTON (2005), p. 122. Those findings support the validity of internalization benefits as stipulated by FDI theories (see Section 2.3.4).

194 For example the study by KPMG (2004a) emphasized the importance of an in-depth cultural post-merger integration of the target, especially in the case of cross-border transactions. Research in the finance literature probing the effect of the cultural fit of the involved entities on the success of transactions is still rather limited; refer to for example the studies by CHAKRABARTI ET AL. (2004) and LICHT ET AL. (2003), who use Hofstede measures to approximate cultural dimensions.

195 A study by KUIPERS ET AL. (2003) found that when target companies were incorporated in the U.S. state of Delaware, foreign acquiring companies faced significant additional costs in completing the transaction, resulting in a negative wealth effect. The authors attribute their observation to the well developed and far-reaching corporate state law in Delaware (see Section 3.6.2), which poses additional challenges for the acquirer especially in the legal planning and documentation phase of the transaction.

196 The predominant method in the finance literature to measure relatedness is by comparing the Standard Industry Classification codes of the acquirer and the target company. Typically, companies operating in the same 2-digit code are classified as related.

197 As shown for example in the studies by MOELLER and SCHLINGEMANN (2005), CORNETT ET AL. (2003), DELONG (2003), FAN and GOYAL (2002), ANDRADE ET AL. (2001), and MULHERIN and BOONE (2000).

198 MARTIN and SAYRAK (2003) provide a survey of other empirical studies on corporate diversification.

199 See DATTA and PUIA (1995), p. 340; HARRIS and RAVENSCRAFT (1991), p. 827. In this context, SINGH and MONTGOMERY (1987) hypothesized that related transactions have more potential for creating value since all forms of synergistic gains discussed in Section 2.3.3.2 are theoretically available in related acquisitions.

transactions might be attributable to inefficient internal markets,[200] agency costs,[201] or to conflicting operational styles or corporate cultures of the various businesses.[202] In this context, some authors posit the existence of a "diversification discount", i.e. companies operating in multiple lines trade at a discount relative to non-diversifying companies.[203]

Several hypotheses in the empirical research suggest both positive and negative correlations between transaction success and the use of shares as the form of payment. According to the bidder overvaluation hypothesis, management is likely to offer shares as the form of payment when due to asymmetric information between them and outside investors it deems its shares overvalued.[204] The outside investors realize this negative signal about the intrinsic value of the acquirer and revise their estimate of its value, which drives down the share price upon announcement of the transaction.[205] However, in cross-border transactions the sellers are frequently unwilling to accept equity of a foreign company, thereby forcing the acquirer to pay with cash.[206]

Another hypothesis of negative cumulative abnormal returns to acquirer shareholders implies that exchange offers signal a lack of internal growth opportunities or a perception that the transaction is a negative net present value project.[207] On the other hand, if shares are used in the acquisition of private companies with a highly concentrated ownership, the target's owners may form a blockholder position that enables them to monitor the acquirer's

---

200 See WHITED (2001), p. 1667; BERGER and OFEK (1995), p. 57f. A study by COMMENT and JARRELL (1995) on the creation of an internal capital market within companies concluded that diversified companies do not rely significantly less on external capital markets than non-diversified companies.

201 See CHOI and TSAI (2002), p. 23f.

202 See REUER ET AL. (2003), p. 8; LAMONT and POLK (2002), p. 54.

203 As noted for example by LAMONT and POLK (2002), WALKER (2000), and MORCK ET AL. (1990). However, arguments challenging the link between diversification and shareholder value attribute the diversification discount to the observation that companies acquire businesses that are already discounted. GRAHAM ET AL. (2002) for example evaluated the pre-diversification valuation of companies that are acquired by conglomerates and concluded that these targets sold at an average discount of approximately 15 percent compared to their value in the last year prior to the transaction. WHITED (2001) and CHEVALIER (2000) contended that the diversification discount is at least partly the result of measurement errors. Recent studies by VILLALONGA (2004) and CAMPA and KEDIA (2002) also contributed the observed diversification discount to bias in the selection of the analyzed sample, arguing that with appropriate measurement techniques the diversification discount disappears or even turns into a premium. MARTIN and SAYRAK (2003) provide an overview of recent studies of the relation between corporate diversification and shareholder value.

204 See GOERGEN and RENNEBOOG (2004), p. 24f. This hypothesis supports the importance of favorable capital markets conditions as a main exogenous factor affecting merger activity, as discussed in Section 2.4.1.2.

205 See BRUNER (2004a), p. 72; DELONG (2003), p. 493.

206 See CONN ET AL. (2005), p. 823. Accordingly, the positive signal from paying with cash might be diminished or essentially non-existent in such cases, see MOELLER and SCHLINGEMANN (2005), p. 538.

207 See BERKOVITCH and NARAYANAN (1990), p. 158f. This explanation assumes that the form of payment already implies the future success of a transaction. If an acquirer is convinced that it can exploit significant synergy potentials, it would prefer a cash offer, since only then would it fully benefit from the realized gains, whereas in an exchange offer it would share those gains with the shareholders of the target.

management and therefore to align their interests, thus creating value.[208] Focusing on tax implications, another hypothesis suggests that sellers generally prefer to receive shares since cash payments create an immediate tax liability, but exchange offers allow for a tax deferral.[209] Therefore, the sellers may be willing to sell their shares at a lower price.[210] The vast majority of the 21 studies analyzing the impact of the choice of payment method support the validity of the various hypotheses. While acquisitions of public targets paid for with shares were associated with significantly negative cumulative abnormal returns, exchange offers involving a private target appeared to be shareholder value generating on average.[211] In contrast, CONN ET AL. (2005) concluded that in cross-border acquisitions of public targets the method of payment has no significant influence.

The method of payment is typically closely connected to the form of the acquisition given that exchange offers generally only apply to share deals. None of the reviewed studies has addressed specifically the impact of the acquisition structure on the success of transactions, though other researchers have observed that, especially as a result of the respective tax benefits, acquirers in asset deals are typically willing to pay a higher premium.[212] However, those studies did not provide an assessment on the directional influence of this determinant. In case the target is a public company, the form of acquisition needs to be further distinguished into whether it is a tender offer, proxy solicitation, exchange offer, or merger. It is hypothesized that compared to mergers, transactions structured as a tender offer better stimulate the market for corporate control and therefore lead to a more auction type process, which in turn may increase the premium paid for the target.[213] However, in the case of U.S. domestic transactions, MOELLER ET AL. (2004) found that tender offers generated higher cumulative abnormal returns for acquirer shareholders, while for U.S. cross-border transactions the impact of this determinant was insignificant.[214] A possible explanation for

---

[208] See FULLER ET AL. (2002), p. 1785. According to these authors, this argument also explains their observation of significantly lower CARs for acquisitions of subsidiaries paid for with shares, given that such subsidiaries are owned by public companies with a more diverse ownership, accordingly blockholder formation is rather unlikely in such a case. Additionally, this reasoning would also presume a positive correlation between the relative size of the target and transaction success.

[209] See BROWN and RYNGAERT (1991), p. 653. In support of this hypothesis, POULSEN and STEGEMOLLER (2006) observed that 36 percent of private target owners list favorable tax consequences as a reason for selling to a public company.

[210] See TOYNE and TRIPP (1998), p. 53f.

[211] See for example the studies by CONN ET AL. (2005), BRADLEY and SUNDARAM (2004), and FULLER ET AL. (2002). Opposite observations are reported only by BEITEL ET AL. (2004) and GOERGEN and RENNEBOOG (2004). HERON and LIE (2002), DELONG (2001), and GHOSH (2001) did not find a significant relation. BHARADWAJ and SHIVDASANI (2003) computed the highest CARs for cash transactions entirely financed with bank debt. These authors suggest that the perceived monitoring role from blockholder formation in private exchange offers apparently can also be assumed by banks. On a more conceptual reference, ANDRADE ET AL. (2001) point out that the announcement period reaction to a share-financed transaction represents a combination of a merger and an equity issues announcement.

[212] As shown for example in studies by AYERS ET AL. (2004) and ERICKSON and WANG (2000). For a discussion of the tax implications of asset and share acquisitions in the United States refer to Section 3.4.

[213] See DATTA ET AL. (1992), p. 70.

[214] Similar results were found in older event studies by GREGORY (1997) and LOUGHRAN and VIJH (1997).

this observation might be linked to the method of payment, since mergers are more often paid for with shares.

Several studies analyzed the role of external advisors, i.e. investment banks, on the success of transactions, assuming that in light of higher complexity and information asymmetry in cross-border transactions, external advice may add considerable value.[215] However, RAU and RODGERS (2002) and SAUNDERS and SRINIVASAN (2001) observed that for U.S. acquirers the inclusion of external advisors in the transaction process was negatively correlated to shareholder wealth creation. BEITEL (2004) documented the same conclusion for transactions by German acquirers, LOWINSKI ET AL. (2004) for Swiss acquirers in cross-border transactions. Agency problems are predominantly cited as an explanation for these results. Due to the fee structure of investment banks, in which a proportion of the fees is contingent on the completion and size of the transaction, the advisors have an incentive to recommend their clients to not walk away from a transaction and to negotiate the highest possible purchase price.[216] Hence, large transactions involving investment banks create high absolute costs that must at least be compensated in order for the transaction to generate wealth gains for its shareholders.[217]

While the participation of several bidders in an acquisition process is generally viewed as a stimulation of the market for corporate control, ROLL (1986) argued that takeover auctions induce a "winner's curse", i.e. that overconfident acquirers overpay for targets.[218] However, the studies by CONN ET AL. (2005), MOELLER and SCHLINGEMANN (2005), MOELLER ET AL. (2004), and DELONG (2001) did not find significant differences between the cumulative abnormal returns to shareholders in auctions and negotiations.[219] No significant correlation was found by the majority of those studies analyzing the impact of the attitude of the offer on cumulative abnormal returns.[220] Out of 11 studies, only FULLER ET AL. (2002) noted higher wealth effects for unsolicited bids. The studies by GOERGEN and RENNEBOOG (2004) and RAU and RODGERS (2002) found support for the assumption that in a hostile transaction,

---

215 See SERVAES and ZENNER (1996), p. 787f. BEITEL (2004) found evidence that German acquiring companies predominantly engage investment banks when the transaction value is relatively high.

216 See RAU (2000), p. 293f. The author found that top-tier advisors, such as Goldman Sachs and Merrill Lynch, tend to advise their clients to offer larger premiums. Corresponding to these observations, ALLEN ET AL. (2004) for example note that abnormal returns decrease if the advisor is a top-tier investment bank. On the other hand, RAU (2000, p. 322) also found that top-tier advisors are more capable of completing a transaction. HUNTER and JAGTIANI (2000) confirmed this observation.

217 See LOWINSKI ET AL. (2004), p. 325. With regard to the contingent fee, SAUNDERS and SRINIVASAN (2001) for example observed that these average 0.70 percent of the transaction volume and tend to be higher if the acquirer had a long-term relationship with the advisor.

218 The reasoning of a "winner's curse" is employed in the study by BCG (2002) as the main reason for the observed high failure rate of transactions.

219 Only BRUNER (2005) observed opposite results, though with weak statistical significance.

220 As shown for example in the studies by CONN ET AL. (2005), GREGORY and MCCORRISTON (2005), CAMPA and HERNANDO (2004), and MOELLER ET AL. (2004).

acquirer shareholders might assume that the company is overpaying for the target or that management's motives for the bid are hubris or agency related.

Other positive success determinants cited in the observed empirical studies with regard to the transaction structuring and management were conducting an expanded due diligence of the target company,[221] retention of the target's key employees,[222] and high speed for the post-merger integration phase.[223]

4.5.5 Influences of the economic environment

Compared to relatively weak overall economic conditions, in times of strong economic growth the current and future prospects of companies' businesses are perceived generally more favorably by the financial community, thereby expected to result in more positive share price reactions to the announcement of a transaction. Additionally, given that the main analytical models for valuing a target company predominantly include assumptions on the future growth rates of the economy and of the target's business, an upward post-merger economic trend might result in surpassing the initial projections of cash flows, thereby creating additional value for the acquirer that was not reflected in the premium paid for the target.[224] However, DÖRR (2000) did not find significant evidence supporting a correlation between economic growth and cumulative abnormal returns.

Closely correlated to the overall economic trend is the performance of the capital markets. During the fifth merger wave, the years from 1998 to 2000 were marked by "hot" market conditions with a high level of M&A activity, particularly for large transactions.[225] Acquiring companies might overpay for targets in such market conditions, either due to mania or in case of exchange offers due to the recognition that their shares are overvalued, which would imply an association between time period and method of payment.[226] MOELLER ET AL. (2004) found that during those years transactions on average created wealth for acquirer shareholders, however the aggregate wealth losses of a relatively few large acquisitions more than offset

221 As for example highlighted in the three consecutive studies by KPMG (2004a, 2001, 1999).

222 As shown for example in the studies by BCG (2002) and PWC (2000), which concluded that an early use of a transition team facilitates an enhanced retention of the target's employees. A similar correlation was also shown in an older study by CANNELLA and HAMBRICK (1993). Studies of top-management departures from U.S. targets that were acquired by foreign companies were performed by KRUG and NIGH (2001, 1998).

223 As noted for example by MERCER CONSULTING (2001) and PWC (2000), arguing that when acquirers carry out the integration faster than their normal operating speed, they are able to reduce costs imposed by incompatible information technology systems, divergent leadership philosophies, and incongruent management practices between the involved entities.

224 See BAMBERGER (1994), p. 190f.

225 See BRUNER (2004a), p. 13.

226 As argued for example by SHELTON (2000).

those gains on a dollar-valued basis.[227] The studies by BRADLEY and SUNDARAM (2004) and GOERGEN and RENNEBOOG (2004) both found that the cumulative abnormal returns for their subsamples of transactions during 1998 to 2000 did not significantly differ from those in the early 1990s.

Although the theoretical literature on international capital markets generally argues that under prefect mobility of capital, exchange rates should not affect the costs of capital for cross-border and domestic acquirers,[228] the studies by GREGORY and MCCORRISTON (2005) and DÖRR (2000) observed a positive correlation between the relative strength of an acquirer's currency and transaction success. Such findings corroborate arguments by FROOT and STEIN (1991) that in light of asymmetric information, foreign acquirers with a relatively strong exchange rate have a comparative financing advantage. MOELLER and SCHLINGEMANN (2005) found in their sample of U.S. acquirers that when the U.S. dollar is relatively strong, cross-border transactions created less value than domestic ones, though the difference was not significant.

4.6 Conclusions and testable hypotheses for the further analysis

The goal of this chapter was to provide a comprehensive review of the existing recent empirical research on the success of cross-border transactions and its determinants, focusing on the three main methodologies for measuring success, capital market based event studies, financial statements based studies, and surveys of executives.

Overall, the reviewed short-term event studies observed on average positive wealth effects for acquirer shareholders in cross-border transactions. Some studies interpreted these findings as evidence corroborating the validity of the synergy hypothesis as the main motive for pursuing transactions,[229] while unsuccessful transactions are deemed to support irrational management-related hypotheses and the existence of agency conflicts.[230] The results of the financial statements based studies were inconclusive. The long-term share-based quantitative

[227] In their sample, MOELLER ET AL. (2004) identified out of 4,136 acquisitions 87 large deals that generated losses of $397b during the years 1998 through 2001, compared to total gains of all transactions of $157b. These large transactions represented only 2.1 percent of the number of acquisitions during those years, but they accounted for 43.4 percent of the total transaction volume.

[228] See MOELLER and SCHLINGEMANN (2005), p. 550.

[229] Various studies by consulting firms concluded that while cost synergies are more readily achieved and simply offset the premium paid for the target, successful transactions are often the result of a focus on revenue benefits, see KPMG (2004a); MCKINSEY & CO. (2001). Older event studies by GUPTA and MISRA (1997) and BERKOVITCH and NARAYANAN (1993) found evidence that synergies are the prime motive for mergers and acquisitions.

[230] As noted for example in the study by GOERGEN and RENNEBOOG (2004). However, it might also be the case that investors principally support the strategic implications of a transaction, but do not concur with its execution, for example the premium paid is deemed too high.

studies by consulting firms yielded on average unsuccessful cross-border activity,[231] but in their survey of executives cross-border acquisitions were deemed on average successful. These results seem to support the assumed methodological weakness of surveys of typically overrepresenting successful transactions. But there are also several difficulties in interpreting cumulative abnormal returns in event studies, as summarized by BRUNER (2004b): "In short, contaminating events, overvalued shares, and industry shocks could all easily mislead thoughtful practitioners into believing that M&A is fundamentally unprofitable even though these effects may have nothing to do with the transactions themselves. Even more important, buyers are typically much larger than targets, which means that the impact of smaller deals is difficult to measure with any precision."[232]

The empirical evidence seems to suggest that internalization of a foreign target's specific resources contributes to the success of cross-border transactions, as postulated by FDI theories. The nationality of the acquiring companies does not seem to be of importance, since the reported results are robust regardless of the geographic focus of the acquisition.[233] However, the majority of studies across the various methodologies did not conclude that such internalization benefits provide an argument for relatively higher success rates in cross-border compared to domestic acquisitions, even though the tendency for cross-border acquisitions to be more prevalent in the 1990s in industries with high levels of research and development and technology may support this assumption.[234] Apparently, higher information asymmetries in cross-border transactions make it more difficult to accurately value the target, as evidenced in transaction premiums that on average exceeded those in domestic acquisitions.[235] In addition, cultural dissonance could pose additional challenges for the integration phase that may increase the possibility of transaction failure.[236] FATEMI and FURTADO (1988) cited as a possible explanation for differences in abnormal returns between

---

231 As pointed out by PAUTLER (2003, p. 35), those studies recently noted an improvement of acquisition performance during the end of the fifth merger wave though.

232 BRUNER (2004b), p. 67. In this context MITCHELL and MULHERIN (1996) suggest that underperformance of acquiring companies is not a consequence of the transaction itself but the result of economic turbulence in the industry.

233 These observations contradict the assumption of several authors that different economic, regulatory, and corporate structures yield different results for shareholders depending on the country of origin of the company. For example, CYBO-OTTONE and MURGIA (2000, p. 857) analyzing bank acquisitions in Europe conclude: "Our research on European bank mergers reaches different conclusions from those of many related studies conducted in the US banking industry. We explain our different results as stemming from the different structure and regulation of EU banking markets, which are shown to be more similar between them than as compared with the US one".

234 See CONN ET AL. (2005), p. 821. The effects of internalization in the context of cross-border transactions are also inconsistent in older empirical studies by MARKIDES and OYON (1998), YOOK and MCCABE (1996), MARKIDES and ITTNER (1994), and MORCK and YEUNG (1992).

235 KOHERS and KOHERS (2000, p. 40f.) interpret such premiums in the case of cross-border acquisitions as payments for the special immediate access to local know-how and markets that the target provides, which by itself is considered being value enhancing.

236 See CONN ET AL. (2005), p. 865.

domestic and cross-border transactions segmentation in capital markets and markets for corporate control.[237]

Primarily focusing on characteristics of the entities involved in a transaction and various aspects of the acquisition execution phase, the finance literature does not provide conclusive evidence with regard to the potential determinants of wealth creation and their interdependence. Generally, the vast majority of acquisitions of private targets elicit significant positive announcement effects that typically exceed those for public targets, regardless of the form of payment. For public targets, only transactions paid for with cash seem likely to generate shareholder gains, while exchange offers unanimously were found to be shareholder wealth destroying, especially for larger transactions. However, shares are rarely used in cross-border transactions as the method of payment. Other determinants most likely to create shareholder wealth according to findings in event studies were relatedness of the business sector of both entities, relatively poor pre-merger performance of the target company, and managerial ownership in the acquiring company. Within the influences of the economic environment, a relatively strong exchange rate of the acquirer's currency seems to be value enhancing in a cross-border acquisition.

Considerable disagreement exists with regard to whether the size and financial condition of the acquirer as well as the relative size of the target compared to the acquirer impact the likelihood of shareholder wealth creation. No significant influence on transaction success is deemed to apply from the participation of multiple bidders, the attitude of the offer, nor the relative strength of the economic growth and the capital markets.

In deviation to the finance literature, the general recommendations for pursuing successful transactions drawn from studies by consulting firms are directed more towards the strategic conception as well as the post-closing integration phase. The consultants highlight a sufficient and effective planning of the post-closing integration, fast-paced integration of the acquired business, and retention of the target company's key employees.

With regard to the success and its determinants of acquisitions of U.S. targets by German acquirers the literature does not provide sufficient research yet.[238] In light of the significant

---

237 The potential influence of the degree of capital market integration was also pointed out in studies by McCann (2001) and Danbolt (1995).

238 A study by Schiereck and Strauss (2000) solely analyzed the impact of the acquisition of *Bankers Trust* by *Deutsche Bank* in 1999, reporting a negative CAR of -9.6 percent for the [-20,20] event window. In addition, Kröger (2005) analyzed German acquirers of U. S. targets based on their share price performance two years subsequent to the closing of the transaction and noted that of 154 transactions only 35 percent were successful. The author contributed the high failure rate to issues during the post-closing integration phase and concluded that the "apparently high cultural affinity between Germans and Americans did not lead to a higher success rate than the global average", Kröger (2005), p. 57.

importance of the U.S. market for German companies and the anticipated future volume of German M&A activity in the United States,[239] such an analysis becomes increasingly relevant. Accordingly, the empirical analysis in the following Chapter 5 aims at filling this existing gap. Since it could be assumed that on the basis of globally integrated capital markets the empirical observations for the transactions predominantly carried out by U.S. and U.K. acquirers are transferable to different institutional environments,[240] the reviewed findings regarding the main[241] determinants and their observed correlation with transaction success are condensed to hypotheses that will be tested in the further analysis. Table 4.11 summarizes the observed average success for cross-border transactions and the empirical impact of 16 determinants on transaction success. Based on these findings, 18 hypotheses applicable to the U.S. cross-border transactions by German companies are derived, as also shown in Table 4.11. For those determinants for which the prior research either found contradicting results or an insignificant correlation, a non-impact on transaction success is hypothesized. These determinants comprise the size (H_3) and financial condition (H_4) of the acquirer, the relative size of the target company compared to the acquirer (H_{10}), and the relative strength of the economic growth (H_{16}) and of the capital markets (H_{17}). In absence of available empirical observations, for the impact of the acquisition structure the respective hypothesis (H_{13}) was derived from the theoretical discussions in Sections 2.2.2 and 3.2.2.

---

239 See Section 2.4.2.

240 See MUKHERJEE ET AL. (2004), p. 7.

241 Due to the composition of the sample and the availability of information and data for the transactions within this study, not all previously discussed determinants are included in the analysis.

Table 4.11: Testable hypotheses for the study

Determinants of transaction success	Empirical results	Hypothesis Average success* of German acquirers of U.S. targets will be …	No.
Overall success of U.S. cross-border transactions			
• Average success	+	… positive	H_1
• Cross-border versus domestic transactions	-	… lower than in domestic acquisitions	H_2
Characteristics of acquiring companies			
• Bigger absolute size	+/-	… unaffected by the size of the acquirer	H_3
• High level of free cash flow and debt	+/-	… unaffected by the financial condition of the acquirer	H_4
• Relatively high market-to-book-value ("MTBV")	-	… higher for companies with a relatively low MTBV	H_5
• Pre-transaction ownership	+	… higher when a previous investment in the target was held	H_6
• Prior transaction experience	+	… higher for U.S. experienced acquirers	H_7
Characteristics of target companies			
• Regulated industry sector	-	… higher for acquisitions of a target in a non-regulated industry	H_8
• Public company	-	… higher for transactions involving a private target	H_9
• Relative size to the acquirer	+/-	… unaffected by the relative size of the target	H_{10}
Characteristics of transaction structuring and management			
• Relatedness of both entities	+	… higher for transactions involving entities in related industries	H_{11}
• Share payment, especially for public targets	-	… higher for transactions paid for with cash	H_{12}
• Acquisition structure	+/-	… higher for transactions structured as a share deal	H_{13}
• Tender offer versus proxy solicitation	+	… higher for public transactions structured as a tender offer	H_{14}
• Inclusion of external advisors	-	… higher for transactions without inclusion of external advisors	H_{15}
Influences of the economic environment			
• Relatively strong economic growth	0	… unaffected by relatively high U.S. economic growth	H_{16}
• Relatively strong capital markets	0	… unaffected by times of relatively strong capital markets	H_{17}
• Relatively strong foreign exchange rate	+	… higher if the Euro compared to the U.S. dollar in the year of the announcement of the transaction is relatively strong	H_{18}

"+" implies a positive correlation, "-" a negative correlation, and "0" no correlation between the determinants and transaction success; for determinants showing a "+/-" sign the reviewed results were mixed or deemed to be inconclusive; * with regard to wealth creation for acquirer shareholders and subjective assessments by executives

5 Empirical analysis of the success of German acquisitions in the United States

5.1 Introduction

The main focus for the analysis of the success of transactions and its determinants for German cross-border acquisitions of U.S. targets is the perspective of the shareholders of the acquiring company. Accordingly, transaction success is measured using the event study methodology. However, as BRUNER (2002) notes, the "task must be to look for patterns of confirmation across approaches and studies much like one sees an image in a mosaic of stones."[1] In order to obtain a qualitative assessment of transaction success the event study is complemented by a survey that is designed to yield additional insights from a managerial perspective. Accordingly, those executives of German companies that pursued an acquisition in the United States during the period 1990 to 2004 were asked to provide their evaluation of transaction success.

Besides answering the question whether German acquirers were successful in the United States from two different perspectives (Section 5.3), the other goal of this chapter is to detect in a uni- and multivariate analysis statistically significant determinants of transaction success (Sections 5.4 and 5.5). A comparison of the results to a control sample of domestic and European cross-border transactions by German acquirers aims to identify systematic differences for U.S. acquisitions (Section 5.6). The generalizations drawn from the deductive verification of the hypothesized directional influences serve as a basis to derive conclusions and implications for future U.S. transactions by German companies (Section 5.7).

5.2 Methodologies for measuring success

5.2.1 Capital market based event study

5.2.1.1 Sample design and description

The U.S. transactions to be included in the sample for this event study are identified using data from Thomson Financial SDC, Frankfurter Allgemeine Zeitung, Bloomberg, Mergers & Acquisitions Rooster, and the Lexis/Nexis database.[2] Returns on individual shares as well as acquirer-specific financial data (for example total assets, cash, liquidity and market-to-book

---

[1] BRUNER (2002), p. 50.

[2] The Securities Data Company mergers and acquisitions database is provided by Thomson Financial Securities Services and is the main source of data for this study. The other sources are used to verify and confirm the announcement dates provided by SDC, whereby Lexis/Nexis provides prospectuses and registration statements only from April 1993 to the present.

ratios) are obtained from Datastream.[3] In order to be included in the sample, the transactions have to meet all of the following selection criteria:

- The acquirer is a German company, publicly traded at least 273 trading days prior and 20 trading days after the initial public announcement of the transaction.[4]
- The target is a U.S. company, either public or private, or a subsidiary, division, or branch of a U.S. group.
- The transaction volume exceeds either $100m or 5 percent of the acquiring company's total assets on the balance sheet date preceding the announcement date.[5]
- In case of a share deal, the acquirer purchases at least 50 percent of the voting power of the target company, or in case it previously owned already a stake in the target before, enough shares were purchased to obtain effective control.
- The transaction was announced between January 1, 1990, and December 31, 2004 (the "observation period").w
- The transaction was completed.

78 transactions by German companies satisfied these selection criteria. Analogous to the vast majority of the reviewed prior empirical research, this event study sample comprises acquisitions of target companies in all business sectors, hence transactions of targets in the financial services industry are also included. Table 5.1 provides a list of the sample, sorted by year of announcement.

These 78 transactions were pursued by 42 companies, of which 74 percent were listed in the DAX30 at the time of the announcement.[6] The most active acquirer in this sample was *Siemens AG* with nine transactions, followed by *BASF AG* with six, and *Bayer AG* with five transactions. A participation in the target company prior to gaining effective control was held in seven cases, while such "toehold" stakes varied from 10.93 percent to 48.9 percent.[7] None of the targets was acquired in a hostile transaction.

---

3 Datastream is also provided by Thomson Financial Securities Services.

4 This timeframe is determined by the choice of the estimation period and the longest event window, as shown in Section 5.2.1.2. An identical timeframe was used for example in the study by BEITEL ET AL. (2004).

5 Using such a transaction volume as a cut-off point ensures that only acquisitions are included in the analysis that have received sufficient attention from the capital markets. Some of the reviewed prior studies, for example those by MOELLER ET AL. (2004) and FULLER ET AL. (2002), employed a cut-off point for the transaction volume of either $1m or one percent of the acquirer's market value of assets in the year before the announcement date.

6 Of those companies listed in the DAX30 as of December 31, 2004, only *BMW AG* did not acquire a U.S. target during the observation period, as it chose to enter the U.S. market via greenfield investments in 1992.

7 These were the transactions by *Siemens AG* in 1995, *Henkel KGaA* in 1996 (of *Loctite Corp.*), *Merck KGaA* in 1999, *Deutsche Bank AG* in 2000, *DaimlerChrysler AG* in 2000, *Lufthansa AG* in 2001, and *Schering AG* in 2002 (of *Collateral Therapeutics Inc.*).

Table 5.1: U.S. acquisitions by German acquirers in the event study sample

No.	Year	Name of target	Industry of target	Status of target*	Name of acquirer	Volume ($m)
1	1990	*Fireman's Fund Insurance*	Financial		*Allianz AG*	3,100
2	1990	*Undisclosed biotechnology company*	Healthcare		*Schering AG*	100
3	1990	*Vista Chemical*	Chemicals	Public	*RWE AG*	582
4	1991	*Consolidation Coal*	Other		*RWE AG*	890
5	1991	*GTE Electricial Prods - Sylvania*	Consumer		*Siemens AG*	1,000
6	1992	*Mobil Chemical -Polystyrene Resin*	Chemicals		*BASF AG*	300
7	1994	*Ino-Delaval Turbine, Turbocare*	Industrial		*Mannesmann AG*	124
8	1994	*ElectroCom Automation Inc.*	Industrial	Public	*AEG AG*	266
9	1995	*Pyramid Technology Corp.*	Technology	Public	*Siemens AG*	205
10	1995	*Marion Merrell Dow Inc.*	Healthcare	Public	*Hoechst AG*	7,265
11	1995	*Monsanto Co-Styrenics Plastics*	Chemicals		*Bayer AG*	580
12	1995	*RCM Capital Mgmt (Travelers)*	Financial		*Dresdner Bank AG*	300
13	1996	*Tyco Intl-Curad and Futuro*	Consumer		*Beiersdorf AG*	165
14	1996	*National Medical Care Inc*	Healthcare		*Fresenius AG*	4,236
15	1996	*O/Brien Powder Products Inc.*	Chemicals		*Hoechst AG*	130
16	1996	*American Re-Insurance Company*	Financial	Public	*Münchner Rückversicherungs AG*	3,280
17	1996	*Sandoz AG-US and Canada Corn*	Chemicals		*BASF AG*	778
18	1996	*Novamax Technologies (Molson)*	Chemicals		*Henkel KGaA*	275
19	1996	*Loctite Corp.*	Chemicals	Public	*Henkel KGaA*	1,289
20	1996	*Johnson Controls - Plastic Division*	Chemicals		*Viag AG*	650
21	1997	*Montgomery Securities - Money*	Financial		*Commerzbank AG*	250
22	1997	*Giddings & Lewis Inc.*	Industrial	Public	*Thyssen AG*	703
23	1997	*Wyle Electronics*	Technology	Public	*VEBA AG*	633
24	1997	*Philips Car Systems*	Industrial		*Mannesmann AG*	754
25	1997	*Westinghouse Power Generation*	Industrial		*Siemens AG*	1,525
26	1998	*Cyprus Foote Mineral Co.*	Chemicals		*Metallgesellschaft AG*	305
27	1998	*Chrysler Corp.*	Consumer	Public	*Daimler-Benz AG*	40,466
28	1998	*Clarendon Insurance Group*	Financial		*Hannover Rückversicherungs AG*	500
29	1998	*Chiron Diagnostics Corp.*	Healthcare		*Bayer AG*	1,100
30	1998	*Gustafson-Seed Treatment Business*	Other		*Bayer AG*	180
31	1998	*Boullioun Aviation Services*	Financial		*Deutsche Bank AG*	120
32	1998	*Millenium Petrochemicals*	Other		*Linde AG*	123
33	1998	*Dover Corp-Elevator Business*	Industrial		*ThyssenKrupp AG*	1,100
34	1998	*Bankers Trust New York Corp.*	Financial	Public	*Deutsche Bank AG*	9,082
35	1999	*Castle Networks*	Technology		*Siemens AG*	300
36	1999	*Argon Networks Inc.*	Technology		*Siemens AG*	240
37	1999	*Eastman Kodak-Copier Division*	Industrial		*Heidelberger Druckmaschinen AG*	200
38	1999	*Premier Manufacturing Support*	Industrial		*Dürr Beteiligungs AG*	76
39	1999	*VWR Scientific Products Corp.*	Healthcare	Public	*Merck KGaA*	581
40	1999	*Turner Corp.*	Industrial	Public	*Hochtief AG*	395
41	1999	*Lone Star Industries Inc.*	Industrial	Public	*Dyckerhoff AG*	1,075
42	1999	*PIMCO Advisors Holdings LP*	Financial	Public	*Allianz AG*	1,930
43	1999	*Lyondell Chemical-Polyils Business*	Chemicals		*Bayer AG*	2,450

* Status of the target company is private if not otherwise noted.

Table 5.1 (cont.): U.S. acquisitions by German acquirers in the event study sample

No.	Year	Name of target	Industry of target	Status of target*	Name of acquirer	Volume ($m)
44	1999	*Chemdal Corp*	Chemicals		*BASF AG*	657
45	1999	*EIS International Inc.*	Technology	Public	*SER Systems AG*	67
46	1999	*Morton Industrial Coatings*	Chemicals		*BASF AG*	175
47	2000	*Total Renal Care Holdings-Intl*	Healthcare		*Fresenius Medical Care AG*	145
48	2000	*Diehl Graphsoft Inc.*	Technology	Public	*Nemetschek AG*	29
49	2000	*Jim Henson Productions Inc.*	Other		*EM.TV AG*	680
50	2000	*Entex Information Services Inc.*	Technology	Public	*Siemens AG*	105
51	2000	*American Cyanamid Agri Product*	Chemcials		*BASF AG*	3,900
52	2000	*Shared Medical Systems*	Healthcare	Public	*Siemens AG*	2,060
53	2000	*CFW Information Services*	Technology		*telegate AG*	36
54	2000	*GemStone Systems Inc.*	Technology		*Brokat Infosystems AG*	300
55	2000	*Blaze Software Inc.*	Technology	Public	*Brokat Infosystems AG*	441
56	2000	*Detroit Diesel*	Industrial	Public	*DaimlerChrysler AG*	581
57	2000	*VoiceStream Wireless Corp.*	Technology	Public	*Deutsche Telekom AG*	29,404
58	2000	*Sybron Chemicals Inc.*	Chemcials	Public	*Bayer AG*	210
59	2000	*Air Products & Chemicals-Poly*	Chemicals		*Celanese AG*	326
60	2000	*Wasserstein Perella Group Inc.*	Financial		*Dresdner Bank AG*	1,255
61	2000	*Acuson Corp.*	Healthcare	Public	*Siemens AG*	668
62	2000	*National Discount Brokers*	Financial	Public	*Deutsche Bank AG*	899
63	2000	*Automated Financial Systems*	Technology	Public	*Brokat Infosystems AG*	35
64	2000	*Nicholas-Applegate Capt Mgmt*	Financial		*Allianz AG*	2,220
65	2000	*SAGA Systems, Inc.*	Technology		*Software AG*	348
66	2001	*Treev, Inc.*	Technology	Public	*CE Computer Equipment AG*	103
67	2001	*Sky Chefs Inc.*	Other		*Deutsche Lufthansa AG*	1,300
68	2001	*TopTier Software Inc.*	Technology		*SAP AG*	400
69	2001	*Catamaran Communications*	Technology		*Infineon Technologies AG*	250
70	2001	*American Water Works Co Inc.*	Other	Public	*RWE AG*	7,726
71	2001	*Zurich Scudder Investments Inc.*	Financial		*Deutsche Bank AG*	2,500
72	2001	*Industrial Computer Source Inc.*	Technology		*Kontron AG*	23
73	2002	*Collateral Therapeutics Inc.*	Healthcare	Public	*Schering AG*	141
74	2002	*Immunex Corp-Leukine Business*	Healthcare		*Schering AG*	380
75	2003	*Honeywell Intl-Engineering Business*	Chemicals		*BASF AG*	170
76	2003	*Dial Corp.*	Consumer	Public	*Henkel KGaA*	2,914
77	2004	*US Filter Corp.*	Industrial		*Siemens AG*	993
78	2004	*Sovereign Specialty Chemicals*	Chemicals		*Henkel KGaA*	575

* Status of the target company is private if not otherwise noted.

While for 1993 no transaction was identified, more than half of the transactions were announced in the period from 1998 to 2000, as displayed in Figure 5.1. Analogous to the worldwide transaction volume, with 19 announced deals the highest transaction activity in the sample was observed for the year 2000. Since achieving this peak the German M&A activity in the United States has significantly decreased.[8] As a result, for the years 2002, 2003, and 2004 only two annual transactions were identified for this sample.

8 As shown in Section 2.4.2.2.

Figure 5.1: Number of transactions in the event study sample by year

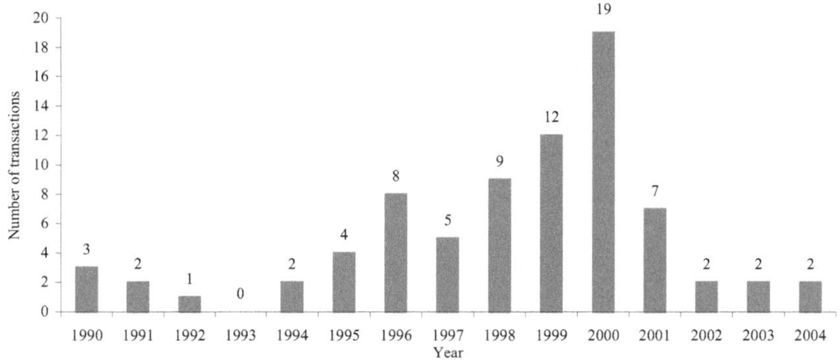

The individual transaction volume ranges from \$23m to \$40.5b and averages \$1.9b.[9] As a result of a few mega-deals, the median of the entire event study sample is \$538m, well below the mean. Since such mega-deals primarily concerned U.S. public companies, the disparity is even higher for the subsample of public transactions, which account for 75 percent of the transaction volume, but only for 38 percent of the total number of transactions.[10] Table 5.2 reports summarizing descriptive statistics for the sample.

Table 5.2: Descriptive statistics of the event study sample

	All	**Public**	**Private**
Number of transactions	78	29	49
in %	*100%*	*38%*	*62%*
Total volume (\$m)	151,619	113,137	38,482
in %	*100%*	*75%*	*25%*
Mean volume (\$m)	1,944	3,901	785
Median volume (\$m)	538	633	348
Standard deviation (\$m)	5,711	9,043	973
Maximum volume (\$m)	40,466	40,466	4,236
Minimum volume (\$m)	23	29	23

Table 5.3 classifies the transactions into various size groups and further highlights the dominance of mega-deals, which account for less than one-third of the total number of transactions but for 87 percent of the total transaction volume.

9 The transaction volume comprises the entire purchase price paid for with cash and shares.

10 This difference in absolute transaction volume between public and private targets has been frequently observed in prior empirical research, most recently in the study by MOELLER ET AL. (2004).

Table 5.3: Size of the transactions in the event study sample

Size of transactions	Number of transactions		Value of transactions ($m)	
< $100m	6	8%	266	0%
$100m - $249m	17	22%	2,636	2%
$250m - $499m	16	21%	5,336	4%
$500m - $999m	16	21%	11,203	7%
≥ $1b	23	29%	132,178	87%
Sum	78	100%	151,619	100%

In light of the earlier mentioned deregulation efforts and technological changes during the observation period,[11] acquisitions of target companies in the financial services, technology, and healthcare sectors comprise approximately half of the transactions by number and volume of the entire sample (see Table 5.4).

Table 5.4: Industry sectors of the transactions in the event study sample

Industry of target company	Number of transactions		Value of transactions ($m)	
Financial services	12	15%	25,437	17%
Technology	17	22%	32,919	22%
Chemicals	17	22%	13,352	9%
Healthcare	10	13%	16,676	11%
Industrial & Automotive	12	15%	7,791	5%
Consumer markets	4	5%	44,545	29%
Other	6	8%	10,899	7%
Sum	78	100%	151,619	100%

The majority of the transactions involved an acquirer and target company in related industries, measured by an identity of at least the first two digits of the respective Standard Industry Classification ("SIC") codes (see Table 5.5). The number of horizontal acquisitions, i.e. transactions with an identical four digit SIC code for the acquirer and target, is almost equal to the number of conglomerate acquisitions. Accordingly, nearly a third of the transactions in the sample were pursued to diversify not only geographically, but also industrially.

11 See Section 2.4.1.2.

Table 5.5: Strategic direction of the transactions in the event study sample

Relatedness of acquisitions	**Number of transactions**		**Value of transactions ($m)**	
Related				
2-digit SIC codes	22	28%	41,491	27%
3-digit SIC codes	8	10%	34,976	23%
4-digit SIC codes	23	30%	60,257	40%
Unrelated	25	32%	14,895	10%
Sum	78	100%	151,619	100%

While the fraction of transactions in those sectors marked by the influence of "industry shocks" is relatively higher than in private transactions, the relatedness between the entities in these public transactions is similar to that of the overall sample.[12] The majority of these public acquisitions were pursued via a cash tender offer, only in six cases did the acquiring company pay at least partially with its own shares. One transaction was pursued through a proxy solicitation, as shown in Table 5.6.[13]

Table 5.6: Form of acquisition of public U.S. targets in the event study sample

Form of transaction	**Number of transactions**	
Cash offer		
Tender offer	22	76%
Proxy solicitation	1	3%
Exchange offer	6	21%
Sum	29	100%

5.2.1.2 Estimation of abnormal returns

Analogous to the majority of the reviewed event studies,[14] abnormal shareholder returns are measured applying the standard market model as shown in equation (6) in Section 4.3.1.1:

$$AR_{it} = R_{it} - E(R_{it}) = R_{it} - (\alpha_i + \beta_i R_{mt})$$

Accordingly, the average abnormal return for event day t and cumulative abnormal returns for event window T are computed using equations (7) and (8) of Section 4.3.1.1:

$$\overline{AR}_t = \left(\frac{1}{n}\right)\sum_{i=1}^{n} AR_{it} \cdot \; CAR_T = \sum_{t=t_1}^{t_2} \overline{AR}_t$$

12 A separate display of the number and volume of those public transactions classified by industry and SIC-code is omitted.

13 This is the acquisition of *Dial Corp.* by *Henkel KGaA*, which was announced in December 2003.

14 As shown in Table 4.2 in Section 4.3.1.2.

The systematic risk β_i is determined for each acquirer in an OLS regression using daily returns over a 253 day estimation period that ends 21 days prior to the acquisition announcement date.[15] For the market return R_{mt} either the DAX30, M-DAX,[16] S-DAX,[17] or NEMAX[18] is employed, depending on in which index the respective acquiring company was included at the time of the announcement of the transaction. Assuming that the companies included in these indices are inherently similar in market capitalization to the acquirers in the event study sample, using different market indices might provide a better prediction of abnormal returns. For comparison purposes, the broader portfolio of the Morgan Stanley Capital International ("MSCI") Standard Market Index for Germany[19] is used alternatively as the market return proxy for all acquirers in the sample.[20] Changes in the share prices and index levels are computed using a total return, hence effects of dividend payments are included.[21]

In order to facilitate the comparison of the results of this study to the prior research on cross-border acquisitions, cumulative abnormal returns are estimated for event windows that are centered around the announcement date ({0}, [-1,1], [-2,2], [-5,5], [-10,10], [-20,20]), designed to capture any pre-announcement effects ([-1,0], [-10,-1], [-20,-1], [-2,1], [-5,1], [-10,1], [-20,1],) and are defined to assess the post-announcement performance of the acquirers' shares ([0,1], [0,10], [1,10], [1,20], [-1,10], and [-1,20]). The broader event windows are used based on the assumption that capital markets are not always capable of predicting the full implications of a transaction immediately upon its announcement.[22]

15 As mentioned in Section 4.3.1.1, there is little consensus in the literature about the appropriate definition of the estimation period, evidenced by the observed range of such periods in the reviewed empirical research from 60 to 280 days. The use of a full calendar year estimation period for the purpose of this study follows for example GREGORY and MCCORRISTON (2005); BEITEL ET AL. (2004); DELONG (2001).

16 At the German stock exchange, the M-DAX is the share index for mid cap companies. It is provided by *Deutsche Börse AG* and comprises 50 medium-sized companies, see PERRIDON and STEINER (2004), p. 247. Within the event study sample, the following companies were listed in the M-DAX at the time of the announcement of the acquisitions: *Beiersdorf AG*, *Celanese AG*, *Fresenius AG* (1996), *Hannover Rückversicherungs AG*, *Heidelberger Druckmaschinen AG*, *Hochtief AG*, *Merck KGaA*, and *Metallgesellschaft AG*.

17 At the German stock exchange, the S-DAX is the share index for small cap companies; similar to the M-DAX, it comprises 50 companies. Within the sample, the following companies were listed in the S-DAX at the time of the announcement of the acquisitions: *Dürr Beteiligungs AG* and *Dyckerhoff AG*.

18 The NEMAX was created in 1997 predominantly for young companies in the new economy and was replaced on March 24, 2003 by the Tec-DAX.

19 This index represents 85 percent of the market capitalization of all publicly traded companies. For information on the composition of this index refer to www.msci.com/methodology/methodology.html.

20 Unless no significant differences between the results from the alternative market return indices are observed, the computed CARs obtained from the MSCI index are provided in the footnotes or the appendix only.

21 Computing total returns is based on the assumption that dividend payments are used to purchase additional shares at the daily closing price, see THOMSON FINANCIAL (2000), p. 66.

22 See DATTA and PUIA (1995), p. 347.

For completeness purposes, abnormal returns for the shareholders of the acquired public target companies are computed as well. However, following the majority of the reviewed empirical research on cross-border transactions, no conclusion is drawn on the combined creation and distribution of shareholder value of the transactions.

5.2.1.3 Definition and distributional properties of significance tests

BOEHMER ET AL. (1991) demonstrated that even with minor increases in event-induced variances, the conventional test statistics as proposed by DODD and WARNER (1983) reject the null hypothesis of zero average abnormal returns too often when it is actually true. Accordingly, in order to avoid potential influences from event-induced variances the test statistics for the average abnormal return on day t and cumulative abnormal return for the event window T are calculated using the following equations (12) and (13):[23]

$$Z_{AR_t} = \overline{SAR}_t \bigg/ \sqrt{\frac{1}{n(n-1)} \sum_{i=1}^{n} \left(SAR_{it} - \sum_{i=1}^{n} \frac{SAR_{it}}{n} \right)^2} \, , \tag{12}$$

$$Z_{CAR_T} = \frac{\sqrt{\sum_{t=t_1}^{t_2} Z_{AR_t}^2}}{\sqrt{(t_2 - t_1 + 1)}} \tag{13}$$

For comparison purposes, the test statistics suggested by DODD and Warner (1983) are displayed as well, but only for the discussion of the overall success of the analyzed transactions and not for the subsamples in the univariate analysis (referred to as "Z-value B").

In order to assess whether the means of two paired subsamples X and Y within the univariate analysis of various determinants of transaction success are statistically different from each other, the following t-statistics are used:[24]

$$\text{t-statistic} = \frac{\overline{CAR}_{TX} - \overline{CAR}_{TY}}{\sqrt{\left(\frac{N_X s_X^2 + N_Y s_Y^2}{n_X + n_Y - 2} \right) \left(\frac{n_X + n_Y}{n_X n_Y} \right)}} \, , \tag{14}$$

---

[23] See CHATTERJEE and KUENZI (2001), p. 22; BOEHMER ET AL. (1991), p. 269f. The test statistics developed by BOEHMER ET AL. (1991) take into account observed increases in both the time-series abnormal returns' variance and the cross-sectional abnormal returns' variance around the event date, see AKTAS ET AL. (2004), p. 9. For a detailed discussion of this "event-induced variance phenomenon" refer to for example HARRINGTON and SHRIDER (2002). These authors provide a detailed overview of other test statistics, including non-parametric tests.

[24] See CHATTERJEE and KUENZI (2001), p. 23f.

$$\text{with } \overline{CAR}_{TX} = \frac{\sum_{i=1}^{n_X} CAR_T}{n_X}, \quad \overline{CAR}_{TY} = \frac{\sum_{i=1}^{n_Y} CAR_T}{n_Y},$$

$$s_X^2 = \frac{\sum_{i=1}^{n_X}\left(CAR_{Ti} - \overline{CAR}_{TX}\right)^2}{N_X}, \quad s_Y^2 = \frac{\sum_{i=1}^{n_Y}\left(CAR_{Ti} - \overline{CAR}_{TY}\right)^2}{N_Y},$$

with $N_X = n_X - 1$, $N_Y = n_Y - 1$,

where:

n_X : number of transactions in subsample X

n_Y : number of transactions in subsample Y

s_X^2 : variance of CAR_T in subsample X

s_Y^2 : variance of CAR_T in subsample Y

Under the null hypothesis that there are no differences in the abnormal returns between the analyzed subsamples, the t-statistics follow a Student-t distribution.[25]

These tests of statistical significance for the cumulative abnormal returns and the mean differences of subsamples rely on the assumptions of independence of the samples and normal distribution of the cumulative abnormal returns. In order to test for normal distribution of the event study sample, a Kolmogorov-Smirnov test based on a Monte Carlo simulation is performed.[26] The results of this test are displayed in Table 5.7 and show that for a confidence level of 10 percent the null hypothesis of normal distribution of the sample cannot be rejected.

---

25 See BAMBERG and BAUR (1993), p. 193. For sample sizes (n_A+n_B - 2) bigger than 30 the t-statistics approximately follow a normal distribution N(0,1), see BLEYMÜLLER ET AL. (2004), p. 63. Given that almost all hypotheses formulated in Section 4.6 are directional, one-tailed tests are applied. For a given probability of committing a "type one" error, i.e. rejecting the null hypothesis when it is actually true, the critical t-value is smaller under a one-tailed test compared to a two-tailed test, thereby resulting in a less frequent rejection of the null hypothesis. BROWN and WARNER (1980, p. 227) noted "when the sign of the abnormal performance is not known a priori, the ability to discern abnormal performance is reduced markedly".

26 See BLEYMÜLLER ET AL. (2004), p. 133f.; BROWN and WARNER (1980), p. 218f.

Table 5.7: Summary of the Kolmogorov-Smirnov test

Inputs		Results	
Number of days in the estimation period	253	Kolmogorov-Smirnov Z-value	0.5296
Number of shares in the sample	78	Asymptotic Significance [b]	0.9418
Average cumulative abnormal returns [a]		Monte-Carlo Significance [b]	
Mean	0.0000	Estimate	0.9313
Standard deviation	0.0029	95% confidence interval lower limit	0.9263
Median	-0.0001	95% confidence interval upper limit	0.9363
Maximum value	0.0077		
Minimum value	-0.0091		

a: normal test distribution; b: two-tailed test.

5.2.1.4 Operationalization of determinants of transaction success

The hypothesized influence of the presumed determinants of transaction success is tested in a uni- and multivariate analysis, which requires for each determinant the definition and operationalization of explanatory variables. Binary dummy variables are assigned for the majority of determinants, while for others various alternative metric variables are used. The respective variables for the determinants are displayed in Table 5.8.

The variables are defined as follows:

- "DAX": The dummy variable is set to 1 if the acquirer was included in the DAX30 index at the time of the announcement of the transaction.
- "LIQUIDITY": The liquidity ratio is defined as the ratio of the acquirer's current assets to its current liabilities on the balance sheet date preceding the announcement date of the transaction.
- "CASH/ASSETS": A proxy for measuring the financial condition of the acquiring company is the ratio of its cash to the total assets on the balance sheet date preceding the announcement date of the transaction.
- "MTBV": Acquirers are categorized either as "value" or "glamour" companies, depending on the comparison of their market-to-book value at the beginning of the year in which the acquisition was announced with the median MTBV for all acquirers. Acquirers with a MTBV below the median are defined as value companies and acquirers with a MTBV above the median are defined as glamour companies.[27]

[27] CONN ET AL. (2005) for example use a less categorical approach for their large sample size, by comparing companies depending on their MTBV quintile at the beginning of the year of the announcement. The respective quintiles are calculated by ranking all acquirers by their MTBV and creating five equally sized groups in terms of number. Acquirers in the quintile with the lowest MTBVs are defined as value companies, and acquirers in the quintile with the highest MTBVs are defined as glamour companies.

- "TOEHOLD": The dummy variable is set to 1 if the acquirer owned already a stake in the target company before gaining effective control.
- "FREQUENT": The dummy variable is set to 1 if the acquirer pursued at least two acquisitions of a U.S. target during the observation period from January 1, 1990 to December 31, 2004.
- "REGULATED": The dummy variable is set to 1 if the business sector of the target company is in a regulated industry, i.e. the financial services, telecommunications, or utilities sectors.[28]
- "STATUS": The dummy variable is set to 1 if the target is a public company.
- "VOLUME$≥1B": The dummy variable is set to 1 if the transaction volume is at least $1b, i.e. if it is considered a "mega-deal".
- "VOLUME$": For conducting the multivariate linear regression, the absolute size of the transaction is transformed by taking the natural log of the purchase price.
- "VOLUME/ASSETS": For both private and public acquisitions, the transaction volume is divided by the amount of total assets[29] of the acquirer on the balance sheet date preceding the announcement date of the transaction.
- "2-DIGIT SIC": Relatedness is measured on a 2-digit SIC code identity, setting the dummy variable to 1 in case of related businesses of the acquirer and target.[30]
- "PAYMENT": The dummy variable is set to 1 in case the transaction was at least partially paid for with shares of the acquirer.
- "FORM": The dummy variable is set to 1 if the transaction was structured as an asset deal.
- "TENDER OFFER": The dummy variable is set to 1 if the acquisition of a public target was pursued via a cash tender offer.
- "IB": The dummy variable is set to 1 if professional external advisors were assisting the acquiring company in the transaction process.
- "GDP": The relative strength of the economic growth of the United States is measured by comparing the growth rate of the gross domestic product ("GDP") in the year of the announcement of the transaction to the average rate for the observation period from January 1, 1990 to December 31, 2004.[31]
- "TIME": The dummy variable is set to 1 if the transaction was announced during the period from January 1, 1998 to December 31, 2000.

---

28 This definition follows GOERGEN and RENNEBOOG (2004).

29 Other studies such as MOELLER ET AL. (2004) used the equity market capitalization of the acquirer as the denominator, but given that especially for new economy companies these are quite high, they do not reflect the size of the acquirer and its capacities. Hence, total assets were used as a proxy in this study.

30 Additionally, 3-digit and 4-digit SIC code identities are also measured.

31 According to data obtained from the Bureau of Economic Analysis, the average annual GDP growth during the observation period was 2.9 percent.

- "EUR": The strength of the Euro relative to the U.S. dollar is measured as the absolute deviation of the average exchange rate for the year of the transaction announcement from the average exchange rate for the observation period from January 1, 1990 to December 31, 2004.[32] A positive value suggests the Euro is strong relative to the dollar.

Table 5.8: Operationalization of determinants of transaction success

Determinant	Name of variable	Category/Proxy	Var.	Hyp.
Characteristics of acquiring companies				
• Absolute size	DAX	1 = DAX30 0 = Non-DAX30	A	H_3
• Financial condition	LIQUIDITY	in percent	Ba	H_4
	CASH/ASSETS	in percent	Bb	H_4
• Valuation ratio	MTBV	in percent	C	H_5
• Previous participation	TOEHOLD	1 = yes 0 = no	D	H_6
• Transaction experience	FREQUENT	1 = frequent 0 = non-frequent	E	H_7
Characteristics of target companies				
• Industry	REGULATED	1 = regulated 0 = non-regulated	F	H_8
• Status	STATUS	1 = public 0 = private	G	H_9
• Absolute and relative size	VOLUME ≥$1B	1 = more than $1b 0 = less than $1b	Ha	H_{10}
	VOLUME$	in $ or ln$	Hb	H_{10}
	VOLUME/ASSETS	in percent	Hc	H_{10}
Characteristics of transaction structuring and management				
• Strategic direction	2-DIGIT SIC	1 = yes 0 = no	I	H_{11}
• Form of payment	PAYMENT	1 = shares 0 = cash	J	H_{12}
• Acquisition structure	FORM	1 = asset deal 0 = share deal	K	H_{13}
• Form of acquisition of public targets	TENDER OFFER	1 = tender offer 0 = other	L	H_{14}
• Inclusion of professional advisors	IB	1 = yes 0 = no	M	H_{15}
Influences of the economic environment				
• Relative strength of economic growth	GDP	in percent	N	H_{16}
• Relative strength of capital markets	TIME	1 = 1998 to 2000 0 = other	O	H_{17}
• Relative strength of the Euro	EUR	in percent	P	H_{18}

32 During the observation period the average exchange rate was 1.1443 USD/EUR.

As mentioned earlier, due to the limited availability of certain data of the acquiring companies and the transactions, not all of the determinants identified in Section 4.5 can be analyzed for the purpose of this study.

5.2.2 Survey of executives

5.2.2.1 Sample design and response data

For the purpose of the survey, the chief financial officers ("CFO") or heads of in-house M&A departments of those public companies identified in the sample for the event study were asked to provide a success assessment for their U.S. cross-border acquisition.[33] This sample was expanded by also including CFOs of those public companies for which their U.S. acquisition did not meet the selection criteria of the event study sample as well as of those non-public German companies that pursued U.S. acquisitions during the observation period valued at more than $100m. In total, 58 companies were selected for inclusion in the mailing list for a standardized questionnaire, as displayed in Table 5.9.

Table 5.9: Mailing list for the survey of executives

German companies in the mailing list sample		
*Adidas-Salomon AG**	*Dykerhoff AG*	*Medigene AG**
Allianz AG	*Em.TV AG*	*Merck KGaA*
*Altana AG**	*E.ON AG*	*Metro AG**
BASF AG	*Epcos AG**	*mg technologies AG*
Bayer AG	*Fresenius Medical Care AG*	*Münchner Rückversicherungs-Gesellschaft AG*
Bayerische Hypo- u. Vereinsbank AG	*Fresenius AG*	*Nemetschek AG*
Beiersdorf AG	*Gerling-Konzern Versicherungs-Beteiligungs AG**	*Otto GmbH & CoKG**
*Bertelsmann AG**	*GfK AG**	*Ruhrkohle Coal International Aktiengesellschaft**
*Bilfinger Berger AG**	*Gildemeister AG**	*Rheinmetall AG**
*BSH GmbH**	*Hannover Rückversicherungs AG*	*Robert Bosch GmbH**
Celanese AG	*Heidelberger Druckmaschinen AG*	*RWE AG*
Commerzbank AG	*Henkel KGaA*	*SAP AG*
DaimlerChrysler AG	*Hochtief AG*	*Schering AG*
Degussa AG	*Hugo Boss AG*	*Schwarz Pharma AG**
Deutsche Bank AG	*Infineon Technologies AG*	*Siemens AG*
Deutsche Lufthansa AG	*Klöckner-Werke AG**	*Software AG*
*Deutsche Post AG**	*Koenig & Bauer AG**	*Telegate AG*
Deutsche Telekom AG	*Kontron Embedded Computers AG*	*ThyssenKrupp AG*
Dresdner Bank AG	*Linde AG*	
Dürr Beteiligungs AG	*MAN AG**	

* denotes acquiring companies not included in the event study sample.

[33] It should be noted that as a result of mergers, bankruptcies, and corporate restructurings not all of the 42 acquiring companies in the event study sample were still existent at the time of this study.

Of 58 mailed questionnaires 20 were returned, which represents a relatively high response rate of 34 percent.[34] In four cases the executives filed out the questionnaire for multiple transactions, while in one case no success evaluation was given.[35] Overall, the survey responses provide a success assessment for 25 cross-border transactions.

In order to test for potential non-response bias, the returned questionnaires are compared to the companies in the mailing list, using the three criteria industry classification, DAX30 listing, and year of the acquisition.[36] The representativeness of the response data with regard to the entire survey sample is confirmed based on the results of a chi-square goodness-of-fit test.[37] Whether the responses are representative for the assessment of the transaction success cannot be evaluated, as pointed out by INGHAM and KRAN (1992), given that "those companies whose past acquisitions were viewed as successful were more likely to respond. Such problems are, however, inevitable with questionnaire-based research".[38]

The classification by industry sectors of the assessed transactions and the respective portion of acquisitions by DAX30 companies are shown in Table 5.10.

Table 5.10: Industry sectors of the surveyed U.S. transactions

Industry of target company	**Number of transactions**		**thereof DAX30 acquirers**	
Financial services	5	20%	3	20%
Technology	2	8%	1	7%
Chemicals	2	8%	1	7%
Healthcare	2	8%	1	7%
Industrial & Automotive	8	32%	6	40%
Consumer markets	3	12%	1	7%
Other	3	12%	2	13%
Sum	25	100%	15	100%

Acquirers in the industrial goods sector represent with 32 percent the highest portion in the response sample, while in the event study sample transactions in the technology and

---

34 As pointed out in Section 4.3.3.3, the average response rate usually is very low. For example, in the study by BAMBERGER (1994, p. 38) a response rate of 22 percent was observed, which the author deemed already relatively high.

35 That questionnaire dealt with a transaction pursued in 2005, for which it was too early to conclude on its success.

36 For a general discussion of employing various criteria for measuring the objectivity, reliability, and validity of samples refer to for example BÜHNER (1990a), p. 98f.; MÖLLER (1983), p. 43f.

37 The following χ^2-values were computed for the applied criteria: for the industrial classification 5.933 (with 6 degrees of freedom ("nf")), for the DAX30 listing 2.04 (with nf=1), and for the year of the transaction 22.70 (with nf=14). For a general discussion of the applicability of the chi-square goodness-of-fit test refer to for example BACKHAUS ET AL. (2005).

38 INGHAM and KRAN (1992), p. 201.

chemicals sectors were the most frequent. As a result of the inclusion of private companies acquisitions by DAX30 companies account for only 60 percent of the transactions in the response sample, compared to 74 percent in the event study sample. Analogous to the peak of the worldwide M&A activity in the 1990s, the majority of the transactions evaluated by the CFOs concern the years 1998, 1999, and 2000 (see Figure 5.2). The number of transactions in the response sample before and subsequent to this period of "hot" capital markets is nearly evenly split.

Figure 5.2: Number of transactions in the response sample by year

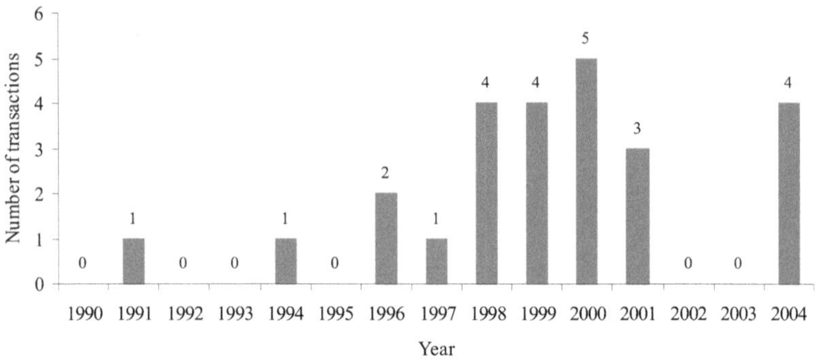

5.2.2.2 Structure of the standardized questionnaire

The standardized questionnaire, which is attached in Appendix A1, is divided into two areas of inquiry. The first section, Part A, asks for general information about the acquiring company, such as its

- industry and status,
- previous domestic and cross-border transaction experience, both in general as well as specific to the United States,
- general perception of priorities and concerns with regard to conducting a due diligence for a U.S. target company,
- general approach of measuring the success of a transaction, i.e. which evaluation criteria for which time horizon subsequent to the closing of the transactions are applied, and
- overall assessment of the success of its previous M&A activity, including a comparison between domestic and cross-border transactions.

Part B of the questionnaire examines various aspects of the structure and success for a specific U.S. transaction, including the

- motives for pursuing the transaction,
- characteristics of the target company, such as its industry classification, status, and relative size compared to the acquirer,
- characteristics of the transaction execution, such as the acquisition structure, strategic direction, form of payment, areas of conducted due diligence, inclusion of external advisors, applied valuation method as well as the degree of post-merger integration, and
- assessment of the success of the transaction and the main factors contributing to it. For the overall success assessment a five-point equal-interval scale was provided, comprising "very successful", "somewhat successful", "neutral", "partial failure", and "full failure". With regard to the success factors the participants were asked to list those individually.

In case the acquiring company pursued multiple acquisitions of U.S. targets during the observation period, the executives were asked to fill out Part B for each of them.[39]

5.2.2.3 Measures of statistical inference

In order to test in a uni- and multivariate analysis the statistical significance of the hypothesized influence of the success determinants, the dependent variable "success" is measured on a nominal scale by grouping the survey responses into the categories "yes" and "no" as an answer to the question whether the transaction was deemed a success. The responses "very successful" and "partly successful" are included in category "yes", consequently category "no" comprises the responses "neutral", "partial failure", and "full failure".[40]

Standard measures of statistical influence for nominal categorical data are contingency coefficients.[41] Such coefficients are a function of Pearson's chi-square statistics and are derived from r x c contingency tables.[42] Contingency tables tabulate in each cell the observed absolute and relative frequencies of the analyzed independent variables.[43] The observed frequencies for the k cells of the contingency table are then compared to their expected

---

39 A copy of the cover letter for the survey request is attached in Appendix A2.

40 In light of the potential positive bias of subjective success assessments the categorization of the "neutral" scaled evaluations as non-successful is deemed being conservative and follows a similar approach by BAMBERGER (1994).

41 See BAMBERGER (1994), pp. 53-58. These measures include Cramer's V coefficient, Phi coefficient, Sakoda coefficient, Tschuprov coefficient, and Pearson's coefficient, see BLACK (1999), pp. 630-642. All these measure have an identical two-sided p-value for testing the null hypothesis of no association, and this p-value equals Pearson's chi-square p-value.

42 See BACKHAUS ET AL. (2005), p. 230f.

43 See BAMBERGER (1994), p. 54.

frequencies, which are determined through the use of probability theory.[44] If the expected frequency of one or more cells is less than 5 and $k>2$, as it is the case for most independent variables in this study, the use of chi-square based coefficients is generally not recommended.[45] Instead, either Fisher's exact test for 2 x 2 contingency tables[46] or the Freeman-Halton exact test for r x c contingency table is employed.[47] In interpreting the p-value obtained from these measures, a value of 0.05 is considered to be the cutoff for acceptability of statistical significance for the rejection of the null hypothesis that there is no correlation between the dependent variable and the independent determinants.[48]

5.3 Overall success of the analyzed transactions

5.3.1 Results of the capital market based event study

5.3.1.1 Cumulative abnormal returns to target shareholders

The announcement of the takeover bid by a German company caused substantial positive cumulative abnormal returns for the shareholders of the U.S. targets, as shown in Table 5.11.

For example, within the [-1,1] event window the cumulative abnormal return, which is calculated employing the Standard & Poor's 500 index, averages 23.00 percent and is highly significant at the 1 percent level.[49] Compared to prior empirical research, these results indicate that German companies paid a relatively high premium for their U.S. public target, given that only one of the reviewed studies reported higher cumulative abnormal returns.[50] However, for two target companies (i.e. 8 percent) the announcement of the transactions generated negative share price reactions. Gradually increasing the event window centered on the announcement date results in even higher shareholder wealth gains, which can be attributed primarily to abnormal share price reactions in the pre-announcement period. Apparently, as it was observed in the majority of previous studies, the transaction was anticipated, either as a result of rumors or insider trading. Subsequent to the announcement

---

44 See BLACK (1999), p. 644f.

45 See SHESKIN (1997), p. 96, who points out that some scholars deem the criteria for when chi-square goodness-of-fit tests should be used too restrictive.

46 Fisher's exact test assesses the probability of replicating a table that simply due to the chance of sampling is at least as strong as the observed one, whereby "strong" is defined by the proportion on the diagonal with the most cases, see BACKHAUS ET AL. (2005), p. 243.

47 An alternative measure of association for categorical data is Goodman-Kruskal's Tau. However, using this measure did not yield a different indication of statistical dependence between the analyzed variables of this study than Fisher's exact test. Accordingly, these results are not separately displayed.

48 Within this study the p-values are calculated using StatXact, Version 6.2.0 (2004).

49 It should be noted that due to the limited availability of sufficient share price data, CARs are computed only for 26 transactions in the event study sample.

50 See Section 4.4.1.1.

date the cumulative abnormal returns decrease slightly, as additional information about the proposed transaction becomes available.

Table 5.11: Cumulative abnormal returns for U.S. target companies

(n=26) Event window	CAR%	Positive %	Negative %	Z-statistic	Z-statistic B
Period surrounding the announcement					
{0}	15.59***	85	15	3.7429	28.6519
[-1,1]	23.00***	92	8	2.6764	24.4232
[-2,2]	28.00**	92	8	2.2014	21.0859
[-5,5]	29.60**	96	4	1.7342	14.9077
[-10,10]	32.61*	88	12	1.5194	11.5413
[-20,20]	35.68	85	15	1.2618	9.4856
Pre-announcement period					
[-1,0]	17.17***	85	15	2.8677	24.2400
[-10,-1]	11.12*	69	31	1.4177	5.2338
[-20,-1]	13.50	77	23	1.1698	5.1937
[-2,1]	27.58***	92	8	2.4612	23.5741
[-5,1]	30.55**	96	4	1.9953	19.2224
[-10,1]	32.54**	96	4	1.8062	15.3646
[-20,1]	34.92*	81	19	1.4526	12.7709
Post-announcement period					
[0,1]	21.42***	92	8	3.0864	25.9322
[0,10]	21.49*	92	8	1.6062	10.9563
[1,10]	5.90	54	46	1.1988	2.4306
[1,20]	6.60	69	31	0.1509	1.9808
[-1,10]	23.07*	88	12	1.6026	12.1147
[-1,20]	23.77*	81	19	1.3543	9.1972

This table shows the results for an event study analyzing 26 acquisitions of public U.S. target companies by German acquirers during the period from 1990 to 2004. Cumulative abnormal returns are calculated employing the standard market model, using an estimation period of 253 trading days prior to the event window [-20,20] and the Standard & Poor's 500 index to measure market returns. Tests for statistical significance follow BOEHMER ET AL. (1991), while Z-statistic B is computed following DODD and WARNER (1983). *, **, *** denote significance at the 10%, 5% , and 1% level, respectively (based on a one-tailed Z-test).

The comparison of both measures of statistical significance shows how controlling for event-induced variances results in substantially lower Z-values compared to those following DODD and WARNER (1983) (columns "Z-statistic" and "Z-statistic B" in Table 5.11). Accordingly, in deviation to Z-statistic B, the null hypothesis that the cumulative abnormal returns are equal to zero is not rejected for all event windows when employing the test statistic by BOEHMER ET AL. (1991).

5.3.1.2 Cumulative abnormal returns to acquirer shareholders

The cumulative abnormal returns for shareholders of German acquirers for the various event windows are presented in Table 5.12.

Table 5.12: Cumulative abnormal returns for German acquirers

(n=78) Event window	CAR%	Positive %	Negative %	Z-statistic	Z-statistic B
Period surrounding the announcement					
{0}	0.37	59	41	1.0988	1.7707
[-1,1]	0.82*	50	50	1.3208	2.3084
[-2,2]	-0.23*	51	49	1.4397	0.1457
[-5,5]	-1.66*	45	55	1.3209	-0.7622
[-10,10]	-2.06	49	51	1.2481	-0.8189
[-20,20]	-2.43	51	49	1.0813	-0.6733
Pre-announcement period					
[-1,0]	0.98*	53	47	1.5613	3.2832
[-10,-1]	-0.54*	41	59	1.3608	-0.0728
[-20,-1]	-1.09	45	55	1.1149	-0.5118
[-2,1]	0.40*	47	53	1.4138	1.1172
[-5,1]	-0.22	54	46	1.2761	0.6364
[-10,1]	-0.32*	51	49	1.2937	0.2586
[-20,1]	-0.88	49	51	1.0960	-0.2479
Post-announcement period					
[0,1]	0.22	49	51	0.8848	0.7961
[0,10]	-1.52	45	55	1.1360	-1.0621
[1,10]	-1.89	45	55	1.1397	-1.6738
[1,20]	-1.71	33	67	1.0458	-0.8481
[-1,10]	-0.91	45	55	1.2201	-0.1876
[-1,20]	-0.74	46	54	1.1026	0.1813

This table shows the results for an event study analyzing 78 acquisitions of U.S. target companies by German acquirers during the period from 1990 to 2004. Cumulative abnormal returns are calculated employing the standard market model, using an estimation period of 253 trading days prior to the event window [-20,20] and various DAX indices to measure market returns. Tests for statistical significance follow BOEHMER ET AL. (1991), while Z-statistic B is computed following DODD and WARNER (1983). * denotes significance at the 10% level (based on a one-tailed Z-test).

On the announcement date as well as in the short time period immediately surrounding it, the transactions yield on average significant positive cumulative abnormal returns for acquirer shareholders, while for almost all other event windows the cumulative abnormal returns are insignificant.[51] For example, the [-1,1] event window displays a positive cumulative abnormal return of 0.82 percent, which is significant at the 10 percent level.[52] These results are essentially in line with the majority of the overall findings in the prior empirical research on cross-border acquisitions, but compared to U.S. transactions by U.K. and Dutch companies reveal higher shareholder gains for German companies.[53]

51 When using the MSCI Germany index for the market model regression, the CAR for the [-1,1] event window amounts to 1.16 percent (significant at the 1 percent level). Overall, the CARs based on the MSCI Germany index are essentially similar to those using DAX indices, as shown in Appendix B.1.1, though more event windows exhibit statistical significance.

52 Employing the test statistics by DODD and WARNER (1983) yields significance at the 5 percent level.

53 See Section 4.4.1.3. GREGORY and MCCORRISTON (2005) and CORHAY and RAD (2000) observed only slightly positive CARs for their subsamples of U.K. and Dutch acquirers, respectively, which were insignificant though in both cases.

The abnormal returns are the highest for the day before and of the event, which hints at an anticipation of the transaction, either due to rumors or insider trading.[54] Gradually extending the length of the pre- and post-announcement periods yields negative returns though.[55] These findings may indicate that the information processing in the capital market was not finished on the event date or that additional information became available with the effect that subsequent to the announcement the initial positive reaction is increasingly corrected. The negative pre-announcement share price reactions may be attributable to short selling by merger arbitrageurs.[56]

While for the announcement date a majority of transactions generate insignificant positive cumulative abnormal returns, for the [-1,1] event window the sample is evenly split between "winners" and "losers".[57] Moreover, the cumulative abnormal returns for the [-1,1] event window are scattered and vary in a broad range from -10.75 percent to +23.01 percent, as illustrated in Table 5.13 and Figure 5.3.

Table 5.13: Statistical distribution of CARs for various event windows

	Event window [-1,1]		**Event window [-1,10]**	
(n=78)	Positive CAR (%)	Negative CAR (%)	Positive CAR (%)	Negative CAR (%)
Proportion	50	50	45	55
Maximum	23.01	-10.75	24.08	-28.28
Minimum	0.01	-0.03	0.34	-0.03
Mean	4.54	-2.90	4.43	-5.27
Median	3.46	-1.62	3.55	-3.58
Std.	4.89	2.93	4.41	5.75

Noteworthy within these results for the [-1,1] event window is the positive cumulative abnormal return of 13.67 percent for the announcement of the *Daimler-Chrysler* merger, which several years after its consummation was widely perceived a failure from the perspective of the previous shareholders of *Daimler-Benz AG*.[58]

54 Such a positive pre-announcement effect on the basis of information leakage was a common finding in the reviewed prior empirical research, see for example LOWINSKI ET AL. (2004). BHATTACHARYA and DAOUK (2002) analyzed the effect of insider trading laws on the cost of capital across countries and rated countries from 0 (worst) to 5 (best) in terms of shareholder rights. While the United States was ranked with a 5, Germany was included in the group with a 1 ranking.

55 Insignificant negative CARs for longer event windows centered on the announcement date were also observed in older event studies. For example, for their subsample of 14 acquisitions of U.S. targets by German acquirers during the period 1983 to 1992, CAKICI ET AL. (1996) report an insignificant CAR of -1.78 percent for the [-10,10] event window.

56 See MITCHELL ET AL. (2004).

57 With the exception of LOWINSKI ET AL. (2004), none of the reviewed studies of cross-border transactions in Chapter 4 provided the split of positive and negative CARs for the observed event windows. LOWINSKI ET AL. (2004) noted with 54 percent transactions with positive CARs a fairly similar split.

58 See for example TAYLOR (2001), p. 52; TIERNEY (2000), p. 24. These authors pointed out that two years after the announcement of the transaction the value of *DaimlerChrysler AG*'s shares was lower than that of *Daimler-Benz AG* alone before the merger.

Figure 5.3: CAR for each transaction within the [-1,1] event window

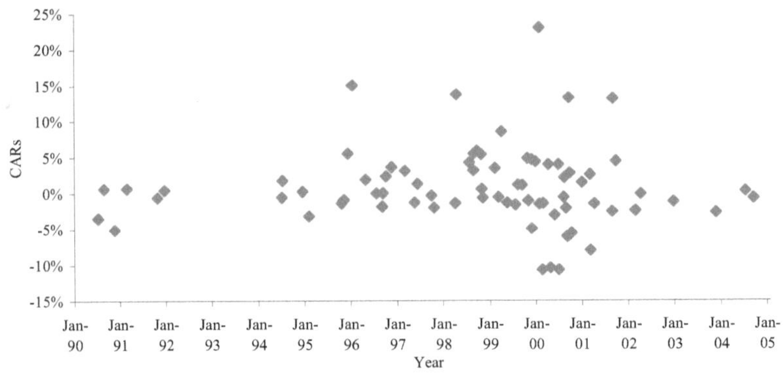

In addition to the cumulative abnormal returns for the [-1,1] event window, Table 5.13 also displays the statistical distribution of these values for the [-1,10] event window, which are on average negative at -0.91 percent, though not significant. A further analysis of these cumulative abnormal returns reveals that they are largely driven by a small number of transactions of acquirers in the new economy. Given the "exuberance"[59] associated with the share prices of such companies during the period of the internet bubble and its subsequent burst, for the further analysis the sample is reduced by transactions of new economy acquirers. As a proxy, all acquisitions by companies that were listed on the NEMAX at the time of the announcement of the transaction are eliminated from the sample, in total ten transactions, which were pursued by *Brokat Infosystems AG* (three acquisitions), *CE Computer Equipment AG*, *EM.TV & Merchandising AG*, *Kontron AG*, *Nemetschek AG*, *SER Systems AG*, *Software AG*, and *telegate AG*. Of these eight acquiring companies, *Brokat Infosystems AG* went into insolvency in November 2001 and *EM.TV & Merchandising AG* went through a major restructuring in 2003. Except for two transactions in 2001, all others were announced in the years 1999 and 2000. Table 5.14 shows the cumulative abnormal returns for German acquirers excluding the NEMAX companies (n=68), while Table 5.15 displays the cumulative abnormal returns for the transactions announced by those companies listed on the NEMAX (n=10).

59 As labeled by the chief of the Federal Reserve Bank, Alan Greenspan, in a speech to the American Enterprise Institute on December 5, 1996, see FEDERAL RESERVE BOARD (1996). This quote was frequently cited in connection with the capital market's peak in the years 1999 and 2000.

Table 5.14: CARs for German acquirers excluding NEMAX companies

(n=68) **Event window**	**CAR%**	**Positive %**	**Negative %**	**Z-statistic**	**Z-statistic B**
Period surrounding the announcement					
{0}	0.44	62	38	1.2350	1.9468
[-1,1]	0.60	50	50	1.0874	1.9949
[-2,2]	0.00	53	47	1.1038	0.3938
[-5,5]	-0.42	49	51	0.9825	-0.0703
[-10,10]	-0.50	53	47	1.0180	-0.1303
[-20,20]	-0.70	56	44	0.9492	-0.1693
Pre-announcement period					
[-1,0]	0.68*	49	51	1.2928	2.8058
[-10,-1]	-0.59	41	59	1.0525	-0.1953
[-20,-1]	-0.75	46	54	0.9286	-0.4932
[-2,1]	0.33	49	51	1.1391	1.0375
[-5,1]	-0.04	57	43	1.0302	0.7078
[-10,1]	-0.23	53	47	1.0525	0.2357
[-20,1]	-0.39	50	50	0.9286	-0.1645
Post-announcement period					
[0,1]	0.36	50	50	0.9301	1.0141
[0,10]	0.09	50	50	0.9857	0.0062
[1,10]	-0.35	49	51	0.9572	-0.6091
[1,20]	-0.38	37	63	0.9532	-0.1845
[-1,10]	0.33	51	49	1.0208	0.5894
[-1,20]	0.30	50	50	0.9889	0.6700

This table shows the results for an event study analyzing 68 acquisitions of U.S. target companies by German acquirers during the period from 1990 to 2004, excluding transactions by companies listed on the NEMAX. Cumulative abnormal returns are calculated employing the standard market model, using an estimation period of 253 trading days prior to the event window [-20,20] and various DAX indices to measure market returns. Tests for statistical significance follow BOEHMER ET AL. (1991), while Z-statistic B is computed following DODD and WARNER (1983). * denotes significance at the 10% level (based on a one-tailed Z-test).

Overall, for the three days immediately surrounding the announcement of the transaction, the cumulative abnormal return for the non-NEMAX sample is smaller than that of the entire sample, but still positive at 0.60 percent. The even split between "winners" and "losers" remains unchanged for this subsample, although for the extended event windows the portion of transactions with positive cumulative abnormal returns is slightly higher than in the total event study sample.

A positive cumulative abnormal return is also generated by the NEMAX acquirers within the [-1,1] event window, which with 2.30 percent is substantially higher, though also not significant. Compared to the non-NEMAX companies, the share price reactions of the NEMAX acquirers show a stronger pre-announcement effect for the day immediately before the announcement. However, while for the [-1,10] event window the cumulative abnormal return for the non-NEMAX companies is positive at 0.33 percent (not significant), for the NEMAX acquirers the cumulative abnormal return is significantly negative at -9.36 percent.[60] None of the 10 transactions by the NEMAX acquirers yields a positive cumulative

60 It should be pointed out that the CARs for NEMAX acquisitions bear statistical significance due to the small sample size.

abnormal return during this post-announcement window, i.e. the substantial shareholder wealth gains observed in the short run event window are not materialized in the days subsequent to the announcement of the transaction. Apparently, the negative post-announcement cumulative abnormal returns observed for the entire sample are mainly attributable to the reaction of investors to the specific subsample of transactions involving acquirers in the new economy.[61]

Table 5.15: CARs for German acquirers listed on the NEMAX

(n=10) **Event window**	**CAR%**	**Positive %**	**Negative %**	**Z-statistic**	**Z-statistic B**
Period surrounding the announcement					
{0}	-0.05	40	60	0.0688	-0.1314
[-1,1]	2.30	50	50	1.1743	1.2450
[-2,2]	-1.76*	40	60	1.4522	-0.6198
[-5,5]	-10.07*	20	80	1.4307	-1.9452
[-10,10]	-12.62	20	80	1.2757	-1.9474
[-20,20]	-14.26	20	80	1.1377	-1.4388
Pre-announcement period					
[-1,0]	3.02*	80	20	1.3327	1.8528
[-10,-1]	-0.19	40	60	1.2006	0.3059
[-20,-1]	-3.41	40	60	1.1201	-0.1433
[-2,1]	0.89	40	60	1.2250	0.4148
[-5,1]	-1.47	30	70	1.1573	-0.0683
[-10,1]	-0.95	40	60	1.1182	0.1074
[-20,1]	-4.17	40	60	1.0804	-0.2635
Post-announcement period					
[0,1]	-0.76	40	60	0.5427	-0.4209
[0,10]	-12.43*	10	90	1.3403	-2.9823
[1,10]	-12.38*	20	80	1.4056	-3.0863
[1,20]	-10.80	10	90	1.1826	-1.8875
[-1,10]	-9.36*	0	100	1.3937	-2.0610
[-1,20]	-7.78	20	80	1.1970	-1.2410

This table shows the results for an event study analyzing 10 acquisitions of U.S. target companies by German acquirers during the period from 1990 to 2004. Cumulative abnormal returns are calculated employing the standard market model, using an estimation period of 253 trading days prior to the event window [-20,20] and the NEMAX index to measure market returns. Tests for statistical significance follow BOEHMER ET AL. (1991), while Z-statistic B is computed following DODD and WARNER (1983). * denotes significance at the 10% level (based on a one-tailed Z-test).

Analogous to the discussion of the results for the entire event study sample, the statistical distributions of the cumulative abnormal returns for the event windows [-1,1] and [-1,10] for the two subsamples are illustrated in Tables 5.16 and 5.17. Both tables highlight the fact that the scattered cumulative abnormal returns of the entire sample are significantly driven by the reactions of the capital markets to the acquisition announcements by NEMAX companies.

61 Subsequent divestitures of the U.S. target in later years, for example of *Henson Productions* by *EM.TV & Merchandising AG*, corroborate the short-term assessment of investors. However, it should also be noted that the negative performance of the NEMAX acquirers in the extended event window partly occurred during a period of a general down-side bias in the capital markets with the burst of the internet bubble; this effect cannot be fully controlled for.

Table 5.16: Statistical distribution of CARs for various event windows excluding German acquirers listed on the NEMAX

	Event window [-1,1]		**Event window [-1,10]**	
(n=68)	Positive CAR (%)	Negative CAR (%)	Positive CAR (%)	Negative CAR (%)
Proportion	50	50	51	49
Maximum	15.04	-10.75	24.08	-17.77
Minimum	0.01	-0.03	0.34	-0.03
Mean	3.84	-2.63	4.43	-4.02
Median	3.13	-1.45	3.55	-3.12
Std.	3.75	2.79	4.41	3.89

Table 5.17: Statistical distribution of CARs for various event windows for German acquirers listed on the NEMAX

	Event window [-1,1]		**Event window [-1,10]**	
(n=10)	Positive CAR (%)	Negative CAR (%)	Positive CAR (%)	Negative CAR (%)
Proportion	50	50	0	100
Maximum	23.01	-10.44	n/a	-28.28
Minimum	1.45	-1.55	n/a	-0.16
Mean	9.35	-4.74	n/a	-9.36
Median	4.63	-3.07	n/a	-6.85
Std.	8.81	3.50	n/a	8.72

5.3.2 Results of the survey of executives

In inquiring about the general approach of how they measure success of transactions, the CFOs were asked to specify which criteria they use and to which entity those are applied (acquirer, target, or combination of both). Notably, the change in the company's share price, i.e. the creation of shareholder value, was deemed relatively insignificant or was not listed as a criterion at all.[62] Instead, growth of profit as well as of the closely correlated EBIT, and growth of cash flows were ranked as the most important measurement criteria. Those measurement criteria are predominantly applied to the combined entity, while 39 percent of the responses indicated that the performance of the target is still measured on a stand-alone basis. Figure 5.4 summarizes these responses.

62 However, as shown in "The Shareholder Value Network" by RAPPAPORT (1986), the main criteria identified by the executives are defined as value drivers that indirectly contribute to shareholder value creation.

Figure 5.4: Criteria for measuring transaction success

Rank	Measurement criteria	Mean*	Mode*	Skew
1	Profit growth	1.58	1	0.81
2	Cash flow growth	1.89	1	1.77
3	EBIT growth	1.89	2	1.96
4	Increase in market share	2.16	2	-0.21
5	Realization of synergies	2.32	2	1.04
6	Revenue growth	2.42	2	0.95
7	Risk reduction	2.84	3	0.88
8	Change in share price	3.32	5	-0.01
9	Other financial ratios (e.g. EVA, EBITDA)	3.76	5	-0.83
10	Other acquisition objectives (e.g. debt coverage)	4.30	5	-1.72

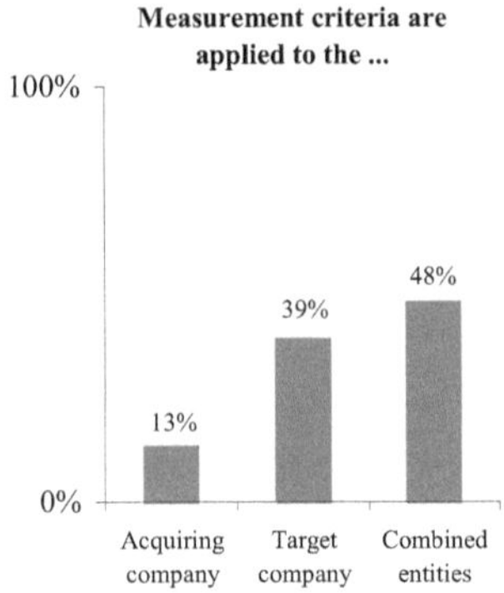

*: 1=very high; 2=high; 3=low; 4=very low; 5=not relevant.

While the vast majority of the executives noted that a period of at least one to three years subsequent to the consummation of the transaction is necessary to allow for an assessment of its success,[63] they do not believe that acquisitions of cross-border targets are on average more successful than those of domestic ones (see Figure 5.5). Hence, the CFOs reject the existence of a positive or negative cross-border effect.

Figure 5.5: Minimum period for measuring success and comparison of success between cross-border and domestic acquisitions

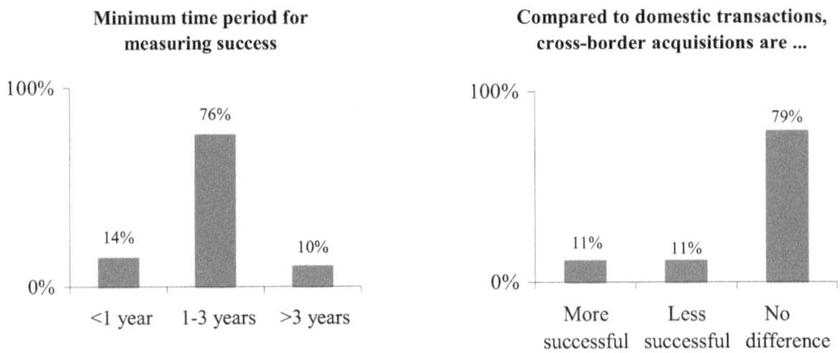

Based on these general principles of measuring success, a slight majority of the executives deemed their acquisition of a U.S. company either very or somewhat successful. Figure 5.6 displays the distribution of the survey responses among the five success categories. The on

63 Such an assessment can be found frequently in the literature, for example in SÜVERKRÜP (1992, p. 177) and BUONO and BOWDITCH (1989, p. 12).

average positive evaluation of U.S. transactions matches the overall observations in previous surveys of executives as shown in Section 4.4.3. Two assessments were provided for transactions by NEMAX acquirers. Similar to their cumulative abnormal returns for the [-1,10] event window in the event study, both transactions were not considered successful.

The assessments for the U.S. transactions closely correlate with the CFOs' evaluation of the total success of their prior domestic and cross-border transactions, given that 75 percent of those executives that deemed their overall prior M&A activity a success also considered their U.S. transaction successful, while 60 percent of those who did not view their prior transactions a success expressed the same conclusion for their individual U.S. transaction.

Figure 5.6: Success assessment for U.S. cross-border acquisitions

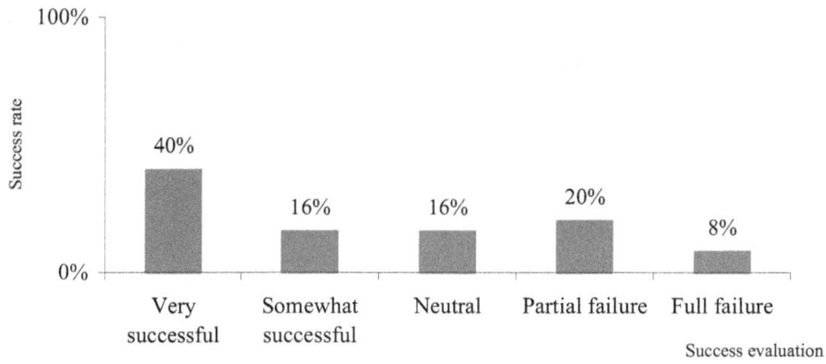

5.3.3 Comparison of the results

Given that some CFOs identified their company in the questionnaire, they allowed for 16 transactions a direct comparison of their subjective success assessment to the cumulative abnormal returns. As shown in Table 5.18, in only 56 percent of these cases both methodologies yielded basically the same conclusion. The executive evaluation differed distinctly from that of the capital market in three cases, given that for theses transactions the cumulative abnormal returns for the [-1,1] event window had an opposite sign and substantially exceeded two percent (in absolute values).

Table 5.18: Comparison of the event study and survey results

Event study - CAR [-1,1]*	Survey of executives - success assessments	Congruence	
+++	Very successful	Yes	
+++	Partial failure		No
---	Somewhat successful		No
++	Somewhat successful	Yes	
--	Neutral	Yes	
+++	Somewhat successful	Yes	
+++	Partial failure		No
---	Neutral	Yes	
--	Somewhat successful		No
---	Full failure	Yes	
---	Very successful		No
---	Very successful		No
+++	Very successful	Yes	
-	Neutral	Yes	
+	Very successful	Yes	
--	Very successful		No

In order to preserve the anonymity of the surveyed executives exact CARs are not shown; *: +, ++, +++ denote CARs positive at 0 to 1%, 1 to 2%, and more than 2%, respectively; -, --, --- denote CARs negative at 0 to -1%, -1 to -2%, and less than -2%, respectively.

A similar comparison for the cumulative abnormal returns for the [-20,20] event window produced with 63 percent a relatively stronger congruence between the results of the event study and the survey responses. Within that comparison, all transactions with non-congruent success assessments were distinctly different between both methodologies.[64]

Overall, the success assessment by the CFOs for 25 transactions is in conformity with the findings from the event study, especially when controlling for new economy transactions: on average, German acquisitions in the United States during the period 1990 to 2004 were a success. Hence, hypothesis H_1 ("Average success of German acquirers of U.S. target companies will be positive") is confirmed, although for individual transactions the observed success may vary significantly. Accordingly, uni- and multivariate analyses are performed to identify factors that positively influenced transaction success.

5.4 Univariate analysis of the determinants of transaction success

5.4.1 Overview

In order to test the hypothesized influences of the previously identified determinants of transaction success, dichotomous analyses are performed, in which both the event study sample and the survey responses are divided into two non-overlapping subsamples. The simultaneous influence of numerous determinants is assessed in the cross-sectional regression analysis in Section 5.5. For simplification purposes, for each subsample within the event

64 Results are not separately displayed.

study the cumulative abnormal returns for only two event windows are shown, which are the three day period centered on the announcement date, as it is the most commonly used event window in the prior empirical research,[65] and the [-1,10] event window, in order to evaluate the impact of the determinant on the post-announcement effect.[66] In light of the influence of the new economy transactions on the results of the event study sample, for each subsample the cumulative abnormal returns for all 78 transactions, referred to as "Panel A", as well as for the 68 acquisitions excluding the NEMAX companies, referred to as "Panel B", are presented. The cumulative abnormal returns for each subsample computed using the MSCI Germany index as the alternative market return index are provided in appendices B2 to B5. Only material differences between these cumulative abnormal returns and those obtained from employing the DAX indices are explicitly pointed out in the discussion.

Following the structure of the review of prior research in Chapter 4, first characteristics of the acquiring and target companies are analyzed, before various aspects of transaction structuring and management are evaluated.

5.4.2 Characteristics of acquiring companies

5.4.2.1 Absolute size

To proxy for the absolute size of the acquiring companies, the event study sample is divided based on whether the acquirer is included in the DAX30 index on the date of the announcement of the transaction. Table 5.19 shows the distinct differences between the two subsamples "DAX30" and "Non-DAX30".

Smaller companies, i.e. non-DAX30 companies, achieve significantly higher wealth effects for their shareholders than DAX30 acquirers, for which the observed cumulative abnormal return for the [-1,1] event window is only slightly positive (though insignificant). Accordingly, the observed overall significant wealth creation for the entire event study sample can predominantly be attributed to non-DAX30 acquirers.[67] As seen for the overall success of all 78 transactions in the sample, for this determinant of transaction success the inclusion of NEMAX companies also negatively influences the post-announcement cumulative abnormal returns. Once these companies are controlled for, within the [-1,10] event window shareholders of relatively smaller acquirers experience significantly higher

---

65 See Table 4.6 in Section 4.4.1.2 and Table 4.7 in Section 4.4.1.3. In this context, CONN ET AL. (2005) point out that the results for short event windows, such as the [-1,1], are generally insensitive to the model chosen for estimating the expected abnormal returns. Accordingly, using this event window allows for a meaningful comparison to other research studies.

66 In case there are noteworthy significant results for other event windows, those are mentioned in the discussions of the respective success determinant.

67 For example the study by MOELLER ET AL. (2004) noted also higher CARs for relatively smaller acquirers.

wealth gains than those of DAX30 acquirers. Given that most DAX30 companies have pursued numerous U.S. transactions during the observation period, it might be concluded that smaller companies do not immediately engage in a transaction once the opportunity presents itself, but rather only when the transaction opportunity fully matches their corporate strategic goals and is perhaps also considered being a relative bargain (so-called "cherry picking").[68] The analysis of whether frequent acquirers are more successful than non-frequent acquirers will shed more light on this observation.[69]

Table 5.19: CARs by size of the acquirer

Var. A	**DAX30**			**Non-DAX30**			**Difference test**	
Event	(1)			(2)			(1)-(2)	
window	CAR%	Z-stat.	pos. %	CAR%	Z-stat.	pos. %	CAR%	t-stat.
Panel A: All transactions								
[-1,1]	0.16	0.9495	48	2.73*	1.3449	55	-2.57**	-1.8391
[-1,10]	-0.13	0.9717	50	-3.18	1.0946	30	3.05**	1.6816
(n)	(58)			(20)				
Panel B: No NEMAX transactions								
[-1,1]	0.16	0.9495	48	3.17*	1.5562	60	-3.01**	-1.9367
[-1,10]	-0.13	0.9717	50	3.00	1.0474	60	-3.13*	-1.5562
(n)	(58)			(10)				

The table shows the results of the univariate analysis of the impact of the acquirer's size on the cumulative abnormal returns, including mean-difference tests. A transaction is included in subgroup (1) if the acquirer was listed in the DAX30 at the time of the announcement of the transaction. CARs are calculated as shown in Section 5.2.1.2. Tests for statistical significance follow BOEHMER ET AL. (1991). *, ** denote significance at the 10%, and 5% level, respectively (based on a one-tailed Z-test or one-tailed t-test).

Another explanation for these results might be potential weaknesses of the event study methodology, such as the possible impact of the "small firm-effect". The insignificant results of the DAX30 acquirers might be attributable to the fact that for them the announced transactions are not as significant and therefore trigger relatively smaller effects on their share prices.[70] In addition, for such companies the announcement of a transaction may be less surprising than for non-DAX30 acquirers, since for the DAX30 companies the capital markets, mainly institutional investors such as hedge funds etc., expect a worldwide growth strategy that includes cross-border acquisitions. Hence, at the time of the announcement of the U.S. transaction, the share price may have already incorporated the external growth strategy.[71] As a result, the cumulative abnormal returns for the DAX30 companies may be pulled towards zero compared to the non-DAX30 subsample.[72]

---

68 In this context it should be noted that data with regard to which entity initiated the transaction was not available for this sample; the results of the survey of executives in Section 5.4.4.6 provide some conclusions on this presumed influence.

69 See Section 5.4.2.5.

70 The simultaneous effect of whether the acquirer is a DAX30 company and whether the transaction is relatively large in size is analyzed in Section 5.5.2.

71 Or as mentioned in Section 4.3.1.3, the announcement of a specific transaction might be part of an acquisition program that was previously announced.

72 Similar findings involving large U.S. acquirers in both domestic and cross-border transactions were also observed in the study by MOELLER ET AL. (2004).

The results of the survey responses are in distinct contrast to the respective findings of the event study. Within the survey, DAX30 acquirers consider themselves with a relative success rate of 69 percent more successful than non-DAX30 public companies, for which the majority of the transactions were deemed a failure, as shown in Figure 5.7.

For private acquirers the assessments were equally balanced. Apparently, for private companies the absence of growth expectations and pressure from the capital markets does not translate into a more cautious M&A activity that allows for better "cherry picking" while screening potential acquisition opportunities. However, the low sample size and statistical significance do not allow for a final conclusion on the impact of the acquirer's status and its absolute size on the transaction success.

Figure 5.7: Correlation between status of the acquirer and transaction success

	Status of the acquirer			
Success?	**Private**	**DAX30**	**Non-DAX30**	Sum
Yes	2	9	3	14
No	2	4	5	11
Sum	4	13	8	25

(p-value:0.3613)

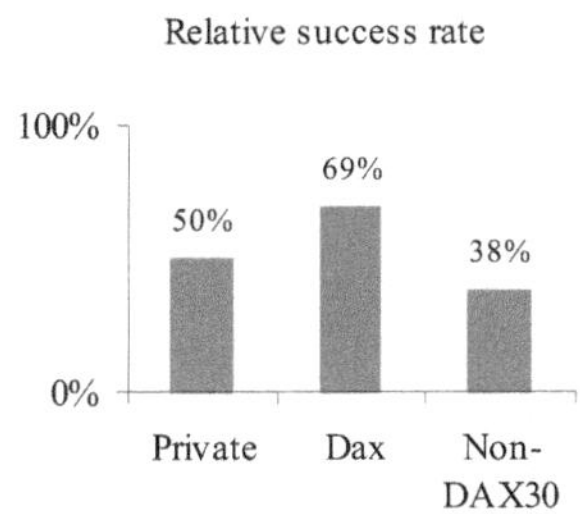

Overall, different conclusions are drawn based on the applied methodology for measuring success. However, in light of the statistically significant observations in the event study, hypothesis H_3 ("Average success of German acquirers of U.S. target companies will be unaffected by the size of the acquirer") is rejected.

5.4.2.2 Financial condition

As defined in Section 5.2.1.4, the financial condition of the acquiring company is measured based on its liquidity and cash-to-assets ratio. With regard to the liquidity ratio, the event study sample is split based on the overall average ratio of all acquiring companies during the observation period.[73] The results in Table 5.20 reveal that acquirers with a relatively high

[73] Based on the financial information for acquirers in 67 transactions, the mean ratio of current assets to current liabilities amounted to 1.83.

liquidity ratio, i.e. a stronger financial position, generate higher cumulative abnormal returns for their shareholders from the announcement of the transaction.[74]

Table 5.20: CARs by liquidity ratio

Var. Ba	**<Mean liquidity**			**≥Mean liquidity**			**Difference test**	
Event	(1)			(2)			(1)-(2)	
window	CAR%	Z-stat.	pos. %	CAR%	Z-stat.	pos. %	CAR%	t-stat.
Panel A: All transactions								
[-1,1]	0.11*	1.3205	51	2.12	0.9514	54	-2.01*	-1.6594
[-1,10]	-0.45	1.0176	46	-0.54	0.9727	46	0.09	0.0637
(n)	(39)			(28)				
Panel B: No NEMAX transactions								
[-1,1]	-0.01	1.1663	50	1.01	0.6580	50	-1.02	-1.0222
[-1,10]	-0.46	0.9568	47	0.94	0.6763	54	-1.40	-1.0545
(n)	(38)			(24)				

The table shows the results of the univariate analysis of the impact of the acquirer's financial position on the cumulative abnormal returns, including mean-difference tests. A transaction is included in subgroup (1) if the acquirer's ratio of current assets to its current liabilities on the balance sheet date preceding the announcement date of the transaction was below the mean ratio of all acquiring companies during the observation period. CARs are calculated as shown in Section 5.2.1.2. Tests for statistical significance follow BOEHMER ET AL. (1991).
* denotes significance at the 10% level (based on a one-tailed Z-test or one-tailed t-test).

For the cash-to-assets ratio the event study sample is separated using a cut-off ratio of 10 percent.[75] The results show that acquirers with a relatively stronger cash position yield higher cumulative abnormal returns, though the difference between both subsamples is not significant (see Table 5.21). It should be noted that for variables Ba and Bb within Panel B, acquirers in subsample (2) used shares as a form of payment in only one transaction.

Table 5.21: CARs by cash-to-assets ratio

Var. Bb	**<10%**			**≥10%**			**Difference test**	
Event	(1)			(2)			(1)-(2)	
window	CAR%	Z-stat.	pos. %	CAR%	Z-stat.	pos. %	CAR%	t-stat.
Panel A: All transactions								
[-1,1]	0.73	0.8083	48	1.29	1.2128	60	-0.56	-0.3965
[-1,10]	-0.87	0.9476	44	-0.35	1.0207	44	-0.52	-0.3267
(n)	(48)			(25)				
Panel B: No NEMAX transactions								
[-1,1]	0.62	0.6968	49	0.77	1.1266	58	-0.15	-0.1136
[-1,10]	-0.06	0.8771	47	0.93	0.9627	58	-0.99	-0.6020
(n)	(45)			(19)				

The table shows the results of the univariate analysis of the impact of the acquirer's financial position on the cumulative abnormal returns, including mean-difference tests. A transaction is included in subgroup (1) if the acquirer's ratio of cash to total assets on the balance sheet date preceding the announcement date of the transaction was below 10 percent. CARs are calculated as shown in Section 5.2.1.2. Tests for statistical significance follow BOEHMER ET AL. (1991).

74 Again, the post-announcement effect for the NEMAX acquirers distorts the analysis of the entire sample, given that for Panel A the CARs for the [-1,10] window are negative, while the results of Panel B are essentially reversed (though not significant).

75 The respective financial information was available only for acquirers in 73 transactions.

Questions regarding the financial condition of the acquirer at the time of the transaction were not part of the questionnaire. Accordingly, results from the survey of executives cannot be presented for this determinant.

Overall, for both variables the observed cumulative abnormal returns for acquiring companies with a relatively stronger financial condition are on average higher than those for acquirers with a relatively weaker financial position. Therefore, hypothesis H_4 ("Average success of German acquirers of U.S. target companies will be unaffected by the financial condition of the acquirer") is rejected.

5.4.2.3 Valuation ratio

In order to test the relationship between the acquirer's stock market valuation and the generated cumulative abnormal returns, the event study sample is divided into two groups based on the average market-to-book value for all acquirers in the sample.[76] The results in Table 5.22 suggest that acquirers with a relatively low MTBV outperform those with a relatively high ratio. For the [-1,10] event window in Panel A the mean difference is highly significant at the one percent level.

Table 5.22: CARs by market-to-book ratio

Var. C	**<Mean MTBV**			**≥Mean MTBV**			**Difference test**	
Event	(1)			(2)			(1)-(2)	
window	CAR %	Z-stat.	pos. %	CAR %	Z-stat.	pos. %	CAR %	t-stat.
Panel A: All transactions								
[-1,1]	0.98*	1.3259	56	0.79	0.5351	43	0.19	0.1297
[-1,10]	0.43	1.1241	54	-3.46	0.9294	19	3.89***	2.4191
(n)	(52)			(21)				
Panel B: No NEMAX transactions								
[-1,1]	0.91*	1.3046	55	-0.28	0.4017	38	1.19	0.8025
[-1,10]	0.59	1.1392	55	-1.14	0.7796	31	1.73	0.9335
(n)	(51)			(13)				

The table shows the results of the univariate analysis of the impact of the acquirer's market valuation on the cumulative abnormal returns, including mean-difference tests. A transaction is included in subgroup (1) if the acquirer's market-to-book value ("MTBV") at the beginning of the year in which the acquisition was announced was below the median MTBV for all acquirers. CARs are calculated as shown in Section 5.2.1.2. Tests for statistical significance follow BOEHMER ET AL. (1991). *, *** denote significance at the 10% and 1% level, respectively (based on a one-tailed Z-test or one-tailed t-test).

One explanation offered by previous empirical research for this distinct difference between both subsamples is the "equity signaling hypothesis", i.e. those acquirers that offer shares as the form of payment for the transaction signal that their shares are overvalued, which causes investors to reassess the company's share price.[77] The composition of subsample (2) in Panel

[76] The use of the MTBV, or alternatively of "Tobin's q", as a proxy for overvaluation of a company's shares is widespread in the event study research, as shown for example in the study by DONG ET AL. (2003).

[77] See Section 4.5.2.

A seems to support this explanation: of the 21 transactions by "glamour" acquirers, seven were financed with equity, which approximately represents two-thirds of all transactions paid for with shares in the entire event study sample.[78] Of those seven transactions, companies within the new economy pursued six during the years 1999 and 2000. In addition, the findings also support the validity of management-related motives for pursuing transactions, since a high equity valuation may increase managerial discretion, allowing management to act out of overconfidence or hubris.[79]

Questions regarding the perceived market valuation of the acquirer at the time of the transaction were not part of the questionnaire in the survey, since not all companies in the mailing list sample are publicly listed. Accordingly, results from the survey of executives cannot be presented for this determinant.

Overall, the results from the event study confirm hypothesis H_5 ("Average success of German acquirers of U.S. target companies will be higher for companies with a relatively low MTBV").

5.4.2.4 Previous participation in the target

Less than 10 percent of the transactions in the event study sample were pursued by acquirers that had a pre-transaction ownership in the target company. As shown in Table 5.23, for the three-day event window a toehold stake was not viewed by the capital market as important in order for the acquirers to execute a more successful deal.

Table 5.23: CARs by previous investment in the target

Var. D	**No toehold stake**			**Toehold stake**			**Difference test**	
Event		(1)			(2)		(1)-(2)	
window	CAR %	Z-stat.	pos. %	CAR %	Z-stat.	pos. %	CAR %	t-stat.
Panel A: All transactions								
[-1,1]	0.91	1.2240	49	-0.10	1.1289	57	1.01	0.4631
[-1,10]	-1.02	1.1429	44	0.20	0.9078	57	-1.22	-0.4322
(n)	(71)			(7)				
Panel B: No NEMAX transactions								
[-1,1]	0.68	0.9962	49	-0.10	1.1289	57	0.78	0.4214
[-1,10]	0.34	0.9180	51	0.20	0.9078	57	0.14	0.0621
(n)	(61)			(7)				

The table shows the results of the univariate analysis of the impact of the acquirer's previous investment in the target on the cumulative abnormal returns, including mean-difference tests. A transaction is included in subgroup (1) if the acquirer did not own a previous stake in the target company. CARs are calculated as shown in Section 5.2.1.2. Tests for statistical significance follow BOEHMER ET AL. (1991).

78 See Section 5.4.4.2.
79 See Section 2.3.3.3.

The same conclusions apply to the longer post-announcement event window, once NEMAX-listed acquiring companies are controlled for, though as in Panel A the mean differences are insignificant.

Within the survey, a previous participation was held in two transactions, i.e. the portion of acquirers with toehold stakes is equally low in the samples for both methodologies. The success rates of both subsamples are reversed in the survey responses, given that both transactions with a prior participation were deemed a success by the CFOs (see Figure 5.8). However, in light of the low sample size for this category not too much weight is placed on this observation.

Figure 5.8: Correlation between previous participation and transaction success

	Previous participation?		
Success?	**Yes**	**No**	Sum
Yes	2	12	14
No	0	11	11
Sum	2	23	25

(p-value: 0.3033)

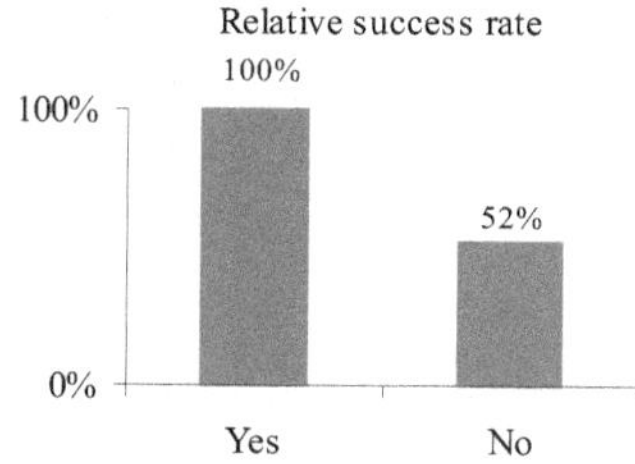

Overall, based on the tendency in the results of the event study, hypothesis H_6 ("Average success of German acquirers of U.S. target companies will be higher when a previous investment in the target was held") is rejected, although the mean difference tests are not significant for this determinant.

5.4.2.5 U.S. transaction experience

In order to examine the impact of the transaction experience on the cumulative abnormal returns, the event study sample is divided based on whether the acquisition represents a subsequent U.S. transaction by a company during the observation period. Subsequent transactions, which are with one exception carried out only by DAX30 companies, account for nearly half of the entire sample and result in Panel A in relatively higher share price reactions, but the sample means are not significantly different from each other (see Table 5.24).

Table 5.24: CARs by frequency of U.S. transactions

Var. E	**Non-frequent/frequent-first**			**Frequent-subsequent**			**Difference test**	
Event	(1)			(2)			(1)-(2)	
window	CAR%	Z-stat.	pos. %	CAR%	Z-stat.	pos. %	CAR%	t-stat.
Panel A: All transactions								
[-1,1]	0.71	1.2174	49	0.94	0.9278	51	-0.23	-0.1789
[-1,10]	-1.45	1.0450	37	-0.32	0.9406	54	-1.13	-0.7031
(n)	(41)			(37)				
Panel B: No NEMAX transactions								
[-1,1]	0.61	0.8503	50	0.60	0.8063	50	0.01	0.0096
[-1,10]	0.40	0.8423	47	0.26	0.8401	56	0.14	0.0946
(n)	(32)			(36)				

The table shows the results of the univariate analysis of the impact of the acquirer's U.S. acquisition experience on the cumulative abnormal returns, including mean-difference tests. A transaction is included in subgroup (1) if it either reflects the acquirer's first or only acquisition of a U.S. target during the observation period. CARs are calculated as shown in Section 5.2.1.2. Tests for statistical significance follow BOEHMER ET AL. (1991).

Excluding the NEMAX transactions reveals quite balanced results between the subsamples. Essentially similar conclusions are drawn when only the first (n=14) and subsequent transactions (n=36) of the frequent acquirers in Panel B are compared.[80] Apparently, for subsequent transactions, the capital markets do not seem to assign additional value to potential advantages that might result from U.S. specific acquisition experience.[81] As mentioned earlier, the findings might be distorted though by the fact that subsequent acquisitions could be part of an announced growth initiative and therefore do not induce significant share price reactions any longer.[82]

Simultaneously controlling for the size of frequent acquirers yields results that are congruent with the earlier findings (see Table 5.25). Non-DAX30 companies significantly outperform their complementary subsample of DAX30 acquirers, when including only those companies in the analysis that carried out solely one U.S. acquisition during the observation period. The higher CARs for subsample (2) support the conclusion that these companies seem to focus more on "cherry picking" rather than on an overall external growth strategy, as it is assumed to be the case for DAX30 companies.

80 CARs are not separately displayed. These findings are line with those by FULLER ET AL. (2002), but contradict observations in an older study by ASQUITH ET AL. (1983), who argued that the first transaction should capture the highest wealth effects.

81 However, a final conclusion on whether transactions by frequent German acquirers yield different shareholder wealth effects than those by non-frequent acquirers would require analyzing all transactions of such acquirers, and not just the U.S. acquisitions.

82 In order to validate the existence of this argument it would be necessary to compute the abnormal returns for the dates of the announcement of such programs. However, such an analysis is outside the scope of this study.

Table 5.25: CARs for non-frequent acquirers by size of the acquirer

Var. E	**DAX30**			**Non-DAX30**			**Difference test**	
Event	(1)			(2)			(1)-(2)	
window	CAR%	Z-stat.	pos. %	CAR%	Z-stat.	pos. %	CAR%	t-stat.
Panel A: All transactions								
[-1,1]	-0.47	0.6904	56	2.04	1.2458	56	-2.51	-0.9013
[-1,10]	-2.59 **	2.2726	33	-3.04	1.2505	31	0.45	0.1526
(n)	(9)			(16)				
Panel B: No NEMAX transactions								
[-1,1]	-0.47	0.6904	56	1.85**	1.6588	56	-2.32	-1.0609
[-1,10]	-2.59 **	2.2726	33	0.65*	1.6414	56	-3.24*	-1.3842
(n)	(9)			(9)				

The table shows the results of the univariate analysis of the impact of the acquirer's size on the cumulative abnormal returns for the first or only transaction in the United States, including mean-difference tests. A transaction, either an acquirer's first or only one during the observation period, is included in subgroup (1) if the acquirer was listed in the DAX30 at the time of the announcement of the transaction. CARs are calculated as shown in Section 5.2.1.2. Tests for statistical significance follow BOEHMER ET AL. (1991). *, ** denote significance at the 10% and 5% level, respectively (based on a one-tailed Z-test or one-tailed t-test).

The survey responses reveal a significant correlation between the acquirer's general transaction experience and the evaluation of the success of the specific U.S. acquisition, as shown in Figure 5.9. 68 percent of those acquirers with more than ten transactions during the observation period deemed themselves successful.[83] These results confirm the assessments by practitioners reported in the majority of the reviewed prior studies by consulting firms.[84]

Figure 5.9: Correlation between transaction experience and transaction success

Success?	Previous transactions **<10**	**>10**	Sum
Yes	1	13	14
No	5	6	11
Sum	6	19	25

(p-value: 0.0391)*

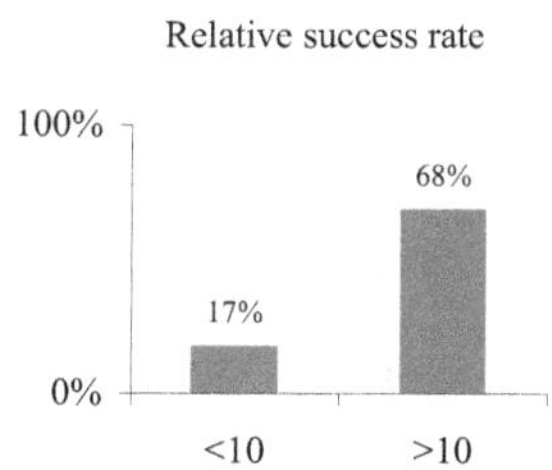

* denotes statistical significance based on Fisher's exact test.

Further differentiating the prior experience by geographic focus of the M&A activity does not yield significant results. For those companies in the response sample for which cross-border transactions represent more than 50 percent of their prior M&A activity,[85] the CFOs deemed their U.S. transaction on average successful.

83 Of these frequent acquirers, 90 percent closed more than 20 transactions during the period from 1990 to 2004.

84 For example in the survey of mid-size German acquirers by KPMG (2005).

85 Interestingly, this portion amounts to 88 percent, which reflects the importance of cross-border M&A activity for German companies, regardless whether listed on the DAX30 or not.

Figure 5.10: Correlation between portion of cross-border transactions in prior acquisition experience and transaction success

	Cross-border portion			
Success?	**<25%**	**25-50%**	>**50%**	Sum
Yes	0	1	13	14
No	1	1	9	11
Sum	1	2	22	25

(p-value:0.7099)

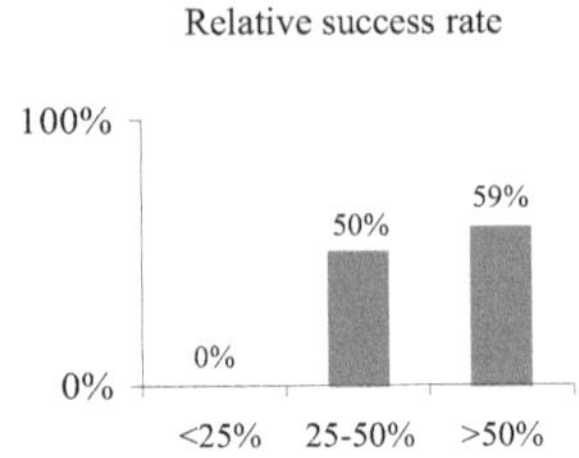

A slight majority of the acquiring companies already acquired a U.S. company before 1990. Accordingly, these companies are expected to have been able to benefit from their U.S. specific experience. The relative success rate of these acquirers confirms this expectation, though the observed correlation is not significant (see Figure 5.11).

Acquirers without prior U.S. acquisitions responded evenly with regard to their success assessment, thereby not allowing for a final evaluation of this determinant.

Figure 5.11: Correlation between prior U.S. experience and transaction success

	Prior U.S. experience?		
Success?	**Yes**	**No**	Sum
Yes	8	6	14
No	5	6	11
Sum	13	12	25

(p-value: 0.4296)

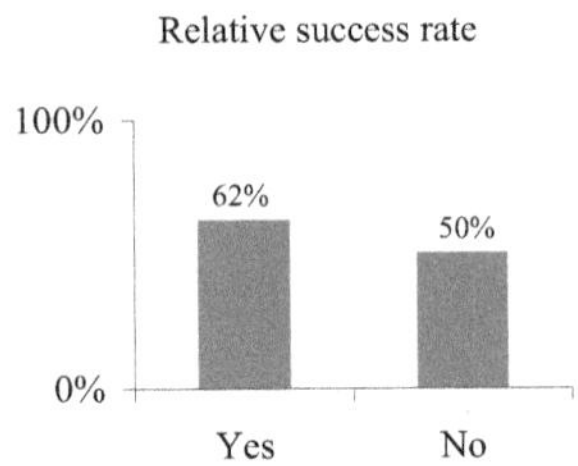

Overall, the results of the event study and the survey do not posit a significant correlation between U.S. specific transaction experience and success, accordingly hypothesis H_7 ("Average success of German acquirers of U.S. target companies will be higher for U.S. experienced acquirers") is rejected. In contrast, the survey responses indicate a significant positive correlation between overall (i.e. not only U.S. specific) transaction experience and success of U.S. transactions.

5.4.3 Characteristics of target companies

5.4.3.1 Industry classification

The cumulative abnormal returns for subsamples split by industry groupings are displayed in Table 5.26. With the exception of transactions in the technology and chemicals sectors, in all other industries positive wealth effects for acquirer shareholders are generated. Eliminating new economy acquirers from the technology subsample only marginally improves the cumulative abnormal return for the [-1,10] window, but substantially decreases the value for the short-term period.[86]

Table 5.26: CARs by industry sectors

Event	Financial services			Technology			Chemicals		
window	CAR%	Z-stat.	pos. %	CAR%	Z-stat.	pos. %	CAR%	Z-stat.	pos. %
Panel A: All transactions									
[-1,1]	1.41	1.2155	50	0.12	0.7405	53	-0.27	0.6201	41
[-1,10]	0.84*	1.3238	42	-5.77	0.9732	18	-0.70	0.7504	41
(n)	(12)			(17)			(17)		
Panel B: No NEMAX transactions									
[-1,1]				-2.81	0.6772	50			
[-1,10]		Same as above		-4.08	1.1789	38		Same as above	
(n)				(8)					

Event	Healthcare			Industrial & Automotive			Consumer markets		
window	CAR%	Z-stat.	pos. %	CAR%	Z-stat.	pos. %	CAR%	Z-stat.	pos. %
Panel A: All transactions									
[-1,1]	1.39	0.4424	50	0.81	0.7862	50	3.96	1.2553	50
[-1,10]	1.96	1.2591	40	0.70	0.6879	67	2.66*	1.2885	75
(n)	(10)			(12)			(4)		
Panel B: No NEMAX transactions									
[-1,1]									
[-1,10]		Same as above			Same as above			Same as above	
(n)									

Event	Others		
window	CAR%	Z-stat.	pos. %
Panel A: All transactions			
[-1,1]	1.66	0.9967	67
[-1,10]	-1.67	1.1800	83
(n)	(6)		
Panel B: No NEMAX transactions			
[-1,1]	2.30	1.1918	80
[-1,10]	3.65	1.2403	100
(n)	(5)		

The table shows the results of the univariate analysis of the impact of the target's industry classification on the cumulative abnormal returns. CARs are calculated as shown in Section 5.2.1.2. Tests for statistical significance follow BOEHMER ET AL. (1991). * denotes significance at the 10% level (based on a one-tailed Z-test).

86 Nine transactions by NEMAX acquirers were included in this sector. The remaining acquisition concerned a target in the media business, which was categorized as "Others".

Apparently, acquisitions by companies in the industry that was most affected by technological developments during the fifth merger wave were not viewed favorably by investors. Within the [-1,1] event window, cumulative abnormal returns are highest for transactions involving a target in the consumer markets industry, which may be attributable to the general strength and importance of this sector in the United States compared to Germany.[87]

Following the approach by CAMPA and HERNANDO (2004), the industry sectors in Table 5.26 are aggregated into regulated industries, i.e. the financial services, telecommunication, and utilities sectors, and non-regulated industries. The results in Table 5.27 do not show significant differences between both groups.[88]

Table 5.27: CARs by regulated industries

Var. F	**Regulated**			**Non-regulated**			**Difference test**	
Event	(1)			(2)			(1)-(2)	
window	CAR%	Z-stat.	pos. %	CAR%	Z-stat.	pos. %	CAR%	t-stat.
Panel A: All transactions								
[-1,1]	-0.39	0.2895	44	1.13*	1.4881	52	-1.52	-0.9874
[-1,10]	-0.09	1.1412	44	-1.13	1.1892	45	1.04	0.5198
(n)	(16)			(62)				
Panel B: No NEMAX transactions								
[-1,1]	0.28	0.3618	47	0.69	1.1671	51	-0.41	-0.3001
[-1,10]	0.19*	1.2830	47	0.37	0.9013	53	-0.18	-0.1017
(n)	(15)			(53)				

The table shows the results of the univariate analysis of the impact of the target's industry classification on the cumulative abnormal returns, including mean-difference tests. A transaction is included in subgroup (1) if the target was operating in a regulated industry. CARs are calculated as shown in Section 5.2.1.2. Tests for statistical significance follow BOEHMER ET AL. (1991). * denotes significance at the 10% level (based on a one-tailed Z-test).

A further analysis of the composition of the "regulated" subsample reveals that the relatively better performance of acquirers in non-regulated industries is primarily attributable to the shareholder wealth losses of four acquisitions in the telecommunications and utilities sectors, while the 12 transactions in the financial services sector generated significant shareholder wealth, as shown in Table 5.26.[89] Given the fairly small subsample size, the observations may only be seen as an indicator for the presumed negative impact of existing regulatory frameworks in certain industries. As mentioned earlier, in cross-border transactions such general adverse conditions might be perceived even more negatively by investors.[90]

---

87 Closely correlated to this observation is the impact of economic growth in the United States, which is assessed in Section 5.4.5.1.

88 However, for the [-2,2] and [-5,5] the t-statistics are significant at the 10% and 5% level, respectively, with negative CARs for transactions in regulated and positive CARs for transactions in non-regulated industries.

89 Compared to the previously mentioned CAR of -9.6 percent for the [-20,20] event window in the study by SCHIERECK and STRAUSS (2000), the CAR calculated in this study for the acquisition of *Bankers Trust New York Corp.* by *Deutsche Bank AG* amounts to -7.04 percent. The difference is attributable to the use of a dissimilar estimation period and market return index, while employing the standard market model.

90 CAMPA and HERNANDO (2004) show similar results for their sample of European cross-border transactions.

The split of the survey responses by industry groupings is displayed in Table 5.28. Similar to the event study, acquisitions of targets in the chemicals business are deemed on average unsuccessful. In contrast, with one exception, CFOs of financial services companies viewed their acquisition as a failure, while in the event study such transactions generated significant positive cumulative abnormal returns. For two transactions in the technology sector, the subjective assessments are inconclusive, while for all other sectors the acquisitions are considered on average a success.

Table 5.28: Success of transactions by target's industry sector

	Industry of the target							
Success?	**Financial services**	**Technology**	**Chemicals**	**Healthcare**	**Industrial goods**	**Consumer goods**	**Other**	Sum
Yes	1	1	2	2	4	2	2	14
	(20%)	(50%)	(40%)	(100%)	(80%)	(67%)	(67%)	
No	4	1	3	0	1	1	1	11
	(80%)	(50%)	(60%)	(0%)	(20%)	(33%)	(33%)	
Sum	5	2	5	2	5	3	3	25

Grouping these transactions into regulated and non-regulated industries confirms the findings of the event study of on average relatively higher success rates of transactions in non-regulated industries (see Figure 5.12).

Figure 5.12: Correlation between industry of the target and transaction success

	Regulated industry?		
Success?	**Yes**	**No**	Sum
Yes	2	12	14
No	4	7	11
Sum	6	19	25

(p-value: 0.2087)

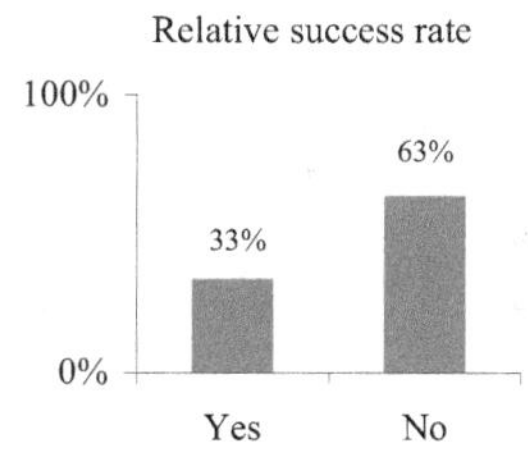

Overall, based on these findings hypothesis H_8 ("Average success of German acquirers of U.S. target companies will be higher for acquisitions of a target in a non-regulated industry") is confirmed, even though for both methodologies the evidence is not statistically significant.

5.4.3.2 Status

Analyzing the impact of the status of the target companies on shareholder wealth creation produces findings consistent with the majority of previous empirical research.[91] For acquisitions of private targets, the cumulative abnormal returns in both panels significantly exceeded those of public acquisitions, as shown in Table 5.29.

Table 5.29: CARs by status of the target

Var. G	Private			Public			Difference test	
Event	(1)			(2)			(1)-(2)	
window	CAR%	Z-stat.	pos. %	CAR%	Z-stat.	pos. %	CAR%	t-stat.
Panel A: All transactions								
[-1,1]	1.03 *	1.3445	53	0.47	0.8720	45	0.56	0.4353
[-1,10]	0.44	0.9881	51	-3.20	1.1381	34	-3.64**	2.2504
(n)	(49)			(29)				
Panel B: No NEMAX transactions								
[-1,1]	1.51 *	1.5591	57	-1.07	0.8257	38	2.58**	2.2691
[-1,10]	1.74	1.0247	57	-2.26	0.9430	42	4.00***	2.7918
(n)	(44)			(24)				

The table shows the results of the univariate analysis of the impact of the target's status on the cumulative abnormal returns, including mean-difference tests. A transaction is included in subgroup (1) if the target was a private company. CARs are calculated as shown in Section 5.2.1.2. Tests for statistical significance follow BOEHMER ET AL. (1991). *, **, *** denote significance at the 10%, 5%, and 1% level, respectively (based on a one-tailed Z-test or one-tailed t-test).

As pointed out in Section 4.5.3, there are numerous explanations suggested in the literature for the observed results: the (i) existence of a liquidity discount for private targets, i.e. the likelihood of higher premiums for public targets,[92] the (ii) more stringent SEC disclosure and procedural requirements applicable to acquisitions of U.S. public targets, and the (iii) potentially limited competition in private acquisitions resulting in a better bargaining position for the acquirer. Overall, investors do not seem to be convinced that tentatively higher prices paid for public targets can be overcompensated by the expected benefits of the transactions, such as the realization of synergy gains.

The results of the survey responses are diametrically opposite to the cumulative abnormal returns. As displayed in Figure 5.13, acquisitions of public targets were deemed distinctly more successful than those of private targets, though unlike in the event study the statistical inference between status and success is not significant.

---

91 For example in the most recent studies by CONN ET AL. (2005) and MOELLER and SCHLINGEMANN (2005).

92 According to a study by YAGO ET AL. (2000), the premiums paid for public target companies in the period 1993 to 1997 were even as high as 46 percent of the pre-offer target value. A study by KOELPIN ET AL. (2000) of multiples based valuations found that in the United States private targets sell for a significant discount compared to public targets. In contrast, ANG and KOHERS (2001) found that private targets sell for a significantly higher premium than public targets.

Figure 5.13: Correlation between status of the target and transaction success

	Status of the target		
Success?	**Private**	**Public**	Sum
Yes	7	7	14
No	9	2	11
Sum	16	9	25

(p-value: 0.1095)

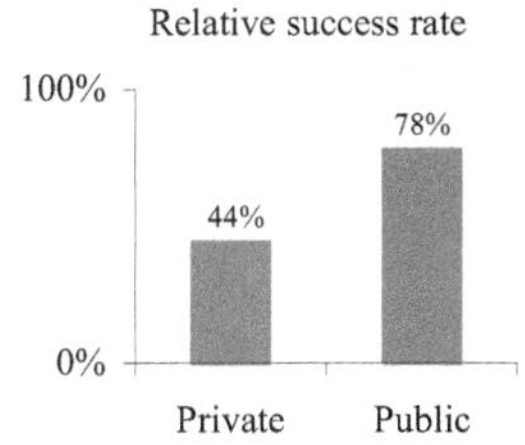

Overall, based on the findings from the event study, hypothesis H_9 ("Average success of German acquirers of U.S. target companies will be higher for transactions involving a private target") is confirmed, even though the survey responses do not provide support for this conclusion.

5.4.3.3 Absolute transaction value and relative size compared to the acquirer

Three variables are used for examining the influence of the absolute transaction volume and the relative size of the target company on transaction success: (i) a split of the sample by mega-deals, i.e. deals with a transaction value of at least \$1b, the (ii) absolute transaction volume, and the (iii) ratio of the transaction volume to the total assets of the acquirer.

A sole differentiation of the event study sample into whether the transaction is a mega-deal or not exhibits distinct results, as shown in Table 5.30.[93]

Table 5.30: CARs by mega-deals

Var. Ha		**<\$1b**			**≥\$1b**		**Difference test**	
Event		(1)			(2)		(1)-(2)	
window	CAR%	Z-stat.	pos. %	CAR%	Z-stat.	pos. %	CAR%	t-stat.
Panel A: All transactions								
[-1,1]	0.54	1.0564	49	1.50	0.9112	52	-0.96	-0.7063
[-1,10]	-2.14	1.1374	36	2.01	1.0422	65	-4.15***	-2.4352
(n)	(55)			(23)				
Panel B: No NEMAX transactions								
[-1,1]	0.14	0.6399	49	1.50	0.9112	52	-1.36	-1.1477
[-1,10]	-0.53	0.9094	44	2.01	1.0422	65	-2.54**	-1.6972
(n)	(45)			(23)				

The table shows the results of the univariate analysis of the impact of the transaction volume on the cumulative abnormal returns, including mean-difference tests. A transaction is included in subgroup (1) if the transaction volume was less than \$1b. CARs are calculated as shown in Section 5.2.1.2. Tests for statistical significance follow BOEHMER ET AL. (1991). **, *** denote significance at the 5% and 1% level, respectively (based on a one-tailed t-test).

[93] In this context it should be pointed out again that these findings may be in part driven by the fact that larger transactions generally induce a more material reaction of an acquirer's share price.

In both panels, mega-deals achieved substantially higher cumulative abnormal returns than smaller transactions, with significant mean differences for the [-1,10] event window. These findings are diametrically opposite to conclusions by practitioners, for example by LUCKS (2005b), who stated that "large-scale transatlantic M&A projects have a particularly low success rate".[94]

Breaking down the cumulative abnormal returns for non-mega-deals into more refined size groups does not produce clear results, as displayed in Table 5.31. In addition to mega-deals, smaller sized deals of less than $250m volume were on average shareholder value enhancing, while mid-size acquisitions, i.e. transactions between $250m and $1b, generated wealth losses in both panels.

Table 5.31: CARs by transaction volume

Var. Hb	**<$100m**		**$100m-$249m**		**$250m-$499m**		**$500m-$999m**		**≥$1b**	
Event	(1)		(2)		(3)		(4)		(5)	
window	CAR%	pos. %	CAR%	pos. %	CAR%	pos. %	CAR%	pos. %	CAR%	pos. %
Panel A: All transactions										
[-1,1]	7.23**	83	0.77	59	-0.96	40	-0.74**	35	1.50	52
[-1,10]	-4.85*	17	0.14	59	-2.30	27	-3.31*	29	2.01	65
(n)	(6)		(17)		(15)		(17)		(23)	
Panel B: No NEMAX transactions										
[-1,1]	8.54 [a]	100	0.73	56	-0.22	50	-0.69*	38	1.50	52
[-1,10]	7.11 [a]	100	0.48	63	-0.89	33	-1.75	31	2.01	65
(n)	(1)		(16)		(12)		(16)		(23)	

The table shows the results of the univariate analysis of the impact of the transaction volume on the cumulative abnormal returns; transactions are split into various subgroups based on their volume. CARs are calculated as shown in Section 5.2.1.2. Tests for statistical significance follow BOEHMER ET AL. (1991). a: since the subsample includes only one transaction, a Z-value cannot be computed. *, ** denote significance at the 10% and 5% level, respectively (based on a one-tailed Z-test).

Controlling further for the status of the target yields a more refined differentiation of the success of "mega deals". Table 5.32 shows that for companies in Panel B acquisitions of private targets are generally shareholder wealth creating, with those gains being positively correlated to the transaction size. Apparently for these transactions the capital market is more focused on the higher absolute synergy potential, rather than on potentially negative implications from a presumed higher complexity in the post-merger integration process for large transactions.[95]

[94] LUCKS (2005b), p. 11, who argued that particularly large transatlantic deals are generally driven by management-related motives.

[95] Similar evidence is offered recently for example in the study by LOWINSKI ET AL. (2004).

Table 5.32: CARs by mega-deals for private targets

Var. Ha		**<$1b**			**≥$1b**			**Difference test**
Event		(1)			(2)			(1)-(2)	
window	CAR%	Z-stat.	pos. %	CAR%	Z-stat.	pos. %	CAR%	t-stat.
Panel A: All transactions								
[-1,1]	0.49	1.0975	51	2.69	1.0569	58	-2.20*	-1.4805
[-1,10]	-0.79	0.9232	43	4.22	1.0170	75	-5.01**	-2.1726
(n)	(37)			(12)				
Panel B: No NEMAX transactions								
[-1,1]	1.07	1.2118	56	2.69	1.0569	58	-1.61	-1.1372
[-1,10]	0.81	0.9553	50	4.22	1.0170	75	-3.41**	-1.8290
(n)	(32)			(12)				

The table shows the results of the univariate analysis of the impact of the transaction volume on the cumulative abnormal returns, including mean-difference tests. A transaction involving a private target is included in subgroup (1) if the transaction volume was less than $1b. CARs are calculated as shown in Section 5.2.1.2. Tests for statistical significance follow BOEHMER ET AL. (1991). *, ** denote significance at the 10% and 5% level, respectively (based on a one-tailed t-test).

In contrast, acquisitions of smaller public targets produce on average losses for acquirer shareholders, as shown in Table 5.33.[96]

Table 5.33: CARs by mega-deals for public targets

Var. Ha		**<$1b**			**≥$1b**			**Difference test**
Event		(1)			(2)			(1)-(2)	
window	CAR%	Z-stat.	pos. %	CAR%	Z-stat.	pos. %	CAR%	t-stat.
Panel A: All transactions								
[-1,1]	0.63	0.7494	44	0.21	0.5136	45	0.42	0.1569
[-1,10]	-4.91	1.0197	22	-0.39	0.8502	55	-4.52**	-1.9497
(n)	(18)			(11)				
Panel B: No NEMAX transactions								
[-1,1]	-2.15	1.0461	31	0.21	0.5136	45	-2.36	-1.1641
[-1,10]	-3.84	0.8866	31	-0.39	0.8502	55	-3.45*	-1.5315
(n)	(13)			(11)				

The table shows the results of the univariate analysis of the impact of the transaction volume on the cumulative abnormal returns, including mean-difference tests. A transaction involving a public company is included in subgroup (1) if the transaction volume was less than $1b. CARs are calculated as shown in Section 5.2.1.2. Tests for statistical significance follow BOEHMER ET AL. (1991). *, ** denote significance at the 10% and 5% level, respectively (based on a one-tailed t-test).

In order to determine whether relatively higher costs associated with the regulatory burden in public transactions provide an explanation for these observations, the cumulative abnormal returns based on the relation of the transaction volume to the size of the acquiring company need to be assessed. Analyzing the impact of the relative size of the target company compared to that of the acquirer shows that in Panel B transaction volumes exceeding 30 percent of the acquirer's total assets create substantially higher cumulative abnormal returns than relatively smaller transactions, while for transactions in Panel A this relation is reversed

96 While the findings for large transactions involving private targets are similar to the observations by FULLER ET AL. (2002), for mega-deals involving public targets the CARs are essentially opposite. Other studies drew divergent conclusions, for example BEITEL ET AL. (2004) for acquisitions by European banks.

(see Table 5.34).[97] However, the difference is not statistically significant[98] and the sample size for the larger transactions is fairly small.

Using a cut-off ratio of 10 percent of the acquirer's total assets yields less distinct results. The cumulative abnormal return for the [-1,1] event window is comparably higher for relatively smaller targets, while for the [-1,10] event window this relation is reversed.[99] Overall, these findings for the event study do not corroborate the evidence from recent empirical research for example by CONN ET AL. (2005).

Table 5.34: CARs by relative size of the target

Var. Hc	**<30%**			**≥30%**			**Difference test**	
Event	(1)			(2)			(1)-(2)	
window	CAR %	Z-stat.	pos. %	CAR%	Z-stat.	pos. %	CAR%	t-stat.
Panel A: All transactions								
[-1,1]	0.79	0.9472	53	-0.24*	1.5148	42	1.03	0.6409
[-1,10]	-0.52	1.1311	47	-1.33	1.0116	33	0.81	0.3941
(n)	(60)			(12)				
Panel B: No NEMAX transactions								
[-1,1]	0.51	0.7893	52	2.20*	1.2912	50	-1.69	-0.8256
[-1,10]	-0.04	1.0424	48	2.93	0.7250	67	-2.97	-1.1668
(n)	(58)			(6)				

The table shows the results of the univariate analysis of the impact of the relative size of the target on the cumulative abnormal returns, including mean-difference tests. A transaction is included in subgroup (1) if the transaction volume represented less than 30 percent of the acquirer's total assets on the balance sheet date preceding the announcement. CARs are calculated as shown in Section 5.2.1.2. Tests for statistical significance follow BOEHMER ET AL. (1991). * denotes significance at the 10% level (based on a one-tailed Z-test).

A further distinction of the findings by controlling for the status of the target company does not provide evidence that for public targets a relatively large transaction volume translates into a higher burden from the procedural requirements that might negatively influence transaction success.[100]

Splitting the survey responses into various size groups produces results that are essentially similar to those in the event study, as highlighted in Figure 5.14. Mega-deals as well as transactions with a volume of less than $250m were deemed on average a success, whereas mid-size transactions were almost unanimously considered a failure.[101]

---

97 Apparently, the majority of transactions by NEMAX companies concerned targets with a relatively large size, which especially for the extended post-announcement period generated negative CARs. When employing the MSCI as the market index, in deviation to the results in Table 5.34 the CAR for subsample (2) for event window [-1,1] in Panel A is positive (0.36 percent, see Appendix B3.8)

98 The t-statistics are significant at the 10 percent level for the [-1,0] event window.

99 The results are not separately displayed.

100 While for acquisitions with a relative size of less than 10 percent the CAR in Panel B is -0.56 percent for the
[-1,1] event window, for the complementary subsample it is -0.37 percent. The mean difference test is not significant though (the results are not separately displayed).

101 A split of the response sample using the $1b cutoff replicates the findings from the event study, including its high level of statistical significance (p-value of 0.0421). The results are not separately displayed.

Figure 5.14: Correlation between transaction volume and success

Success?	Transaction volume **<$250m**	**$250m-$999m**	**≥$1b**	Sum
Yes	6	1	7	14
No	3	7	1	11
Sum	9	8	8	25

(p-value:0.019)*

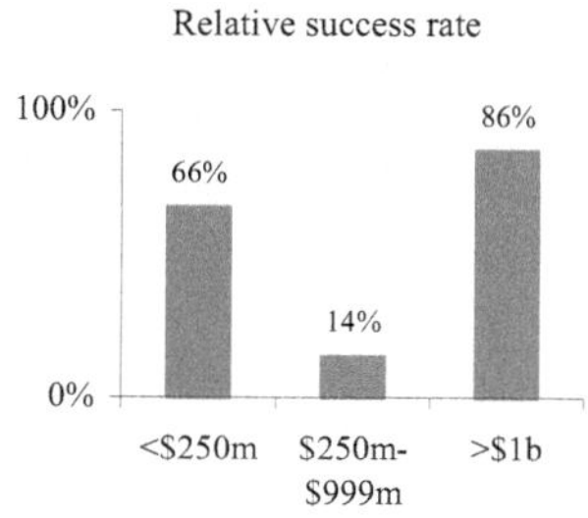

* denotes statistical significance based on Freeman-Halton's exact test.

When comparing the transaction volume to the size of the acquiring company, the directional influence of this determinant deviates from the observation in the event study. Acquisitions of target companies representing at least 25 percent of the acquirer's size were not viewed successful, contrary to those of relatively smaller targets (see Figure 5.15).

Figure 5.15: Correlation between relative size of the target and transaction success

Success?	Relative size of the target **<10%**	**10-25%**	**>25%**	Sum
Yes	7	5	2	14
No	6	1	4	11
Sum	13	6	6	25

(p-value:0.2483)

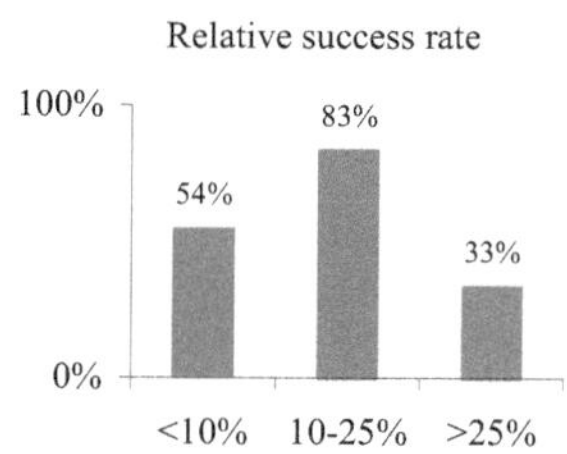

Overall, the results of both methodologies show that with regard to the absolute volume of the transactions, mega-deals tend to be more successful that mid-size transactions. However, when comparing the transaction volume to the acquirer's size, the results are less distinct. Accordingly, based on the available evidence hypothesis H_{10} ("Average success of German acquirers of U.S. target companies will be unaffected by the relative size of the target") is confirmed.

5.4.4 Characteristics of transaction structuring and management

5.4.4.1 Strategic direction

The results of the analysis of the influence of the strategic direction of the transaction notably do not confirm the contention that conglomerate diversification destroys value. For both panels in Table 5.35, the cumulative abnormal returns for non-related transactions are substantially higher than those for related acquisitions, with significant mean differences for the [-1,1] event window in Panel A[102] and for the [-1,10] event window in Panel B.[103] It appears as if for this sample of U.S. transactions the potential benefits from simultaneous geographic and industrial diversification dominate those derived from the synergy hypothesis.[104]

Table 5.35: CARs by strategic direction

Var. I	**Non-related**			**Related**			**Difference test**	
Event	(1)			(2)			(1)-(2)	
window	CAR %	Z-stat.	pos. %	CAR %	Z-stat.	pos. %	CAR%	t-stat.
Panel A: All transactions								
[-1,1]	1.99 *	1.3190	68	0.27	0.9772	42	1.72*	1.2993
[-1,10]	0.33	0.9433	52	-1.50	1.1153	42	1.83	1.0643
(n)	(25)			(53)				
Panel B: No NEMAX transactions								
[-1,1]	1.59	1.1086	68	0.13	0.7009	41	1.46	1.2214
[-1,10]	1.75	0.9497	59	-0.35	1.0116	48	2.10*	1.3756
(n)	(22)			(46)				

The table shows the results of the univariate analysis of the impact of the relatedness of the involved entities on the cumulative abnormal returns, including mean-difference tests. A transaction is included in subgroup (1) if the acquirer's and the target's first two digits of their primary SIC codes are not identical. CARs are calculated as shown in Section 5.2.1.2. Tests for statistical significance follow BOEHMER ET AL. (1991). *, ** denote significance at the 10% and 5% level, respectively (based on a one-tailed Z-test or one-tailed t-test).

However, splitting subsample (2) further based on a 2-, 3-, and 4-digit SIC-code identity between the acquirer and the target company generates more distinct results, as displayed in Table 5.36. In case both entities were fully related, i.e. a horizontal transaction was pursued, shareholder wealth was created on average. The cumulative abnormal returns for this subgroup in Panel B are positive for both event windows, contrary to those within the other subgroups. These findings are congruent with the evidence in prior research that focused

102 The mean difference for this event window is not significant when using MSCI-based CARs, as shown in Appendix B4.1.

103 Employing MSCI-based CARs yields significant t-statistics also for the [-1,1] event window for transactions in Panel B (see Appendix B4.1). LOWINSKI ET AL. (2004) note similar results for Swiss acquirers in cross-border transactions, unlike MOELLER and SCHLINGEMANN (2005) for U.S. acquirers. However, in his analysis of the resource-fit of acquirers and targets, BECKER (2005) points out that applying the SIC-code for measuring relatedness of two entities only reveals information with regard to the business sector affinity of both entities, but it does not indicate differences or similarities with regard to the available resources of the target.

104 In this context, BEITEL (2002) cites as an example for a very specific product diversification the acquisition of *National Discount Brokers* by *Deutsche Bank AG* in 2000, since nine months after the closing, *Deutsche Bank AG* sold the online brokerage business of *National Discount Brokers*, thereby solely retaining the target's market maker function for over 4000 shares traded on the NASDAQ.

transactions, in which the acquirers expand their core business, are positively related with cumulative abnormal returns.[105] Accordingly, the results in Table 5.35 and 5.36 provide simultaneous evidence with regard to the validity of both the synergy as well as the diversification hypotheses.

Table 5.36: CARs for related transactions

Var. I	**2-digit SIC**	**3-digit SIC**	**4-digit SIC**	**Difference tests**		
Event window	(1) CAR%	(2) CAR%	(3) CAR%	(1)-(2) CAR%	(1)-(3) CAR%	(2)-(3) CAR%
Panel A: All transactions						
[-1,1]	-0.62	1.82	0.58	-2.44	-1.20	1.24
[-1,10]	-1.46	-1.46	-1.55	0.00	0.09	0.09
(n)	(22)	(8)	(23)			
Panel B: No NEMAX transactions						
[-1,1]	-0.62	-2.15**	1.80	1.53	-2.42**	-3.95
[-1,10]	-1.46	-0.20**	0.95	-1.26	-2.41**	-1.15
(n)	(22)	(6)	(18)			

The table shows the results of the univariate analysis of the impact of the relatedness of the involved entities on the cumulative abnormal returns, including mean-difference tests. The transactions are split into various subgroups based on the SIC-code identity between the acquirer and the target company. CARs are calculated as shown in Section 5.2.1.2. Tests for statistical significance follow BOEHMER ET AL. (1991). ** denotes significance at the 5% level (based on a one-tailed Z-test or one-tailed t-test).

Since none of the CFOs in the survey classified the evaluated transaction as a conglomerate one, a direct comparison between the subjective assessments and the success observed in the event study is not possible. However, similar to the cumulative abnormal returns for transactions with a 4-digit SIC-code identity, focused acquisitions yield a relatively higher success rate than vertical ones, as displayed in Figure 5.16. The difference between the relative success rates is fairly minor though, hence the inference is not statistically significant.[106]

Figure 5.16: Correlation between strategic direction and transaction success

Success?	Strategic direction: **Horizontal**	**Vertical**	Sum
Yes	11	2	13
No	9	2	11
Sum	20	4	24

(p-value: 0.6366)

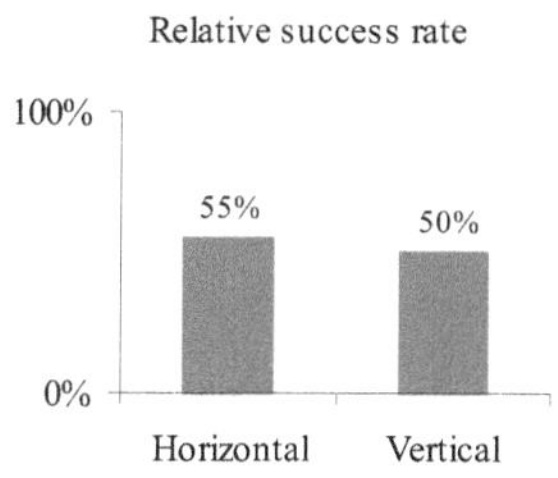

[105] Opposite observations are reported in older studies, for example by TRAVLOS (1987) and ASQUITH ET AL. (1983), which supports the presumed differences between the main factors motivating M&A activity in the 1990s compared to those of earlier merger waves.

[106] It should be noted that for one transaction no information regarding its strategic direction was given.

Overall, based on the findings of both methodologies the validity of hypothesis H_{11} ("Average success of German acquirers of U.S. target companies will be higher for transactions involving entities in related industries") cannot be determined.

5.4.4.2 Form of payment

Of 11 transactions paid for with shares, more than half were pursued by companies in the new economy with an above average MTBV during the period of buoyant capital markets, which supports the assumption in the finance literature that shares are more likely to be chosen as the method of payment if the acquirer deems its shares overvalued.[107] However, as shown for example by CONN ET AL. (2005) for cross-border transactions by U.K. acquirers, the low portion of transactions in the event study sample financed at least partially with shares provides support for the notion that in cross-border acquisitions sellers are frequently unwilling to accept equity of a foreign company.[108]

Table 5.37 provides the cumulative abnormal returns for the subsamples split based on the chosen form of payment. Analogous to the findings on the influence of the strategic direction of the U.S. transaction, the results for this determinant do not fully support the conclusions drawn in the majority of prior empirical research. While the cumulative abnormal returns for both event windows in Panel A provide opposite results, acquirer shareholder wealth gains for exchange offers in Panel B exceed their complementary subsample in both event windows. Although the mean difference tests for transactions in Panel B are not significant, the tendency of the results can be seen as an indicator that the capital markets do not generally view the choice of shares as a negative signal and that the premise of asymmetric information between the acquirer's management and investors about the acquirer's share market value does not necessarily lead to negative cumulative abnormal returns.[109] In addition, the results also hint at the importance of the different tax implications of the respective choice of payment, as discussed in Section 3.4.[110]

---

107 See Section 4.5.4.

108 See CONN ET AL. (2005), p. 823.

109 The analysis of the MTBV variable showed that high market valuations of the acquirers' shares led to negative CARs. However, only a minority of those transactions used shares to pay for the acquisition.

110 AYERS ET AL. (2004) point to the *Daimler-Chrysler* merger as a good example of the importance of shareholder taxation in structuring a transaction and quote the description of the merger discussions in the proxy statement filed by *Chrysler* on September 18, 1998: "During the course of these discussions and thereafter, representatives of Chrysler stated that it was important to Chrysler that any potential transaction maximize value for its shareholders, that it be tax-free to Chrysler's U.S. shareholders and tax efficient for DaimlerChrysler AG ... Representatives of Daimler-Benz indicated that it was important to Daimler-Benz that any potential transaction maximize value for its shareholders, that it be tax-free to Daimler-Benz' German shareholders and tax efficient for DaimlerChrysler AG.", AYERS ET AL. (2004), p. 883.

Table 5.37: CARs by form of payment

Var. J	**Cash**			**Shares**			**Difference test**	
Event	(1)			(2)			(1)-(2)	
window	CAR%	Z-stat.	pos. %	CAR%	Z-stat.	pos. %	CAR%	t-stat.
Panel A: All transactions								
[-1,1]	0.81	1.0552	52	0.90**	1.7150	36	-0.09	-0.0531
[-1,10]	-0.12	1.0523	48	-5.75*	1.3631	27	5.63***	2.5258
(n)	(67)			(11)				
Panel B: No NEMAX transactions								
[-1,1]	0.44	0.8749	51	2.68	0.8897	40	-2.24	-1.0435
[-1,10]	0.14	0.9654	51	2.74	0.8014	60	-2.60	-0.9431
(n)	(63)			(5)				

The table shows the results of the univariate analysis of the impact of the form of payment on the cumulative abnormal returns, including mean-difference tests. A transaction is included in subgroup (1) if the transaction was fully paid for with cash. CARs are calculated as shown in Section 5.2.1.2. Tests for statistical significance follow BOEHMER ET AL. (1991). *, **, *** denote significance at the 10%, 5%, and 1% level, respectively (based on a one-tailed Z-test or one-tailed t-test).

Simultaneously controlling for the form of payment and the status of the target reveals that cumulative abnormal returns to acquirers of private targets were significantly positive regardless of the choice of payment (see Panel B in Table 5.38). Similar to the observations for example by BRADLEY and SUNDARAM (2004) and FULLER ET AL. (2002), transactions financed with shares significantly outperform those paid for with cash in Panel B. As mentioned earlier, these findings might be explained by potential benefits from the blockholder role that the seller assumes in exchange for its concentrated ownership in the target.[111] Another interpretation offered by BEITEL ET AL. (2004) is that the German capital markets are still not as efficient as in the United States and therefore do not consider the valuation signal sent by the acquirer when using shares.[112] However, due to the small absolute size of the sample, these conclusions should be interpreted with caution.

Table 5.38: CARs by form of payment in private transactions

Var. J	**Cash**			**Shares**			**Difference test**	
Event	(1)			(2)			(1)-(2)	
window	CAR%	Z-stat.	pos. %	CAR%	Z-stat.	pos. %	CAR%	t-stat.
Panel A: All transactions								
[-1,1]	1.20*	1.2957	57	-0.43**	1.7503	20	1.63	0.7591
[-1,10]	0.85	0.9684	52	-3.20	1.2341	40	4.05	1.1989
(n)	(44)			(5)				
Panel B: No NEMAX transactions								
[-1,1]	1.28*	1.3621	57	6.45	0.8136	50	-5.17*	-1,7398
[-1,10]	1.22	0.9364	55	12.71***	108.1628	100	-11.49***	-3.0722
(n)	(42)			(2)				

The table shows the results of the univariate analysis of the impact of the form of payment on the cumulative abnormal returns, including mean-difference tests. A transaction involving a private company is included in subgroup (1) if the transaction was fully paid for with cash. CARs are calculated as shown in Section 5.2.1.2. Tests for statistical significance follow BOEHMER ET AL. (1991). *, **, *** denote significance at the 10%, 5%, and 1% level, respectively (based on a one-tailed Z-test or one-tailed t-test).

111 See FULLER ET AL. (2002), p. 1785.
112 See BEITEL ET AL. (2004), p. 130.

Using cash to pay for the acquisition of a public U.S. target generates on average shareholder wealth losses (see Table 5.39). These results as well as the low rate of transactions with positive cumulative abnormal returns in subgroup (1) do not confirm conclusions drawn for example by MOELLER ET AL. (2004) and BHARADWAJ and SHIVDASANI (2003) that only exchange offers for public targets generate negative abnormal returns. Analogous to subsample (2) for transactions involving a private target, the small number of transactions in this case limits the meaningfulness of the observations.

Table 5.39: CARs by form of payment in public transactions

Var. J	**Cash**			**Shares**			**Difference test**	
Event	(1)			(2)			(1)-(2)	
window	CAR %	Z-stat.	pos. %	CAR%	Z-stat.	pos. %	CAR%	t-stat.
Panel A: All transactions								
[-1,1]	0.06	0.7433	43	2.01	0.9982	50	-1.95	-0.6104
[-1,10]	-1.98	0.9808	39	-7.87*	1.5688	17	5.89**	2.1458
(n)	(23)			(6)				
Panel B: No NEMAX transactions								
[-1,1]	-1.25	0.9730	38	0.16	0.5994	33	-1.41	-0.4507
[-1,10]	-2.03	1.0017	43	-3.91	1.2349	33	1.88	0.5302
(n)	(21)			(3)				

The table shows the results of the univariate analysis of the impact of the form of payment on the cumulative abnormal returns, including mean-difference tests. A transaction involving a public company is included in subgroup (1) if the transaction was fully paid for with cash. CARs are calculated as shown in Section 5.2.1.2. Tests for statistical significance follow BOEHMER ET AL. (1991). *, ** denote significance at the 10% and 5% level, respectively (based on a one-tailed Z-test or one-tailed t-test).

The survey responses do not provide evidence for a significant relation between the form of payment and transaction success. The relative success rates for cash and share payments are almost equal, as displayed in Figure 5.17. Controlling for the status of the target does not produce more definitive results, given that for both public and private targets the relative success rate in case of share payments remains at 50 percent.[113]

Figure 5.17: Correlation between form of payment and transaction success

Form of payment

Success?	**Cash**	**Shares**	Sum
Yes	12	2	14
No	9	2	11
Sum	21	4	25

(p-value: 0.6043)

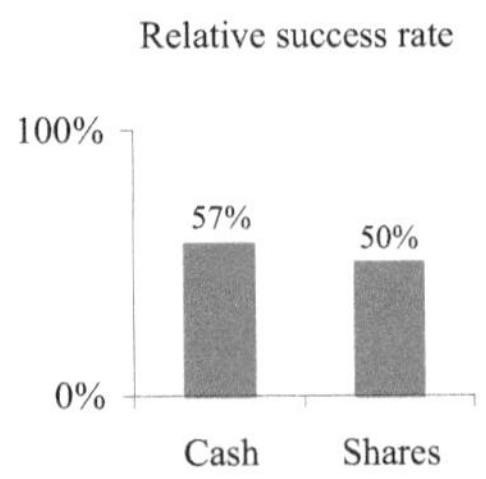

[113] Results are not separately displayed.

Overall, based on these results hypothesis H_{12} ("Average success of German acquirers of U.S. target companies will be higher for transactions paid for with cash rather than shares") is rejected.

5.4.4.3 Acquisition structure

Of the 78 transactions in the event study sample, only 19 (28 percent) were structured as an asset deal, which confirms the conclusion drawn in Section 3.4.2.3 that as a result of the seller's single level of capital gains tax, the majority of taxable acquisitions are structured as a share deal in the United States. As shown in Table 5.40, asset deals were less successful than share deals on average, with the exception of cumulative abnormal returns for transactions in Panel A in the event window [-1,10]. Although the difference tests are not statistically significant for both panels, the results provide an indication for a perception in the capital market that asset deals are more complex and more difficult to manage than share deals.[114]

Table 5.40: CARs by acquisition structure

Var. K	**Asset deal**			**Share deal**			**Difference test**	
Event	(1)			(2)			(1)-(2)	
window	CAR%	Z-stat.	pos. %	CAR%	Z-stat.	pos. %	CAR%	t-stat.
Panel A: All transactions								
[-1,1]	0.43	0.8072	42	0.95*	1.5813	53	-0.52	-0.3557
[-1,10]	-0.04	0.9963	47	-1.20*	1.3594	44	1.16	0.6167
(n)	(19)			(59)				
Panel B: No NEMAX transactions								
[-1,1]	0.43	0.8072	42	0.67*	1.3529	53	-0.24	-0.1909
[-1,10]	-0.04	0.9963	47	0.47	1.2125	53	-0.51	-0.3161
(n)	(19)			(49)				

The table shows the results of the univariate analysis of the impact of the acquisition structure on the cumulative abnormal returns, including mean-difference tests. A transaction is included in subgroup (1) if the transaction was structured as an asset deal. CARs are calculated as shown in Section 5.2.1.2. Tests for statistical significance follow BOEHMER ET AL. (1991). * denotes significance at the 10% level (based on a one-tailed Z-test).

Analogous to the event study sample, asset deals accounted for less than one third of the transactions evaluated in the survey. The subjective assessments essentially mirrored the observed cumulative abnormal returns, as displayed in Figure 5.18, though the correlation is not statistically significant.

114 For a general comparison of the advantages and disadvantages of asset and share deals refer to Table 2.1 in Section 2.2.2 and the discussion in Section 3.2.2.

Figure 5.18: Correlation between acquisition structure and success

	Acquisition structure		
Success?	**Asset**	**Share**	Sum
Yes	2	12	14
No	5	6	11
Sum	7	18	25

(p-value: 0.1016)

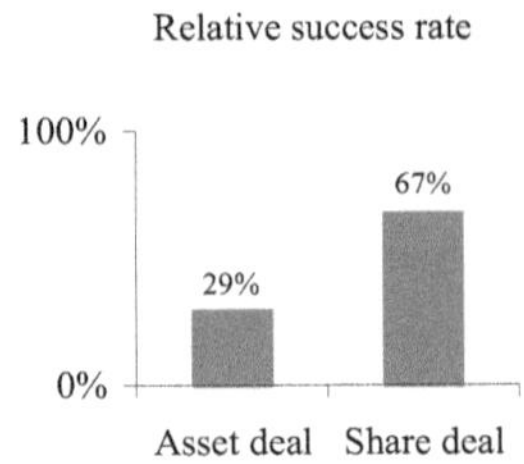

Despite the lack of statistical significance of the results in both methodologies, in light of the observed direction of the influence of this determinant, hypothesis H_{13} ("Average success of German acquirers of U.S. target companies will be higher for transactions structured as a share deal") is deemed confirmed.

5.4.4.4 Form of transaction for public targets

The analysis of the form of acquisition for public U.S. targets can essentially be approximated by the previous analysis of the impact of the form of payment on the cumulative abnormal returns. The respective subsamples for both determinants differ from each other by only one transaction, which was structured as a proxy solicitation[115] and grouped into the subsample "Other form" in Table 5.41, together with exchange offers.

Table 5.41: CARs by form of acquisition for public targets

Var. L	**Tender offer**			**Other form**			**Difference test**	
Event	(1)			(2)			(1)-(2)	
Window	CAR%	Z-stat.	pos. %	CAR%	Z-stat.	pos. %	CAR%	t-stat.
Panel A: All transactions								
[-1,1]	0.19	0.5074	45	1.34	1.1377	43	-1.15	-0.3774
[-1,10]	-2.18	1.0142	36	-6.40	1.1602	29	4.22*	1.5721
(n)	(22)			(7)				
Panel B: No NEMAX transactions								
[-1,1]	-1.17	0.8208	40	-0.56	0.8348	25	-0.61	-0.2204
[-1,10]	-2.25	1.0245	40	-2.34	0.9274	50	0.09	0.0300
(n)	(20)			(4)				

The table shows the results of the univariate analysis of the impact of the acquisition structure on the cumulative abnormal returns, including mean-difference tests. A transaction involving a public company is included in subgroup (1) if the acquisition was pursued via a tender offer. CARs are calculated as shown in Section 5.2.1.2. Tests for statistical significance follow BOEHMER ET AL. (1991). * denotes significance at the 10% level (based on a one-tailed t-test).

115 This is the acquisition of *Dial Corp.* by *Henkel KGaA*, which was announced in December 2003.

The general conclusions drawn from this determinant are essentially the same as for the choice of form of payment, i.e. on average an acquisition of a public company does not benefit acquirer shareholders, regardless of how it is structured. Although for all event windows in both panels the cumulative abnormal returns are insignificant, the observed tendency of the results hints on the one hand at the notion that for all types of public acquisitions the associated regulatory requirements in the United States create essentially a tax on the acquirer, which cannot be overcompensated by the potentially inherent economic benefits of the transaction.[116] On the other hand the SEC disclosure and filing requirements may facilitate a more profound release of information, thereby enabling investors to better assess the economic substance of the announced transaction.[117]

Only two transactions were structured as a direct merger between the ultimate German acquiring company and the U.S. target. Both transactions generated a positive cumulative abnormal return for the [-1,1] event window,[118] which is higher than for the remaining 27 acquisitions of public targets, for which the cumulative abnormal return for the [-1,1] event window is -0.06 percent.[119] The limited size of the subsample does not provide sufficient evidence though to draw a final conclusion on whether investors deem transactions pursued through a direct merger more beneficial.

An assessment of the survey responses would allow drawing a link to individual transactions in the sample and would therefore reveal the identity of participants. Accordingly, in order to protect their anonymity a detailed presentation of the findings is omitted. However, the observed results essentially confirm the above conclusions for the event study that no form of structuring a public transaction is more beneficial than another. As pointed out earlier, unlike in the event study, within the survey responses the overall success rate for acquisitions of public targets is positive though.

---

116 BRADLEY ET AL. (1988) provide this explanation for the observed underperformance of acquirers in their sample of domestic U.S. tender offers prior to the fifth merger wave.

117 LOWENGRUB ET AL. (2003) examined evidence from U.S. and German capital markets in order to determine whether differences in corporate governance matters impact the share price reactions to announcements of transactions. The authors based their study on the premise that "German executives can make misleading statements regarding merger activities while U.S. executives must either state 'no comment' or provide a truthful statement", LOWENGRUB ET AL. (2003, p. 1). As a result of a U.S. Supreme Court ruling in 1988, which stated that a company could be sued if it falsely denied engaging in merger negotiations, U.S. executives typically state "no comment" when asked if they are engaged in transaction negotiations. For example *E.ON AG* (formerly *Veba AG*) was sued for fraud by the U.S. SEC for allegedly misleading investors by denying merger talks with *Viag AG* only days before the merger was announced. Following the SEC's inquiry into *E.ON AG*'s denial, German regulators announced that the SEC inquiry is of no concern in Germany as denying merger talks was not in violation of German law. However, the authors did not observe price-relevant differences arising from the differences in corporate governance. The introduction of the Act Enhancing Investor Protection ("AnSVG") in 2004 provided new regulation in Germany that is closer to the U.S. rules.

118 These are the *Daimler-Chrysler* (CAR of 13.67 percent) and the *CE-Treev* merger (CAR of 1.45 percent).

119 Results for the [-1,10] event window and for transactions in Panel B are not separately displayed.

Overall, based on the results for this determinant in both methodologies hypothesis H_{14} ("Average success of German acquirers of U.S. target companies will be higher for transactions of target companies structured as a tender offer") is rejected, although the evidence is not statistically significant.

5.4.4.5 Inclusion of external advisors

While according to BEITEL (2004) the average inclusion rate for transactions by German acquirers during the period 1992 to 2001 amounted to 12 percent, for this sample of U.S. acquisitions advisors were involved in 62 percent of the transactions.[120] The higher inclusion rate in this sample hints at the presumed higher complexity in U.S. cross-border transactions, as mentioned in Section 2.5.5 and Section 3.8. Companies that pursued their U.S. transaction in-house, i.e. without the help of an investment bank, created on average higher gains for their shareholders than those that were supported by external advisors (see Table 5.42). Although the mean differences between the subsamples are not significant for both event windows,[121] the results indicate the possibility that acquiring companies have developed their own analytical capabilities similar to those of investment banks[122] and that the benefits obtained from the external advise do not compensate for the incurred additional fees.[123]

Table 5.42: CARs by inclusion of external advisors

Var. M	**No advisors**			**Advisors**			**Difference test**	
Event	(1)			(2)			(1)-(2)	
window	CAR%	Z-stat.	pos. %	CAR%	Z-stat.	pos. %	CAR%	t-stat.
Panel A: All transactions								
[-1,1]	1.71*	1.2938	63	0.27*	1.3305	42	1.44	1.1297
[-1,10]	-1.07*	1.3019	50	-0.82	1.1676	42	-0.25	-0.1523
(n)	(30)			(48)				
Panel B: No NEMAX transactions								
[-1,1]	0.92	1.2128	62	0.41	1.2030	43	0.51	0.4382
[-1,10]	0.46	1.1372	58	0.25	1.0112	48	0.21	0.1440
(n)	(26)			(42)				

The table shows the results of the univariate analysis of the impact of the inclusion of external advisors on the cumulative abnormal returns, including mean-difference tests. A transaction is included in subgroup (1) if external advisors were not included in the transaction execution. CARs are calculated as shown in Section 5.2.1.2. Tests for statistical significance follow BOEHMER ET AL. (1991). * denotes significance at the 10% level (based on a one-tailed Z-test).

---

120 It should be pointed out that BEITEL (2004) included in his sample transactions exceeding a volume of EUR25m; it could be assumed that the inclusion rate of external advisors might be lower for small-sized transactions. ALLEN ET AL. (2000) observed for U.S. acquirers an inclusion rate of 84 percent; apparently in the United States investment banks are an integral part of the acquisition management.

121 Significant differences at the 10 percent level were found for the [-2,2] and [-5,5] event windows, in which only the "No advisors" subsample displayed positive CARs.

122 Such capabilities are frequently centralized in corporate M&A departments, as mentioned for example by MIDDELMANN and HELMES (2005) for *ThyssenKrupp AG* or by *Lucks* (2005d) for *Siemens AG*.

123 These are some fees for transactions in the event study sample: *Dyckerhoff-LoneStar* \$6.7m, *Hochtief-Turner* \$2.2m, *Daimler-Chrysler* \$44.9m, and *Fresenius-National Medical Care* \$19.1m, see BEITEL (2004), p. 49.

To evaluate whether the cumulative abnormal returns are related to the choice of the advisor, subsample (2) is further divided into "top-tier" and "second-tier" groups, based on the listing of investment banks in the Top10-League table of Thomson Financial for Germany in the year preceding the acquisition.[124] The results reveal a more differentiated verdict on the benefits of external advice, as shown in Table 5.43.

Table 5.43: CARs by level of external advisors

Var. M	**No advisors**	**Top-tier**	**Second-tier**		**Difference tests**	
Event window	(1) CAR%	(2) CAR%	(3) CAR%	(1)-(2) CAR%	(1)-(3) CAR%	(2)-(3) CAR%
Panel A: All transactions						
[-1,1]	1.71*	-0.34	1.48	2.04*	0.23	-1.82
[-1,10]	-1.07*	-1.00	-0.45	-0.07	-0.62	-0.55
(n)	(30)	(32)	(16)			
Panel B: No NEMAX transactions						
[-1,1]	0.92	-0.17	2.03	1.09	-1.11	-2.20
[-1,10]	0.46	-0.83	3.29	1.29	-2.83	-4.12*
(n)	(26)	(31)	(11)			

The table shows the results of the univariate analysis of the impact of the inclusion of external advisors on the cumulative abnormal returns, including mean-difference tests. The transactions are split into subgroups based on the status of the included advisor, if any. CARs are calculated as shown in Section 5.2.1.2. Tests for statistical significance follow BOEHMER ET AL. (1991). * denotes significance at the 10% level (based on a one-tailed Z-test or one-tailed t-test).

While for the "top-tier" subgroup in both panels the cumulative abnormal returns are negative, for the "second-tier" subgroup they are not only positive, but also substantially higher than for the "no advisors" subsample in Panel B. The results suggest that advisors in the "second-tier" subsample, which tend to be smaller than their peers, may offer a more client-tailored and therefore better expertise for such particular and comparably rather infrequent transactions like cross-border acquisitions in the United States.[125]

A main advantage normally associated with the inclusion of external advisors is that it is a way for non-frequent acquirers to obtain external transaction experience.[126] In order to test whether for the previously identified non-frequent acquirers in the sample the inclusion of advisors generated additional shareholder wealth, the sample of transactions by non-frequent acquirers of Table 5.25 in Section 5.4.2.5 is split based on whether an investment bank was involved in the transaction or not. The findings are unambiguous, as shown in Table 5.44. The inclusion of advisors does not seem to make up for the presumed lack of experience

124 Thomson Financial compiles this ranking annually based on the deal value of the transactions the advisors were engaged with. The composition of this ranking remained fairly consistent during the observation period of this sample.

125 As mentioned earlier, SAUNDERS and SRINIVASAN (2001) observed that top-tier advisors charge generally higher fees than lower-tier advisors and that for the recurring involvement of the same investment bank acquiring companies tend to pay a relationship premium that is also highest for top advisors. This observation not withstanding, RAU (2000) points out a positive relationship between the ranking of advisors and transaction completion rates.

126 See PORRINI (2006), p. 91.

(with significant mean difference tests for both Panels). In contrast, cumulative abnormal returns are higher for infrequent acquirers when no external advisors were involved.[127]

Table 5.44: CARs for non-frequent acquirers by inclusion of external advisors

Var. M Event window	**No advisors** (1) CAR%	Z-stat.	pos. %	**Advisors** (2) CAR%	Z-stat.	pos. %	**Difference test** (1)-(2) CAR%	t-stat.
Panel A: All transactions								
[-1,1]	4.21*	1.3205	73	-1.28	0.9332	43	5.49**	2.2119
[-1,10]	-3.21**	1.8368	45	-2.62*	1.4581	21	-0.59	-0.2034
(n)	(11)			(14)				
Panel B: No NEMAX transactions								
[-1,1]	2.71**	2.2334	71	-0.59	1.0930	45	3.30*	1.5275
[-1,10]	1.25**	1.9136	71	-2.38**	1.7577	27	3.63*	1.5295
(n)	(7)			(11)				

The table shows the results of the univariate analysis of the impact of the inclusion of external advisors on the cumulative abnormal returns, including mean-difference tests. A transaction by one-time only acquirers during the observation period is included in subgroup (1) if no external advisors were involved in the transaction execution. CARs are calculated as shown in Section 5.2.1.2. Tests for statistical significance follow BOEHMER ET AL. (1991). *, ** denote significance at the 10% and 5% level, respectively (based on a one-tailed Z-test or one-tailed t-test).

89 percent of the surveyed CFOs declared that the inclusion of external advisors is generally more important in a cross-border than in a domestic transaction, thereby hinting at the potentially higher complexity of cross-border acquisitions. Despite this assessment, an investment bank was involved in the transaction structuring in only 64 percent of the surveyed cases (see Figure 5.19). Contrary to the evidence of the event study, according to the CFOs the inclusion of external advisors was on average beneficial, with a relative success rate of 63 percent. Since only a few executives identified their advisors, a further differentiation by the level of the involved investment bank is not possible.

Figure 5.19: Correlation between inclusion of external advisors and transaction success

External advisors?

Success?	Yes	No	Sum
Yes	10	4	14
No	6	5	11
Sum	16	9	25

(p-value: 0.3245)

Relative success rate

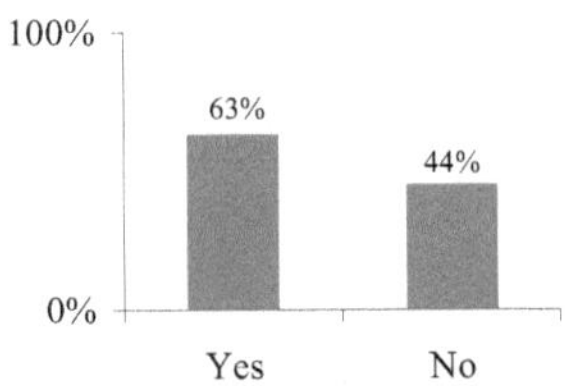

127 It should be noted though that the sample sizes are relatively small.

Overall, the results of the event study are not conclusive with regard to hypothesis H_{15} ("Average success of German acquirers of U.S. target companies will be higher for transactions without inclusion of external advisors"). The survey responses suggest a positive influence of external advisors, though the observed inference is not statistically significant.

5.4.4.6 Other aspects of the survey

Other determinants of transaction success for which no data was available for the event study sample but for which the responses in the survey produced some evidence comprise the motives for the transaction, the initiator of the transaction, the existence of multiple bidders in the acquisition process, the retention of the target's management, and the degree of post-closing integration of the target company.

When asked which motives drove the U.S. acquisition, the executives confirmed the prevailing dominance of the synergy, diversification, and market power hypotheses as endogenous factors for pursuing transactions. The majority of the transactions that were induced by those motives were considered a success (see Table 5.45).[128]

Table 5.45: Correlation between transaction motives and success

	Motives for the transaction					
Success?	**Realize synergies**	**International diversification**	**Enter U.S. market**	**Market share**	**Competitive advantage**	**Comparative advantage**
Yes	7	6	7	8	5	3
	(54%)	(50%)	(64%)	(67%)	(63%)	(50%)
No	6	6	4	3	3	3
	(46%)	(50%)	(36%)	(33%)	(37%)	(50%)
Sum	13	12	11	11	8	6
	Excess cash	**Personal reasons**	**Replacement cost**	**Increase efficiency**	**Tax attributes**	**Other**
Yes	0	0	1	1	1	2
	(0%)	(0%)	(100%)	(100%)	(100%)	(100%)
No	2	2	0	0	0	0
	(100%)	(100%)	0%	0%	(0%)	(0%)
Sum	2	2	1	1	1	2

[128] The questionnaire allowed multiple answers for this question.

The majority of the transactions were aimed at realizing synergies, whereby the enhancement of revenue was cited as the most important synergy category (see Table 5.46).[129] Interestingly, transactions for which the importance of revenue enhancements was deemed "very high" achieved a success rate of only 50 percent.[130] As could be expected, the potential to benefit from realizing overhead costs reductions was considered relatively unimportant for the observed cross-border transactions. Other synergies listed by the CFOs comprise "marketing activities" and "creativity knowledge".

Table 5.46: Relative importance of synergy categories

Rank	Synergy category	Mean*	Mode*	Skew
1	Revenue enhancements	1.69	1	0.66
2	Operational cost reductions	2.33	2	0.59
3	Financial	2.50	2	0
4	Differential	2.60	2	1.26
5	Overhead cost reductions	2.83	3	-0.41
6	Other	1.50	-	-

*: 1=very high importance; 2=high importance; 3=low importance.

Transactions were pursued in order to expand or preserve the market share of the acquirer in 11 cases, which essentially confirms the findings in the study by KPMG (2001) that executives consider gaining market share as the single-most important reason for undertaking global transactions. In the response sample these transactions experienced a relative success rate of 67 percent. Four transactions were carried out primarily on the basis of management-related motives, i.e. either for the use of excess cash or personal reasons. All four were deemed a failure. Other motives such as the exploitation of comparative or competitive advantages or the tax attributes of the target company were not considered being important.

The survey results reveal a significant correlation between the initiator of a transaction and success, as displayed in Figure 5.20.[131] Target companies initiated exactly half of the surveyed transactions, and only 33 percent of those were deemed a success. In case the acquirer proactively contacted the target, a relative success rate of 75 percent was achieved. Accordingly, transactions that are actively initiated as an outflow of the acquirer's external growth strategy seem to offer a higher likelihood of success than those that are presumably pursued once the opportunity presents itself.[132] These findings are in line with a study by

---

129 These responses are in line with the results of the studies by KPMG (2004a) and McKINSEY & CO. (2001).

130 These results do not confirm the conclusions in the study by KPMG (2004a), in which a focus on realizing revenue synergies was deemed being a key factor for success of cross-border transactions.

131 It should be noted that for one transaction information regarding the initiator was not provided.

132 A similar conclusion was reached by WIEANDT and SANTIAGO (2005, p. 94f.), who listed the consistency of the M&A activity with the overall corporate strategy as a key factor for the success of *Deutsche Bank AG* in the United States, as well as by STEINEBACH ET AL. (2005, p. 109), who based on *Henkel KGaA*'s U.S. experience noted that a good strategic fit "leads to a friendly approach that … can achieve a number of

KPMG (2005), which noted a comparably low success rate of 38 percent for opportunistic transactions. However, since the success rate in the subsample of transactions initiated by the target company is evenly split between DAX30 and non-DAX30 acquirers, the survey responses do not support the presumed differences between those subgroups in their strategic approach to transactions as discussed in Sections 5.4.2.1 and 5.4.2.5

Figure 5.20: Correlation between transaction initiator and success

	Initiator of transaction		
Success?	**Acquirer**	**Target**	Sum
Yes	9	4	13
No	3	8	11
Sum	12	12	24

(p-value: 0.0498)*

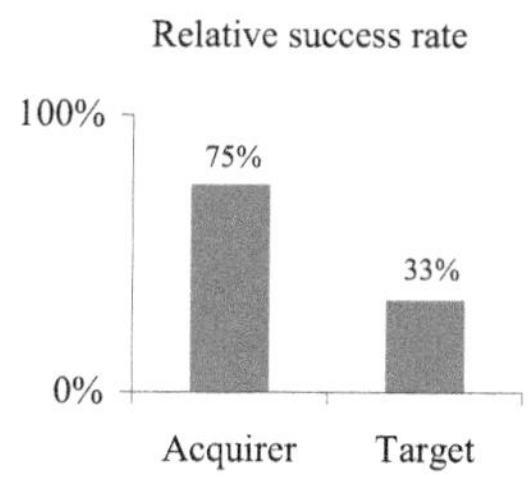

* denotes statistical significance based on Fisher's exact test.

The existence of multiple bidders in the acquisition process seems to negatively impact the transaction success, though the inference is not significant (see Figure 5.21). However, the direction of the results might provide an indication that in a competitive auction environment the acquiring company may overpay for the target, which negatively affects the success of the transaction.[133]

Figure 5.21: Correlation between multiple bidders and transaction success

	Multiple bidders?		
Success?	**Yes**	**No**	Sum
Yes	7	6	13
No	8	3	11
Sum	15	9	24

(p-value: 0.3001)

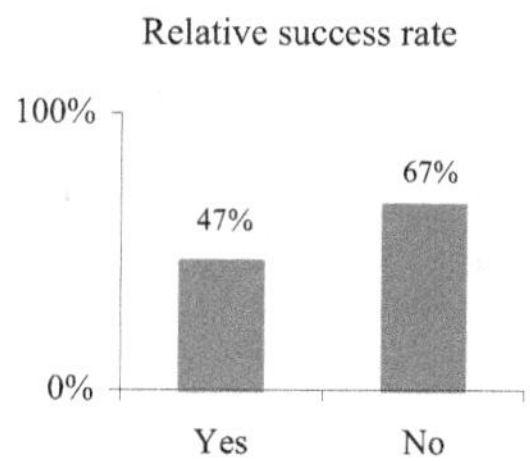

advantages such as getting a better insight into the acquired company during the due diligence and contract negotiation." These observations do not support concerns that companies initiating an acquisition would be required to offer the sellers in order for them to approve the transaction additional incentives, for example a higher purchase premium, which would adversely impact transaction success, see LORANGE and KOTLARCHUK (1994), p. 8.

133 BAMBERGER (1994) observed for his survey of German acquirers opposite responses and concluded that the existence of multiple interested parties in the target company signals its attractiveness.

Retaining the management of the target company subsequent to the closing of the acquisition did not significantly impact transaction success in the survey, as shown in Figure 5.22. In only 44 percent of those cases where entering the U.S. market was cited as a main motive for pursuing the transaction, was the management of the target company retained. This seems surprising given that it could be assumed that the knowledge and experience of the management would be deemed important to the acquirer. The vast majority of those transactions were deemed a success. Accordingly, retaining the business knowledge of the target's executives seemed to have been beneficial in successfully entering the U.S. market.[134]

Figure 5.22: Correlation between management retention and transaction success

	Management retained?		
Success?	**Yes**	**No**	Sum
Yes	11	3	14
No	7	4	11
Sum	18	7	25

(p-value: 0.3515)

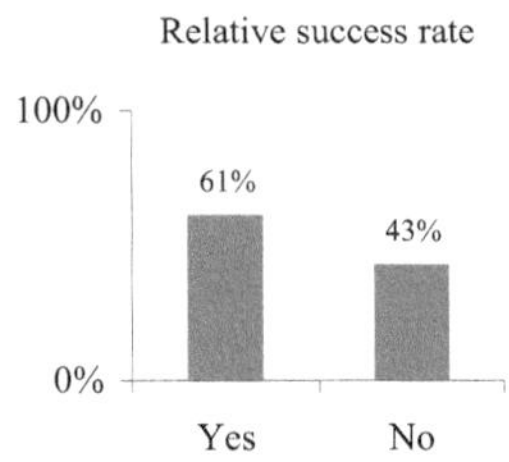

With regard to the influence of the degree of post-closing integration of the target company on transaction success the survey results are inconclusive and not significant, as shown in Figure 5.23.

Figure 5.23: Correlation between intensity of post-merger integration of the target and transaction success

	Integration of the target			
Success?	**Strong**	**Medium**	**Little**	Sum
Yes	6	4	4	14
No	5	4	2	11
Sum	11	8	6	25

(p-value:0.7925)

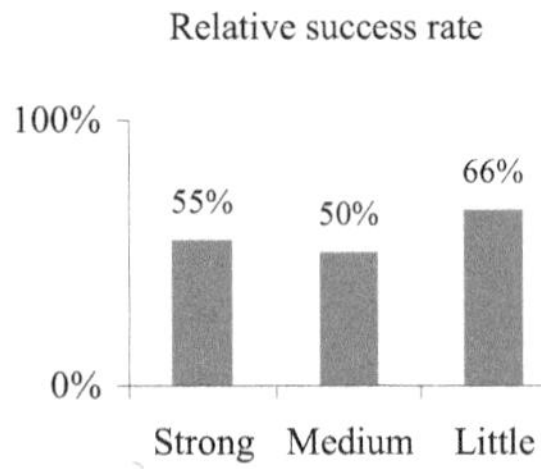

[134] Results are not separately displayed.

On average slightly positive success assessments were provided for transactions either with a strong degree of integration, i.e. a full integration into the acquirer's corporate group, or a low degree of integration, i.e. the target remains economically independent. Apparently, in case of a strong integration the opposing influences from the realization of potential synergy gains versus the potential losses from cultural frictions (and vice versa in case of a loose integration) do not seem to outweigh each other. Similar results were found in a survey of German mid-size companies by KPMG (2005), in which approximately half of the surveyed executives argued for a full integration in order for a cross-border transaction to be successful, while the other half viewed a loose integration as more beneficial.[135]

5.4.5 Influences of the economic environment

5.4.5.1 Relative strength of U.S. economic growth

In order to test the impact of the relative strength of the economic growth in the United States on the shareholder wealth creation, the event study sample is divided based on whether the transaction was announced in years of above average growth of the inflation-adjusted U.S. gross domestic product. Based on this approach, it was determined that 1990, 1991, 1995, 2001, 2002, and 2003 were years of relatively weak economic growth.

The results for Panel B in Table 5.47 show that transactions in years of relatively strong GDP growth significantly outperform their corresponding subsample.

Table 5.47: CARs by relative strength of U.S. economic growth

Var. N	**Relatively strong GDP**			**Relatively weak GDP**			**Difference test**	
Event	(1)			(2)			(1)-(2)	
window	CAR%	Z-stat.	pos. %	CAR%	Z-stat.	pos. %	CAR%	t-stat.
Panel A: All transactions								
[-1,1]	1.28*	1.5314	55	-0.51	1.2813	35	1.79	1.2659
[-1,10]	-0.97	1.2566	48	-0.77	1.0459	35	-0.20	-0.1079
(n)	(58)			(20)				
Panel B: No NEMAX transactions								
[-1,1]	1.14*	1.4429	58	-0.90*	1.3074	28	2.04**	1.6224
[-1,10]	0.49	1.0743	56	-0.13	1.1401	39	0.62	0.3821
(n)	(50)			(18)				

The table shows the results of the univariate analysis of the impact of U.S. economic growth on the cumulative abnormal returns, including mean-difference tests. A transaction is included in subgroup (1) if it was pursued during a year of above average growth of the U.S. GDP. The mean growth rate was computed for the observation period from 1990 to 2004. CARs are calculated as shown in Section 5.2.1.2. Tests for statistical significance follow BOEHMER ET AL. (1991). *, ** denote significance at the 10% and 5% level, respectively (based on a one-tailed Z-test or one-tailed t-test).

The split of the event study sample also confirms the presumed link between overall economic growth and the general volume of M&A activity, since transactions in years with a

[135] See KPMG (2005), p. 423.

relatively weak GDP growth rate only represent 26 percent of all transactions in the event study sample. More than half of the 78 transactions were announced in the years from 1998 to 2000, which not only represent a period of high economic growth, but also a period of buoyant capital markets marked by the internet bubble and a general euphoria towards merger activities by companies.[136]

The success assessments of the CFOs corroborate the conclusions drawn from the cumulative abnormal returns, as shown in Figure 5.24. 75 percent of those transactions pursued during a year of relatively weak economic growth were deemed a failure, which compares to a failure rate for years of a relatively strong GDP growth of only 38 percent. However, the relation is not statistically significant.

Figure 5.24: Correlation between economic growth and transaction success

	Relatively strong GDP?		
Success?	**Yes**	**No**	Sum
Yes	13	1	14
No	8	3	11
Sum	21	4	25

(p-value: 0.2087)

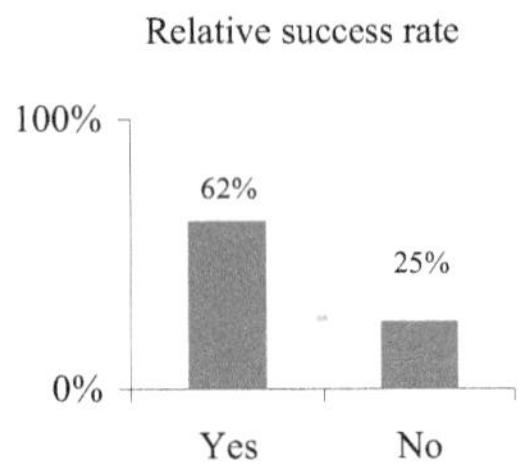

Overall, based on the results from the event study hypothesis H_{16} ("Average success of German acquirers of U.S. target companies will be unaffected by relatively high U.S. economic growth") is rejected.

5.4.5.2 Relative strength of capital markets

The effects of the booming capital markets during the years 1998 to 2000 on the cumulative abnormal returns are evident for the days immediately surrounding the announcement of the acquisition, as shown in Table 5.48. For both panels the cumulative abnormal returns in the [-1,1] event window are higher compared to those of acquisitions that were announced before and after the time of "hot" capital markets, though the mean difference is not significant. The observed cumulative abnormal returns might be attributable to the significant rise of private investors in Germany at the end of the 1990s, given that "... private investors in a rather naïve way might welcome transaction hoping they would create shareholder value".[137]

---

136 See Section 2.4.1.2.

137 LOWINSKI ET AL. (2002), p. 17f. The authors cite this argument in their study of Swiss acquirers during that period.

Examining the post-announcement period reveals that acquirer shareholders generally benefited more from transactions that did not fall within this period of "exuberance". The years 1998 to 2000 account in Panel A for a disproportionate share of the best and worst acquisitions.[138] Analogous to the decline in the capital markets beginning in 2000, the observed cumulative abnormal returns deteriorated for transactions in subsample (3). Although the mean tests are not significant, the general tendency of the results does not support the conclusion of improving success rates of acquisitions over the observation period, as drawn for example in numerous studies by KPMG.[139] It appears that investors are more cautious in their assessment of cross-border transaction announcements, given that before 1998 shareholders experienced positive gains, whereas after 2000 the cumulative abnormal returns are negative in Panel B (though not significant).

Table 5.48: CARs for various time periods

Var. O	Before 1998	1998-2000	After 2000	Difference tests		
Event	(1)	(2)	(3)	(1)-(2)	(1)-(3)	(2)-(3)
window	CAR%	CAR%	CAR%	CAR%	CAR%	CAR%
Panel A: All transactions						
[-1,1]	0.62	1.15	0.20	-0.53	0.42	0.95
[-1,10]	0.86	-1.93	-1.18	2.79*	2.04	-0.75
(n)	(25)	(40)	(13)			
Panel B: No NEMAX transactions						
[-1,1]	0.62	0.90	-0.30	-0.28	0.92	1.20
[-1,10]	0.86	0.11	-0.22	0.75	1.08	0.33
(n)	(25)	(32)	(11)			

The table shows the results of the univariate analysis of the impact of the relative strength of capital markets on the cumulative abnormal returns, including mean-difference tests. The transactions are split into subgroups based on whether they were announced before, during, or after a period of buoyant capital markets. CARs are calculated as shown in Section 5.2.1.2. Tests for statistical significance follow BOEHMER ET AL. (1991). * denotes significance at the 10% level (based on a one-tailed t-test).

The results of the survey support the observed tendency of the post-announcement effect within the event study that transactions prior to 1998 are on average most successful, though the relation is not significant (see Figure 5.25). In deviation to the event study, transactions past the year 2000 were viewed by the majority of the CFOs as a success.

138 Also the studies by BRUNER (2005) and MOELLER ET AL. (2004) noted that the most extreme outliers in their samples occurred for transactions during the years 1998 to 2000. In addition, the high transaction volume during these years supports arguments by GORT (1969) that M&A activity increases in periods of buoyant capital markets when shares are likely to be overvalued.

139 See Section 4.4.3.

Figure 5.25: Correlation between year and transaction success

	Year of the transaction			
Success?	**<1998**	**1998-2000**	**>2000**	Sum
Yes	3	7	4	14
No	2	6	3	11
Sum	5	13	7	25

(p-value:0.7099)

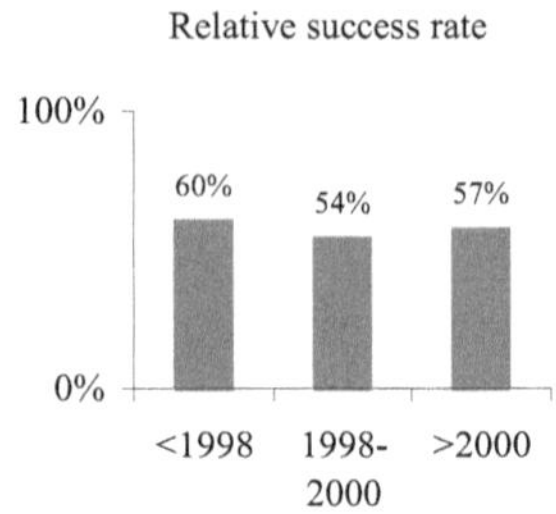

Overall, based on the findings hypothesis H_{17} ("Average success of German acquirers of U.S. acquirers will be unaffected by times of relatively strong capital markets") is confirmed.

5.4.5.3 Relative strength of the Euro

The USD/EUR exchange rate fluctuated from 0.8264USD/EUR to 1.4457USD/EUR during the years from 1990 to 2004. Based on the mean exchange rate for the observation period of 1.1443USD/EUR, the sample was divided into whether the transaction was announced during a time of a relatively strong Euro.[140] The results in Table 5.49 show that shareholder gains were higher for acquisitions of targets that were relatively cheaper for the German acquiring company at the time of a strong Euro. Accordingly, cumulative abnormal returns appear to be significantly correlated with the foreign exchange rate.

Table 5.49: CARs by relative strength of the Euro

Var. P	**Relatively strong EUR**			**Relatively weak EUR**			**Difference test**	
Event	(1)			(2)			(1)-(2)	
window	CAR%	Z-stat.	pos. %	CAR%	Z-stat.	pos. %	CAR%	t-stat.
Panel A: All transactions								
[-1,1]	0.97	1.2245	56	0.71	0.7792	46	0.26	0.2040
[-1,10]	1.73	1.1027	53	-2.75*	1.2894	39	4.48***	2.8790
(n)	(32)			(46)				
Panel B: No NEMAX transactions								
[-1,1]	0.97	1.2245	56	0.27	0.6252	44	0.70	0.6206
[-1,10]	1.73	1.1027	53	-0.92	1.1580	50	2.65**	1.8721
(n)	(32)			(36)				

The table shows the results of the univariate analysis of the impact of the relative strength of the USD/EUR exchange rate on the cumulative abnormal returns, including mean-difference tests. A transaction is included in subgroup (1) if it was pursued during a year of an above average Euro valuation. The mean USD/EUR exchange rate was computed for the observation period from 1990 to 2004. CARs are calculated as shown in Section 5.2.1.2. Tests for statistical significance follow BOEHMER ET AL. (1991). *, **, *** denote significance at the 10%, 5%, and 1% level, respectively (based on a one-tailed Z-test or one-tailed t-test).

140 Or respectively the DM before the introduction of the Euro on January 1, 2002. The USD/DM exchange rates for the years 1990 to 2001 were converted based on the fixed rate of 1.95583DM/EUR.

These findings are supported by the results of the survey, which show for transactions pursued during times of a relatively strong Euro with 70 percent a higher success rate than for those that were pursued during a time of a relatively weak Euro (see Figure 5.26).

Figure 5.26: Correlation between relative strength of the Euro and transaction success

	Relatively strong Euro?		
Success?	**Yes**	**No**	**Sum**
Yes	7	6	13
No	3	9	12
Sum	10	15	25

(p-value: 0.1442)

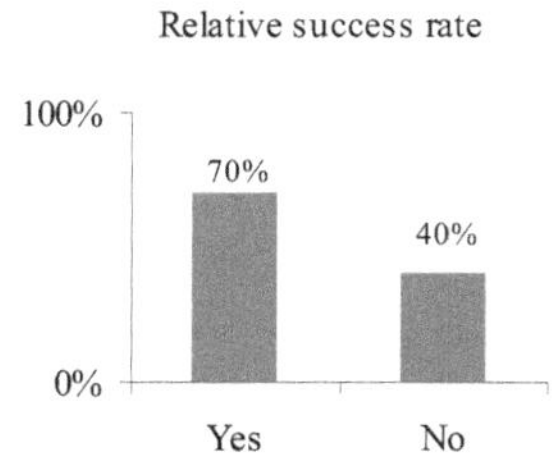

Overall, the results of the event study and the survey confirm hypothesis H_{18} ("Average success of German acquirers of U.S. target companies will be higher if the Euro compared to the U.S. dollar in the year of the announcement of the transaction is relatively strong").

5.4.6 Summary

The main event study results for the univariate analysis of determinants of transaction success are summarized in Tables 5.50 and 5.51. Both tables display the cumulative abnormal returns for the [-1,1] and [-1,10] event windows for transactions in Panel A (Table 5.50) and Panel B (Table 5.51). The statistical significance of the mean difference tests is given in parentheses. A comparison of these results to the cumulative abnormal returns obtained when using the MSCI index shows that the findings are essentially not impacted by the choice of the market index.[141]

The observed directional influence on the cumulative abnormal returns was confirmed by the survey responses for the impact of the industry and relative size of the target, the acquisition structure, and the relative strength of the capital markets and the foreign exchange rate. The differences between the event study subsamples regarding the size and U.S. transaction experience of the acquirer, a previous participation in the target company, the status of the target, and the inclusion of external professional advisors were not corroborated by the survey responses. However, the opposite influence was statistically significant only for the impact of general prior transaction experience. Other determinants in the survey with a statistically significant inference were the transaction volume and the initiator of the transaction.

[141] The CARs for the majority of transactions in Panel B are nearly identical, while for the NEMAX-listed companies the differences between the CARs are more pronounced, as shown in Appendix B6.

Table 5.50: Summary of the univariate analysis of transactions in Panel A

Panel A (n=78)		**CAR% [-1,1]**			**CAR% [-1,10]**		
Variable		**(a)**	**(b)**	**Diff.**	**(a)**	**(b)**	**Diff.**
A: Absolute size of the acquirer							
(a) DAX	(b) Non-DAX	0.16	2.73 *	(**)	-0.13	-3.18	(**)
B: Financial condition of the acquirer							
Ba (a) <Mean liquidity	(b) ≥Mean liquidity	0.11 *	2.12	(*)	-0.45	-0.54	
Bb (a) <Mean c-a ratio	(b) ≥Mean c-a ratio	0.73	1.29		-0.87	-0.35	
C: Valuation ratio of the acquirer							
(a) <Mean MTBV	(b) ≥Mean MTBV	0.98 *	0.79		0.43	-3.46	(***)
D: Previous participation of the acquirer							
(a) No	(b) Yes	0.91	-0.10		-1.02	0.20	
E: U.S. transaction experience of the acquirer							
(a) No	(b) Yes	0.71	0.94		-1.45	-0.32	
F: Industry of the target company							
(a) Regulated	(b) Non-regulated	-0.39	1.13 *		-0.09	-1.13	
G: Status of the target company							
(a) Private	(b) Public	1.03 *	0.47		0.44	-3.20	(**)
H: Relative size to the acquirer							
Ha (a) <$1b	(b) ≥$1b	0.54	1.50		-2.14	2.01	(***)
Hc (a) <30%	(b) ≥30%	0.79	-0.24 *		-0.52	-1.33	
I: Relatedness							
(a) No	(b) Yes	1.99 *	0.27	(*)	0.33	-1.50	
J: Form of payment							
(a) Cash	(b) Shares	0.81	0.90 **		-0.12	-5.75 *	(***)
K: Acquisition structure							
(a) Asset deal	(b) Share deal	0.43	0.95 *		-0.04	-1.20 *	
L: Form of transaction public target							
(a) Tender offer	(b) Other	0.19	1.34		-2.18	-6.40	(*)
M: Inclusion of advisors							
(a) No	(b) Yes	1.71 *	0.27 *		-1.07 *	-0.82	
N: Relative strength of economic growth							
(a) <Mean GDP	(b) ≥Mean GDP	-0.51	1.28 *		-0.77	-0.97	
O: Relative strength of capital markets [a]							
(a) <1998,>2000	(b) 1998-2000	0.48	1.15		0.16	-1.93	(*)
P: Relative strength of the Euro							
(a) <Mean USD/EUR	(b) ≥Mean USD/EUR	0.71	0.97		-2.75 *	1.73	(***)

a: In deviation to the presentation in Section 5.4.5.2., transactions before 1998 and after 2000 were grouped together; CARs are calculated as shown in Section 5.2.1.2. Tests for statistical significance follow BOEHMER ET AL. (1991). *, **, *** denote significance at the 10%, 5%, and 1% level, respectively (based on a one-tailed Z-test or one-tailed t-test).

Table 5.51: Summary of the univariate analysis of transactions in Panel B

Panel B (n=68)		**CAR% [-1,1]**			**CAR% [-1,10]**		
Variable		**(a)**	**(b)**	**Diff.**	**(a)**	**(b)**	**Diff.**
A: Absolute size of the acquirer							
(a) DAX	(b) Non-DAX	0.16	3.17 *	(**)	-0.13	3.00	(*)
B: Financial condition of the acquirer							
Ba (a) <Mean liquidity	(b) ≥Mean liquidity	-0.01	1.01		-0.46	0.94	
Bb (a) <Mean c-a-ratio	(b) ≥Mean c-a-ratio	0.62	0.77		-0.06	0.93	
C: Valuation ratio of the acquirer							
(a) <Mean MTBV	(b) ≥Mean MTBV	0.91 *	-0.28		0.59	-1.14	
D: Previous participation of the acquirer							
(a) No	(b) Yes	0.68	-0.10		0.34	0.20	
E: U.S. transaction experience of the acquirer							
(a) No	(b) Yes	0.61	0.60		0.40	0.26	
F: Industry of the target company							
(a) Regulated	(b) Non-regulated	0.28	0.69		0.19 *	0.37	
G: Status of the target company							
(a) Private	(b) Public	1.51 *	-1.07	(**)	1.74	-2.26	(***)
H: Relative size to the acquirer							
Ha (a) <$1b	(b) ≥$1b	0.14	1.50		-0.53	2.01	(**)
Hc (a) <30%	(b) ≥30%	0.51	2.20 *		-0.04	2.93	
I: Relatedness							
(a) No	(b) Yes	1.59	0.13		1.75	-0.35	(*)
J: Form of payment							
(a) Cash	(b) Shares	0.44	2.68		0.14	2.74	
K: Acquisition structure							
(a) Asset deal	(b) Share deal	0.43	0.67 *		-0.04	0.47	
L: Form of transaction public target							
(a) Tender offer	(b) Other	-1.17	-0.56		-2.25	-2.34	
M: Inclusion of advisors							
(a) No	(b) Yes	0.92	0.41		0.46	0.25	
N: Relative strength of economic growth							
(a) <Mean GDP	(b) ≥Mean GDP	-0.90 *	1.14 *	(**)	-0.13	0.49	
O: Relative strength of capital markets [a]							
(a) <1998, >2000	(b) 1998-2000	0.16	-1.93	(*)	0.53	0.11	
P: Relative strength of the Euro							
(a) <Mean USD/EUR	(b) ≥Mean USD/EUR	0.27	0.97		-0.92	1.73	(**)

a: In deviation to the presentation in Section 5.4.5.2., transactions before 1998 and after 2000 were grouped together.; CARs are calculated as shown in Section 5.2.1.2. Tests for statistical significance follow BOEHMER ET AL. (1991). *, **, *** denote significance at the 10%, 5%, and 1% level, respectively (based on a one-tailed Z-test or one-tailed t-test).

5.5 Multivariate analysis of the determinants of transaction success

5.5.1 Methodology

In order to provide evidence for the simultaneous explanatory power of the observed determinants of transaction success, a cross-sectional analysis is conducted, employing standard linear ordinary least squares ("OLS") regressions. The observed cumulative abnormal returns for the [-1,1] and [-1,10] event windows are the dependent variables that are regressed on those independent variables for which the sample mean tests in the univariate analysis showed significant differences. These variables are the absolute size, liquidity ratio (variable Ba for Panel A only), and market-to-book value (variable C for Panel A only) of the acquirer, status of the target, the transaction volume, strategic direction, and form of payment (variable J for Panel A only). External factors of the economic environment are not included, since only the impact of those determinants that the acquirer may actually influence are assessed in the multivariate analysis. Equations (15) and (16) show the basic model specifications applied for the multivariate analysis.

Multivariate analysis for transactions in Panel A:

$$CAR_T = ß_0 + ß_1\,DAX + ß_2\,LIQUIDITY + ß_3\,MTBV + ß_4\,STATUS + ß_5\,VOLUME{\geq}\$1B + ß_6\,2\text{-}DIGIT\ SIC + ß_7\,PAYMENT \quad (15)$$

Multivariate analysis for transactions in Panel B:

$$CAR_T = ß_0 + ß_1\,DAX + ß_2\,STATUS + ß_3 VOLUME{\geq}\$1B + ß_4\,2\text{-}DIGIT\ SIC \quad (16)$$

where:
$ß_0$: intercept of the regression model
$ß_X$: coefficient of the independent variable

Applying multivariate regressions generally requires testing the independent variables for multicollinearity, autocorrelation, and heteroskedasticity.[142] Multicollinearity occurs when two or more variables are correlated, leading to smaller t-statistics of the regression coefficients, i.e. less precision of the analysis,[143] whereby the computed multicollinearity values for the independent variables in the regressions indicate absence of significant collinearity.[144] Autocorrelation refers to the case in which the residual error terms from different observations in the regression are correlated, which can be caused for example by the omission of an important explanatory variable.[145] Positive autocorrelation yields inflated t-statistics, meaning that the regression coefficients will be found to be significantly different from zero when in fact they are not. Autocorrelation can be detected applying the Durbin-

142 See for example BACKHAUS ET AL. (2005).
143 See SCHROEDER ET AL. (1986), p. 71f.
144 The results of the correlation matrix of the independent variables are not separately displayed.
145 See BERRY and FELDMAN (1985), p. 73f.

Watson test, which in this case did not indicate positive or negative autocorrelation.[146] Heteroskedasticity exists when the error term in the OLS regression is not independent from the factors included in the analysis. Analogous to autocorrelation, by affecting the size of the standard error of the regression coefficient, heteroskedasticity evokes bias on the results.[147] In order to control for potential problems arising from heteroskedasticity, standardized cumulative abnormal returns are used for this regression.[148]

Due to the categorical measurement of the dependent variable "success" in the survey responses, a logistic instead of a linear regression model is employed.[149] A logistic regression generally computes the probability $\hat{p}$ that the dependent variable is equal to 1, as shown in equation (17):[150]

$$\ln\left(\frac{\hat{p}}{1-\hat{p}}\right) = \beta_0 + \beta_1 x_{i1} + \ldots + \beta_j x_{ij}, \qquad (17)$$

with $\hat{p} = \dfrac{1}{1+e^{-(\beta_0+\beta_1 x_{i1}+\ldots+\beta_j x_{ij})}}$

The fit of this regression model is gauged based on a chi-square test, while for the linear regression the adjusted R-square values are used. Otherwise, the techniques for testing the hypotheses with logistic regressions are quite similar to those of linear regressions.

Analogous to the approach for the event study results, the logistic regression includes as independent variables only those determinants that revealed a significant inference with transaction success. These variables are the prior transaction experience, the transaction volume, and the initiator of the transaction. For comparison purposes those determinants that were found to be significant in the event study are also included in the logistic regression, i.e. the variables "DAX", "STATUS", and "PAYMENT".[151]

---

146 The results of the Durbin-Watson test are not separately displayed.
147 See SCHROEDER ET AL. (1986), p. 77.
148 This approach follows for example CEBENOYAN ET AL. (1991).
149 See CHRISTENSEN (1997), p. 116ff.
150 See BEITEL (2004), p. 130f.
151 The variables "LIQUIDITY", "MTBV", and "SIC 2-DIGIT" are not included, given that they were not quantifiable within the survey.

5.5.2 Results of the capital market based event study

The results of the multiple linear regressions for Panels A and B are displayed in Tables 5.52 and 5.53, respectively. Along with the sample sizes,[152] the adjusted R-square and F-values are reported for each regression model at the bottom of the table. For Panel A, regression models (1) to (7) show binary regressions for each independent variable, and models (8) and (9) display the results of the multivariate analysis for the [-1,1] and [-1,10] event window, respectively. For Panel B, the results of the multivariate regressions for those two event windows are documented in models (5) and (6), respectively.

The signs for the independent variables and for the intercepts in the regressions for Panels A and B confirm the results of the univariate analysis. While for transactions in Panel A only the variable "DAX" is significantly associated with cumulative abnormal returns for the [-1,1] event window,[153] in Panel B a significant correlation is observed also for the variable "STATUS". The negative signs of the "DAX" and "STATUS" variables replicate the findings in Sections 5.4.2.1 and 5.4.3.2 that the capital markets attach less value to transactions by DAX30 companies as well as to acquisitions of public targets.

The majority of the independent variables do not remain insignificant in the multivariate analysis, especially while regressing against the cumulative abnormal returns for the [-1,10] event window. In deviation to the multivariate analyses for transactions in Panel A, both cross-sectional models employed for transactions in Panel B display a high explanatory power (see Table 5.53). The intercepts in these models are positive (though not significant for the [-1,10] window), indicating that in case all dummy variables are equal to zero, acquiring a U.S. target generally creates value for acquirer shareholders.[154] When all determinants discussed in the univariate analysis are employed in the multivariate regression, in addition to the aforementioned variables a significant coefficient is found for variable "INDUSTRY" for transactions in Panel B. Within the [-1,1] event window that variable displays a negative sign, thereby implying that transactions in regulated industries yield on average negative cumulative abnormal returns.[155]

Overall, the cross-sectional analysis corroborates the conclusions from the univariate analysis regarding the hypothesized influence of the determinants of shareholder value creation.

---

152 Since the required data was not available for all variables, some regression model subsamples are smaller than others.

153 For the [-1,10] event window, coefficients significant at various levels in the binary regressions are found for the "DAX", "STATUS", "MTBV", and "VOLUME ≥$1B" variables. The results are not separately displayed.

154 While performing binary regressions for the determinants in the [-1,10] event window in Panel B, only the variable "STATUS" is found to be consistently significant for both event windows.

155 Results are not separately displayed.

Table 5.52: Regression results for significant determinants of transaction success in Panel A

	Event window	[-1,1]	[-1,1]	[-1,1]	[-1,1]	[-1,1]	[-1,1]	[-1,1]	[-1,1]	[-1,10]
	Variable	(1)	(2)	(3)	(4)	(5)	(6)	(7)	(8)	(9)
	Intercept	2.734 **	-3.305	1.089	1.029	0.536	1.989 *	0.807	-1.399	-0.653
	(*t*-stat.)	(2.265)	(-1.630)	(0.995)	(1.308)	(0.879)	(1.823)	(1.197)	(-0.674)	(-0.337)
A	DAX[a]	-2.574 *							-1.827 **	0.934
	(*t*-stat.)	(-1.838)							(-2.229)	(1.219)
Ba	LIQUIDITY[b]		2.079 **						2.299 **	-0.616
	(*t*-stat.)		(2.007)						(2.397)	(-0.688)
C	MTBV[c]			-0.159					0.077	0.206
	(*t*-stat.)			(-0.251))					(0.124)	(0.357)
G	STATUS[d]				-0.563				-0.300	-1.357 *
	(*t*-stat.)				(-0.436)				(-0.413)	(-1.994)
Ha	VOLUME≥$1B[e]					0.965			1.621 *	2.176 **
	(*t*-stat.)					(0.673)			(1.864)	(2.676)
I	2-DIGIT SIC[f]						-1.720		-1.121	-1.665 **
	(*t*-stat.)						(-1.299		(-1.393)	(-2.214)
J	PAYMENT[g]							0.096	-0.103	-1.604
	(*t*-stat.)							(0.054)	(-0.090)	(-1.499)
	n	78	67	73	78	78	78	78	67	67
	Adjusted-R^2	4.26% *	6.39% **	0.01%	0.25%	0.65%	2.17%	0.01%	23.1% *	27.5% **
	F-value	3.379	4.030	0.063	0.190	0.499	1.688	0.003	2.100	2.651

This table shows the results of the OLS-regression models run for CARs of the acquirers measured in the [-1,1] and [-1,10] event windows; values of the t-statistic are given in parentheses. *a*: The dummy variable "DAX" is set to 1 if the acquirer was included in the DAX30 stock index at the time of the announcement of the transaction; *b*: The liquidity ratio is defined as the ratio of the acquirer's current assets to its current liabilities on the balance sheet date preceding the announcement date; *c*: Acquirers are categorized either as "value" or "glamour" companies, depending on the comparison of their MTBV at the beginning of the year in which the acquisition was announced with the median MTBV for all acquirers; *d*: The dummy variable "STATUS" is set to 1 if the target is a public company; *e*: The dummy variable "VOLUME≥$1B" is set to 1 if the transaction volume is at least $1b; *f*: The dummy variable "2-DIGIT SIC" is set to 1 if the first two digits of the primary SIC-code for both entities are equal; *g*: The dummy variable "PAYMENT" is set to 1 in case the transaction was at least partially paid for with shares of the acquirer.
*, ** denotes significance at the 10% and 5% level, respectively.

Table 5.53: Regression results for significant determinants of transaction success in Panel B

	Event window	[-1,1]	[-1,1]	[-1,1]	[-1,1]	[-1,1]	[-1,10]
Variable		**(1)**	**(2)**	**(3)**	**(4)**	**(5)**	**(6)**
	Intercept	3.165 **	1.515 **	0.1431	1.589	5.416***	2.406
	(*t*-stat.)	(-0.208)	(2.238)	(0.208)	(1.617)	(3.451)	(1.615)
A	DAX[a]	-3.005 *				-3.374**	-1.802
	(*t*-stat.)	(-1.936)				(-2.343)	(-1.318)
G	STATUS[b]		-2.585 **			-3.254***	-2.658**
	(*t*-stat.)		(-2.270)			(-2.990)	(-2.573)
Ha	VOLUME≥$1B[c]			1.357		3.067**	2.733**
	(*t*-stat.)			(1.148)		(2.653)	(2.491)
I	2-DIGIT SIC[d]				-1.459	-2.698**	-1.777
	(*t*-stat.)				(-1.221)	(-2.357)	(-1.636)
	n	68	68	68	68	68	68
	Adjusted R^2	5.37% *	7.24% **	1.96%	2.21%	23.65%***	16.26%**
	F-value	3.747	5.151	1.317	1.492	4.880	3.057

This table shows the results of the OLS-regression models run for CARs of the acquirers measured in the [-1,1] and [-1,10] event windows; values of the t-statistic are given in parentheses; *a*: The dummy variable "DAX" is set to 1 if the acquirer was included in the DAX30 stock index at the time of the announcement of the transaction; *b*: The dummy variable "STATUS" is set to 1 if the target is a public company; *c*: The dummy variable "VOLUME≥$1B" is set to 1 if the transaction volume is at least $1b; *d*: The dummy variable "2-DIGIT SIC" is set to 1 if the first two digits of the primary SIC-code for both entities are equal. *, **, *** denote significance at the 10%, 5%, and 1% level, respectively.

5.5.3 Results of the survey of executives

A consistency between the findings in the univariate analysis and the results from the binary regressions is also observed for the results of the survey responses, as shown in models (1) to (6) in Table. 5.54.[156] Significant coefficients are found in the binary regressions for the variables "FREQUENT",[157] "VOLUME≥$1B", and the initiator of the transactions ("INITIATOR").

None of these variables remains significant in the multiple logistic regression though, as shown in model (7). Compared to the binary regression, within the multiple regression the sign of the coefficient for the variable "DAX" is notably reversed and corresponds to the direction of the influence in the linear regressions for the event study sample. Similar signs for the coefficients in the linear regression for Panel A in the event study (see Table 5.52) and the logistic regression for the survey responses are also found for the impact of the absolute size of the transaction and the form of payment. An opposite direction is noted for the variable "STATUS", i.e. while in the event study acquisitions of private targets significantly outperform those of public targets, the survey responses yield a reverse conclusion. This

156 Within this regression model, the signs of the regression coefficients have to be inversely interpreted.

157 It should be pointed out that within the survey this variable not only reflects the acquirer's number of U.S. transactions, but all domestic and cross-border acquisitions during the observation period.

difference in the observed results between both methodologies was also found in the univariate analysis. However, the explanatory power of the multiple logistic regression for the survey responses is fairly low, accordingly not too much weight is put on these conclusions.

Table 5.54: Regression results for significant determinants of transaction success in the survey

	Variable	(1)	(2)	(3)	(4)	(5)	(6)	(7)
	Intercept	0.406	-0.773	0.251	0.357	-0.288	-1.099 *	-1.330
	(*t*-stat.)	(0.628)	(-1.567)	(0.499)	(0.723)	(-0.652)	(-1.649)	(-0.693)
A	DAX[a]	-1.099						0.030
	(*t*-stat.)	(-1.298)						(0.018)
E	FREQUENT[b]		2.383 *					2.553
	(*t*-stat.)		(1.983)					(1.155)
G	STATUS[c]			-1.504				-0.030
	(*t*-stat.)			(-1.589)				(-0.018)
Ha	VOLUME≥$1B[d]				-2.303 *			-8.787
	(*t*-stat.)				(-1.959)			(-0.316)
J	PAYMENT[e]					0.288		7.655
	(*t*-stat.)					(0.263)		(0.275)
	INITIATOR[f]						1.792 *	2.022
	(*t*-stat.)						(1.981)	(1.545)
	N	25	25	25	25	25	24	24
	Residual deviance	32.556	29.105	31.465	29.063	34.227	28.772	19.073

This table shows the results of the logistic regression model; values of the t-statistic are given in parentheses; *a*: The dummy variable "DAX" is set to 1 if the acquirer was included in the DAX30 stock index at the time of the announcement of the transaction; *b*: The dummy variable "FREQUENT" is set to 1 if the acquirer has general M&A experience from less than ten transactions during the period 1990 to 2004 (note: for the survey this definition deviates from the one laid out in section 5.2.1.4 for the event study); *c*: The dummy variable "STATUS" is set to 1 if the target is a public company; *d*: The dummy variable "VOLUME≥$1B" is set to 1 if the transaction volume is at least $1b; *e*: The dummy variable "PAYMENT" is set to 1 in case the transaction was at least partially paid for with shares of the acquirer; *f*: The dummy variable "INITIATOR" is set to 1 in case the acquirer initiated the transaction. * denotes significance at the 10% level.

5.6 Comparison of the U.S. transactions to domestic and European cross-border transactions by German acquirers

5.6.1 Overview

In order to gain additional perspective on the relative success of the U.S. cross-border transactions, the cumulative abnormal returns are compared to those of two samples of domestic and European cross-border transactions by German acquirers. For these control samples the same selection criteria as for the U.S transactions apply, except that the choice of the acquirer is constrained. Only acquiring companies in the U.S event study sample were also chosen for the control samples, i.e. the acquirers in all three samples are essentially identical.[158] Holding constant the characteristics of acquirers allows for a more direct examination of the influence of the characteristics of target companies and the transaction management on the variations of the abnormal returns.[159] 35 domestic and 82 European transactions satisfied the selection criteria,[160] which are listed in Appendix B7. Since only the European sample includes one transaction by a company listed on the NEMAX at the time of the announcement, a differentiation of the analysis analogous to the U.S. event study sample is not deemed necessary.[161] Accordingly, for the following comparison of the cumulative abnormal returns the results of Panel B of the U.S. sample are used.

5.6.2 Overall success of the analyzed transactions

5.6.2.1 German domestic transactions

Of the 42 acquiring companies in the U.S. sample, only 15 pursued domestic acquisitions that met the sample selection criteria. With one exception, all acquirers were listed on the DAX30 at the time of the announcement of the transaction. The mean and median of the domestic transaction volume are similar to those of the U.S. sample, though the range of the transaction volume is not as broad (see Table 5.55). Accordingly, the overall complexity level for both sub-samples is assumed to be comparable, although with 45 percent the proportionate share of the volume of public transactions is much lower than in the U.S. sample (75 percent).

Table 5.55: Descriptive statistics of the sample of German domestic transactions

	All	**Public**	**Private**
Number of transactions	35	10	25
in %	*100%*	*29%*	*71%*
Total volume ($m)	67,478	30,482	36,996
in %	*100%*	*45%*	*55%*
Mean volume ($m)	1,874	3,048	1,480
Median volume ($m)	472	1,740	466
Standard deviation ($m)	3,890	6,584	1,038
Maximum volume ($m)	19,656	19,656	5,373
Minimum volume ($m)	101	122	101

158 A similar research design was employed for example in the study by FULLER ET AL. (2002).

159 As pointed out by FULLER ET AL. (2002), assuming that the same acquirers pursue different types of acquisitions with randomly varying acquisition patterns among them, the variation in the acquirer's abnormal returns are mainly due to determinants other than new information about the characteristics of the acquirer itself.

160 Based on the results of the Kolmogorov-Smirnov-test as described in Section 5.2.1.2, for both control samples normal distribution is confirmed (results are not separately displayed).

161 This transaction concerns the acquisition of the British *SLEC Holdings LTD* by *EM.TV & Merchandising AG* in 2000.

Similar to the U.S. sample, acquisitions of German targets generate on average wealth gains for shareholders of the acquiring companies in the days immediately surrounding the announcement of the transaction (see Table 5.56). The cumulative abnormal return for the [-1,1] event window of 0.63 percent is almost identical to the U.S. sample value of 0.60 percent.[162]

Table 5.56: CARs for German acquirers in domestic transactions

(n=35) **Event window**	**CAR%**	**Positive %**	**Negative %**	**Z-statistic**	**Z-statistic B**
Period surrounding the announcement					
{0}	0.34**	57	43	1.8031	1.6238
[-1,1]	0.63	51	49	1.2068	1.7423
[-2,2]	0.31	57	43	1.0770	0.7124
[-5,5]	-0.23	49	51	1.0203	-0.5486
[-10,10]	-0.96	40	60	0.9632	-1.4722
[-20,20]	-3.13	37	63	1.0172	-2.0103
Pre-announcement period					
[-1,0]	0.28	49	51	1.2790	1.2855
[-10,-1]	0.07	51	49	0.7932	-0.9492
[-20,-1]	-1.51	46	54	1.0228	-2.1059
[-2,1]	0.64	54	46	1.0581	1.3814
[-5,1]	0.76	57	43	1.0224	0.6249
[-10,1]	0.76	54	46	0.9416	-0.0514
[-20,1]	-0.82	51	49	1.0718	-1.4040
Post-announcement period					
[0,1]	0.69*	54	46	1.4746	1.9966
[0,10]	-1.03	37	63	1.0951	-1.1291
[1,10]	-1.37	40	60	0.9971	-1.6978
[1,20]	-1.97	31	69	0.0461	-1.1375
[1,20]	-1.09	46	54	1.0493	-1.0250
[-1,10]	-0.28	49	51	1.1087	-0.5661
[-1,20]	-1.69	34	66	0.9889	-0.6970

This table shows the results for an event study analyzing 35 acquisitions of domestic target companies by German acquirers during the period from 1990 to 2004. Cumulative abnormal returns are calculated employing the standard market model, using an estimation period of 253 trading days prior to the event window [-20,20] and various DAX indices to measure market returns. Tests for statistical significance follow BOEHMER ET AL. (1991), while Z-statistic B is computed following DODD and WARNER (1983). *, ** denote significance at the 10%, and 5% level, respectively (based on a one-tailed Z-test).

The split in "winners" and "losers" for this event window shows essentially similar results between both samples as well. Deviations are found in a more positive upward pre-announcement price movement for the German transactions, whereas the post-announcement effect yields negative returns in this sample. For the extended event window [-20,20] the domestic transactions yield a negative cumulative abnormal return of -3.13 percent, compared to negative cumulative abnormal return of -0.70 percent for the U.S. acquisitions.

162 When using the MSCI Germany index for the market model regression, the CAR for the [-1,1] event window also amounts to 0.63 percent, though not significant. Overall, the results (including the levels of statistical significance) based on the MSCI Germany index are essentially similar to those using DAX indices, as shown in Appendix B8.

For the shareholders of the German target companies, the cumulative abnormal return for the [-1,1] event window is 9.51 percent,[163] which compares to 23.00 percent for the shareholders of targets in the U.S. sample. Apparently, compared to their domestic transactions, U.S. cross-border acquisitions were more expensive for German acquirers. These results corroborate the conclusion drawn in Section 3.5 of higher purchase price premiums in U.S. transactions and contradict the assessment of the surveyed CFOs.

5.6.2.2 European cross-border transactions

23 acquiring companies, of which 20 were listed on the DAX30 at the time of the announcement of the acquisition, are included in the European transactions sample. The mean and median volume of the 82 European cross-border transactions are only slightly lower than those of the U.S. targets sample (see Table 5.57). Accordingly, a similar complexity level is assumed also for the second control sample. The range of the transaction volumes is wider than in the German domestic sample, but is still not as broad as for the U.S. transactions. Acquisitions involving a public target account for slightly more than half of the total transaction volume.

Table 5.57: Descriptive statistics of the sample of European cross-border transactions

	All	**Public**	**Private**
Number of transactions	82	20	62
in %	*100%*	*24%*	*76%*
Total volume ($m)	127,588	67,737	59,851
in %	*100%*	*53%*	*47%*
Mean volume ($m)	1,556	3,387	965
Median volume ($m)	371	486	356
Standard deviation ($m)	4,135	7,325	2,131
Maximum volume ($m)	32,595	32,595	13,629
Minimum volume ($m)	100	100	101

In contrast to the reviewed evidence in the majority of prior empirical research and the analysis of the U.S. cross-border transactions, the results in Table 5.58 show that acquiring a European target on average destroyed wealth for shareholders of German acquiring companies. The cumulative abnormal returns are negative for almost every event window, though statistically significant only for the event day.[164]

---

[163] Significant at the 10 percent level. CARs are computed for nine German targets employing the MSCI Germany (for one public target company sufficient data was not available). For the event day, the abnormal return is 3.40 percent (significant at the 10 percent level); the detailed CARs are not separately displayed.

[164] These results contradict an assumption by DÖRR (2000, p. 183), who posits that German acquisitions of target companies in the United States would not be more successful than European cross-border transactions.

Table 5.58: CARs for German acquirers in European cross-border transactions

(n=82) Event window	CAR%	Positive %	Negative %	Z-statistic	Z-statistic B
Period surrounding the announcement					
{0}	-0.31*	40	60	1.3912	-1.4493
[-1,1]	-0.18	45	55	1.0019	-0.4754
[-2,2]	-0.20	48	52	0.8111	-0.4264
[-5,5]	-0.45	50	50	0.7344	-0.7123
[-10,10]	-0.34	51	49	0.9365	-0.3071
[-20,20]	-1.50	40	60	0.9588	-1.3450
Pre-announcement period					
[-1,0]	-0.13	40	60	1.2123	-0.3930
[-10,-1]	0.12	56	44	0.6834	0.4576
[-20,-1]	-0.92	44	56	0.9607	-0.7842
[-2,1]	-0.26	44	56	0.8958	-0.6091
[-5,1]	-0.23	56	44	0.7260	-0.2004
[-10,1]	-0.24	48	52	0.7460	-0.0779
[-20,1]	-1.28	40	60	0.9645	-1.1137
Post-announcement period					
[0,1]	-0.36	44	56	1.0018	-1.2140
[0,10]	-0.46	48	52	1.1179	-0.8606
[1,10]	-0.15	50	50	1.0868	-0.4443
[1,20]	-0.27	48	52	0.0451	-0.8175
[-1,10]	-0.28	49	51	1.1087	-0.5661
[-1,20]	-0.40	46	54	0.9591	-0.8980

This table shows the results for an event study analyzing 82 acquisitions of European target companies by German acquirers during the period from 1990 to 2004. Cumulative abnormal returns are calculated employing the standard market model, using an estimation period of 253 trading days prior to the event window [-20,20] and various DAX indices to measure market returns. Tests for statistical significance follow BOEHMER ET AL. (1991), while Z-statistic B is computed following DODD and WARNER (1983). * denotes statistical significance at the 10% level.

The distinction between "winners" and "losers" in the sample yields similar results, given that for only two event windows the portion of acquirers with positive cumulative abnormal returns exceeds 50 percent.[165]

5.6.2.3 Comparison of the results

Comparing all three samples shows that the mean differences tests are significant between the U.S.-European and the German domestic-European transactions, as shown in Table 5.59. The comparison between the U.S. and domestic transactions does not hint at the existence of a positive or negative cross-border effect, which confirms the assessment given by the surveyed CFOs (see Figure 5.5 in Section 5.3.2).

In order to further enhance the comparability of the results, the intersection of identical acquirers in all three subsamples is created. Overall, 13 acquiring companies are represented

165 When using the MSCI Germany index for the market model regression, the CAR for the [-1,1] event window amounts to -0.26 percent (not significant). Overall, the results based on the MSCI Germany index are essentially similar to those using DAX indices, as shown in Appendix B9, including the split of "winners" and "losers" and the absence of statistical significance for CARs in all event windows.

simultaneously in all three samples.[166] For the three days surrounding the announcement of the transaction, the shareholder wealth gains reveal a pattern that is essentially similar to that for transactions in Panel B. The post-announcement effect in both cross-border subsamples shows inverse findings though, given that the European transactions yield a positive cumulative abnormal return, while the U.S. transactions yield shareholder losses. However, the t-statistics for the difference tests for these subsamples are not significant.

Table 5.59: Comparison of the CARs for the three samples

	U.S. targets	**German targets**	**European targets**		**Difference tests**	
Event window	(1) CAR%	(2) CAR%	(3) CAR%	(1)-(2) CAR%	(1)-(3) CAR%	(2)-(3) CAR%
All transactions						
[-1,1]	0.82*	0.63	-0.18	0.19	1.00*	0.81*
[-1,10]	-0.91	-1.09	-0.28	-0.18	-0.63	-0.81
(n)	(78)	(35)	(82)			
Panel B: No NEMAX transactions						
[-1,1]	0.60	0.63	-0.22	-0.03	0.82*	0.85*
[-1,10]	0.33	-1.09	-0.21	1.42	0.54	-0.88
(n)	(68)	(35)	(81)			
Intersection						
[-1,1]	0.28	0.36	-0.08	-0.08	0.36	0.44
[-1,10]	-0.19	-0.99	0.10	0.80	-0.29	-1.09
(n)	(42)	(33)	(68)			

The table shows the comparison of the generated cumulative abnormal returns, including mean-difference tests, for all transactions in the U.S., German domestic, and European samples and for the intersection of acquirers in each of the three samples. CARs are calculated as shown in Section 5.2.1.2. Tests for statistical significance follow BOEHMER ET AL. (1991). * denotes significance at the 10% level (based on a one-tailed Z-test or one-tailed t-test).

Overall, based on these results hypothesis H_2 ("Average success of German acquirers of U.S. target companies will be lower than in domestic acquisitions") is rejected.

5.6.3 Determinants of transaction success

The analysis of which determinants of transaction success are systematically different between the U.S. and the two control samples is confined to characteristics of the target companies and transaction structures. The cumulative abnormal returns for the univariate analysis of the various subsamples for each determinant are presented in condensed form in Table 5.60 for the German and in Table 5.62 for the European cross-border transactions. The statistical significance of the mean difference tests is given in parentheses. The results of the binary and multivariate regressions are displayed in Table 5.61 for the German transactions and Table 5.63 for the European cross-border transactions.

166 These are *Allianz AG, BASF AG, Bayer AG, Commerzbank AG, Daimler-Chrysler AG, Deutsche Bank AG, Deutsche Lufthansa AG, Deutsche Telekom AG, E.ON AG, Mannesmann AG, RWE AG, Schering AG*, and *Siemens AG*.

5.6.3.1 German domestic transactions

Comparing the results of the univariate analysis for the German domestic transactions with those for the U.S. sample[167] yields the following findings:

- Similar to the U.S. transactions, cumulative abnormal returns for non-regulated acquisitions are relatively higher in domestic transactions, though the mean differences are not significant. The direction of the findings provide evidence for the previously mentioned assumption of investors' concerns regarding the impact of the burden of the regulatory framework applicable to such transactions.
- Unlike in the U.S. sample, takeovers of public targets produce higher shareholder wealth gains for the [-1,1] event window in domestic transactions. These results highlight the previously mentioned perception of comparably stricter rules and regulations in the United States applicable to acquisitions of public companies. While in the U.S. sample the cumulative abnormal return for acquisitions of private targets is positive in both event windows, in the domestic sample it is negative for the [-1,10] event window.
- The observed pattern for mega-deals mirrors that of the U.S. sample. Transactions with a volume of at least $1b seem to outperform smaller deals in the [-1,1] window. However, for the extended event window this relation is reversed.
- In deviation to the U.S. sample, diversifying acquisitions did not generate shareholder wealth in domestic transactions. Apparently in domestic transactions the perceived benefits stemming from the synergy and market power hypotheses are more relevant than in cross-border transactions.
- Acquisitions paid for with shares have the same effect on shareholder wealth in the [-1,1] event window as acquisitions of U.S. targets, i.e. significantly higher wealth gains compared to transactions paid for with cash. However, unlike in the U.S. sample, the relation is reversed for the [-1,10] event window, as exchange deals tend to generate relatively higher losses for shareholders. As expected, with a portion of 17 percent of all transactions, shares are more frequently used in domestic transactions than in the U.S. sample, for which a portion of only 7 percent was observed.
- Inconclusive results are found for the impact of the acquisition structure. Unlike in the U.S. sample, the perceived additional complexity of asset deals does not seem to have a negative impact on the short-term cumulative abnormal returns, given that the cumulative abnormal returns for this subsample are higher than those for share deals. The result is reversed for the [-1,10] event window though, with both subsamples displaying a negative cumulative abnormal return.
- Advisors were engaged in only 46 percent of the German transactions, which confirms the earlier assumption of a higher rate of including advisors in cross-border

---

[167] The comparisons apply to the findings for the 68 U.S. transactions in Panel B.

transactions.[168] In deviation to the U.S. transactions, the inclusion of external professional advisors seems to be beneficial in domestic transactions.

Table 5.60: Summary of the univariate analysis for German domestic transactions

		CAR% [-1,1]			CAR% [-1,10]		
Variable		**(a)**	**(b)**	**Diff.**	**(a)**	**(b)**	**Diff.**
F: Industry							
(a) Regulated (n=13)	(b) Non-regulated (n=22)	0.32	0.82 *		-1.25	-0.99 *	
G: Status							
(a) Private (n=25)	(b) Public (n=10)	0.05	2.08 **	(**)	-1.05	-1.17 *	
H: Relative size to the acquirer							
(a) <$1b (n=24)	(b) ≥$1b (n=11)	-0.12	2.27 *	(***)	-1.05	-1.16	
(a) <30% (n=34)	(b) ≥30% (n=1)	0.52	4.38 [a]		-0.95	-5.66 [a]	
I: Strategic direction							
(a) No (n=15)	(b) Yes (n=20)	-0.04 *	1.13 *		-1.24	-0.97 *	
J: Form of payment							
(a) Cash (n=29)	(b) Shares (n=6)	0.05	3.46 ***	(***)	-0.94	-1.80	
K: Acquisition structure							
(a) Asset deal (n=7)	(b) Share deal (n=28)	0.95	0.55		-2.97 **	-0.62	
M: Inclusion of advisors							
(a) No (n=19)	(b) Yes (n=16)	0.36	0.96 *		-1.20	-0.96	

Tests for statistical significance follow BOEHMER ET AL. (1991). a: since the subsample includes only one transaction, a Z-value cannot be computed; *, **, *** denote significance at the 10%, 5%, and 1% level, respectively (based on a one-tailed Z-test or one-tailed t-test).

Analogous to the approach for the U.S. sample, binary and multivariate regressions are performed for those determinants with significant differences for their respective subsample means, i.e. the variables "STATUS", "VOLUME≥$1B", and "PAYMENT". Only the binary regression on the status of the German target company shows a significant coefficient, confirming that for the [-1,1] window acquisitions of public targets are successful. The signs of the other binary regressions as well as of the multiple linear regressions are also in line with the earlier findings, though not significant.

168 As mentioned in Section 5.4.4.5, in the U.S. sample external advisors were included in 62 percent of the transactions.

Table 5.61: Regression results for significant determinants of success for German domestic transactions

	Event window	[-1,1]	[-1,1]	[-1,1]	[-1,1]	[-1,10]
Variable		**(1)**	**(2)**	**(3)**	**(4)**	**(5)**
	Intercept	0.165 ***	0.005	0.004	0.007	-0.004
	(*t*-stat.)	(2.922)	(0.948)	(0.696)	(1.040)	(-0.430)
G	STATUS[a]	0.205 **			-0.006	-0.006
	(*t*-stat.)	(2.036)			(-0.417)	(-0.270)
Ha	VOLUME≥$1B[b]		0.003		-0.012	0.012
	(*t*-stat.)		(0.263)		(-0.860)	(0.545)
J	PAYMENT[c]			0.016	0.032	0.012
	(*t*-stat.)			(1.296)	(1.376)	(-1.417)
	n	35	35	35	35	35
	Adjusted-R^2	4.9% **	2.0%	4.9%	7.3%	16.2%
	F-value	4.146	0.069	1.680	0.809	2.002

This table shows the results of the OLS-regression models run for CARs of the acquirers measured in the [-1,1] and [-1,10] event windows; values of the t-statistics are given in parentheses; *a*: The dummy variable "STATUS" is set to 1 if the target is a public company; *b*: The dummy variable "VOLUME≥$1B" is set to 1 if the transaction volume is at least $1b; *c*: The dummy variable "PAYMENT" is set to 1 if the transaction was at least partially paid for with shares of the acquirer; **, *** denotes significance at the 5%, and 1% level, respectively.

5.6.3.2 European cross-border transactions

Comparing the results of the univariate analysis for the European cross-border transactions with those for the U.S. sample yields the following findings:

- Similar to the U.S. sample, European transactions in non-regulated industries outperformed those of targets in regulated industries, but the cumulative abnormal returns for both subsamples in the two event windows are negative.
- As observed for the U.S. sample, acquisitions of public targets yielded a significantly lower cumulative abnormal return in the [-1,1] event window. Unlike in the German domestic sample, in this case this observation also holds for the [-1,10] event window.
- The observed impact of the absolute size of the transaction deviates from the U.S. sample, given that European mega-deals yielded on average greater shareholder losses than smaller transactions, though the differences are not significant.
- With regard to the strategic direction of the transaction opposite results were found, since diversifying acquisitions of European targets generated greater wealth losses for the acquirer shareholders. Apparently, simultaneous geographical and industrial diversification is not always beneficial for shareholders of German acquirers.
- The findings for the impact of the form of payment are congruent with those for the German sample, in that for the short term exchange offers outperformed cash payments, while in the longer term the relation is reversed. Unlike in the U.S. sample, regardless

which form of payment was chosen, the cumulative abnormal return is negative for the European cross-border transactions in both event windows.

- Whether the European transaction was structured as an asset or share deal did not induce variations in the cumulative abnormal return for the [-1,1] event window. For the [-1,10] event window the observations correspond to the earlier findings for the U.S. and German sample.
- The rate of including external advisors in the transaction process is with 70 percent higher than in the U.S. sample. Those transactions generated relatively higher wealth gains than those that were pursued solely in-house, with a significant mean difference test for the [-1,10] event window.

Table 5.62: Summary of the univariate analysis of European cross-border transactions

		CAR% [-1,1]			CAR% [-1,10]		
Variable		**(a)**	**(b)**	**Diff.**	**(a)**	**(b)**	**Diff.**
F: Industry							
(a) Regulated (n=38)	(b) Non-regulated (n=44)	-0.20	-0.16		-0.34	-0.22	
G: Status							
(a) Private (n=62)	(b) Public (n=20)	0.27	-1.57 *	(***)	-0.02	-1.21 *	
H: Relative size to the acquirer							
(a) <$1b (n=66)	(b) ≥$1b (n=16)	-0.02	-0.81		-0.09	-1.07	
(b) <30% (n=81)	(b) ≥30% (n=1)	-0.10	-6.50 [a]		-0.19	-7.54 [a]	
I: Strategic direction							
(a) No (n=29)	(b) Yes (n=53)	-0.26	-0.13		-1.04	0.14	
J: Form of payment							
(a) Cash (n=76)	(b) Shares (n=6)	-0.19	-0.02 **		-0.14	-2.05	
K: Acquisition structure							
(a) Asset deal (n=15)	(b) Share deal (n=67)	-0.18	-0.18 *		-1.57 *	0.01	
M: Inclusion of advisors							
(a) No (n=24)	(b) Yes (n=58)	-0.21	-0.16		-1.59 *	0.27	(*)

Tests for statistical significance follow BOEHMER ET AL. (1991). a: since the subsample includes only one transaction, a Z-value cannot be computed. *, **, *** denote significance at the 10%, 5%, and 1% level, respectively (based on a one-tailed Z-test or one-tailed t-test).

The results of the binary and multivariate regressions essentially corroborate the findings of the univariate analysis, although only the variable "STATUS" exhibits statistical significance in these regressions, as shown in Table 5.63.[169]

Table 5.63: Regression results for significant determinants of success of European cross-border transactions

	Event window / Variable	[-1,1] (1)	[-1,1] (2)	[-1,1] (3)	[-1,1] (4)	[-1,10] (5)
	Intercept	0.003	-0.000	-0.003	0.003	-0.007
	(*t*-stat.)	(0.775)	(-0.068)	(-0.491)	(0.491)	(-0.656)
G	STATUS[a]	-0.018 **			-0.018 **	-0.010
	(*t*-stat.)	(-2.590)			(-2.380)	(-0.739)
Ha	VOLUME≥$1B[b]		-0.008		-0.004	-0.009
	(*t*-stat.)		(-0.986)		(-0.462)	(-0.634)
I	2-DIGIT SIC[c]			0.001	0.001	0.012
	(*t*-stat.)			(0.199)	(0.119)	(1.054)
	n	82	82	82	82	82
	Adjusted-R^2	7.7% **	1.2%	0.0%	8.0% *	2.9
	F-value	6.713	0.971	0.039	2.260	0.766

This table shows the results of the OLS-regression models run for CARs of the acquirers measured in the [-1,1] and [-1,10] event windows; values of the t-statistics are given in parentheses; *a*: The dummy variable "STATUS" is set to 1 if the target is a public company. *b*: The dummy variable "VOLUME≥$1B" is set to 1 if the transaction volume is at least $1b; *c*: The dummy variable "2-DIGIT SIC" is set to 1 if the first two digits of the primary SIC-code for both entities are equal; *, ** denote significance at the 10% and 5% level, respectively.

5.6.3.3 Comparison of the results

In order to conclude the comparison of the U.S., German domestic, and European cross-border transactions, a multivariate regression analysis was performed on the cumulative abnormal returns for the intersection of identical acquirers in all three subsamples. Over all three subsamples, 13 acquiring companies pursued 143 transactions. Those determinants that showed significant difference tests in the univariate analysis for any of the three subsamples are employed as the independent variables. In addition, a dummy variable "U.S." is introduced, which is set to 1 if the target is a U.S. company and to 0 if the target is incorporated in a European country, including Germany. This variable is individually regressed in models (1) and (3) of Table 5.64 on the cumulative abnormal returns for the [-1,1] and [-1,10] event windows.

[169] Although significant differences between the respective subsamples are only observed for the variable "STATUS", for purposes of comparing both cross-border regressions with each other, the variables "VOLUME≥$1B" and "2-DIGIT SIC" are also included in this analysis.

Table 5.64: Regression results for significant determinants of success for the intersection of German acquirers in all three samples

	Event window	[-1,1]	[-1,1]	[-1,10]	[-1,10]
Variable		(1)	(2)	(3)	(4)
	Intercept	0.065	0.611	-0.520	0.398
	(*t*-stat.)	(0.194)	(1.236)	(-1.071)	(0.549)
	U.S.[a]	0.537	0.7821	0.847	0.985
	(*t*-stat.)	(0.978)	(1.442)	(1.058)	(1.238)
G	STATUS[b]		-2.177		-2.939
	(*t*-stat.)		(-3.608) ***		(-3.323)
Ha	VOLUME≥$1B[c]		0.503		1.405
	(*t*-stat.)		(0.766)		(1.458)
I	2-DIGIT SIC[d]		-0.515		-0.623
	(*t*-stat.)		(-0.936)		(-0.772)
J	PAYMENT[e]		2.119 **		-0.973
	(*t*-stat.)		(2.121)		(-0.665)
	n	143	143	143	143
	Adjusted-R^2	0.5%	8.6% ***	0.6%	2.5% **
	F-value	0.956	3.361	1.120	2.910

This table shows the results of the OLS-regression models run for CARs of the acquirers measured in the [-1,1] and [-1,10] event windows; values of the t-statistics are given in parentheses; *a*: The dummy variable "STATUS" is set to 1 if the target is a U.S. company; *b*: The dummy variable "STATUS" is set to 1 if the target is a public company; *c*: The dummy variable "VOLUME≥$1B" is set to 1 if the transaction volume is at least $1b; *d*: The dummy variable "2-DIGIT SIC" is set to 1 if the first two digits of the primary SIC-code for both entities are equal; *e*: The dummy variable "PAYMENT" is set to 1 if the transaction was at least partially paid for with shares of the acquirer; **, *** denote significance at the 5% and 1% level, respectively.

For both event windows the sign of the regression coefficient for the variable "U.S." indicates that transactions involving a U.S. target create on average value for acquirer shareholders, though the coefficient is not significant. The multivariate regression models (2) and (4) both confirm with a high explanatory power the earlier conclusions that large acquisitions of U.S. private targets in non-related industries are on average successful. A distinct difference between both models was found for the impact of the form of payment. In the [-1,1] event window, transactions financed with shares yield significantly higher shareholder gains than transactions paid for with cash. In the [-1,10] event window this relation is reversed.

5.7 Conclusions and implications

The goal of Chapter 5 was to analyze the success and its determinants of acquisitions by German companies in the United States, employing both a capital market based event study and a survey of executives.

The overall findings in both methodologies confirmed the hypothesis that U.S. cross-border acquisitions are on average successful. Even though none of the surveyed executives explicitly listed shareholder value creation as a motive for pursuing the U.S. transaction, the corresponding success rates observed in both methodologies suggest that the goals of the acquirer's management and its shareholders were fairly congruent.[170] A gradual extension of the event window produced increasingly negative cumulative abnormal returns, though they were not significant. These negative share price reactions are predominantly driven by acquisitions of companies of the new economy during the period of buoyant capital markets in the years 1999 and 2000. When such transactions are excluded, the observed wealth gains for the shareholders of the remaining German acquiring companies are positive and more robust.

The variations in the observed success rates are more refined when numerous determinants of transaction success are controlled for. Overall, as summarized in Table 5.65, the analysis did not confirm for all determinants the hypothesized directional influence, although the evidence did not produce sufficient statistical significance for all determinants.

Given that DAX30 acquirers not only represented the largest but also the most active frequent acquirers in the sample, the observation of higher cumulative abnormal returns for relatively smaller and non-frequent acquirers did not support the hypothesis that U.S. specific transaction experience is positively related to transaction success. Infrequent acquirers seemed to be more successful in screening and timing the appropriate opportunity for a transaction, though these findings were not corroborated by the survey responses. Acquirers in a relatively stronger financial condition and with a relatively lower market-to-book value outperformed their respective peers.

Assessing the impact of various characteristics of the target companies revealed that transactions with an absolute or relatively large volume were more successful than smaller deals. In the event study, this conclusion only holds for acquisitions of private targets though. While acquiring a private target was generally associated with positive wealth impacts for the acquirer shareholders, transactions involving a public target destroyed shareholder value. These findings can mainly be attributed to the presence of the liquidity discount for private companies as well as to potentially negative implications for the process of acquiring U.S. public targets, i.e. the burden of applicable U.S. federal securities laws and tendentiously higher purchase price premiums. With regard to whether the target is in a regulated industry,

---

170 DATTA ET AL. (2001) draw a similar conclusion and explain this observation with the existence of a more shareholder value conscious management as a result of the increasing use of options as a form of managerial compensation in the 1990s, which makes management more likely to undertake acquisitions that increase the share price of the acquirer.

the results provided insignificant support for the hypothesis that relatively stricter regulatory requirements negatively weigh on transaction success.

Table 5.65: Summary of confirmation of tested hypotheses

	Hypothesis	**Confirmation**	
No.	Average success[a] of German acquirers of U.S. target companies will be…	**Event study**	**Survey**
	Overall success of cross-border transactions in the United States		
H_1	… positive	Yes*	Yes
H_2	… lower than in domestic acquisitions	No	n/a
	Characteristics of acquiring companies		
H_3	… unaffected by the size of the acquirer	No*	No
H_4	… unaffected by the financial condition of the acquirer	No*	n/a
H_5	… higher for companies with a relatively low MTBV	Yes*	n/a
H_6	… higher when a previous investment in the target was held	No	Yes
H_7	… higher for U.S. experienced acquirers	No	Yes
	Characteristics of target companies		
H_8	… higher for acquisitions of a target in a non-regulated industry	Yes	Yes
H_9	… higher for transactions involving a private target	Yes*	No
H_{10}	… unaffected by the relative size of the target	Yes	Yes
	Characteristics of transaction structuring and management		
H_{11}	… higher for transactions involving entities in related industries	--	--
H_{12}	… higher for transactions paid for with cash	No*	--
H_{13}	… higher for transactions structured as a share deal	Yes	Yes
H_{14}	… higher for public transactions structured as a tender offer	No	n/a
H_{15}	… higher for transactions without inclusion of external advisors	--	No
	Influences of the economic environment		
H_{16}	… unaffected by relatively high U.S. economic growth	No*	No
H_{17}	… unaffected by times of relatively strong capital markets	Yes	Yes
H_{18}	… higher if the Euro compared to the U.S. dollar in the year of the announcement of the transaction is relatively strong	Yes*	Yes

a: with regard to wealth creation for acquirer shareholders and subjective assessments by executives; n/a implies that sufficient data was not available to assess the impact of the determinant; -- implies that the analysis did not provide sufficient evidence to conclude on the validity of the hypothesis; * denotes statistical significance of the results in the univariate and/or multivariate analysis.

Contrary to what had been hypothesized, diversifying acquisitions achieved on average higher cumulative abnormal returns for acquirer shareholders than transactions involving acquirers and targets in related industries. However, a further differentiated analysis revealed that horizontal transactions focusing on an expansion of the acquirer's core business also yielded significant positive abnormal returns. Similar observations were found in the survey responses. Accordingly, the evidence simultaneously supports the validity of the synergy and the diversification hypotheses as shareholder-related motives for M&A activity. These two motives were among the most frequently cited by the CFOs in the survey. While the share price reaction reflects the perception of the investors at the time of the announcement regarding the transaction's potential to benefit from synergies in the future, the responses of the executives in the survey provided an evaluation whether those were actually achieved post-closing. Given the observed success rates this seemed to have been the case for the majority of the evaluated transactions. Executives deemed transactions undertaken on the premise of management-related motives a failure, as it was expected from the earlier discussion of endogenous factors stimulating M&A activity.[171]

In line with the prior empirical research, acquisitions of private targets paid for at least partially with shares were found to yield higher wealth gains than transactions paid for with cash. Giving the paucity of cross-border transactions involving shares as the form of payment especially for private targets, not too much weight is placed on this finding though. Whether the transaction was structured as an asset or share deal did not generate significant differences, but the direction of the results were consistent with the perception that asset deals are more complex and relatively more expensive for an acquirer. With regard to the form of acquisitions of public targets, the evidence was inconclusive, i.e. the presumed procedural advantage of tender offers compared to proxy solicitations or exchange offers did not seem to be a key success factor.

A confirmed hypothesized directional influence was the apparently non-value creating effect from the inclusion of external advisors. In the event study, abnormal returns for the subsample of transactions pursued solely in-house exceeded those for transactions in which external advisors assisted in the transaction process. A further differentiation of the results showed that negative wealth effects were only found though for the inclusion of top-tier investment banks. Second-tier advisors apparently were more successful in generating benefits for the acquiring companies, which might be explained by a presumed higher degree of client-tailored advice and expertise.

The response data in the survey further revealed that transactions initiated by the target company yielded on average failures, hence opportunistic acquisitions should be approached with caution.

The impact of other characteristics of the acquisition execution phase, such as the extent of due diligence,[172] aspects of the tax planning, method for valuating the target, or the use of contractual measures to protect the transaction or to subsequently adjust the purchase price, could not be analyzed, due to the lack of available data for the event study sample.

---

[171] See Section 2.3.3.3. There is no direct evidence in prior empirical research supporting the validity of management-related motives, since executives typically would not admit in surveys their own interests in "empire building". However, the national and international press expressly dealt in their coverage of certain transactions with the issue of personal motives, see for example MORGENSON (2005), p. 60.

[172] In 24 of the 25 transactions in the survey the CFOs indicated that a due diligence was performed.

The analysis of various exogenous factors of the economic environment essentially supported their hypothesized influence on transaction success. A relatively strong U.S. economic growth and a relatively strong Euro were positively correlated with abnormal shareholder wealth gains, while "hot" capital markets did not seem to contribute to transaction success. Since the sharp decline of the capital markets and the level of M&A activity beginning in 2001, investors seemed to perceive transactions more warily, as evidenced by the on average negative abnormal returns in the period 2001 to 2004. This perception of investors was not shared though by the executives who evaluated the majority of their transactions within those years a success.

Comparing the results for the sample of U.S. cross-border transactions to acquisitions by German companies of either domestic or European targets did not support the existence of a positive cross-border effect, i.e. compared to domestic transactions additional benefits from the exploitation of product and factor market imperfections as suggested by FDI literature. Similar to findings in prior research on comparisons between cross-border and domestic transactions by U.K. and U.S. acquirers,[173] the observed cumulative abnormal returns for the three days centered on the announcement date are essentially equal between the U.S. and German sample. Compared to the observed cumulative abnormal returns for cross-border transactions of U.K acquirers, German companies generate relatively bigger wealth gains for their shareholders, which could be attributable to a corporate governance system in Germany that may enable a more thorough scrutiny of potential transactions, which in turn allows for higher success rates of transactions.[174] However, a further differentiation shows that the capital markets attach a "diversification discount" to German cross-border transactions in Europe.[175] While the results for the U.S. sample also indicate that the German capital market is highly integrated with international capital markets,[176] in contrast the findings for the European transactions simultaneously hint at an intra-European market integration that

---

173 As pointed out in the studies by CONN ET AL. (2005) and MOELLER and SCHLINGEMANN (2005), respectively. GOERGEN and RENNEBOOG (2004) report for a subgroup of German, Austrian, and Swiss acquirers in their European sample similar findings, i.e. higher CARs in domestic rather than in cross-border transactions. In an older study, ECKBO and THORBURN (2000) computed comparable shareholder wealth effects for their sample of transactions by Canadian acquirers before the fifth merger wave.

174 In addition, especially for acquirers that are listed in the DAX30, frequently members of the supervisory board are executives of another DAX30 company and thereby they most likely have their own experience with acquisitions in the U.S. In his analysis of long-term shareholder effects of cross-border transactions, BÜHNER (1990) does not support this assumption though. However, it should be noted that his sample includes transactions from the 1980s and since then the corporate governance environment has substantially evolved.

175 DÖRR (2000) draws opposite conclusions for his sample of German cross-border transactions.

176 LOWINSKI ET AL. (2004) draw similar conclusions for the Swiss capital market based on their analysis of cross-border transactions of Swiss companies. A high degree of market integration might also have negative implications for cross-border acquirers, as pointed out by MOELLER ET AL. (2005). On the one hand an absence of market segmentation might cause an increase in the competitiveness in the market for corporate control, which would cause acquirers to capture only a smaller portion of any potential synergistic gains. On the other hand, increased market integration yields reduced transaction costs for cross-border acquisitions and might induce agency problems and hubris of the acquirer's management.

despite the EU harmonization process is not as advanced as widely perceived. The comparison of the success of the U.S. and German transactions also shows that the market power hypothesis is not of relatively high importance, assuming that market power is more of an argument for success of transactions in the acquirer's domestic market.

The evidence for systematic differences of determinants of transaction success among the U.S., German, and European samples is relatively weak and only indicated that large transactions (in absolute and relative value) seem to negatively impact shareholder wealth in the European sample, opposite to the noted influence for the U.S. transactions. Holding acquirer characteristics constant did not substantially yield additional insights into which U.S. specific factors contribute to transaction success.

Overall, diversifying geographically does not generally seem to be beneficial for German acquirers, but crossing the Atlantic apparently is. Given that compared to domestic transactions, cross-border transactions are more prone to result from an active corporate growth strategy, it seems as if the capital market only rewards those that aim at the U.S. market with its relatively higher growth rates and herewith associated more promising business prospects, and not those that aim at European target companies. Divergent corporate and local cultures and their potentially negative implications for the management of the transaction execution and post-merger integration do not seem to be a major concern of investors for U.S. transactions. However, such aspects may serve as an explanation for transaction failure in addition to other factors cited in the literature,[177] for example overpayment,[178] over-optimistic synergy projections,[179] momentum building,[180] non-fit of the target and its resources and capabilities,[181] and lack of redeployment of key employees from the acquiring company to the target.[182]

Table 5.66 concludes the empirical part of this study by displaying the various reasons cited by the CFOs in the survey for the success or failure of their transactions.

---

177 See BREALEY and MYERS (2000), p. 942. VERY and SCHWEIGER (2001) for example provide an overview that follows the standardized structure of a transaction process to explain the various problem areas faced when pursuing an acquisition.

178 See WIEANDT and SANTIAGO (2005), p. 85; CORDING ET AL. (2002), p. 12. For example SIROWER (1997) found that the higher the premium paid, the bigger the losses for acquirer shareholders. In this context RAPPAPORT (1986) points out that the present value of anticipated synergies must be greater than the premium paid, in order for the transaction to create shareholder wealth gains.

179 See CANTWELL and SANTANGELO (2002), p. 405.

180 HASPESLAGH and JEMISON (1991) point out that momentum builds in unpredictable ways during the transaction process, reflecting increased commitment by the people involved, secrecy, and intensity of the process, as well as the influence of the outside advisors. For example, WIEANDT and SANTIAGO (2005, p. 95) list the ability to "say no" as a critical success factor for *Deutsche Bank AG*.

181 See BECKER (2005); CHATTERJEE and BOURGEOIS (2002), p. 2.

182 See ANAND ET AL. (2005), pp. 206-209; STEINEBACH ET AL. (2005), p. 109.

Table 5.66: Reasons for transaction success cited in the survey

Cited reasons for transaction success / failure
Success
• "Strong growth, realization of synergies, successful rebranding"
• "Complementary product portfolio, international roll-out, cross-selling opportunities"
• "Serves as a platform to further enhance U.S. activities, strengthens our position in the U.S."
• "Vertical integration, market leadership"
• "Higher growth rates, international diversification"
• "Adequate speed of integration"
• "Integration and achieving planned synergies"
• "Increase of market share, internalization"
Failure
• "Strong domestic competition with good connections to U.S. companies"
• "Cultural skills, understanding of specialties in that business model"
• "Not far enough integrated, no member of acquirer installed at management of target"
• "Highly cyclical business, underestimated litigation risks"
• "Customer relationship/dependency was underestimated"
• "No key personnel from acquirer into target, lack of financial control of target"
• "Limited knowledge of markets"

6 Summary and outlook

In light of the position of the United States as the single most important target country for cross-border mergers and acquisitions by German companies during the fifth merger wave, the goals of this study were to (i) detect special aspects that impact the structure and management of a U.S. cross-border transaction, (ii) evaluate from the perspective of the acquirer's shareholders and management how German companies succeeded in the U.S. environment, and (iii) identify potential determinants of cross-border transaction success. This summary condenses the conclusions and implications with regard to these goals discussed at the end of Chapters 3 and 5.

A large number of local institutional peculiarities must be taken into consideration when deciding on the structure of a U.S. cross-border acquisition, including the treatment of the liabilities of the target, the form of payment choice, tax implications, and, especially for public targets, timing, consent, and fiduciary issues resulting from federal securities regulations and applicable state corporate laws.

As shown in the review of the U.S. legal framework in Chapter 3 and confirmed by a survey of executives of German acquirers of U.S. targets, during the various subjects of due diligence the identification of the target company's liabilities should focus on

- pending or potential litigation and product liability claims, which might result in substantial costs due to compensatory and punitive damages,
- environmental matters, given the extended and retroactive responsibility for violations of environmental compliance beyond those parties causing it, and
- specific employee-related issues, particularly workers compensation and discrimination claims and insufficient funding of retirement and post-employment defined benefits plans. Additional matters encountered by a foreign acquirer relate to the U.S. compensation system for executives and to the flexibility of implementing a reduction of the target company's workforce, especially in the presence of a collective bargaining agreement with a labor union.

With certain exceptions such as the bulk sales law, structuring the transaction as an asset deal generally permits the acquirer to avoid inadvertently assuming the target's liabilities. If instead the transaction is structured as a share deal, acquirers in the United States typically rely less on codified law and more on extensive representations and warranties as well as indemnifications in the acquisition agreement in order to shift the responsibility for disclosed and undisclosed liabilities back to the seller.

From a tax perspective, structuring a U.S. acquisition as an asset deal does not allow the acquirer to use the target's tax attributes, such as carryforwards of net operating losses, but it does transform the purchase price into future deductions for amortization and depreciation expense through the step-up of the book value of the acquired assets, including goodwill resulting from the transaction. For the seller such a structure is less favorable, since it creates an immediate double layer of taxes for the target company and its shareholders that frequently exceed the present value of the acquirer's future tax benefit in an asset deal. As a consequence, U.S. transactions are mainly structured as share deals, as shown by the sample transactions in the event study and the survey of executives within the empirical analysis in Chapter 5.

A tax-free treatment of a U.S. transaction is permitted only if shares are used at least partially as the form of payment, which typically requires a secondary listing of the acquirer on a U.S. stock exchange. Besides potential pressure on the acquirer's share price caused by major flow backs of shares initially used as the form of payment, such a listing adds a substantial burden given the required compliance with U.S. accounting standards and federal securities laws, including the onerous provisions of the Sarbanes-Oxley Act. As a result, German companies chose to pay sellers with shares in only 12 percent of the analyzed U.S. acquisitions.

U.S. federal securities laws also contain procedural and disclosure requirements applicable to an acquisition of a public target company that is structured as a tender offer, proxy solicitation, or exchange offer. Those three transaction structures differ in terms of the time and filings needed to pursue the acquisition, and due to applicable state corporate laws, they also differ regarding the required level of the target shareholders' consent, especially in connection with a planned merger of the acquisition vehicle and the target. Regardless of the transaction structure, state corporate laws impose fiduciary duties on the target's directors that might affect negotiation and the price of the acquisition.

Other transactional complications to be considered by a foreign acquirer comprise

- the stronger emphasis in the United States on multiples in the valuation of the target, which could make the cross-border transaction more expensive than a domestic one,
- the differences in the applied financial reporting standards between U.S. GAAP and German GAAP or IFRS, mainly in the accounting for fixed assets, inventory, provisions, and pension and health care plans, and
- the regulatory pre-transaction review requirements under the Hart-Scott-Rodino Act and the Exon-Florio statute.

Against this backdrop, the quantitative and qualitative evaluation of 87[1] transactions during the period from 1990 to 2004 showed that German companies were on average successful in navigating the potential risks inherent in the transaction process. However, the success of individual transactions revealed stark variances, with cumulative abnormal returns to acquirer shareholders ranging from 23.01 percent to -10.75 percent for the three days centered on the announcement date and with responses in the survey of executives ranging from "full success" to "full failure". Transactions by companies in the new economy unanimously generated significant losses for their shareholders over a slightly extended post-announcement event window. Subjective evaluations by executives as well as some divestitures of targets or bankruptcies of acquirers in subsequent years corroborated that initial assessment by investors. The majority of those transactions were structured as an exchange offer during the period of buoyant capital markets in 1999 and 2000, thereby supporting the assumption in the finance literature of a positive correlation between a high market-to-book value of acquirers and the likelihood of choosing shares as the method of payment. Within the 78 transactions in the event study sample, those exchange offers destroyed the most wealth for acquirer shareholders.

Controlling for new economy acquirers provided a more refined perspective for the success rate variations. In most cases the dichotomous and cross-sectional analyses of the event study and survey samples confirmed the hypothesized directional influence of the 16 determinants of transaction success that were inductively derived in Chapter 4 from the review of prior empirical research. However, a statistically significant impact on shareholder wealth gains was only observed for the

- absolute size of the acquiring company,
- status of the target company,
- absolute transaction volume,
- strategic direction of the transaction, and
- relative strength of the U.S. economic growth and of the Euro compared to the U.S. dollar.

Due to increased international competition the majority of the large DAX30 companies in pursuit of becoming a global player acquired multiple U.S. targets during the observation period. However, the higher cumulative abnormal returns for the smaller non-DAX30 companies might hint at a better strategic conception of their less frequent acquisitions. These findings might also demonstrate a weakness of the event study methodology, since the share

[1] The analysis included 78 transactions in the event study and 25 transactions in the survey responses, of which 16 transactions overlapped between both samples.

prices of DAX30 acquirers could have already incorporated the external growth strategy and therefore did not elicit a significant reaction to the announcement of a transaction. While the positive cumulative abnormal returns for acquirers of private target companies indicate the existence of a liquidity discount, the shareholder losses for acquirers of public targets reflect the (i) tendentiously higher purchase price premiums, which are evidenced by high cumulative abnormal returns of 23.00 percent[2] for the shareholders of 26 public targets in the sample, and the (ii) potential burdensomeness of higher transactional complexity due to the procedural SEC requirements. Analogous to the observed success in the survey responses, these differences in shareholder value creation were more distinct for the extended post-announcement event window when partitioning the sample based on transaction volume. For private targets the wealth effects were more positive when the transaction volume was at least $1b. A similar relation was shown for public targets, although the cumulative abnormal returns were still negative. A comparison of the absolute transaction volume to the size of the acquirer did not yield significant implications.

Unlike vertical acquisitions, horizontal acquisitions pursued to extract synergistic gains as well as conglomerate transactions aimed at a simultaneous geographic and industrial diversification were found to create significant shareholder wealth. These findings support the validity of both the strategic management and portfolio theories as endogenous explanations for the occurrence of shareholder value-oriented M&A activity.

Besides the benefit from a strong Euro in the form of a reduced need for relatively costly external financing, an exogenous factor of the business environment found to positively influence transaction success was a relatively high growth of the U.S. gross domestic product. The importance of the economic growth of the United States as the world's most dominant consumer market was further highlighted by the negative cumulative abnormal returns for a control sample of 82 European cross-border acquisitions by the same German acquirers as in the U.S. sample. Apparently, investors seemed to have less confidence in the business expectations for the more heterogeneous and stagnant European markets. In order to determine whether those patterns in abnormal returns were also attributable to differentiating aspects of the execution of the U. S. cross-border transactions, an additional control sample of 35 German domestic transactions was included in the analysis. Creating the intersection of identical companies in all three subsamples allowed for holding acquirer characteristics constant, but did not detect systematic differences with regard to those determinants of transactions success that were identified as being significant for the U.S. cross-border acquisitions.

2 For the [-1,1] event window.

In closing, it can be concluded that this study's main focus on characteristics of the acquiring and target companies and of the acquisition execution phase did not fully explain the variations in the success of U.S. cross-border transactions, whereby the reliance on immediate efficiency of the capital markets and the size of the event study and survey samples might weaken the generalizations of some findings. The responses from the surveyed German executives provided an indication though how the examined determinants interact with the strategic conception of the transaction and the post-closing integration of the target company. Accordingly, an evaluation of an acquirer's ability in an acquisition to formulate a stringent strategy, extract synergies, transfer competencies, and bridge disparate country and corporate cultures would yield further insights into the causes of transaction success. For example, it would be interesting to compare the DAX30 companies' approach to the screening of U.S. targets to that of smaller non-public companies, which are not pressured by the demands of the capital markets and which typically do not maintain broad in-house M&A capabilities, or to that of private equity firms, which increasingly challenge transaction opportunities for strategic investors. Moreover, since the short-term share price reactions only reflect investors' expectations regarding the economic benefit of a transaction at the time of its announcement, a further refinement of the methodology for long-term capital market studies would provide another means to measure the actual realization of synergistic gains. The continuing integration of international capital markets and the market for corporate control accompanied by a sharp recent increase in the level of cross-border mergers and acquisitions by German companies in the United States will offer a fruitful basis for further research into the success of transactions and its determinants.

Appendix

A Survey of executives

A1 Questionnaire

Structure and Success of Acquisitions
of U.S. Target Companies by German Acquirers

General remarks

- All information will be treated strictly confidential.
- The analysis of the completed questionnaires will not allow the reader to draw any conclusions on individual participating companies.
- The names of the acquired U.S. target companies are not relevant. If you prefer, you can return the entire questionnaire anonymously. A neutral return envelope is attached.

Definitions

- The term "acquisition" is used in a generic sense and includes all transactions in which the business of the acquirer and target company is combined through the acquisition of a majority of shares (i.e. > 50%) or assets or through a statutory merger.
- The term "cross-border" is used for all acquisitions in which the target company was incorporated outside of Germany.

Instructions for completing the questionnaire

- In case you cannot respond to particular questions, please leave them unanswered.
- The questionnaire is divided into two parts:

  Part A: General information regarding the acquiring company, the structure of transactions and the evaluation of the success of acquisitions.

  Part B: Specific information regarding a particular acquisition of U.S. target companies in the period January 1, 1990 – December 31, 2004.
- There are 4 copies provided of Part B in case your company had multiple acquisitions of U.S. target companies in the period January 1, 1990 – December 31, 2004.
- The completion of the questionnaire should take not more than 25 minutes (in case of one acquisition).
- If you wish to receive a copy of the results of the study, please attach your business card to the questionnaire or mail it in a separate envelope.
- Please return the questionnaire by July 31, 2005, to:

Attn. Bernd Wübben
345 Park Avenue 40th floor
New York, NY 10154 USA

A. GENERAL INFORMATION *(APPLICABLE TO ALL TRANSACTIONS)*

1. Name of the acquiring company (Can be omitted.) ______________________________

2. Industry *(Please fill in.)* ____

3. Is your company a public company?

- ☐ Yes
- ☐ Yes, listed on the DAX
- ☐ No

4. What was the approximate total number of domestic and cross-border acquisitions of your company during the period January 1, 1990 – December 31, 2004?

- ☐ 1 - 5
- ☐ 6 - 10
- ☐ 11 - 20
- ☐ Above 20

5. Of the total number of those transactions, what was the approximate proportion of cross-border transactions?

- ☐ 1 - 10%
- ☐ 11 - 25%
- ☐ 25 - 50%
- ☐ Above 50%

6. Considering all transactions in the period January 1, 1990 – December 31, 2004, what was the size of deals, measured based on the purchase price?
(Please check all that apply.)

- ☐ Less than $100 million
- ☐ $100 million - $250 million
- ☐ $250 million - $500 million
- ☐ $500 million - $1 billion
- ☐ Over $1 billion

7. Had you had previous experience with acquisitions of U.S. target companies before January 1, 1990?

- ☐ Yes
- ☐ No

8. Is the inclusion of external advisors in a cross-border due diligence process more important than in a domestic transaction?

- ☐ Yes
- ☐ No

9. In the specific context of the acquisition of a U.S. target company, are there any areas of due diligence that are of higher importance than in a domestic transaction?
(Please check all that apply.)

	Importance				
	Very high	High	Low	Very low	N/A
Finance and accounting	☐	☐	☐	☐	☐
Legal	☐	☐	☐	☐	☐
Tax	☐	☐	☐	☐	☐
Environmental	☐	☐	☐	☐	☐
Human resource	☐	☐	☐	☐	☐
Marketing	☐	☐	☐	☐	☐
Organization & IT	☐	☐	☐	☐	☐
Cultural	☐	☐	☐	☐	☐

10. Are there any specific concerns in conducting a due diligence for a U.S. target?

(Please fill in.)

____

11. Aside from usual issues faced with any domestic or cross-border transaction, are there any specific concerns for the process of acquiring a target company in the United States?

(Please fill in.)

____

12. Are the premiums paid in a cross-border transaction higher than in a domestic acquisition?

☐ Yes
☐ No

13. Which criteria do you use for measuring the success of acquisitions?
(Please check all that apply.)

	Importance				
	Very high	High	Low	Very low	N/A
- Change of stock price (if acquirer is public)	☐	☐	☐	☐	☐
CHANGE OF THE FOLLOWING FINANCIAL RATIOS					
- Revenue growth	☐	☐	☐	☐	☐
- Profit	☐	☐	☐	☐	☐
- EBIT	☐	☐	☐	☐	☐
- Cash flow	☐	☐	☐	☐	☐
- Other *(Please fill in.)*________________	☐	☐	☐	☐	☐
ACHIEVEMENT OF OBJECTIVES OF THE ACQUISITION					
- Realization of synergies	☐	☐	☐	☐	☐
- Risk reduction	☐	☐	☐	☐	☐
- Increase/Protection of market share	☐	☐	☐	☐	☐
- Other *(Please fill in.)*________________	☐	☐	☐	☐	☐

14. To the performance of which company do you apply those criteria?

☐ Acquirer
☐ Target
☐ Combined company

15. How many years after the consummation of an acquisition is it possible to evaluate its success?

☐ Within the first year following the closing of the acquisition
☐ 1 year – 3 years
☐ More than 3 years

16. Considering all transactions in the period January 1, 1990 – December 31, 2004, how would you evaluate those? *(Please check all that apply.)*

☐ Success
☐ Failure
☐ Neutral

17. How would you generally compare the success of cross-border acquisitions to those of domestic ones?

☐ More successful
☐ Less successful
☐ No difference

B. INFORMATION REGARDING SPECIFIC U.S. ACQUISITION #1

1. **Industry** (Please fill in.) ______________________________

2. **What was the strategic direction of the acquisition (i.e. business sector affinity)?**

- ☐ Horizontal
- ☐ Vertical
- ☐ Conglomerate

3. **Year of acquisition** *(Please fill in.)* ______________________________

4. **Were there any other bidders for the target company?**

- ☐ Yes
- ☐ No

5. **What was the approximate relative size of the target company compared to your company, measured based on revenue?**

- ☐ Less than 5%
- ☐ 5% - 10%
- ☐ 11% - 25%
- ☐ 26% - 50%
- ☐ Over 50%

6. **What was the approximate purchase price for the acquisition?**

- ☐ Less than $100 million
- ☐ $100 million - $250 million
- ☐ $250 million - $500 million
- ☐ $500 million - $1 billion
- ☐ Over $1 billion

7. **What was the form of payment?**

- ☐ Cash
- ☐ Cash – including post-closing payments based on conditional earn-out agreements
- ☐ Shares of the acquiring company (or a subsidiary)
- ☐ Other *(Please fill in.)* ______________________________

8. **Was there a previous participation in the target (<50%) before the transaction?**

- ☐ Yes
- ☐ No

9. **Who initiated the transaction?**

- ☐ Acquirer
- ☐ Target

10. Did an external advisor assist you in structuring the transaction?

- ☐ Yes *(Please fill in the name.)*__________________________________
- ☐ No

11. What were the reasons (i.e. objectives) for acquiring the U.S. target company?
(If you check more than one, please rank them, with "1" being the most important reason(s)).

- ☐ To enter the U.S. market
- ☐ To diversify internationally
- ☐ To realize synergy potentials
- ☐ To benefit from tax attributes of the target company (e.g. loss carryforwards)
- ☐ To use excess free cash
- ☐ To acquire competitive advantages (e.g. superior technology, marketing skills)
- ☐ To benefit from comparative advantages of the U.S. market (e.g. higher growth rates compared to Germany)
- ☐ To increase/protect market share
- ☐ To benefit from the $/Euro(DM) currency exchange ratio
- ☐ To acquire a target company below its replacement cost
- ☐ To increase efficiency of the target company (e.g. by replacing its management)
- ☐ Personal motives
- ☐ Other *(Please fill in.)*

12. In case the main reason for the acquisition was to realize synergy potentials, which types of synergy were mainly considered?

	Importance				
	Very high	High	Low	Very low	N/A
Operational cost reductions	☐	☐	☐	☐	☐
Overhead cost reductions	☐	☐	☐	☐	☐
Revenue enhancements	☐	☐	☐	☐	☐
Financial	☐	☐	☐	☐	☐
Differential (acquirer's management is more efficient)	☐	☐	☐	☐	☐
Other *(Please fill in.)*________________	☐	☐	☐	☐	☐

13. What was the basic form of the transaction?

- ☐ Asset deal
- ☐ Share deal
- ☐ Merger

14. In case of a share acquisition, what was the transaction form for U.S. tax purposes?

- ☐ Not applicable, since the transaction was not a share acquisition
- ☐ Taxable share acquisition
- ☐ Taxable share acquisition using Section 338(g) election
- ☐ Taxable share acquisition using Section 338(h)(10) election
- ☐ Tax-free transaction

15. Was a due diligence performed before the closing of the transaction?

- ☐ Yes
- ☐ No

If the answer to question #15 is "No", please skip to question #19.

16. In which area was the due diligence conducted? (*Please check all that apply.*)

- ☐ Financial and accounting
- ☐ Legal
- ☐ Tax
- ☐ Environmental
- ☐ Human resource
- ☐ Marketing
- ☐ Organization & IT
- ☐ Cultural

17. Was the performance of the due diligence supported by external advisors?

- ☐ Yes
- ☐ No

If the answer to question #17 is "No", please skip to question #19.

18. Which advisors were involved in the due diligence process?
(Please check all that apply.)

- ☐ Investment bank *(Please fill in the name.)*____________________
- ☐ Auditors *(Please fill in the name.)*____________________
- ☐ Lawyers *(Please fill in the name.)*____________________
- ☐ Tax advisors *(Please fill in the name.)*____________________
- ☐ Environmental specialists
- ☐ Human resource specialists
- ☐ Product specialists (e.g. technicians)
- ☐ Others *(Please fill in.)*____________________

19. In case the U.S. target was a private company, which valuation technique was applied?

- ☐ Not applicable, since no private U.S. target company was acquired
- ☐ Asset-based valuation (at replacement or liquidation value)
- ☐ Comparable market multiples *(Please fill in.)*____________________
- ☐ Discounted future earnings method
- ☐ Discounted cash flow model
- ☐ Combination method *(Please fill in.)*____________________
- ☐ Other *(Please fill in.)*____________________

20. In case the U.S. target was a public company, which valuation technique was applied in determining the share price?

- ☐ Not applicable, since no public U.S. target company was acquired
- ☐ Comparable multiples (Please fill in.)______________________________
- ☐ Discounted cash flow mode
- ☐ Other *(Please fill in.)*______________________________________

If your company does not use a discounted cash flow model in valuing target companies, please skip to question #22.

21. When employing the discounted cash flow model, how was the discount rate determined?

- ☐ Average cost of capital of the acquiring company
- ☐ Cost of equity of the acquiring company
- ☐ Average cost of capital of the target company
- ☐ Cost of equity of the target company
- ☐ Other *(Please fill in.)*______________________________________

22. What was the degree of post-acquisition integration of the target company?

- ☐ Little (the target is still economically independent)
- ☐ Medium (certain activities are shared between the acquirer and the target)
- ☐ Strong (the target is fully integrated into the group of the acquirer)

23. Was the management of the target company retained after the closing?

- ☐ Yes
- ☐ No

24. How would you evaluate the success of this acquisition?

- ☐ Very successful
- ☐ Somewhat successful
- ☐ Neutral
- ☐ Partial failure
- ☐ Full failure

25. What was the main factor for the positive or negative success of this acquisition? (Please fill in.)

____
____
____
____
____
____

Thank you very much for your kind participation.

A2 Cover letter

Bernd Wübben
345 Park Avenue, 40th floor
New York, NY 10154 USA

New York, 7. Juni 2005

Name der Gesellschaft
z.Hd.
Adresse

Sehr geehrter Herr (Name),

im Rahmen einer wissenschaftlichen Dissertation am Institute for Mergers & Acquisitions der Universität Witten-Herdecke sowie mit Unterstützung der KPMG Deutsche Treuhand-Gesellschaft wird eine Studie durchgeführt, die die Struktur und den Erfolg von Akquisitionen deutscher Unternehmen in den USA analysiert. Dabei soll die Studie Antworten auf folgende zentrale Fragestellungen geben:

- Welche Besonderheiten sind hinsichtlich der Transaktionsphase einer Akquisition in den USA aus Sicht eines deutschen Erwerbers zu beachten?
- Wie erfolgreich sind Akquisitionen deutscher Unternehmen in den USA im Zeitraum 1. Januar 1990 bis 31. Dezember 2004 gewesen?
- Welche Faktoren haben maßgeblich zum Erfolg einer Akquisition in den USA beigetragen?

In diesem Zusammenhang möchte ich Sie herzlichst bitten, den beiliegenden Fragebogen zu beantworten. Die Beantwortung wird ungefähr 25 Minuten in Anspruch nehmen, in Fall von multiplen Akquistionen in der Vergangenheit gegebenenfalls etwas mehr. Eine strikt vertrauliche Behandlung der Ergebnisse wird Ihnen an dieser Stelle versichert, zudem wird die Studie keine Rückschlüsse auf Einzelaussagen einzelner Unternehmen oder Personen erlauben.

Ich würde es sehr begrüssen, wenn Sie die Bearbeitung des Fragebogens und somit die Durchführung der Studie unterstützen würden. Gerne übersende ich Ihnen nach Fertigstellung der Dissertation ein Exemplar.

Für Fragen stehe ich Ihnen gerne zur Verfügung.

Mit freundlichen Grüssen

Bernd Wübben

B Capital market based event study

B1 Overall success of the analyzed transactions

B1.1 Cumulative abnormal returns for German acquirers (MSCI)

(n=78) Event window	CAR %	Positive %	Negative %	Z-statistic	Z-statistic B
Period surrounding the announcement					
{0}	0.62 **	62	38	1.7788	2.6942
[-1,1]	1.16 *	50	50	1.4365	2.8158
[-2,2]	-0.01 *	50	50	1.5071	0.5107
[-5,5]	-1.60 *	45	55	1.4162	-0.5724
[-10,10]	-1.73 *	46	54	1.3456	-0.5109
[-20,20]	-2.69	46	54	1.1106	-0.4696
Pre-announcement period					
[-1,0]	1.18 **	50	50	1.7436	3.7038
[-10,-1]	-0.11 *	42	58	1.3492	0.3244
[-20,-1]	-1.08	46	54	1.1095	-0.2398
[-2,1]	0.75 *	49	51	1.4471	1.6697
[-5,1]	0.27	58	42	1.2533	1.2192
[-10,1]	0.50 *	51	49	1.3379	0.9698
[-20,1]	-0.47	49	51	1.1261	0.2688
Post-announcement period					
[0,1]	0.61	53	47	1.2796	1.6499
[0,10]	-1.62 *	46	54	1.3424	-1.0153
[1,10]	-2.24 *	42	58	1.2906	-1.9168
[1,20]	-2.24	32	68	0.0907	-1.0350
[-1,10]	-1.07 *	49	51	1.3765	-0.2378
[-1,20]	-1.06	46	54	1.1455	0.1299

This table shows the results for an event study analyzing 78 acquisitions of U.S. target companies by German acquirers during the period from 1990 to 2004. Cumulative abnormal returns are calculated employing the standard market model, using an estimation period of 253 trading days prior to the event window [-20,20] and the MSCI index to measure market returns. Tests for statistical significance follow BOEHMER ET AL. (1991), while Z-statistic B is computed following DODD and WARNER (1983). *, ** denote significance at the 10% and 5% level, respectively (based on a one-tailed Z-test).

B1.2 Statistical distribution of CARs for various event windows (MSCI)

	Event window [-1,1]		Event window [-1,10]	
(n=78)	Positive CAR (%)	Negative CAR (%)	Positive CAR (%)	Negative CAR (%)
Proportion	50	50	49	51
Maximum	25.32	-9.90	23.85	-22.72
Minimum	0.04	-0.05	0.18	0.00
Mean	5.13	-2.81	4.40	-6.26
Median	3.70	-1.68	2.66	-4.94
Std.	5.25	2.81	4.58	5.30

B1.3 CARs for German acquirers excluding NEMAX companies (MSCI)

(n=68) Event window	CAR %	Positive %	Negative %	Z-statistic	Z-statistic B
Period surrounding the announcement					
{0}	0.50 *	65	35	1.6071	2.4657
[-1,1]	0.62	49	51	1.1781	2.1712
[-2,2]	0.02	51	49	1.1388	0.5476
[-5,5]	-0.43	49	51	1.0335	0.0357
[-10,10]	-0.50	50	50	1.1243	-0.0297
[-20,20]	-0.63	49	51	0.9525	0.0448
Pre-announcement period					
[-1,0]	0.68 *	46	54	1.4088	3.0091
[-10,-1]	-0.50	44	56	1.1112	0.0472
[-20,-1]	-0.66	46	54	0.9274	-0.1947
[-2,1]	0.40	49	51	1.1456	1.3395
[-5,1]	0.10	59	41	1.0000	1.0444
[-10,1]	-0.05	53	47	1.1227	0.6120
[-20,1]	-0.21	49	51	0.9529	0.2346
Post-announcement period					
[0,1]	0.45	53	47	1.1782	1.3936
[0,10]	0.00	51	49	1.1360	-0.0861
[1,10]	-0.50	49	51	1.0777	-0.8700
[1,20]	-0.47	37	63	0.1054	-0.2925
[-1,10]	0.17	54	46	1.1396	0.4343
[-1,20]	0.21	50	50	0.9859	0.6284

This table shows the results for an event study analyzing 68 acquisitions of U.S. target companies by German acquirers during the period from 1990 to 2004, excluding transactions by companies listed on the NEMAX. Cumulative abnormal returns are calculated employing the standard market model, using an estimation period of 253 trading days prior to the event window [-20,20] and the MSCI index to measure market returns. Tests for statistical significance follow BOEHMER ET AL. (1991), while Z-statistic B is computed following DODD and WARNER (1983). * denotes significance at the 10% level (based on a one-tailed Z-test).

B1.4 Statistical distribution of CARs for various event windows excluding German acquirers listed on the NEMAX (MSCI)

	Event window [-1,1]		**Event window [-1,10]**	
(n=68)	Positive CAR (%)	Negative CAR (%)	Positive CAR (%)	Negative CAR (%)
Proportion	49	51	54	46
Maximum	15.01	-9.90	23.85	-17.16
Minimum	0.04	-0.05	0.18	-0.56
Mean	4.04	-2.59	4.29	-4.75
Median	3.43	-1.57	2.66	-3.83
Std.	3.86	2.66	4.60	3.83

B1.5 CARs for German acquirers listed on the NEMAX (MSCI)

(n=10) Event window	CAR %	Positive %	Negative %	Z-statistic	Z-statistic B
Period surrounding the announcement					
{0}	1.48	40	60	0.7554	1.0946
[-1,1]	4.79	60	40	1.2483	2.2024
[-2,2]	-0.19 *	40	60	1.6446	-0.0015
[-5,5]	-9.57 **	20	80	1.8192	-1.6915
[-10,10]	-10.06 *	20	80	1.4770	-1.3495
[-20,20]	-16.74	30	70	1.2146	-1.4285
Pre-announcement period					
[-1,0]	4.57 *	80	20	1.5081	2.4973
[-10,-1]	2.53	30	70	1.2555	0.7830
[-20,-1]	-3.94	50	50	1.1065	-0.1622
[-2,1]	3.15 *	50	50	1.2847	1.1702
[-5,1]	1.42	50	50	1.2160	0.6816
[-10,1]	4.22	40	60	1.1711	1.1124
[-20,1]	-2.25	50	50	1.0699	0.1390
Post-announcement period					
[0,1]	1.69	50	50	0.5901	0.9740
[0,10]	-12.59 **	10	90	1.6528	-2.6112
[1,10]	-14.07 **	0	100	1.7169	-3.0848
[1,20]	-14.28	0	100	0.0582	-2.1279
[-1,10]	-9.49 **	10	90	1.6839	-1.7965
[-1,20]	-9.70 *	20	80	1.3480	-1.2759

This table shows the results for an event study analyzing 10 acquisitions of U.S. target companies by German acquirers during the period from 1990 to 2004. Cumulative abnormal returns are calculated employing the standard market model, using an estimation period of 253 trading days prior to the event window [-20,20] and the MSCI index to measure market returns. Tests for statistical significance follow BOEHMER ET AL. (1991), while Z-statistic B is computed following DODD and WARNER (1983). *, ** denote significance at the 10% and 5% level, respectively (based on a one-tailed Z-test).

B1.6 Statistical distribution of CARs for various event windows for German acquirers listed on the NEMAX (MSCI)

	Event window [-1,1]		**Event window [-1,10]**	
(n=10)	Positive CAR (%)	Negative CAR (%)	Positive CAR (%)	Negative CAR (%)
Proportion	60	40	10	90
Maximum	25.32	-9.38	8.24	-22.72
Minimum	4.20	-1.68	8.24	0.00
Mean	11.14	-4.73	8.24	-11.46
Median	9.11	-3.94	8.24	-10.96
Std.	7.91	3.76	n/a	6.52

B2 Characteristics of acquiring companies (MSCI)

B2.1 CARs by size of the acquirer (MSCI)

Var. A	**DAX30**			**Non-DAX30**			**Difference test**	
Event	(1)			(2)			(1)-(2)	
window	CAR%	Z-stat.	pos. %	CAR%	Z-stat.	pos. %	CAR%	t-stat.
Panel A: All transactions								
[-1,1]	0.13	1.0223	47	4.13 **	1.7364	60	-4.00***	-2.7814
[-1,10]	-0.42	1.0700	53	-2.95 *	1.2854	35	2.53*	1.3503
(n)	(58)			(20)				
Panel B: No NEMAX transactions								
[-1,1]	0.13	1.0223	47	3.47 *	1.5250	60	-3.34**	-2.1420
[-1,10]	-0.42	1.0700	53	3.59	1.1262	60	-4.01**	-1.9226
(n)	(58)			(10)				

The table shows the results of the univariate analysis of the impact of the acquirer's size on the cumulative abnormal returns, including mean-difference tests. A transaction is included in subgroup (1) if the acquirer was listed in the DAX30 at the time of the announcement of the transaction. CARs are calculated as shown in Section 5.2.1.2. Tests for statistical significance follow BOEHMER ET AL. (1991). *, **, *** denote significance at the 10%, 5%, and 1% level, respectively (based on a one-tailed Z-test or t-test).

B2.2 CARs by liquidity ratio (MSCI)

Var. Ba	**<Mean liquidity**			**≥Mean liquidity**			**Difference test**	
Event	(1)			(2)			(1)-(2)	
window	CAR%	Z-stat.	pos. %	CAR%	Z-stat.	pos. %	CAR%	t-stat.
Panel A: All transactions								
[-1,1]	0.15 *	1.4462	49	2.43	1.0959	54	-2.28**	-1.7418
[-1,10]	-0.57	1.1668	49	-0.78	1.1061	54	0.21	0.1316
(n)	(39)			(28)				
Panel B: No NEMAX transactions								
[-1,1]	0.02 *	1.3019	47	0.99	0.7123	50	-0.97	-0.9392
[-1,10]	-0.41	1.0641	50	0.47	0.7307	58	-0.88	-0.6136
(n)	(38)			(24)				

The table shows the results of the univariate analysis of the impact of the acquirer's financial position on the cumulative abnormal returns, including mean-difference tests. A transaction is included in subgroup (1) if the acquirer's ratio of current assets to its current liabilities on the balance sheet date preceding the announcement date of the transaction was below the mean ratio of all acquiring companies during the observation period. CARs are calculated as shown in Section 5.2.1.2. Tests for statistical significance follow BOEHMER ET AL. (1991). *, ** denote significance at the 10% and 5% level, respectively (based on a one-tailed Z-test or t-test).

B2.3 CARs by cash-to-assets ratio (MSCI)

Var. Bb	**<10%**			**≥10%**			**Difference test**	
Event	(1)			(2)			(1)-(2)	
window	CAR%	Z-stat.	pos. %	CAR%	Z-stat.	pos. %	CAR%	t-stat.
Panel A: All transactions								
[-1,1]	0.74	0.8495	50	2.03	1.2327	56	-1.29	-0.8837
[-1,10]	-1.15	1.0773	48	-0.94	1.1817	48	-0.21	-0.1157
(n)	(48)			(25)				
Panel B: No NEMAX transactions								
[-1,1]	0.62	0.7580	51	0.93	1.0622	53	-0.31	-0.2351
[-1,10]	-0.29	1.0301	51	0.97	0.9135	58	-1.26	-0.7328
(n)	(45)			(19)				

The table shows the results of the univariate analysis of the impact of the acquirer's financial position on the cumulative abnormal returns, including mean-difference tests. A transaction is included in subgroup (1) if the acquirer's ratio of cash to total assets on the balance sheet date preceding the announcement date of the transaction was below 10 percent. CARs are calculated as shown in Section 5.2.1.2. Tests for statistical significance follow BOEHMER ET AL. (1991).

B2.4 CARs by market-to-book ratio (MSCI)

Var. C Event window	**<Mean MTBV** (1) CAR%	Z-stat.	pos. %	**≥Mean MTBV** (2) CAR%	Z-stat.	pos. %	**Difference test** (1)-(2) CAR%	t-stat.
Panel A: All transactions								
[-1,1]	1.26*	1.4582	54	0.99	0.5512	48	0.27	0.1704
[-1,10]	0.67	1.2575	60	-5.40	1.1962	19	6.07***	3.4471
(n)	(52)			(21)				
Panel B: No NEMAX transactions								
[-1,1]	1.00*	1.3915	53	-0.42	0.4961	46	1.42	0.9514
[-1,10]	0.52	1.2439	59	-1.63	1.0343	31	2.15	1.1113
(n)	(51)			(13)				

The table shows the results of the univariate analysis of the impact of the acquirer's market valuation on the cumulative abnormal returns, including mean-difference tests. A transaction is included in subgroup (1) if the acquirer's market-to-book value ("MTBV") at the beginning of the year in which the acquisition was announced was below the median MTBV for all acquirers. CARs are calculated as shown in Section 5.2.1.2. Tests for statistical significance follow BOEHMER ET AL. (1991). *, *** denote significance at the 10% and 1% level, respectively (based on a one-tailed Z-test or one-tailed t-test).

B2.5 CARs by previous investment in the target (MSCI)

Var. H Event window	**No toehold stake** (1) CAR%	Z-stat.	pos. %	**Toehold stake** (2) CAR%	Z-stat.	pos. %	**Difference test** (1)-(2) CAR%	t-stat.
Panel A: All transactions								
[-1,1]	1.28*	1.3723	49	-0.04	0.9638	57	1.32	0.5736
[-1,10]	-1.18*	1.3047	48	0.12	0.9705	57	-1.30	-0.4493
(n)	(71)			(7)				
Panel B: No NEMAX transactions								
[-1,1]	0.70	1.1123	48	-0.04	0.9638	57	0.74	0.3960
[-1,10]	0.18	1.0458	54	0.12	0.9705	57	0.06	0.0238
(n)	(61)			(7)				

The table shows the results of the univariate analysis of the impact of the acquirer's previous investment in the target on the cumulative abnormal returns, including mean-difference tests. A transaction is included in subgroup (1) if the acquirer did not own a previous stake in the target company. CARs are calculated as shown in Section 5.2.1.2. Tests for statistical significance follow BOEHMER ET AL. (1991); * denotes significance at the 10% level (based on a one-tailed Z-test)

B2.6 CARs by frequency of U.S. transactions (MSCI)

Var. C Event window	**Non-frequent/frequent-first** (1) CAR%	Z-stat.	pos. %	**Frequent-subsequent** (2) CAR%	Z-stat.	pos. %	**Difference test** (1)-(2) CAR%	t-stat.
Panel A: All transactions								
[-1,1]	1.41	1.2629	49	0.88	0.9291	51	0.53	0.4057
[-1,10]	-1.40	1.2345	44	-0.70	0.9714	54	-0.70	-0.4228
(n)	(41)			(37)				
Panel B: No NEMAX transactions								
[-1,1]	0.65	0.9371	47	0.60	0.8224	50	0.05	0.0452
[-1,10]	0.46	1.0691	53	-0.09	0.8896	56	0.55	0.3622
(n)	(32)			(36)				

The table shows the results of the univariate analysis of the impact of the acquirer's U.S. acquisition experience on the cumulative abnormal returns, including mean-difference tests. A transaction is included in subgroup (1) if it either reflects the acquirer's first or only acquisition of a U.S. target during the observation period. CARs are calculated as shown in Section 5.2.1.2. Tests for statistical significance follow BOEHMER ET AL. (1991).

B2.7 CARs for non-frequent acquirers by size of the acquirer (MSCI)

Var. D Event window	DAX30 (1) CAR%	Z-stat.	pos. %	Non-DAX30 (2) CAR%	Z-stat.	pos. %	Difference test (1)-(2) CAR%	t-stat.
Panel A: All transactions								
[-1,1]	-0.39	0.7172	67	3.76 *	1.6289	63	-4.15 *	-1.3409
[-1,10]	-2.60 ***	2.4704	44	-2.55 *	1.4077	38	-0.05	-0.0179
(n)	(9)			(16)				
Panel B: No NEMAX transactions								
[-1,1]	-0.39	0.7172	67	2.19 *	1.5950	56	-2.58	-1.1159
[-1,10]	-2.60 ***	2.4704	44	1.34 **	2.1422	56	-3.94 *	-1.4629
(n)	(9)			(9)				

The table shows the results of the univariate analysis of the impact of the acquirer's size on the cumulative abnormal returns for the first or only transaction in the United States, including mean-difference tests. A transaction, either an acquirer's first or only one during the observation period, is included in subgroup (1) if the acquirer was listed in the DAX30 at the time of the announcement of the transaction. CARs are calculated as shown in Section 5.2.1.2. Tests for statistical significance follow BOEHMER ET AL. (1991). *, **, *** denote significance at the 10%, 5%, and 1% level, respectively (based on a one-tailed Z-test or one-tailed t-test).

B3 Characteristics of target companies (MSCI)

B3.1 CARs by industry sectors (MSCI)

Event window	Financial services CAR%	Z-stat.	pos. %	Technology CAR%	Z-stat.	pos. %	Chemicals CAR%	Z-stat.	pos. %
Panel A: All transactions									
[-1,1]	1.21	1.2334	58	1.14	0.5038	53	-0.35	0.4095	35
[-1,10]	-0.61 *	1.4226	42	-6.81	1.1234	24	-0.37	0.9455	53
(n)	(12)			(17)			(17)		
Panel B: No NEMAX transactions									
[-1,1]				-2.65	0.6613	50			
[-1,10]	Same as above			-3.97	1.2014	38	Same as above		
(n)				(8)					

Event window	Healthcare CAR%	Z-stat.	pos. %	Industrial goods CAR%	Z-stat.	pos. %	Consumer goods CAR%	Z-stat.	pos. %
Panel A: All transactions									
[-1,1]	1.23	0.3953	40	1.08	0.7454	50	3.95 *	1.3257	50
[-1,10]	1.83 *	1.3091	50	1.19	0.5984	67	2.72 **	2.0972	75
(n)	(10)			(12)			(4)		
Panel B: No NEMAX transactions									
[-1,1]									
[-1,10]	Same as above			Same as above			Same as above		
(n)									

Event window	Other CAR%	Z-stat.	pos. %
Panel A: All transactions			
[-1,1]	3.21	1.0931	83
[-1,10]	1.24 *	1.4593	83
(n)	(6)		
Panel B: No NEMAX transactions			
[-1,1]	2.38	1.1755	80
[-1,10]	3.68 *	1.3795	100
(n)	(5)		

The table shows the results of the univariate analysis of the impact of the target's industry classification on the cumulative abnormal returns. CARs are calculated as shown in Section 5.2.1.2. Tests for statistical significance follow BOEHMER ET AL. (1991). *,** denote significance at the 10% and 5% level, respectively (based on a one-tailed Z-test).

B3.2 CARs by regulated industries (MSCI)

Var. E	Regulated			Non-regulated			Difference test	
Event	(1)			(2)			(1)-(2)	
window	CAR%	Z-stat.	pos. %	CAR%	Z-stat.	pos. %	CAR%	t-stat.
Panel A: All transactions								
[-1,1]	-0.41	0.3506	50	1.56 *	1.6076	50	-1.97	-1.2189
[-1,10]	-1.74	1.2760	44	-0.89 *	1.2968	50	-0.85	-0.4134
(n)	(16)			(62)				
Panel B: No NEMAX transactions								
[-1,1]	0.19	0.4137	53	0.75	1.2643	47	-0.56	-0.4050
[-1,10]	-1.00 *	1.3080	47	0.51	1.0333	57	-1.51	-0.8285
(n)	(15)			(53)				

The table shows the results of the univariate analysis of the impact of the target's industry classification on the cumulative abnormal returns, including mean-difference tests. A transaction is included in subgroup (1) if the target was classified in a regulated industry. CARs are calculated as shown in Section 5.2.1.2. Tests for statistical significance follow BOEHMER ET AL. (1991). * denotes significance at the 10% level (based on a one-tailed Z-test).

B3.3 CARs by status of the target (MSCI)

Var. F	Private			Public			Difference test	
Event	(1)			(2)			(1)-(2)	
window	CAR%	Z-stat.	pos. %	CAR%	Z-stat.	pos. %	CAR%	t-stat.
Panel A: All transactions								
[-1,1]	1.39*	1.5805	51	0.77	0.6252	48	0.62	0.4574
[-1,10]	0.50	1.1091	55	-3.72 *	1.3132	38	4.22***	2.5623
(n)	(49)			(29)				
Panel B: No NEMAX transactions								
[-1,1]	1.45**	1.6482	52	-0.89	0.7019	42	2.34**	2.0158
[-1,10]	1.56	1.0730	59	-2.36	1.1659	46	3.92***	2.5960
(n)	(44)			(24)				

The table shows the results of the univariate analysis of the impact of the target's status on the cumulative abnormal returns, including mean-difference tests. A transaction is included in subgroup (1) if the target was a private company. CARs are calculated as shown in Section 5.2.1.2. Tests for statistical significance follow BOEHMER ET AL. (1991). *, **, *** denote significance at the 10%, 5%, and 1% level, respectively (based on a one-tailed Z-test or one-tailed t-test).

B3.4 CARs by mega-deals (MSCI)

Var. Gb	<$1b			≥$1b			Difference test	
Event	(1)			(2)			(1)-(2)	
window	CAR%	Z-stat.	pos. %	CAR%	Z-stat.	pos. %	CAR%	t-stat.
Panel A: All transactions								
[-1,1]	1.04	1.1096	47	1.43	0.9397	57	-0.39	-0.2702
[-1,10]	-2.11*	1.2844	42	1.44	1.0576	65	-3.55**	-2.0001
(n)	(55)			(23)				
Panel B: No NEMAX transactions								
[-1,1]	0.21	0.7068	44	1.43	0.9397	57	-1.22	-1.0213
[-1,10]	-0.47	0.9820	49	1.44	1.0576	65	-1.91	-1.2039
(n)	(45)			(23)				

The table shows the results of the univariate analysis of the impact of the transaction volume on the cumulative abnormal returns, including mean-difference tests. A transaction is included in subgroup (1) if the transaction volume was less than $1b. CARs are calculated as shown in Section 5.2.1.2. Tests for statistical significance follow BOEHMER ET AL. (1991). *, ** denote significance at the 10% and 5% level, respectively (based on a one-tailed Z-test or one-tailed t-test).

B3.5 CARs by transaction volume (MSCI)

Var. Ga Event window	<$100m (1) CAR%	pos. %	$100m-$249m (2) CAR%	pos. %	$250m-$499m (3) CAR%	pos. %	$500m-$999m (4) CAR%	pos. %	≥$1b (5) CAR%	pos. %
Panel A: All transactions										
[-1,1]	9.42**	83	0.88	53	-0.74	33	-0.18*	41	1.43	57
[-1,10]	-3.64*	33	-0.26	59	-2.96	33	-2.67	35	1.44	65
(n)	(6)		(17)		(15)		(17)		(23)	
Panel B: No NEMAX transactions										
[-1,1]	10.62[a]	100	0.67	50	-0.13	42	-0.65	38	1.43	57
[-1,10]	12.14[a]	100	0.47	63	-0.54	42	-2.16	38	1.44	65
(n)	(1)		(16)		(12)		(16)		(23)	

The table shows the results of the univariate analysis of the impact of the transaction volume on the cumulative abnormal returns; transactions are split into various subgroups based on their volume. CARs are calculated as shown in Section 5.2.1.2. Tests for statistical significance follow BOEHMER ET AL. (1991). a: since the subsample includes only one transaction, a Z-value cannot be computed. *, ** denote significance at the 10% and 5% level, respectively (based on a one-tailed Z-test).

B3.6 CARs by mega-deals for private targets (MSCI)

Var. Gb Event window	<$1b (1) CAR%	Z-stat.	pos. %	≥$1b (2) CAR%	Z-stat.	pos. %	Difference test (1)-(2) CAR%	t-stat.
Panel A: All transactions								
[-1,1]	1.02	1.2164	49	2.52	1.1394	58	-1.50	-0.8913
[-1,10]	-0.35	0.9668	51	3.13	0.9578	67	-3.48*	-1.4804
(n)	(37)			(12)				
Panel B: No NEMAX transactions								
[-1,1]	1.05	1.2246	50	2.52	1.1394	58	-1.47	-0.9846
[-1,10]	0.97	0.9338	56	3.13	0.9578	67	-2.16	-1.0571
(n)	(32)			(12)				

The table shows the results of the univariate analysis of the impact of the transaction volume on the cumulative abnormal returns, including mean-difference tests. A transaction involving a private target is included in subgroup (1) if the transaction volume was less than $1b. CARs are calculated as shown in Section 5.2.1.2. Tests for statistical significance follow BOEHMER ET AL. (1991). * denotes significance at the 10% level (based on a one-tailed t-test).

B3.7 CARs by mega-deals for public targets (MSCI)

Var. Gb Event window	<$1b (1) CAR%	Z-stat.	pos. %	≥$1b (2) CAR%	Z-stat.	pos. %	Difference test (1)-(2) CAR%	t-stat.
Panel A: All transactions								
[-1,1]	1.08	0.4010	44	0.25	0.4708	55	0.83	0.3112
[-1,10]	-5.74	1.2133	22	-0.41	1.1337	64	-5.33**	-2.1710
(n)	(18)			(11)				
Panel B: No NEMAX transactions								
[-1,1]	-1.85	0.8470	31	0.25	0.4708	55	-2.10	-1.0609
[-1,10]	-4.02	1.1681	31	-0.41	1.1337	64	-3.61*	-1.5663
(n)	(13)			(11)				

The table shows the results of the univariate analysis of the impact of the transaction volume on the cumulative abnormal returns, including mean-difference tests. A transaction involving a public company is included in subgroup (1) if the transaction volume was less than $1b. CARs are calculated as shown in Section 5.2.1.2. Tests for statistical significance follow BOEHMER ET AL. (1991). *, ** denote significance at the 10% and 5% level, respectively (based on a one-tailed t-test).

B3.8 CARs by relative size of the target (MSCI)

Var. Gc	<30%			≥30%			Difference test	
Event	(1)			(2)			(1)-(2)	
window	CAR%	Z-stat.	pos. %	CAR%	Z-stat.	pos. %	CAR%	t-stat.
Panel A: All transactions								
[-1,1]	0.94	1.1780	53	0.36	1.2502	42	0.58	0.3502
[-1,10]	-0.44*	1.2890	52	-4.37	0.9990	33	3.93**	1.7142
(n)	(60)			(12)				
Panel B: No NEMAX transactions								
[-1,1]	0.54	0.9791	52	2.37	1.2410	50	-1.83	-0.8853
[-1,10]	-0.20	1.1737	52	2.84	0.9502	67	-3.04	-1.1375
(n)	(58)			(6)				

The table shows the results of the univariate analysis of the impact of the relative size of the target on the cumulative abnormal returns, including mean-difference tests. A transaction is included in subgroup (1) if the transaction volume represented less than 30 percent of the acquirer's total assets on the balance sheet date preceding the announcement. CARs are calculated as shown in Section 5.2.1.2. Tests for statistical significance follow BOEHMER ET AL. (1991). *, ** denote significance at the 10% and 5% level, respectively (based on a one-tailed Z-test or one-tailed t-test).

B4 Characteristics of transaction structuring and management (MSCI)

B4.1 CARs by strategic direction (MSCI)

Var. J	Non-related			Related			Difference test	
Event	(1)			(2)			(1)-(2)	
window	CAR%	Z-stat.	pos. %	CAR%	Z-stat.	pos. %	CAR%	t-stat.
Panel A: All transactions								
[-1,1]	2.05*	1.5685	64	0.74	0.7808	43	1.31	0.9304
[-1,10]	-0.27	1.1932	56	-1.44	1.1210	45	1.17	0.6632
(n)	(25)			(53)				
Panel B: No NEMAX transactions								
[-1,1]	1.69*	1.3590	64	0.11	0.5829	41	1.58*	1.3026
[-1,10]	1.47	1.1288	64	-0.45	1.0574	50	1.92	1.1989
(n)	(22)			(46)				

The table shows the results of the univariate analysis of the impact of the relatedness of the involved entities on the cumulative abnormal returns, including mean-difference tests. A transaction is included in subgroup (1) if the acquirer's and the target's first two digits of their primary SIC codes are not identical. CARs are calculated as shown in Section 5.2.1.2. Tests for statistical significance follow BOEHMER ET AL. (1991). * denotes significance at the 10% level (based on a one-tailed Z-test or one-tailed t-test).

B4.2 CARs for related transactions (MSCI)

Var. J	2-digit SIC	3-digit SIC	4-digit SIC	Difference tests		
Event	(1)	(2)	(3)	(1)-(2)	(1)-(3)	(2)-(3)
window	CAR%	CAR%	CAR%	CAR%	CAR%	CAR%
Panel A: All transactions						
[-1,1]	-0.56	3.10	1.16	-3.66*	-1.72	1.94
[-1,10]	-1.46	0.80	-2.20	-2.26	0.74	3.00
(n)	(22)	(8)	(23)			
Panel B: No NEMAX transactions						
[-1,1]	-0.56	-2.46**	1.80	1.90	-2.36**	-4.26
[-1,10]	-1.46	-0.30**	0.74	-1.16	-2.20*	-1.04
(n)	(22)	(6)	(18)			

The table shows the results of the univariate analysis of the impact of the relatedness of the involved entities on the cumulative abnormal returns, including mean-difference tests. The transactions are split into various subgroups based on the SIC code identity between the acquirer and the target company. CARs are calculated as shown in Section 5.2.1.2. Tests for statistical significance follow BOEHMER ET AL. (1991). *, ** denote significance at the 10% and 5% level, respectively (based on a one-tailed Z-test or t-test).

B4.3 CARs by form of payment (MSCI)

Var. K	Cash			Shares			Difference test	
Event	(1)			(2)			(1)-(2)	
window	CAR%	Z-stat.	pos. %	CAR%	Z-stat.	pos. %	CAR%	t-stat.
Panel A: All transactions								
[-1,1]	0.99	1.2746	51	2.17*	1.4045	45	-1.18	-0.6236
[-1,10]	-0.26	1.2653	52	-5.97*	1.4605	27	5.71***	2.4904
(n)	(67)			(11)				
Panel B: No NEMAX transactions								
[-1,1]	0.45	1.0786	49	2.83	0.9467	40	-2.38	-1.0991
[-1,10]	-0.01	1.1080	54	2.44	0.7711	60	-2.45	-0.8475
(n)	(63)			(5)				

The table shows the results of the univariate analysis of the impact of the form of payment on the cumulative abnormal returns, including mean-difference tests. A transaction is included in subgroup (1) if the transaction was fully paid for with cash. CARs are calculated as shown in Section 5.2.1.2. Tests for statistical significance follow BOEHMER ET AL. (1991). *, *** denote significance at the 10% and 1% level, respectively (based on a one-tailed Z-test or one-tailed t-test).

B4.4 CARs by form of payment in private transactions (MSCI)

Var. K	Cash			Shares			Difference test	
Event	(1)			(2)			(1)-(2)	
window	CAR%	Z-stat.	pos. %	CAR%	Z-stat.	pos. %	CAR%	t-stat.
Panel A: All transactions								
[-1,1]	1.34*	1.4210	52	1.79*	1.5652	40	-0.45	-0.1875
[-1,10]	0.77	1.1025	57	-1.80*	1.3616	40	2.57	0.7577
(n)	(44)			(5)				
Panel B: No NEMAX transactions								
[-1,1]	1.22*	1.4606	52	6.33	0.8055	50	-5.11*	-1.6286
[-1,10]	1.05	1.0149	57	12.24***	25.7034	100	-11.19***	-2.7540
(n)	(42)			(2)				

The table shows the results of the univariate analysis of the impact of the form of payment on the cumulative abnormal returns, including mean-difference tests. A transaction involving a private company is included in subgroup (1) if the transaction was fully paid for with cash. CARs are calculated as shown in Section 5.2.1.2. Tests for statistical significance follow BOEHMER ET AL. (1991). *, *** denote significance at the 10% and 1% level, respectively (based on a one-tailed Z-test or one-tailed t-test).

B4.5 CARs by form of payment in public transactions (MSCI)

Var. L	Cash			Shares			Difference test	
Event	(1)			(2)			(1)-(2)	
window	CAR%	Z-stat.	pos. %	CAR%	Z-stat.	pos. %	CAR%	t-stat.
Panel A: All transactions								
[-1,1]	0.32	0.5210	48	2.48	0.8130	50	-2.16	-0.6746
[-1,10]	-2.22	1.1779	43	-9.45*	1.6404	17	7.23***	2.5149
(n)	(23)			(6)				
Panel B: No NEMAX transactions								
[-1,1]	-1.09	0.7850	43	0.50	0.6330	33	-1.59	-0.5228
[-1,10]	-2.12	1.2218	48	-4.09*	1.4183	33	1.97	0.5422
(n)	(21)			(3)				

The table shows the results of the univariate analysis of the impact of the form of payment on the cumulative abnormal returns, including mean-difference tests. A transaction involving a public company is included in subgroup (1) if the transaction was fully paid for with cash. CARs are calculated as shown in Section 5.2.1.2. Tests for statistical significance follow BOEHMER ET AL. (1991). *,*** denote significance at the 10% and 1% level, respectively (based on a one-tailed Z-test or one-tailed t-test).

B4.6 CARs by acquisition structure (MSCI)

Var. I	**Asset deal**			**Share deal**			**Difference test**	
Event	(1)			(2)			(1)-(2)	
window	CAR%	Z-stat.	pos. %	CAR%	Z-stat.	pos. %	CAR%	t-stat.
Panel A: All transactions								
[-1,1]	0.40	0.4990	42	1.40 *	1.5905	53	-1.00	-0.6569
[-1,10]	0.05	0.9733	53	-1.42 *	1.5645	47	1.47	0.7632
(n)	(19)			(59)				
Panel B: No NEMAX transactions								
[-1,1]	0.40	0.4990	42	0.71 *	1.3435	51	-0.31	-0.2470
[-1,10]	0.05	0.9733	53	0.22 *	1.3876	55	-0.17	-0.1045
(n)	(19)			(49)				

The table shows the results of the univariate analysis of the impact of the acquisition structure on the cumulative abnormal returns, including mean-difference tests. A transaction is included in subgroup (1) if the transaction was structured as an asset deal. CARs are calculated as shown in Section 5.2.1.2. Tests for statistical significance follow BOEHMER ET AL. (1991). * denotes significance at the 10% level (based on a one-tailed Z-test).

B4.7 CARs by form of acquisition for public targets (MSCI)

Var. L	**Tender offer**			**Other form**			**Difference test**	
Event	(1)			(2)			(1)-(2)	
window	CAR%	Z-stat.	pos. %	CAR%	Z-stat.	pos. %	CAR%	t-stat.
Panel A: All transactions								
[-1,1]	0.46	0.2766	50	1.74	0.9851	43	-1.28	-0.4200
[-1,10]	-2.43	1.2607	41	-7.77	1.1687	29	5.34**	1.8792
(n)	(22)			(7)				
Panel B: No NEMAX transactions								
[-1,1]	-1.01	0.6159	45	-0.31	0.8704	25	-0.70	-0.2585
[-1,10]	-2.34	1.2787	45	-2.49	1.0156	50	0.15	0.0472
(n)	(20)			(4)				

The table shows the results of the univariate analysis of the impact of the acquisition structure on the cumulative abnormal returns, including mean-difference tests. A transaction involving a public company is included in subgroup (1) if the acquisition was pursued via a tender offer. CARs are calculated as shown in Section 5.2.1.2. Tests for statistical significance follow BOEHMER ET AL. (1991). ** denotes significance at the 5% level (based on a one-tailed t-test).

B4.8 CARs by inclusion of external advisors (MSCI)

Var. M	**No advisors**			**Advisors**			**Difference test**	
Event	(1)			(2)			(1)-(2)	
window	CAR%	Z-stat.	pos. %	CAR%	Z-stat.	pos. %	CAR%	t-stat.
Panel A: All transactions								
[-1,1]	2.46*	1.4105	63	0.34	1.2263	42	2.12*	1.5855
[-1,10]	0.05	1.2532	60	-1.76 *	1.3124	42	1.81	1.0722
(n)	(30)			(48)				
Panel B: No NEMAX transactions								
[-1,1]	0.87	1.0360	58	0.47	1.1436	43	0.40	0.3407
[-1,10]	0.63	0.9979	65	-0.11	1.1436	48	0.74	0.4695
(n)	(26)			(42)				

The table shows the results of the univariate analysis of the impact of the inclusion of external advisors on the cumulative abnormal returns, including mean-difference tests. A transaction is included in subgroup (1) if external advisors were not included in the transaction execution. CARs are calculated as shown in Section 5.2.1.2. Tests for statistical significance follow BOEHMER ET AL. (1991). * denotes significance at the 10% level (based on a one-tailed Z-test or one-tailed t-test).

B4.9 CARs by level of external advisors (MSCI)

Var. M	No advisors	Top-tier	Second-tier	Difference tests		
Event	(1)	(2)	(3)	(1)-(2)	(1)-(3)	(2)-(3)
window	CAR%	CAR%	CAR%	CAR%	CAR%	CAR%
Panel A: All transactions						
[-1,1]	2.46*	-0.33	1.69	2.79**	0.77	-2.02
[-1,10]	0.05	-1.76	-1.77	1.81	1.82	0.01
(n)	(30)	(32)	(16)			
Panel B: No NEMAX transactions						
[-1,1]	0.87	-0.14	2.18	1.01	-1.31	-2.32
[-1,10]	0.63	-1.22	3.03	1.85	-2.40	-4.25**
(n)	(26)	(31)	(11)			

The table shows the results of the univariate analysis of the impact of the inclusion of external advisors on the cumulative abnormal returns, including mean-difference tests. The transactions are split into subgroups based on the status of the included advisor, if any. CARs are calculated as shown in Section 5.2.1.2. Tests for statistical significance follow BOEHMER ET AL. (1991). *,** denote significance at the 10% and 5% level, respectively (based on a one-tailed Z-test or one-tailed t-test).

B4.10 CARs for non-frequent acquirers by inclusion of external advisors (MSCI)

Var. M	No advisors			Advisors			Difference test	
Event	(1)			(2)			(1)-(2)	
window	CAR%	Z-stat.	pos. %	CAR%	Z-stat.	pos. %	CAR%	t-stat.
Panel A: All transactions								
[-1,1]	6.43**	2.1504	82	-1.01	1.0742	50	7.44***	2.7617
[-1,10]	-0.07**	1.7895	64	-4.53*	1.6334	21	4.46*	1.5310
(n)	(11)			(14)				
Panel B: No NEMAX transactions								
[-1,1]	2.80**	2.0424	71	-0.31	1.2111	55	3.11	1.3285
[-1,10]	1.99**	2.2157	86	-2.30**	2.1707	27	4.29*	1.5631
(n)	(7)			(11)				

The table shows the results of the univariate analysis of the impact of the inclusion of external advisors on the cumulative abnormal returns, including mean-difference tests. A transaction by one-time only acquirers during the observation period is included in subgroup (1) if no external advisors were involved in the transaction execution. CARs are calculated as shown in Section 5.2.1.2. Tests for statistical significance follow BOEHMER ET AL. (1991). *, **, *** denote significance at the 10%, 5%, and 1% level, respectively (based on a one-tailed Z-test or one-tailed t-test).

B5 Influences of the economic environment (MSCI)

B5.1 CARs by relative strength of U.S. economic growth (MSCI)

Var. P	Relatively strong GDP			Relatively weak GDP			Difference test	
Event	(1)			(2)			(1)-(2)	
window	CAR%	Z-stat.	pos. %	CAR%	Z-stat.	pos. %	CAR%	t-stat.
Panel A: All transactions								
[-1,1]	1.54**	1.6640	57	0.04	1.0432	30	1.50	1.0024
[-1,10]	-1.26*	1.3592	50	-0.49	1.0850	45	-0.77	-0.4052
(n)	(58)			(20)				
Panel B: No NEMAX transactions								
[-1,1]	1.20*	1.4685	58	-0.98	1.1814	22	2.18**	1.7216
[-1,10]	0.36	1.1009	58	-0.34	1.1054	44	0.70	0.4074
(n)	(50)			(18)				

The table shows the results of the univariate analysis of the impact of U.S. economic growth on the cumulative abnormal returns, including mean-difference tests. A transaction is included in subgroup (1) if it was pursued during a year of above average growth of the U.S. GDP. The mean growth rate was computed for the observation period from 1990 to 2004. CARs are calculated as shown in Section 5.2.1.2. Tests for statistical significance follow BOEHMER ET AL. (1991). *, ** denote significance at the 10% and 5% level, respectively (based on a one-tailed Z-test or one-tailed t-test).

B5.2 CARs for various time periods (MSCI)

Var. N	Before 1998	1998-2000	After 2000	Difference tests		
Event window	(1) CAR%	(2) CAR%	(3) CAR%	(1)-(2) CAR%	(1)-(3) CAR%	(2)-(3) CAR%
Panel A: All transactions						
[-1,1]	0.63	1.50*	1.12	-0.87	-0.49	0.38
[-1,10]	0.72	-2.36	-0.51	3.08*	1.23	-1.85
(n)	(25)	(40)	(13)			
Panel B: No NEMAX transactions						
[-1,1]	0.63	0.95	-0.36	-0.32	0.99	1.31
[-1,10]	0.72	-0.10	-0.26	0.82	0.98	0.16
(n)	(25)	(32)	(11)			

The table shows the results of the univariate analysis of the impact of the relative strength of the capital markets on the cumulative abnormal returns, including mean-difference tests. The transactions are split into subgroups based on whether they were announced before, during, or after a period of buoyant capital markets. CARs are calculated as shown in Section 5.2.1.2. Tests for statistical significance follow BOEHMER ET AL. (1991). * denotes significance at the 10% level (based on a one-tailed Z-test or one-tailed t-test).

B5.3 CARs by relative strength of the Euro (MSCI)

Var. O	Relatively strong EUR			Relatively weak EUR			Difference test	
Event	(1)			(2)			(1)-(2)	
window	CAR%	*Z*-stat.	pos. %	CAR%	*Z*-stat.	pos. %	CAR%	t-stat.
Panel A: All transactions								
[-1,1]	0.94	1.2715	53	1.31	0.9805	48	-0.37	-0.2784
[-1,10]	1.58	1.0814	59	-2.91*	1.3818	41	4.49***	2.7956
(n)	(32)			(46)				
Panel B: No NEMAX transactions								
[-1,1]	0.94	1.2715	53	0.34	0.7098	44	0.60	0.5202
[-1,10]	1.58	1.0814	59	-1.08	1.1803	50	2.66**	1.7956
(n)	(32)			(36)				

The table shows the results of the univariate analysis of the impact of the relative strength of the USD/EUR exchange rate on the cumulative abnormal returns, including mean-difference tests. A transaction is included in subgroup (1) if it was pursued during a year of an above average Euro valuation. The mean USD/EUR exchange rate was computed for the observation period from 1990 to 2004. CARs are calculated as shown in Section 5.2.1.2. Tests for statistical significance follow BOEHMER ET AL. (1991). *, **, *** denote significance at the 10%, 5% and 1% level, respectively (based on a one-tailed Z-test or one-tailed t-test).

B6 Comparison of the DAX- and MSCI-based cumulative abnormal returns for the [-1,1] event window

B6.1 CARs for transactions in Panel A (DAX and MSCI)

Panel A (n=78)		**DAX-based**			**MSCI-based**		
Variable		**(a)**	**(b)**	**Diff.**	**(a)**	**(b)**	**Diff.**
A: Absolute size of the acquirer							
(a) DAX	(b) Non-DAX	0.16	2.73*	(**)	0.13	4.13**	(***)
B: Financial condition of the acquirer							
(a) <Mean liquidity	(b) ≥Mean liquidity	0.11 *	2.12	(*)	0.15*	2.43	(**)
(a) <Mean c-a ratio	(b) ≥Mean c-a ratio	0.73	1.29		0.74	2.03	
C: Valuation ratio of the acquirer							
(a) <Mean MTBV	(b) ≥Mean MTBV	0.98*	0.79		1.26*	0.99	
D: Previous participation of the acquirer							
(a) No	(b) Yes	0.91	-0.10		1.28*	-0.04	
E: U.S. transaction experience of the acquirer							
(a) No	(b) Yes	0.71	0.94		1.41	0.88	
F: Industry of the target company							
(a) Regulated	(b) Non-regulated	-0.39	1.13*		-0.41	1.56*	
G: Status of the target company							
(a) Private	(b) Public	1.03*	0.47		1.39*	0.77	
H: Relative size to the acquirer							
(a) <$1b	(b) ≥$1b	0.54	1.50		1.04	1.43	
(a) <30%	(b) ≥30%	0.79	-0.24*		0.94	0.36	
I: Relatedness							
(a) No	(b) Yes	1.99*	0.27	(*)	2.05*	0.74	
J: Form of payment							
(a) Cash	(b) Shares	0.81	0.90**		0.99	2.17*	
K: Acquisition structure							
(a) Asset deal	(b) Share deal	0.43	0.95*		0.40	1.40*	
L: Form of transaction public target							
(a) Tender offer	(b) Other	0.19	1.34		0.46	1.74	
M: Inclusion of advisors							
(a) No	(b) Yes	1.71*	0.27*		2.46*	0.34	
N: Relative strength of economic growth							
(a) <Mean GDP	(b) ≥Mean GDP	-0.51	1.28*		0.04	1.54**	
O: Relative strength of capital markets [a]							
(a) <1998,>2000	(b) 1998-2000	0.48*	1.15		0.80*	1.50*	
P: Relative strength of the Euro							
(a) <Mean USD/EUR	(b) ≥Mean USD/EUR	0.71	0.97		1.31	0.94	

a: In deviation to the presentation in Section 5.4.5.2., transactions before 1998 and after 2000 were grouped together; CARs are calculated as shown in Section 5.2.1.2. Tests for statistical significance follow BOEHMER ET AL. (1991). *, **, *** denote significance at the 10%, 5%, and 1% level, respectively (based on a one-tailed Z-test or one-tailed t-test).

B6.2 CARs for transactions in Panel B (DAX and MSCI)

Panel B (n=68)		**DAX-based**			**MSCI-based**		
Variable		**(a)**	**(b)**	**Diff.**	**(a)**	**(b)**	**Diff.**
A: Absolute size of the acquirer							
(a) DAX	(b) Non-DAX	0.16	3.17*	(**)	0.13	3.47*	(**)
B: Financial condition of the acquirer							
(a) <Mean liquidity	(b) ≥Mean liquidity	-0.01	1.01		0.02*	0.99	
(a) <Mean c-a-ratio	(b) ≥Mean c-a-ratio	0.62	0.77		0.62	0.93	
C: Valuation ratio of the acquirer							
(a) <Mean MTBV	(b) ≥Mean MTBV	0.91*	-0.28		1.00*	-0.42	
D: Previous participation of the acquirer							
(a) No	(b) Yes	0.68	-0.10		0.70	-0.04	
E: U.S. transaction experience of the acquirer							
(a) No	(b) Yes	0.61	0.60		0.65	0.60	
F: Industry of the target company							
(a) Regulated	(b) Non-regulated	0.28	0.69		0.19	0.75	
G: Status of the target company							
(a) Private	(b) Public	1.51*	-1.07	(**)	1.45**	-0.89	(**)
H: Relative size to the acquirer							
(a) <$1b	(b) ≥$1b	0.14	1.50		0.21	1.43	
(a) <30%	(b) ≥30%	0.51	2.20*		0.54	2.37	
I: Relatedness							
(a) No	(b) Yes	1.59	0.13		1.69*	0.11	(*)
J: Form of payment							
(a) Cash	(b) Shares	0.44	2.68		0.45	2.83	
K: Acquisition structure							
(a) Asset deal	(b) Share deal	0.43	0.67*		0.40	0.71*	
L: Form of transaction public target							
(a) Tender offer	(b) Other	-1.17	-0.56		-1.01	-0.31	
M: Inclusion of advisors							
(a) No	(b) Yes	0.92	0.41		0.87	0.47	
N: Relative strength of economic growth							
(a) <Mean GDP	(b) ≥Mean GDP	-0.90*	1.14*	(**)	-0.98	1.20*	(**)
O: Relative strength of capital markets [a]							
(a) <1998,>2000	(b) 1998-2000	0.34*	0.90		0.33	0.95	
P: Relative strength of the Euro							
(a) <Mean USD/EUR	(b) ≥Mean USD/EUR	0.27	0.97		0.34	0.94	

a: In deviation to the presentation in Section 5.4.5.2., transactions before 1998 and after 2000 were grouped together.; CARs are calculated as shown in Section 5.2.1.2. Tests for statistical significance follow BOEHMER ET AL. (1991). *, **, *** denote significance at the 10%, 5%, and 1% level, respectively (based on a one-tailed Z-test or one-tailed t-test).

B7 Control sample design

B7.1 Domestic acquisitions by German acquirers in the sample

No.	Year	Name of target	Industry of target	Status of target*	Name of acquirer	Volume ($m)
1	1990	*Hochtief AG*	Industrial	Public	*RWE AG*	354
2	1990	*International German-Certain Assets*	Other		*Deutsche Lufthansa AG*	150
3	1990	*Gerresheimer Glas AG*	Industrial	Public	*E.ON AG*	190
4	1990	*Deutsche Bank Kreditbank*	Finance		*Deutsche Bank AG*	425
5	1991	*Continental Can Europe*	Industrial		*E.ON AG*	999
6	1991	*VDO Adolph Schindling*	Industrial		*Commerzbank AG*	177
7	1992	*Deutscher Herold Versicherungs*	Finance		*Deutsche Bank AG*	251
8	1992	*Bayernwerk AG*	Other	Public	*E.ON AG*	3,125
9	1995	*Hoechst AG-Printing Business*	Consumer		*Bayer AG*	498
10	1996	*Jenapharm GmbH(Gehe AG)*	Healthcare		*Schering AG*	336
11	1996	*Linotype-Hell AG*	Industrial	Public	*RWE AG*	122
12	1997	*Urbana Systemtechnik AG*	Other		*E.ON AG*	320
13	1997	*GFC GmbH*	Chemicals		*E.ON AG*	1,731
14	1997	*EI du Pont-Graphic Films*	Consumer		*Bayer AG*	600
15	1997	*E-Plus Mobilfunk GmbH(Otelo)*	Technology		*E.ON AG*	1,566
16	1997	*Fried Krupp AG Hoesch-Krupp*	Industrial	Public	*Thyssen Krupp AG*	3,381
17	1998	*Degussa AG*	Chemicals	Public	*E.ON AG*	4,740
18	1998	*Huels AG-Solvents & Surfactant*	Chemicals		*RWE AG*	271
19	1998	*Vianova Resins GmbH(Hoechst)*	Chemicals		*Deutsche Bank AG*	472
20	1998	*Otelo Communications-Cable TV*	Technology		*Deutsche Bank AG*	546
21	1999	*Adtranz Group*	Industrial		*Daimler-Chrysler AG*	472
22	1999	*Allgemeine Deutsche Investment*	Finance		*Commerzbank AG*	337
23	1999	*Tele Columbus GmbH*	Other		*Deutsche Bank AG*	775
24	1999	*Mannesmann Arcor AG*	Technology		*Mannesmann AG*	534
25	1999	*Siemens-Surge Arresters Units*	Technology		*Siemens AG*	1,044
26	1999	*VIAG AG*	Other	Public	*E.ON AG*	13,153
27	1999	*VEW AG*	Other	Public	*RWE AG*	3,432
28	2000	*Debis Systemhaus GmbH*	Technology		*Deutsche Telekom AG*	5,373
29	2000	*Varta AG*	Industrial	Public	*Deutsche Bank AG*	222
30	2001	*Dresdner Bank AG*	Finance	Public	*Allianz AG*	19,656
31	2002	*Hermes Kreditversicherung*	Finance		*Allianz AG*	461
32	2002	*RWW*	Other		*RWE AG*	175
33	2002	*Clariant AG-European Emulsions*	Chemicals		*Celanese AG*	144
34	2002	*Bayer CropScience*	Chemicals		*BASF AG*	1,157
35	2003	*T-Info GmbH*	Technology		*Deutsche Telekom AG*	101

* Status of the target company is private if not otherwise noted.

B7.2 European acquisitions by German acquirers in the sample

No.	Year	Name of target	Industry of target	Status of target*	Name of acquirer	Volume ($m)
1	1990	*Selby (Rhone-Poulenc SA/France)*	Chemicals		*Bayer AG*	101
2	1990	*Sturge Holdings PLC*	Finance	Public	*Bayer AG*	105
3	1990	*Skoda KP Plzen-Locomotive Mnfr*	Industrial		*Siemens AG*	105
4	1991	*Skoda KP Plzen-Energy Division*	Industrial		*Siemens AG*	170
5	1992	*Barnangen (Nobel Industrier)*	Consumer		*Henkel KGaA*	552
6	1992	*Banco de Madrid*	Finance		*Deutsche Bank AG*	353
7	1993	*Caisse Centrale de Reescompte*	Finance		*Commerzbank AG*	112
8	1993	*Banca Popolare di Lecco*	Finance	Public	*Deutsche Bank AG*	280
9	1993	*GCR SpA*	Industrial	Public	*Siemens AG*	174
10	1993	*Roussel-Uclaf-Agro-Veterinary*	Healthcare		*Hoechst AG*	256
11	1994	*Lloyd Adriatico SpA*	Finance	Public	*Allianz AG*	719
12	1994	*Elf Sanofi SA-Bioactivities*	Consumer		*VEBA AG*	832
13	1994	*Boots Co PLC-Pharmaceutical Op*	Healthcare		*BASF AG*	1,584
14	1994	*Delaval Stork VOF*	Industrial		*Mannesmann AG*	124
15	1994	*Sanofi Bio-Industries*	Consumer		*VEBA AG*	824
16	1995	*Inntrepreneur Estates-1750 Pub*	Consumer		*Deutsche Bank AG*	404
17	1995	*Jupiter Tyndall Group PLC*	Finance	Public	*Commerzbank AG*	272
18	1995	*Enichem Augusta SpA*	Chemicals	Public	*RWE AG*	179
19	1995	*Kleinwort Benson Group PLC*	Finance	Public	*Dresdner Bank AG*	1,554
20	1995	*Amper Telematica,Amper Datos*	Technology		*Siemens AG*	110
21	1995	*Mercury Commune-Customer Premises*	Technology		*Siemens AG*	125
22	1996	*Zeneca Textile Color*	Chemicals		*BASF AG*	210
23	1996	*Leiras*	Healthcare		*Schering AG*	314
24	1996	*Plant Genetic Systems*	Healthcare	Public	*Hoechst AG*	550
25	1996	*Master Builders Technologies*	Chemicals		*VEBA AG*	1,081
26	1997	*Elektrowatt AG*	Other		*Siemens AG*	816
27	1997	*Skandia International Ins Corp*	Finance		*Hannover RückversicherungsAG*	137
28	1997	*AGF*	Finance	Public	*Allianz AG*	5,118
29	1997	*Reale Riassicurazioni*	Finance		*Münchner RückversicherungsAG*	227
30	1997	*Royal Nederland Verzekeringsgr*	Finance		*Allianz AG*	758
31	1998	*Tele.Ring*	Technology		*Mannesmann AG*	157
32	1998	*EACgraphics*	Other		*RWE AG*	273
33	1998	*Pharmacia & Upjohn-Nutrition*	Healthcare		*Fresenius AG*	472
34	1998	*Credit Lyonnais Belgium*	Finance		*Deutsche Bank AG*	594
35	1999	*BTL AB*	Industrial	Public	*VEBA AG*	421
36	1999	*Ing C Olivetti-Telecom*	Technology		*Mannesmann AG*	8,404
37	1999	*Construcciones Aeronauticas SA*	Industrial		*Daimler-Chrysler AG*	747
38	1999	*EZH*	Other		*VEBA AG*	950
39	1999	*One 2 One*	Technology		*Deutsche Telekom AG*	13,629
40	1999	*AGA AB*	Industrial	Public	*Linde AG*	4,083
41	1999	*Immobiliere Batibail*	Finance	Public	*Deutsche Telekom AG*	264
42	1999	*Soleri*	Technology	Public	*Daimler-Chrysler AG*	100
43	1999	*Aerospatiale Matra*	Industrial	Public	*Daimler-Chrysler AG*	6,748

* Status of the target company is private if not otherwise noted.

B7.2 (cont.) European acquisitions by German acquirers in the sample

No.	Year	Name of target	Industry of target	Status of target*	Name of ultimate acquirer	Volume ($m)
44	1999	*Orange PLC*	Technology	Public	*Mannesmann AG*	32,595
45	1999	*SIRIS SAS*	Technology		*Allianz AG*	723
46	1999	*Cariplo-Property Portfolio*	Finance		*Münchner RückversicherungsAG*	382
47	2000	*Radiomobil*	Technology		*Deutsche Telekom AG*	765
48	2000	*Club Internet*	Technology		*Deutsche Telekom AG*	2,334
49	2000	*Schroder Leasing Ltd*	Finance		*Siemens AG*	156
50	2000	*SLEC Holdings Ltd*	Other		*EMTV*	2,618
51	2000	*Sisas-Belgian Chemical Op*	Chemicals		*BASF AG*	144
52	2000	*Pocket Phone Co Ltd*	Consumer		*Deutsche Telekom AG*	109
53	2000	*Smith & Nephew-Elastoplast*	Healthcare		*Beiersdorf AG*	121
54	2000	*Slovenske Telekomunikacie SP*	Technology		*Deutsche Telekom AG*	953
55	2000	*Bayerische Vita*	Finance	Public	*Münchner RückversicherungsAG*	589
56	2000	*Ya.com*	Technology		*Deutsche Telekom AG*	495
57	2000	*Zwolsche Algemeene NV*	Finance		*Allianz AG*	553
58	2000	*Thames Water PLC*	Other	Public	*RWE AG*	6,256
59	2000	*Novartis AG-Flint Business*	Chemicals		*Bayer AG*	751
60	2000	*Turbogas*	Other		*RWE AG*	156
61	2000	*Thomas Cook Holdings Ltd*	Other		*Deutsche Lufthansa AG*	794
62	2000	*Portugen Energia SA*	Other		*RWE AG*	166
63	2000	*Societe Edification Logement*	Finance		*Deutsche Bank AG*	708
64	2000	*Maktel*	Technology		*Deutsche Telekom AG*	323
65	2001	*Hrvatski Telecom*	Technology		*Deutsche Telekom AG*	500
66	2001	*Syngenta AG-Mikado Herbicide*	Chemicals		*Bayer AG*	106
67	2001	*Obragas Holding NV*	Other		*RWE AG*	302
68	2001	*Fairbar Ltd*	Consumer		*Deutsche Bank AG*	2,328
69	2001	*Berner Versicherung AG*	Finance	Public	*Allianz AG*	154
70	2001	*Aventis CropScience Hldg SA*	Chemicals		*Bayer AG*	6,646
71	2001	*Ceske Radiokomunikace*	Technology	Public	*Henkel KGaA*	179
72	2001	*Hotel Arts(Sogo Co Ltd)*	Other		*Deutsche Bank AG*	258
73	2001	*Slovenska Poistovna*	Finance		*Allianz AG*	127
74	2001	*Highland Energy Holding Ltd*	Other		*RWE AG*	156
75	2002	*Innogy Holdings PLC*	Other	Public	*RWE AG*	7,396
76	2002	*Telefon AB LM Ericsson*	Technology		*Infineon Technologies AG*	451
77	2002	*Electric Utility Stoen SA*	Other		*RWE AG*	360
78	2003	*Alstom SA*	Industrial		*Siemens AG*	1209
79	2003	*Bodio Properties Srl*	Finance		*Allianz AG*	234
80	2003	*Scout24 Schweiz AG*	Technology		*Deutsche Telekom AG*	220
81	2003	*Banca BNL Investimenti SpA*	Finance		*Allianz AG*	124
82	2004	*Hansen Transmissions BV*	Other		*Allianz AG*	159

* Status of the target company is private if not otherwise noted.

B8 Overall success of German domestic transactions (MSCI)

(n=35) Event window	CAR%	Positive %	Negative %	Z-statistic	Z-statistic B
Period surrounding the announcement					
{0}	0.38*	54	46	1.3775	1.2170
[-1,1]	0.63	46	54	1.1415	1.5486
[-2,2]	0.29	54	46	1.0638	0.6860
[-5,5]	-0.31	43	57	1.0525	-0.6142
[-10,10]	-1.05	37	63	0.9749	-1.3840
[-20,20]	-3.27	34	66	1.0833	-2.2953
Pre-announcement period					
[-1,0]	0.26	49	51	0.9763	0.7695
[-10,-1]	0.12	51	49	0.5783	-0.6371
[-20,-1]	-1.67	46	54	1.1542	-2.1195
[-2,1]	0.66	57	43	0.9967	1.4410
[-5,1]	0.76	49	51	0.9372	0.7496
[-10,1]	0.87	51	49	0.7770	0.2299
[-20,1]	-0.92	51	49	1.1783	-1.4216
Post-announcement period					
[0,1]	0.75*	57	43	1.3965	1.9877
[0,10]	-1.17	34	66	1.2289	-1.3048
[1,10]	-1.55	34	66	1.2131	-1.7533
[1,20]	-1.98	29	71	0.1048	-1.4390
[-1,10]	-1.28	43	57	1.1769	-1.2864
[-1,20]	-1.72	34	66	0.9882	-1.1400

This table shows the results for an event study analyzing 35 acquisitions of domestic target companies by German acquirers during the period from 1990 to 2004. Cumulative abnormal returns are calculated employing the standard market model, using an estimation period of 253 trading days prior to the event window [-20,20] and various DAX indices to measure market returns. Tests for statistical significance follow BOEHMER ET AL. (1991), while Z-statistic B is computed following DODD and WARNER (1983).
* denotes significance at the 10% level (based on a one-tailed Z-test).

B9 Overall success of European cross-border transactions (MSCI)

(n=82) Event window	CAR%	Positive %	Negative %	Z-statistic	Z-statistic B
Period surrounding the announcement					
{0}	-0.33	41	59	1.1453	-1.2072
[-1,1]	-0.26	46	54	1.0885	-0.3707
[-2,2]	-0.29	48	52	0.8981	-0.3877
[-5,5]	-0.59	52	48	0.7810	-0.6719
[-10,10]	-0.65	50	50	0.9340	-0.4507
[-20,20]	-1.63	41	59	0.9627	-1.2852
Pre-announcement period					
[-1,0]	-0.17	45	55	1.2505	0.0124
[-10,-1]	0.08	54	46	0.8294	0.2914
[-20,-1]	-0.89	45	55	1.0063	-0.7790
[-2,1]	-0.35	44	56	0.9877	-0.5960
[-5,1]	-0.36	56	44	0.8628	-0.3181
[-10,1]	-0.35	45	55	0.8475	-0.2729
[-20,1]	-1.32	43	57	0.9998	-1.1407
Post-announcement period					
[0,1]	-0.43	41	59	0.9324	-1.3201
[0,10]	-0.73	46	54	1.0197	-0.9005
[1,10]	-0.40	51	49	1.0063	-0.5627
[1,20]	-0.40	52	48	0.0074	-0.7912
[-1,10]	-0.56	50	50	1.0510	-0.5086
[-1,20]	-0.57	48	52	0.9429	-0.7506

This table shows the results for an event study analyzing 82 acquisitions of European target companies by German acquirers during the period from 1990 to 2004. Cumulative abnormal returns are calculated employing the standard market model, using an estimation period of 253 trading days prior to the event window [-20,20] and various DAX indices to measure market returns. Tests for statistical significance follow BOEHMER ET AL. (1991), while Z-statistic B is computed following DODD and WARNER (1983).

B10 Comparison of the overall results for the three analyzed samples (MSCI)

	U.S. targets	German targets	European targets	Difference tests		
Event window	(1) CAR%	(2) CAR%	(3) CAR%	(1)-(2) CAR%	(1)-(3) CAR%	(2)-(3) CAR%
All transactions						
[-1,1]	1.16*	0.63	-0.26	0.53	1.42**	0.89*
[-1,10]	-1.07*	-1.28	-0.56	0.21	-0.51	-0.72
(n)	(78)	(35)	(82)			
Panel B: No NEMAX transactions						
[-1,1]	0.62	0.63	-0.22	-0.01	0.84*	0.85*
[-1,10]	0.17	-1.28	-0.20	1.45	0.37	-1.08
(n)	(68)	(35)	(81)			
Intersection						
[-1,1]	0.27	0.28	-0.06	-0.01	0.33	0.34
[-1,10]	-0.51	-1.16	0.10	0.65	-0.61	-1.26*
(n)	(42)	(33)	(68)			

The table shows the comparison of the generated cumulative abnormal returns, including mean-difference tests, for all transactions in the U.S., German domestic, and European samples and for the intersection of acquirers in each of the three samples. CARs are calculated as shown in Section 5.2.1.2. Tests for statistical significance follow BOEHMER ET AL. (1991). *, ** denote significance at the 10% and 5% level, respectively (based on a one-tailed Z-test or one-tailed t-test).

B11 Determinants of transaction success for the control samples (MSCI)

B11.1 Summary of the univariate analysis for the German domestic transactions (MSCI)

Variable		CAR% [-1,1] (a)	(b)	Diff.	CAR %[-1,10] (a)	(b)	Diff.
F: Industry							
(a) Regulated (n=13)	(b) Non-regulated (n=22)	0.20	0.88*		-1.29	-1.28*	
G: Status							
(a) Private (n=25)	(b) Public (n=10)	-0.01	2.22	(**)	-1.25	-1.37*	
H: Relative size to the acquirer							
(a) <$1b (n=24)	(b) ≥$1b (n=11)	-0.11	2.24	(**)	-1.32	-1.20	
(a) <30% (n=34)	(b) ≥30% (n=1)	0.47	5.97[a]		-1.15	-5.71[a]	
I: Relatedness							
(a) No (n=15)	(b) Yes (n=20)	-0.17*	1.23*	(*)	-1.34	-1.24*	
J: Form of payment							
(a) Cash (n=29)	(b) Shares (n=6)	0.03	3.55	(***)	-1.14	-1.98*	
K: Acquisition structure							
(a) Asset deal (n=7)	(b) Share deal (n=28)	1.25	0.48		-3.42**	-0.75*	
M: Inclusion of advisors							
(a) No (n=19)	(b) Yes (n=16)	0.41	0.89		-1.50	-1.02	

Tests for statistical significance follow BOEHMER ET AL. (1991). a: since the subsample includes only one transaction, a Z-value cannot be computed. *, **, *** denote significance at the 10%, 5%, and 1% level, respectively (based on a one-tailed Z-test or one-tailed t-test).

B11.2 Summary of the univariate analysis of European cross-border transactions (MSCI)

Variable		CAR% [-1,1] (a)	(b)	Diff.	CAR% [-1,10] (a)	(b)	Diff.
F: Industry							
(a) Regulated (n=38)	(b) Non-regulated (n=44)	-0.20	-0.32		-0.28	-0.81	
G: Status							
(a) Private (n=62)	(b) Public (n=20)	0.15	-1.55*	(***)	-0.37	-1.18*	
H: Relative size to the acquirer							
(a) <$1b (n=66)	(b) ≥$1b (n=16)	-0.02	-1.25		-0.06	-2.67	
(a) <30% (n=81)	(b) ≥30% (n=1)	-0.19	-6.41[a]		-0.48	-7.30[a]	
I: Relatedness							
(a) No (n=29)	(b) Yes (n=53)	-0.48	-0.14		-1.69	0.05	
J: Form of payment							
(a) Cash (n=76)	(b) Shares (n=6)	-0.19	-1.18*		-0.15	-5.78	(**)
K: Acquisition structure							
(a) Asset deal (n=15)	(b) Share deal (n=67)	-0.26	-0.26*		-1.67	-0.32	
M: Inclusion of advisors							
(a) No (n=24)	(b) Yes (n=58)	-0.48	-0.17		-2.62*	0.29	(**)

Tests for statistical significance follow BOEHMER ET AL. (1991). a: since the subsample includes only one transaction, a Z-value cannot be computed. *, **, *** denote significance at the 10%, 5%, and 1% level, respectively (based on a one-tailed Z-test or one-tailed t-test).

References

ABAHONIE, E./BRENNER, J. (1994): Tax Planning for Mergers and Acquisitions, in: Rock, M./Rock, R./Sikora, M. (Ed.), The Mergers & Acquisitions Handbook, 2nd edition, New York 1994, pp. 219-226.

ACHLEITNER, A.-K. (2002): Handbuch Investment-Banking, 3rd revised and enhanced edition, Wiesbaden 2002.

AGRAWAL, A./JAFFE, J. (2000): The Post-Merger Performance Puzzle, Advances in Mergers and Acquisitions, Volume 1, Stamford 2000, pp. 7-41.

AGRAWAL, P./MAEBIUS, S. (2004): Conducting an Intellectual Property Due Diligence Review, http://www.foley.com/files/tbl_s31Publications/FileUpload137/2340/1283319_1.pdf.

AKTAS, H./DE BODT, E./COUSIN, J. (2004): Event Study Under Contaminated Estimation Period, Working Paper University of Lille 2004.

ALBRECHT, S. (1994): Erfolgreiche Zusammenschlußstrategien, Wiesbaden 1994.

ALFORD, A./BERGER, P. (1998): The Role of Taxes, Financial Reporting, and Other Market Imperfections in Structuring Divisive Reorganizations, Working Paper Wharton School, University of Pennsylvania 1998.

ALLEN, L./JAGTIANI, J./PERISTIANI, S./SAUNDERS, A. (2004): The Role of Bank Advisors in Mergers and Acquisitions, in: Journal of Money, Credit, and Banking, 36(2), pp. 197-224.

ALLEN, L./JAGTIANI, J./SAUNDERS, A. (2000): The Role of Bank Advisors in Mergers and Acquisitions, Emerging Issues Series, Supervision and Regulation Department Federal Reserve Bank of Chicago, May 2000, S&R-2000-1R.

ALTHAUS, S. (1996): Henkel Optimistic Following 6% Rise, in: The Financial Times, November 13, 1996, p. 27.

AMIHUD, Y./LEV, B. (1981): Risk Reduction as a Managerial Motive for Conglomerate Mergers, in: Rand Journal of Economics, 12, pp. 605-618.

ANAND, J./CAPRON, L./MITCHELL, W. (2005): Using Acquisitions to Access Multinational Diversity: Thinking Beyond the Domestic Versus Cross-Border M&A Comparison, in: Industrial and Corporate Change, 14(2), pp. 191-224.

ANDRADE, G./MITCHELL, M./STAFFORD, E. (2001): New Evidence and Perspectives on Mergers, in: Journal of Economic Perspectives, 15(2), pp. 103-120.

ANDRE, P./KOOLI, M./L'HER, J.-P. (2004): The Long-Run Performance of Mergers and Acquisitions: Evidence from the Canadian Stock Market, in: Financial Management, Winter 2004, pp. 27-43.

ANG, J./KOHERS, N. (2001): The Take-Over Market for Privately Held Companies: the US Experience, in: Cambridge Journal of Economics, 25, pp. 723-748.

ANGERER, L./WINCKLER, C. (2005): US and German Corporate Governance Issues and Their Implications on M&A Transactions, in: Lucks, K. (Ed.), Transatlantic Mergers & Acquisitions, Erlangen 2005, pp. 284-294.

ANSOFF, H. I. (1966): Management-Strategie, München 1966.

ANSOFF, H. I. (1987): Corporate Strategy, London 1987.

ANSOFF, H. I. (1988): The New Corporate Strategy, New York 1988.

APENBRINK, R. (1993): Empirische Kapitalmarktuntersuchung zu Unternehmensakquisitionen in Deutschland, Wien 1993.

ARANOW, E./EINHORN, H./BERLSTEIN, G. (1977): Developments in Tender Offers for Corporate Control, Columbia University Press 1977.

ASQUITH, P. (1983): Merger Bids, Uncertainty, and Stockholder Returns, in: Journal of Financial Economics, 11, pp. 51-83.

ASQUITH, P./BRUNER, R.F./MULLINS, D.W. (1983): The Gains to Bidding Firms from Merger, in: Journal of Financial Economics, 11, pp. 121-139.

A. T. KEARNEY (1999): See HABECK, M./KROGER, F./TRAM, M. (1999).

AUERBACH, A./REISHUS, D. (1988): The Effects of Taxation on the Merger Decision, in: Auerbach, A.J. (Ed.), Corporate Takeovers: Causes and Consequences, Chicago 1988, pp. 157-183.

AYERS, B./LEFANOWICZ, C./ROBINSON, J. (2000): The Effects of Goodwill Tax Deductions on the Market for Corporation Acquisitions, in: Journal of the American Taxation Association, 22 (Supplement), pp. 34-50.

AYERS, B./LEFANOWICZ, C./ROBINSON, J. (2004): The Effect of Shareholder-Level Capital Gains Taxes on Acquisition Structure, in: The Accounting Review, 79(4), pp. 859-887.

AW, M./CHATTERJEE, R. (2004): The Performance of UK Firms Acquiring Large Cross-Border and Domestic Takeover Targets, in: Applied Financial Economics, 14, pp. 337-349.

BACHMANN, C. (2001): Synergie- und Nutzungspotentiale von Unternehmenszusammenschlüssen. Definition, Realisierung, Messung, Wiesbaden 2001.

BACKHAUS, K./ERICHSON, B./PLINKE, W./WEIBER, R. (2005): Multivariate Analysemethoden. Eine anwendungsorientierte Einführung, 11th revised edition, Berlin 2005.

BAETGE, J./NIEMEYER, K./KÜMMEL, J. (2001): Darstellung der Discounted-Cash-Flow Verfahren (DCF-Verfahren) mit Beispiel, in: Peemöller, V. (Ed.), Praxishandbuch der Unternehmensbewertung, Herne 2001, pp. 263-360.

BAKER, P. (1993): Executive Compensation in Mergers and Acquisitions, in: The Practical Lawyer, June 1993, pp. 75-96.

BALLWIESER, W. (1993): Methoden der Unternehmensbewertung, in: Gebhardt, G./Gerke, W./Steiner, M. (Ed.), Handbuch des Finanzmanagements, München 1993, pp. 151-176.

BAMBERG, G./BAUR, F. (1993): Statistik, 8th edition, München 1993.

BAMBERGER, B. (1994): Der Erfolg von Unternehmensakquisitionen in Deutschland, Bergisch-Gladbach 1994.

BAMBERGER, I./WRONA, T. (1996): Der Ressourcenansatz und seine Bedeutung für die strategische Unternehmensführung, in: Zeitschrift für betriebswirtschaftliche Forschung, 2, 1996, pp. 130-153.

BANERJEE, A./OWERS, J. (1992): Wealth Reduction in White Knight Bids, in: Financial Management, 21(3), pp. 48-57.

BARBER, B./LYON, J. (1996): Detecting Abnormal Operating Performance: the Empirical Power and Specification of Test Statistics, in: Journal of Financial Economics, 41(3), pp. 359-399.

BARNEY, J.B. (1991): Firm Resources and Sustained Competitive Advantage, in: Journal of Management, 17(1), pp. 99-120.

BEA, F./HAAS, J. (2001): Strategisches Management, 3rd edition, Stuttgart 2001.

BECKER, D. (2005): Ressourcen-Fit bei M&A Transaktionen, Wiesbaden 2005.

BEEZY, M./PECOT, R. (2004): Caveat Emptor or "let the buyer beware". Applying Diligent Investor Principles to Trademark and Copyright Issues in Mergers and Acquisitions, http://www.ipfrontline.com/downloads/foley.pdf.

BEITEL, D. (2004): Investmentbanken in M&A-Transaktionen, Wiesbaden 2004.

BEITEL, P. (2002): Akquisitionen und Zusammenschlüsse europäischer Banken, Wiesbaden 2002.

BEITEL, P./SCHIERECK, D. (2001): Value Creation at the Ongoing Consolidation of the European Banking Market, Working Paper 05/01 University of Witten/Herdecke.

BEITEL, P./SCHIERECK, D./WAHRENBURG, M. (2004): Explaining M&A Success in European Banks, in: European Financial Management, 2004, 10(1), pp. 109-139.

BEKAERT, G./HARVEY, C.R. (1995): Time-Varying World Market Integration, in: Journal of Finance, 50, pp. 403-443.

BENDANIEL, D./ROSENBLOOM, A. (1998): International M&A, Joint Ventures, and Beyond, New York 1998.

BERENS, W./MERTES, M./STRAUCH, J. (2005): Unternehmensakquisitionen, in: Berens, W./ Brauner, H./Strauch, J. (Ed.), Due Diligence bei Unternehmensakquisitionen, 4th revised and enhanced edition, Stuttgart 2005, pp. 26-74.

BERENS, W./STRAUCH, J. (2002): Due Diligence bei Unternehmensakquisitionen – eine empirische Untersuchung, Frankfurt am Main 2002.

BERENS, W./STRAUCH, J. (2005): Herkunft und Inhalt des Begriffes Due Diligence, in: Berens, W./Brauner, H./Strauch, J. (Ed.), Due Diligence bei Unternehmensakquisitionen, 4th revised and enhanced edition, Stuttgart 2005, pp. 3-25.

BERGER, A./DEMSETZ, R./STRAHAN, P. (1999): The Consolidation of the Financial Services Industry: Causes, Consequences, and Implications for the Future, in: Journal of Banking and Finance, 23(2-4), pp. 135-194.

BERGER, P.G./OFEK, E. (1995): Diversification's Effect on Firm Value, in: Journal of Financial Economics, 37(1), pp. 39-65.

BERK, T. (1996): Sending the Right Merger Message to All Employees, in: Mergers & Acquisitions, 30(4), pp. 30-34.

BERKOVITCH, E./NARAYANAN, M. (1990): Competition and the Medium of Exchange in Takeovers, in: Review of Financial Studies, 3(2), pp. 153-174.

BERKOVITCH, E./NARAYANAN, M. (1993): Motives for Takeovers: An Empirical Investigation, in: Journal of Financial and Quantitative Analysis, 28, pp. 347-361.

BERRY, W./FELDMANN, S. (1985): Multiple Regression in Practice, Beverly Hills 1985.

BERTRAND, O./MUCCHIELLI, J.-L./ZITOUNA, H. (2004): Location Choices of Multinational Firms: The Case of Mergers and Acquisitions, Hamburg Institute of International Economics Discussion Paper 2004.

BETSCH, O./GROH, A.P./LOHMANN, G.E. (2000): Corporate Finance, 2nd edition, München 2000.

BHAGAT, S./BLACK, B. (1999): The Uncertain Relationship Between Board Composition and Firm Performance, in: Business Lawyer, May 1999, 54(3), pp. 941-984.

BHAGAT, S./ROMANO, R. (2001): Event Studies and the Law - Part I: Technique and Corporate Litigation, Yale ICF Working Paper No. 00-31, 2001.

BHARADWAJ, A./SHIVDASANI, A. (2003): Valuation Effects of Bank Financing in Acquisitions, in: Journal of Financial Economics, 67, pp. 113-148.

BHATTACHARYA, U./DAOUK, H. (2002): The World Price of Insider Trading, in: Journal of Finance, 57(1), pp. 75-109.

BLACK, B.S. (1989): Bidder Overpayment in Takeovers, in: Stanford Law Review, 41, pp. 597-660.

BLACK, E./CARNES, T./JANDIK, T. (2001): The Long-Term Success of Cross-Border Mergers and Acquisitions, Working Paper University of Arkansas, May 2001.

BLACK, T. (1999): Doing Quantitative Research in the Social Sciences: an Integrated Approach to Research Design, Beverly Hills 1999.

BLEYMÜLLER, J./GEHLERT, G./GÜLICHER, H. (2004): Statistik für Wirtschaftswissenschaftler, 14th edition, München 2004.

BODNAR, G./DUMAS, B./MARSTON, R. (2002): Cross-Border Valuation: The International Cost of Capital, Working Paper INSEAD Fontainebleau, May 2002.

BODNAR, G./TANG, C./WEINTROP, J. (2003): The Value of Corporate International Diversification, Working Paper John Hopkins University, July 2003.

BÖCKING, H.-J./NOWAK, K. (1998): Der Beitrag der Discounted Cash Flow Verfahren zur Lösung der Typisierungsproblematik bei Unternehmensbewertungen, in: Der Betrieb, 51, pp. 685-690.

BÖGLE, M./BÄTZ, R.: Differences in Valuation Methods - a Comparison of Income Approach Valuation, in: Lucks, K. (Ed.): Transatlantic Mergers & Acquisitions, Erlangen 2005, pp. 346-357.

BOEHMER, E./LÖFFLER, Y. (1997): Kursrelevante Ereignisse bei Unternehmensübernahmen, Arbeitspapier Humboldt-University Berlin, 1997.

BOEHMER, E./MUSUMECI, J./POULSEN, A. (1991): Event-Study Methodology Under Conditions of Event Induced Variance, in: Journal of Financial Economics, 30, pp. 253-272.

BORN, J./TRAHAN, E. (1993): Golden Parachutes: Incentive Aligners, Management Entrenchers, or Takeover Bid Signals, in: Journal of Financial Research, 16, pp. 299-308.

BORN, K. (2003): Unternehmensanalyse und Unternehmensbewertung, 2nd updated and enhanced edition, Stuttgart 2003.

BORN, K. (2005): Rechnungslegung International, 4th updated and completely revised edition, Stuttgart 2005.

BOSSART, R. (2002): Tax Due Diligence, in Rosenbloom, A. (Ed.): Due Diligence in Global Deal Making, Princeton 2002.

BOSTON CONSULTING GROUP (2002): see HENRY AND JESPERSEN (2002).

BOSTON CONSULTING GROUP (2004): Growing Through Acquisitions – the Successful Value Creation Record of Acquisitive Growth Strategies, Boston May 2004.

BOWMAN, R.G. (1983): Understanding and Conducting Event Studies, in: Journal of Business Finance and Accounting, 10, pp. 561-584.

BRADLEY, M. (1980): Interfirm Tender Offers and the Market for Corporate Control, in: Journal of Business, 53(4), pp. 345-376.

BRADLEY, M./SUNDARAM, A. (2004): Do Acquisitions Drive Performance or Does Performance Drive Acquisitions? Working Paper Duke University Durham, September 2004.

BRADLEY, M./DESAI, A./KIM, E. (1982): Specialized Resources and Competition in the Markets for Corporate Control, Working Paper Ann Arbor, University of Michigan, 1982.

BRADLEY, M./DESAI, A./KIM, E. (1983): The Rational Behind Interfirm Tender Offers: Information or Synergy?, in: Journal of Financial Economics, 11(1-4), pp. 183-206.

BRADLEY, M./DESAI, A./KIM, E. (1988): Synergistic Gains from Corporate Acquisitions and Their Division Between the Stockholders of Target and Acquiring Firms, in: Journal of Financial Economics, 21(1), pp. 3-40.

BREALEY, R.A./MYERS, S.C. (2000): Principles of Corporate Finance, 6th edition, New York 2000.

BREBECK, F./BREDY, J. (1999): Due Diligence aus bilanzieller und steuerlicher Sicht, in: Berens, W. & Brauner, H. (Ed.): Due Diligence bei Unternehmensakquisitionen, 2nd edition, Stuttgart 1999, pp. 221 – 249.

BROMILEY, P./GOVEKAR, M./MARCUS, A. (1988): On Using Event-Study Methodology in Strategic Management Research: in: Technovation, 8, pp. 25-42.

BROWN, D./RYNGAERT, M. (1991): The Mode of Acquisition in Takeovers: Taxes and Asymmetric Information, in: Journal of Finance, 46, pp. 653-669.

BROWN, S./WARNER, J. (1980): Measuring Security Price Performance, in: Journal of Financial Economics, 8, pp. 205-258.

BROWN, S./WARNER, J. (1985): Using Daily Stock Returns: the Case of Event Studies, in: Journal of Financial Economics, 14, pp. 3-31.

BRUNER, R. (2002): Does M&A pay? A Survey of Evidence from the Decision-Maker, in: Journal of Applied Finance, 12(1), pp. 48-68.

BRUNER, R. (2004a): Applied Mergers and Acquisitions, Hoboken 2004.

BRUNER, R. (2004b): Where M&A Pays and Where it Strays: A Survey of the Research, in: Journal of Applied Corporate Finance, 16(4), pp. 63-76.

BRUNER, R. (2005): Profiles of Outlying: M&A Transactions 1985-2000, Working Paper Darden Graduate School of Business University of Virginia, March 2005.

BRUNER, R./EADES, K./HARRIS, R./HIGGINS, R. (1998): Best Practices' in Estimating the Cost of Capital: Survey and Synthesis, in: Financial Practice and Education, Spring/Summer, pp. 13-28.

BUCHTER, H. (2006): IBM friert Pensionsfonds ein, in: Financial Times Deutschland, January 9, 2006, p. 4.

BÜHNER, R. (1990a): Erfolg von Unternehmenszusammenschlüssen in der Bundesrepublik Deutschland, Stuttgart 1990.

BÜHNER, R. (1990b): Unternehmenszusammenschlüsse: Ergebnisse empirischer Analysen, Stuttgart 1990.

BÜHNER, R. (1991): Grenzüberschreitende Unternehmenszusammenschlüsse deutscher Unternehmen, Stuttgart 1991.

BÜHNER, R./SPINDLER, H.-J. (1986): Synergieerwartungen bei Unternehmenszusammenschlüssen, in: Der Betrieb, 39, pp. 601-606.

BUONO, A.F./BOWDITCH, J.L. (1989): The Human Side of Mergers and Acquisitions, San Francisco 1989.

BURNHAM, W. (1999): Introduction to the Law and Legal System of the United States, 2nd edition, New York 1999.

CABLE, J./HOLLAND, K.H. (1999): Regression vs. Non-Regression Models of Normal Returns: Implications for Event Studies, in: Economics Letters, 64, pp. 81-85.

CAKICI, N./HESSEL, C./TANDON, K. (1996): Foreign Acquisitions in the United States: Effect on Shareholder Wealth of Foreign Acquiring Firms, in: Journal of Banking and Finance, 20, pp. 307-329.

CAMPA, J./HERNANDO, I. (2004): Shareholder Value Creation in European M&As, in: European Financial Management, 10(1), pp. 47-81.

CAMPA, J./KEDIA, S. (2002): Explaining the Diversification Discount, in: Journal of Finance, 57, pp. 1731-1762.

CANNELLA, A. jr./HAMBRICK, D.C. (1993): Effects of Executive Departures on the Performance of Acquired Firms, in: Strategic Management Journal, 14 (Special Issue), pp. 137-153.

CANTWELL, J.A./SANTANGELO, G.D. (2002): M&As and the Global Strategies of TNCs, in: The Developing Economies, 40(4), pp. 400-434.

CARLINE, N./LINN, S./YADAV, P. (2004): Can the Stock Market Systematically Make Use of Firm- and Deal-Specific Factors When Initially Capitalizing the Real Gains from Mergers and Acquisitions, CFR Working Paper No. 04-08, 2004.

CARROLL, C.A. (2002): A Century of Mergers and Acquisitions, in: B.E. Gup (Ed.), Megamergers in a Global Economy, Westport 2002, pp. 19-43.

CARTWRIGHT, S./COOPER, C. (1996): Managing Mergers, Acquisitions and Strategic Alliances: Integrating People and Cultures, Manchester 1996.

CAVES, R.E./PORTER, M. (1977): From Entry Barriers to Mobility Barriers: Conjectural Decisions and Deterrence to New Competition, in: Quarterly Journal of Economics, 91, pp. 241-261.

CAYTAS, I.G./MAHARI, J.J. (1988): Im Banne des Investment Banking, Stuttgart 1988.

CEBENOYAN, A.S./PAPAIOANNOU, G.J./TRAVLOS, N. (1991): Foreign Takeover Activity in the U.S. and Wealth Effects for Target Firm Shareholders, in: Financial Management, 31(3), pp. 58-68.

CHAPMAN, T.L./DEMPSEY, J.J./RAMSDELL, G./BELL, T.E. (1998): Purchasing's Big Moment-After the Merger, in: The McKinsey Quarterly, 1998, pp. 56-65.

CHAKRABARTI, R./NARAYANAN, J./MUKHERJEE, S. (2004): Mars-Venus Marriages: Culture and Cross-Border M&A, Working Paper College of Management Georgia Institute of Technology, 2004.

CHARKRAVARTHY, B. (1986): Measuring Strategic Performance, in: Strategic Management Journal, 6, pp. 437-458.

CHATTERJEE, R./KUENZI, A. (2001): Mergers and Acquisitions: the Influence of Methods of Payment on Bidder's Share Price, Working Paper University of Cambridge, 2001.

CHATTERJEE, R./LUBATKIN, M. (1990): Corporate Mergers, Stockholders Diversification, and Changes in Systematic Risk, in: Strategic Management Journal, 11, pp. 255-268.

CHATTERJEE, S. (1986): Types of Synergy and Economic Value, in: Strategic Management Journal, 7 (2), pp. 119-140.

CHATTERJEE, S./BOURGEOIS, L. (2002): Framework for Acquisition Success: Post-acquisition Resource Interactions, Working Paper Darden Institute of Business, University of Virginia, 2002.

CHENG, L.T.W./CHAN, K.C. (1995): A Comparative Analysis of the Characteristics of International Takeovers, in: Journal of Business Finance and Accounting, 22, pp. 637-657.

CHEVALIER, J. (2000): Why Do Firms Undertake Diversifying Mergers? An Investigation of the Investment Policies of Merging Firms, Working Paper University of Chicago, January 2000.

CHOI, D./PHILIPPATOS, G.C. (1983): An Examination of Merger Synergism, in: Journal of Financial Research, 6, pp. 239-256.

CHOI, J.J./TSAI, E. (2002): International Mergers and Acquisitions: Wealth Effects and Winning Firm Characteristics, Working Paper Fox School Of Business, Philadelphia, December 2002.

CHRISTENSEN, C. (1997): The Innovator's Dilemma, Boston 1997.

CLARK, E./DANBOLT, J./GADAD, M. (2000): UK Disposals and Abnormal Returns to Cross-Border Acquirers, Working Paper Middlesex University, February 2000.

CLEIS, S. (2005): Guidant Contra Johnson & Johnson, in: Neue Züricher Zeitung, November 8, 2005, p. 23.

COASE, R. (1937): The Nature of the Firm, in: Economica, 4, pp. 386-405.

COCHRAN, P./WOOD, R. (1984): Corporate Social Responsibility and Financial Performance, in: Academy of Management Journal, 27, pp. 42-56.

COENENBERG, A. (2000): Jahresabschluss und Jahresabschlussanalyse: betriebswirtschaftliche, handelsrechtliche, steuerrechtliche und internationale Grundsätze – HGB, IAS, US-GAAP, 17th revised and enhanced edition, Landsberg/Lech, 2000.

COLBERG, W. (1989): Internationale Präsenzstrategien von Industrieunternehmen, Kiel 1989.

COMISKEY, E./MULFORD, C. (2000): Guide to Financial Reporting and Analysis, New York 2000.

COMMENT, R./JARRELL, G. (1995): Corporate Focus and Stock Returns, in: Journal of Financial Economics, 37(1), pp. 67-87.

COMMENT, R./SCHWERT, G.W. (1995): Poison or Placebo? Evidence on the Deterrence and Wealth Effects of Modern Antitakeover Measures, in: Journal of Financial Economics, 39, pp. 3-43.

CONN, R. (1985): A Re-Examination of Merger Studies that Use the Capital Asset Pricing Model Methodology, in: Cambridge Journal of Economics, 9, pp. 43-56.

CONN, R./CONNELL, F. (1990): International Mergers: Returns to U.S. and British Firms, in: Journal of Business Finance and Accounting, 17(5), pp. 689-711.

CONN, R./COSH, A./GUEST, P./HUGHES, A. (2005): The Impact on UK Acquirers of Domestic, Cross-Border, Public, and Private Acquisitions, in: Journal of Business Finance & Accounting, 32(5)(6), pp. 815-870.

CONNER, K. (1991): An Historical Comparison of Resource-Based Logic and Five Schools of Thought Within Industrial Organization Economics: Do We Have a New Theory of the Firm Here?, in: Journal of Management, 17, pp. 121-154.

COOLEY & GODWARD (2001): Hart-Scott-Rodino Quick Reference Outline, http://www.law commerce.com/newsletters/art_cooley_quickref0102.asp.

COPELAND, T./WESTON, J.F. (1988): Financial Theory and Corporate Policy, 3rd edition, New York 1988.

COPELAND, T./KOLLER, T./MURRIN, J. (2000): Valuation: Measuring and Managing the Value of Companies, New York 2000.

CORDING, M./CHRISTMANN, P./BOURGEOIS, L.J. (2002): A Focus on Resources in M&A Success: a Literature Review and Research Agenda to Resolve Two Paradoxes, Working Paper Darden School University of Virginia, 2002.

CORHAY, A./RAD, A.T. (2000): International Acquisitions and Shareholder Wealth: Evidence from the Netherlands, in: International Review of Financial Analysis, 9(2), pp. 163-174.

CORNETT, M.M./HOVAKIMIAN, G./PALIA, D./THERANIAN, H. (2003): The Impact of the Manager-Shareholder Conflict on Acquiring Bank Returns, in: Journal of Banking and Finance, 27, pp. 103-131.

COYLE, R.J. (1995): The McGraw-Hill Handbook of American Depository Receipts, New York 1995.

CULLINAN, G./HOLLAND, T. (2002): Strategic Due Diligence, in: Rosenbloom, A. (Ed.): Due diligence for global deal making, New Jersey 2002, pp. 13-50.

CUSATIS, P./MILES, J.A./WOOLRIDGE, J.R. (2001): Some New Evidence that Spinoffs Create Value, in Chew, D.H. (Ed.), The New Corporate Finance, 3rd edition, New York 2001, pp. 592-599.

CYBO-OTTONE, A./MURGIA, M. (2000): Mergers and Shareholder Wealth in European Banking, in: Journal of Banking and Finance, 24, pp. 831-859.

DALEY, J./MEKROTA, V./SIVAKUMA, R. (1997): Corporate Focus and Value Creation: Evidence from Spin-Offs, in: Journal of Financial Economics, 45(2), pp. 257-281.

DAMS, J./SEIBEL, K. (2006): Deutsche Unternehmen kaufen wieder gern in Amerika ein, in: Die Welt, 5. Januar 2006. p. 12.

DANBOLT, J. (1995): An Analysis of Gains and Losses to Shareholders of Foreign Bidding Companies Engaged in Cross-Border Acquisitions Into the United Kingdom 1986-1991, in: European Journal of Finance, 1, pp. 279-309.

DASILVA, R. (2005): Share Pledges in German/US Mergers and Acquisitions, in: Lucks, K. (Ed.), Transatlantic Mergers & Acquisitions, Erlangen 2005, pp. 340-346.

DATTA, D.K. (1991): Organizational Fit and Acquisition Performance: Effects of Post-Acquisition Integration, in: Strategic Management Journal, 12, 1991, pp. 281-297.

DATTA, S./ISKANDAR-DATTA, M./RAMAN, K (2001): Executive Compensation and Corporate Acquisition Decisions, in: Journal of Finance, 56, pp. 2299-2336.

DATTA, D.K./PINCHES, G.E./NARAYANAN, V.K. (1992): Factors Influencing Wealth Creation from Mergers and Acquisitions: A Meta-Analysis, in: Strategic Management Journal, 13, pp. 67-84.

DATTA, D.K./PUIA, G. (1995): Cross-Border Acquisitions: An Examination of the Influence of Relatedness and Cultural Fit on Shareholder Value Creation in U.S. Acquiring Firms, in: Management International Review, 35(4), pp. 337-359.

DAWSON, S./PENCE, R./STONE, D. (1987): Poison Pill Defensive Measures in: The Business Lawyer, 42(2), pp. 423–39.

DEANDINO, J./MARTINEZ, M./TATE, R./MADDRY, T. (2004): Conducting an Intellectual Property Due Diligence, in: Property & Technology Law Journal, 16(8), pp. 1-3.

DELONG, G. (2001): Stockholder Gains from Focusing Versus Diversifying Bank Mergers, in: Journal of Financial Economics, 59(2), pp. 221-252.

DELONG, G. (2003): The Announcement Effects of U.S. Versus Non-U.S. Bank Mergers: Do They Differ?, in: Journal of Financial Research, 26(4), pp. 487-500.

DEMSETZ, H. (1988): The Theory of the Firm Revisited, in: Journal of Law, Economics, and Organization, 4(1), pp. 141-161.

DEPAMPHILIS, D. (2003): Mergers, Acquisitions, and Other Restructuring Activities, 2nd edition, Academic Press New York 2003.

DEWENTER, K.L. (1995): Does the Market React Differently to Domestic and Foreign Takeover Announcements? Evidence from the U.S. Chemical and Retail Industries, in: Journal of Financial Economics, 37, pp. 421-441.

DIAZ, J. (2002): Financial and Accounting Due Diligence, in: Rosenbloom, A. (Ed.), Due Diligence for Global Deal Making, Princeton 2003, pp. 101-148.

DICKEY, G. (2000): Federal Income Taxation of Acquisitions, in: Morris, J. (Ed.), Mergers and Acquisitions. Business Strategies for Accountants, 2nd edition, New York 2000.

DISSANAIKE, G. (1994): On the Computation of Returns in Tests of the Stock Market Overreaction Hypothesis, in: Journal of Banking and Finance, 18, pp. 1083-1094.

DODD, P. (1980): Merger Proposals, Management Discretion and Stockholder Wealth: An Empirical Analysis, in: Journal of Financial Economics, 8(2), pp. 105-138.

DODD, P./WARNER, J. (1983): On Corporate Governance: A Study of Proxy Contests, in: Journal of Financial Economics, 11, pp. 401-438.

DÖRR, T. (2000): Grenzüberschreitende Unternehmensakquisitionen, Wiesbaden 2000.

DONG, M./HIRSHLEIFER, D./RICHARDSON, S. (2002): Does Investor Misvaluation Drive the Takeover Market? Working Paper York University Toronto, 2003.

DOUKAS, J. (1995): Overinvestment, Tobin's Q and Gains From Foreign Acquisitions, in: Journal of Banking and Finance, 19, pp. 1285-1303.

DOUKAS, J./TRAVLOS, N. G. (1988): The Effect of Corporate Multinationalism on Shareholder Wealth: Evidence from International Acquisitions, in: Journal of Finance, 43, 1988, pp. 1161-1175.

DRAPER, P./PAUDYAL, K. (1999): Corporate Takeovers: Method of Payment, Returns and Trading Activity, in: Journal of Business Finance & Accounting, 26(5), pp. 521-558.

DRIES, V. (1998): Und plötzlich waren es nur noch die Big Two. Gelassenheit in Detroit - Qualitätsspritze fuer Chrysler - Unions in Tuscaloosa?, in: Börsen-Zeitung, May 8, p. 7.

DRUKARCZYK, J. (2001): Unternehmensbewertung, 3rd edition, München 2001.

DUFEY, G./HOMMEL, U. (2000): Mergers & Acquisitions, in: Hagen, J.v./Stein, J. v. (Ed.), Geld-, Bank- und Börsenwesen, Stuttgart 2000, pp. 963–986.

DUNNING, J.H. (1977): Trade, Location of Economic Activity and the MNE: A Search for an Eclectic Approach, in Ohlin, B./Hesselborn, P.O./Wijkman, P.M. (Ed.): The International Allocation of Economic Activity, London 1977, pp. 395-418.

DUNSCH, J. (1998): Wachstumszwang und Grössenwahn, in: Frankfurter Allgemeine Zeitung, 1998, December 2, 1998, p. 1.

ECKARDT, J. (1999): Kurz- und langfristige Kurseffekte beim Erwerb von Beteiligungen deutscher börsennotierter Aktiengesellschaften, Lohmar 1999.

ECKBO, E./THORBURN, K. (2000): Gains to Bidder Firms Revisited: Domestic and Foreign Acquisitions in Canada, in: Journal of Financial and Quantitative Analysis, 35(1), pp. 1-25.

ECKER, M./HECKEMÜLLER, C. (2005): M&A als Instrument der strategischen Unternehmensführung für den Mittelstand, in: M&A Review 10, 2005, pp. 421-426.

EDWARDS, C.D. (1955): Conglomerate Bigness as a Source of Power, in: Business Concentration and Price Policy: A Conference of the Universities-National Bureau Committee for Economic Research, Princeton 1955, pp. 331-352.

EDWARDS, C./LANG, M./MAYDEW, E. (2003): Germany's Repeal of the Corporate Capital Gains Tax: The Equity Market Response, in: Journal of the American Tax Association, 26, Supplement 2004, pp. 73-97.

ENVIRONMENTAL PROTECTION AGENCY (1984): Liability of Corporate Shareholders and Successor Corporations for Abandoned Sites, http://www.epa.gov/compliance/resources/policies/cleanup/superfund/corpshr-aban-mem.pdf.

ERICKSON, M/WANG, S. (2000): The Effect of Transaction Structure on Price: Evidence from Subsidiary Sales, in: Journal of Accounting & Economics, 30(1), pp. 59-97.

ERNST, D./HAUG, M./SCHMIDT, W. (2004): Realoptionen: Spezialfragen für eine praxisorientierte Anwendung, in: Richter, F./Timmreck, C. (Ed), Unternehmensbewertung, Moderne Instrumente und Lösungsansätze, Stuttgart 2004, pp. 397 - 420.

ERNST & YOUNG (1994): International Mergers and Acquisitions: a Comprehensive Country-by-Country Guide, New York 1994.

ERRAMILLI, M.K./D'SOUZA, D.E. (1993): Venturing into Foreign Markets: The Case of Small Service Firms, in: Entrepreneurial Theory Practice, 17(4), pp. 29-41.

ERRUNZA, V./SENBET L. (1981): The Effects of International Operations on the Market Value of the Firm: Theory and Evidence, in: Journal of Finance, 36(2), pp. 401-417.

ESCHEN, E. (2002): Der Erfolg von Mergers and Acquisitions, Wiesbaden 2002.

EUN, C. S./KOLODNY, R./SCHERAGA, C. (1996): Cross-Border Acquisitions and Shareholder Wealth: Test of the Synergy and Internalisation Hypotheses, in: Journal of Banking and Finance, 20, pp. 1559-1582.

FAIRBURN, J.A./KAY, J.A. (1989): Mergers and Merger Policy, Oxford University Press, New York 1989.

FAMA, E.F. (1970): Efficient Capital Markets: A Review of Theory and Empirical Work, in: Journal of Finance, 25, pp. 383-418.

FAMA, E.F. (1980): Agency Problems and the Theory of the Firm, in: Journal of Political Economy, 88, pp. 288-307.

FAMA, E.F. (1998): Market Efficiency, Long-Term Returns, and Behavioral Finance, in: Journal of Financial Economics, 49(3), pp. 283-306.

FAMA, E.F./FISCHER, L./JENSEN, M.C./ROLL, R. (1969): The Adjustment of Stock Prices to New Information, in: International Economic Review, 10, pp. 1-21.

FAMA, E.F./FRENCH, K. (1992): The Cross-Section of Expected Stock Returns, in: Journal of Finance, 47, pp. 427-465.

FAN, J./GOYAL, V. (2002): On the Patterns and Wealth Effects of Vertical Mergers, Working Paper Hong Kong University of Science & Technology, January 2002.

FATEMI, A.M./FURTADO, E.P.H. (1988): An Empirical Investigation of the Wealth Effects of Foreign Acquisitions, in: Khoury, S. J./Ghosh, A. (Ed.): Recent Developments in International Banking and Finance, Volume 2, Lexington 1988.

FEDERAL RESERVE BOARD (1996): Remarks by Chairman Alan Greenspan at the Annual Dinner and Francis Boyer Lecture of the American Enterprise Institute for Public Policy Research, Washington, D.C. December 5, 1996, http://www.federalreserve.gov/ boardDocs/ speeches/1996/19961205.htm.

FELLI, L./ROBERTS, K. (2000): Does Competition Solve the Hold-Up Problem?, Working Paper London School of Economics - Department of Economics, July 2000.

FIRTH, M. (1980): Takeovers, Shareholder Returns, and the Theory of the Firm, in: Quarterly Journal of Economics, 94(2), pp. 235-260.

FISCHER, H. (1989): Bewertung beim Unternehmens- und Beteilgungskauf, in: Hölters, W. (Ed.), Handbuch des Unternehmens- und Beteiligungskaufs, 2nd edition, Köln 1989, pp. 51-176.

FISCHER, N./IANNACONI, T./LECHNER, H. (2001): United States – Individual Accounts, in: Ordelheide, D./KPMG (Ed.): Transnational Accounting, 2nd edition, Hampshire, pp. 2851-2987.

FLEISCHER, H./KOERBER, T. (2001): Wirtschaftsrecht - Due Diligence und Gewährleistung beim Unternehmenskauf, in: BetriebsBerater, 56 (17), pp. 841-848.

FOLEY & LARDNER (2004): SOX Impact on M&A, May 10, 2005: http://www.foley.com/files/tbl_s31Publications/FileUpload137/2689/NDI_SOXMandA_final.pdf.

FRANKS, J.R./BROYLES, J.E./HECHT, M.J. (1977): An Industry Study of the Profitability of Mergers in the UK, in: Journal of Finance, 32, pp. 1513-1525.

FRESENIUS MEDICAL CARE (2005): Fresenius Medical Care Receives Second Request from U.S. Federal Trade Commission, June 15, 2005. http://www.fmc-ag.com/internet/fmc/fmcag/agintpub.nsf/Content/June+15%2C+2005_pr.

FRESENIUS MEDICAL CARE (2006): Fresenius Medical Care Announces Signing of Definitive Agreement to Divest Facilities in Connection with Renal Care Group Acquisition, February 15, 2006. http://www.fmc-ag.com/internet/fmc/fmcag/agintpub.nsf/Content/February+15%2C+2006_pr.

FREYTAG, A./SCHIERECK, D./THOMAS, T. (2005): Consolidation and Market Power of Energy Utilities - the Case of US-American and German Utility Takeovers, Working Paper Friedrich Schiller University Jena, July 2005.

FRITSCHE, M./GRIESE, M. (2005): Legal Due Diligence, in: Berens, W./Brauner, H.U./Strauch, J. (Ed.), Due Diligence bei Unternehmensakquisitionen, 4th revised and enhanced edition, Stuttgart 2005, pp. 457-488.

FROMM, E./LEWIS, E./CORKEN, H. (1997): Allocating Environmental Liabilities in Acquisitions, in: Journal of Corporation Law, 22(3), pp. 429-464.

FROOT, K.A./STEIN, J.C. (1991): Exchange Rates and Foreign Direct Investment: An Imperfect Capital Market Approach, in: Quarterly Journal of Economics, 106, pp. 1191-1217.

FROST, C./KINNEY, W. (1996): Disclosure Choices of Foreign Registrants in the United States, in: Journal of Accounting Research, 34 (Spring), pp. 67-84.

FULLER, K./NETTER, J./STEGEMOLLER, M. (2002): What Do Returns to Acquiring Firms Tell Us? Evidence from Firms that Make Many Acquisitions, in: Journal of Finance, 57(4), pp. 1763-1793.

GARVEY, G./HANKA, G. (1999): Capital Structure and Corporate Control: The Effect of Antitakeover Statutes on Firm leverage, in: Journal of Finance, 54, pp. 519-546.

GAUGHAN, P. (1999): Mergers, Acquisitions, and Corporate Restructurings, 2nd edition, New York 1999.

GEISER, A./JUCHEM, N. (2005): Key Factors for Successful M&A Communications in Germany, in: Lucks, K. (Ed.), Transatlantic Mergers & Acquisitions, Erlangen 2005, pp. 411-425.

GERKE, W./GARTZ, H./OERKE, M. (1995): Die Bewertung von Unternehmensübernahmen auf dem deutschen Aktienmarkt, in: Zeitschrift für die betriebswirtschaftliche Forschung, 47, pp. 805-820.

GERPOTT, T.J. (1993): Integrationsgestaltung und Erfolg von Unternehmensakquisitionen, Stuttgart 1993.

GHOSH, A. (2001): Does Operating Performance Really Improve Following Corporate Acquisitions?, in: Journal of Corporate Finance, 7(2), pp. 151-178.

GLAUM, M. (1996): Internationalisierung und Unternehmenserfolg. Wiesbaden 1996.

GLAUM, M./LINDEMANN, J. (2002): Externes Unternehmenswachstum: Theoretische Überlegungen und empirische Befunde, in: Glaum, M./Hommel, U./ Thomaschewski, D. (Ed.), Wachstumsstrategien internationaler Unternehmungen - internes versus externes Wachstum, Stuttgart 2002, pp. 269-299.

GOERGEN, M./RENNEBOOG, L. (2004): Shareholder Wealth Effects of European Domestic and Cross-Border Takeover Bids, in: European Financial Management, 10(1), pp. 9-45.

GOMEZ, P. (1992): Unternehmensakquisitionen vor dem Hintergrund des Shareholder Value, in: Sieben, G./Stein, H.G. (Ed.), Unternehmensakquisitionen: Strategien und Abwehrstrategien. Berichte der Schmalenbachgesellschaft/Deutsche Gesellschaft für Betriebswirtschaft e.V., Stuttgart 1992, pp. 7-20.

GOMEZ, P./GANZ, M. (1992): Diversifikation mit Konzept - den Unternehmenswert steigern, Harvard Manager, 1, pp. 44-54.

GOMEZ, P./WEBER, B. (1989): Akquisitionsstrategie. Wertsteigerung durch Übernahme von Unternehmungen, Stuttgart 1989.

GOOLD, M./CAMPBELL, A. (1998): Desperately Seeking Synergy, in: Harvard Business Review, 76(5), pp. 130-143.

GORDON, J. (2002): An American Perspective on the New German Anti-Takeover Law, Discussion Paper No. 407 Harvard Law and Economics, February 2002.

GORT, M. (1969): An Economic Disturbance Theory of Mergers, in: Quarterly Journal of Economics, 83, pp. 624-642.

GRAFER, R./BALDASERO, M. (1994): Effective Due Diligence, in: Rock, M./Rock, R./Sikora, M., The Mergers & Acquisitions Handbook, 2nd edition, New York 1994, pp. 341-352.

GRAHAM, J./HARVEY, C. (2001): The Theory and Practice of Corporate Finance: Evidence from the Field, in: Journal of Financial Economics, 60, pp. 187-243.

GRAHAM, J./LEMMON, M./WOLF, J. (2002): Does Corporate Diversification Destroy Value?, in: Journal of Finance, 57, pp. 695-720.

GRANDJEAN, B. (1992): Unternehmenszusammenschlüsse und die Verteilung der abnormalen Renditen zwischen den Aktionären der übernehmenden und übernommenen Gesellschaften: eine empirische Untersuchung, Frankfurt 1992.

GRANT, R.M. (1991): The Resource-Based Theory of Competitive Advantage: Implications for Strategy Formulation, in: California Management Review, 33(3), pp. 114-135.

GREENE, E.F./BELLER, A. ET AL. (1998): U.S. Regulation of the Securities and Derivates Markets, Aspen Law & Business, New York 1998.

GREGORY, A. (1997): An Examination of the Long-Run Performance of U.K. Acquiring Firms, in: Journal of Business Finance and Accounting, 24(7/8), pp. 971-1002.

GREGORY, A./MCCORRISTON, S. (2005): Foreign Acquisitions by UK Limited Companies: Short- and Long-Run Performance, in: Journal of Empirical Finance, 12, pp. 99-125.

GRIESSER, S./SCHWINGELER, T. (2005): Transatlantic M&A Market – Volume and Dynamics, in: Lucks, K. (Ed.), Transatlantic Mergers & Acquisitions, Erlangen 2005, pp. 44-51.

GRINBLATT, M./TITMAN, S. (2002): Financial Markets and Corporate Strategy, 2nd edition, Boston 2002.

GRUBE, R. (2005): The Post-Merger Integration Process of DaimlerChrysler AG, in: Lucks, K. (Ed.): Transatlantic Mergers & Acquisitions, Erlangen 2005, pp. 58-74.

GUGLER, K./MUELLER, D./YURTOGLU, B./ZULEHNER, C. (2003): The Effects of Mergers: An International Comparison, in: International Journal of Industrial Organization, 21, pp. 625-653.

GUPTA, E./MISRA, S. (1997): Regulatory Change, Profitability, and Managerial Motives in Financial Mergers, Working Paper Bentley College Waltham, 1997.

HABECK, M./KROEGER, F./TRAM, M. (1999): After the Merger: Seven Rules for Post-Merger Integration, A.T. Kearney, 1999.

HACHMEISTER, D. (1999): Der Discounted Cash Flow als Maßstab der Unternehmenswertsteigerung, 3rd edition, Frankfurt am Main 1999.

HACHMEISTER, D. (2005): Impairment Test nach IFRS und US GAAP. in: Ballwieser, W./Beyer, S./Zelger, H. (Ed.), Unternehmenskauf nach IFRS und US-GAAP, Stuttgart 2005, pp. 191-224.

HACKETT, R./CRAIG, M. (1999): Letter of Intent, The Cambridge Institute, http://www.fclaw.com/Seminar/Materials/mergerfiles/2.pdf.

HALEBLIAN, J./FINKELSTEIN, S. (1999): The Influence of Organizational Acquisition Experience on Acquisition Performance: in: A Behavioral Perspective, Administrative Science Quarterly (44), pp. 29-56.

HALL, R. (2001): Private Company Acquisitions in the US. A Survival Guide for Overseas Buyers, http://crossborder.practicallaw.com/jsp/binaryContent.jsp?item=26946&tab=3.

HALPERN, P. (1973): Empirical Estimates of the Amount of Distribution of Gains to Companies in Mergers, in: Journal of Business, 46, pp. 554-575.

HALPERN, P. (1983): Corporate Acquisitions: A Theory of Special Cases? A Review of Event Studies Applied to Acquisitions, in: Journal of Finance, 38(2), pp. 297-317.

HAMILTON, D./QUINLAN, J. (2005): U.S.-German Relations: Will the Ties that Bind Grow Stronger or Weaker?, in: Lucks, K. (Ed.), Transatlantic Mergers & Acquisitions, Erlangen 2005, pp. 20-32.

HAND, J./SKANTZ, T. (1999): Tax Planning in Initial Public Offerings: The Case of Equity Carve-Outs, Working Paper University of North Carolina at Chapel Hill, 1999.

HARFORD, J. (2005): What Drives Merger Waves?, in: Journal of Financial Economics, 77(3), pp. 529-560.

HARRINGTON, S./SHRIDER, D. (2002): All Events Induce Variance: Analyzing Abnormal Returns When Effects Vary Across Firms, Working Paper University of South Carolina.

HARRIS, R.S./RAVENSCRAFT, D. (1991): The Role of Acquisitions in Foreign Direct Investment: Evidence from the U.S. Stock Market, in: Journal of Finance, 46, pp. 825-844.

HARRISON, J./OLER, D./ALLEN, M. (2005): Event Studies and the Importance of Longer-Term Measures in Assessing the Performance Outcomes of Complex Events, Working Paper University of Richmond, 2005.

HASPESLAGH, P.C./JEMISON, D.B. (1991): Managing Acquisitions: Creating Value Through Corporate Renewal, New York 1991.

HAUGEN, R.A./LANGENSTIEG, T. (1975): An Empirical Test for Synergism in Merger, in: Journal of Finance, 30(4), pp. 1003-1014.

HAWAWINI, G.A./SWARY, I. (1990): Mergers and Acquisitions in the U.S. Banking Industry: Evidence from the Capital Markets, North Holland, Amsterdam 1990.

HAY, G.A./NYDAM, R.J. (1989): Merger Policy in the United States, in: Fairburn, J./Kay, J. (Ed.), Mergers and Merger Policy, Oxford 1989.

HAYN, C. (1989): Tax Attributes as Determinants of Shareholder Gains in Corporate Acquisitions, in: Journal of Financial Economics, 23, pp. 121-153.

HAYN, S./WALDERSEE, G. (2004): IFRS/US-GAAP/HGB im Vergleich. Synoptische Darstellung für den Einzel- und Konzernabschluss, 5th updated edition, Stuttgart 2004.

HEALY, P./PALEPU, K./RUBACK, R. (1992): Does Corporate Performance Improve after Mergers?, in: Journal of Financial Economics, 31, pp. 135-175.

HEITHECKER, M. (2006): BASF versucht feindliche Übernahme in Amerika, in: Die Welt, January 4, 2006, p. 1, 9.

HELBLING, C. (1993): Unternehmensbewertung und Steuern, 7th edition, Zürich 1993.

HENRY, D./JESPERSEN, F. (2002): Mergers: Why Most Big Deals Don't Pay Off, in: Business Week, October 14, 2002, pp. 60-70.

HENSELMANN, K. (1999): Unternehmensrechnungen und Unternehmenswert, Aachen 1999.

HERING, T. (1999): Finanzwirtschaftliche Unternehmensbewertung, Wiesbaden 1999.

HERON, R./LIE, E. (2002): Operating Performance and the Method of Payment in Takeovers, in: Journal of Financial and Quantitative Analysis, 37, pp. 137-155.

HERZEL, L./SHEPRO, R.W. (1990): Bidders and Targets: Mergers and Acquisitions in the U.S., Oxford 1990.

HERZIG, N. (2004): Step up-Modelle im Vergleich in: Unternehmenskauf im Steuerrecht, in: Schaumburg, H. v. (Ed.), 3. Aufl., Stuttgart 2004, pp. 131-149.

HIETALA, P./KAPLAN, S./ROBINSON, D. (2002): What is the Price of Hubris? Using Takeover Battles to Infer Overpayments and Synergies, NBER Working Paper no. W9264, October 2002.

HILSENRATH, J. (2004): As Two Economists Debate Markets, the Tide Shifts - Belief in Efficient Valuation Yields Ground to Role of Irrational Investors. Mr. Thaler takes on Mr. Fama, in: The Wall Street Journal, October 18, 2004, p. A1.

HITT, M.A. (2000): The New Frontier: Transformation of Management for the New Millennium, in: Organizational Dynamics, 28, pp. 6-17.

HITT, M.A./HARRISON, J.S./IRELAND, R.D. (2001): Mergers and Acquisitions: a Guide to Creating Value for Stakeholders, New York 2001.

HÖLSCHER, L. (1998): Käuferbezogene Unternehmensbewertung, Frankfurt am Main 1998.

HÖLTERS, W. (1992): Handbuch des Unternehmens – Beteiligungskauf. 3rd edition, Köln 1992.

HOHNHAUS, W. (2004): Erfolg der M&A-Beratung bei Unternehmenstransaktionen. Strukturelle Voraussetzungen und funktionale Beiträge aus Kundensicht, Wiesbaden 2004.

HOLDERNESS, C./SHEEHAN, D. (1985): Raiders or Saviors? The Evidence on Six Controversial Investors, in: Journal of Financial Economics, 14, pp. 555-579.

HOLZAPFEL, H./PÖLLATH, R. (2000): Unternehmenskauf in Recht und Praxis – Rechtliche und steuerliche Aspekte, 9th edition, Köln 2000.

HOLZAPFEL, H./PÖLLATH, R. (2003): Recht und Praxis des Unternehmenskaufs, 11th edition, Köln 2003.

HOOPES, D.G./MADSEN, T.L./WALKER, G. (2003): Guest Editors' Introduction to the Special Issue: Why is There a Resource-based View? Toward a Theory of Competitive Heterogeneity, in: Strategic Management Journal, 24(10), pp. 889-902.

HOUSTON, J.F./JAMES, C.M./RYNGAERT, M.D. (2001): Where do Merger Gains Come From? Bank Mergers from the Perspective of Insiders and Outsiders, in: Journal of Financial Economics, 2001, 60(2,3), pp. 285-331.

HUANG, Y.S./WALKING, R.A. (1987): Target Abnormal Returns Associated with Acquisition Announcements: Payment, Acquisition Form, and Managerial Resistance, in: Journal of Financial Economics, 19, pp. 329-349.

HUEMER, F. (1990): Mergers & Acquisitions, strategische und finanzielle Analyse von Unternehmensübernahmen, Frankfurt am Main 1990.

HUNTER, W.C./JAGTIANI, J. (2000): Merger Advisory Fees and Advisors' effort, Emerging Issues Series Federal Reserve Bank of Atlanta S&R-2000-11R.

HUTTER, S./LAWRENCE, J.W. (1999): Übernahmerecht in den USA, in: Rosen, R. v./ Seifert, W.G. (Ed.), Die Übernahme börsennotierter Unternehmen, Schriften zum Kapitalmarkt, Band 2, Eschborn 1999, pp. 95-148.

HYMER, S.H. (1976): The International Operations of National Firms: a Study of Direct Foreign Investment, Cambridge 1976.

INGHAM, H./KRAN, I. ET AL. (1992): Mergers and Profitability: A Managerial Success Story? in: Journal of Management Studies, March 1992, pp. 195-208.

INKPEN, A./SUNDARAM, A./ROCKWOOD, K. (2000): Cross-border Acquisitions of U.S. Technology Assets, in: California Management Review, 42(3), pp. 50-71.

JAENSCH, G. (1992): Unternehmensbewertung bei Akquisitionen in den USA, in: Busse von Colbe, W./Coenenberg, A., Unternehmensakquisition und Unternehmensbewertung, Stuttgart 1992, pp. 377-387.

JANSEN, S. (2001): Mergers & Acquisitions, 4th edition, Wiesbaden 2001.

JANSEN, S./KÖRNER, K. (2000): Fusionsmanagement in Deutschland, Witten/Herdecke 2000.

JARRELL, G./BRADLEY, M. (1980): The Economic Effects of Federal and State Regulations of Cash Tender Offers, in: Journal of Law and Economics, 23(2), pp. 371-407.

JARRELL, G./BRICKLEY, J./NETTER, J. (1988): The Market for Corporate Control: The Empirical Evidence Since 1980, in: Journal of Economic Perspectives, 2(2), pp. 49-68.

JARRELL, G./POULSEN, A. (1987): Shark Repellents and Stock Prices: The Effects of Antitakeover Amendments Since 1980, in: Journal of Financial Economics, 19, pp. 127-168.

JARRELL, G./POULSEN, A. (1989): The Returns to Acquiring Firms in Tender Offers: Evidence from Three Decades, in: Financial Management, 18(3), pp. 12-19.

JEMISON, D./SITKIN, S. (1986): Corporate Acquisitions: A Process Perspective, in: Academy of Management Review, 11(1), pp. 145-163.

JENSEN, M.C. (1984): Takeovers: Folklore and Science, in: Harvard Business Review, November-December, pp. 109-121.

JENSEN, M.C. (1986): Agency Costs of Free Cash Flow, Corporate Finance, and Takeovers, in: American Economic Review, Papers and Proceedings, 76, pp. 323-329.

JENSEN, M.C. (1988): Takeovers: Their Causes and Consequences, in: Journal of Economic Perspectives, 2, pp. 21-48.

JENSEN, M.C./MECKLING, W.H. (1976): Theory of the Firm: Managerial Behavior, Agency Costs and Ownership Structure, in: Journal of Financial Economics, 3, pp. 305-360.

JENSEN, M.C./RUBACK, R.S. (1983): The Market for Corporate Control, in: Journal of Financial Economics, 11, pp. 5-50.

JENSEN, S./WERRES, T. (2001): Verlademeister, in: Manager Magazin, Nr. 7, June 26, 2001.

JESUTHASAN, R./UDER, H. (2005): How HR Contributes to Merger Success, in: Lucks, K. (Ed.), Transatlantic Mergers & Acquisitions, Erlangen 2005, pp. 178-191.

JOHNSON, B.W./NATARAJAN, A. (1985): Shareholder Returns and Corporate Excellence, in: Journal of Business Strategy, Fall 1985, pp. 52-62.

JOHNSON, S.Z. (2001): Amendments to Hart-Scott-Rodino Pre-merger Filing Law, http://www.gtlaw.com/pub/alerts/2001/johnson_02.pdf.

JOVANOVIC, B./BRAGUINSKY, S. (2004): Bidder Discounts and Target Premia in Takeovers, in: American Economic Review, Papers and Proceedings, 94(1), pp. 46-56.

JUNG, H. (1993): Erfolgsfaktoren von Unternehmensakquisitionen, Stuttgart 1993.

KALE, J.R./KINI, O./RYAN, H.E. (1998): On the Participation and Reputation of Financial Advisors in Corporate Acquisitions, Working Paper Georgia State University Atlanta, 1998.

KANG, J.-K. (1993): The International Market for Corporate Control: Mergers and Acquisitions of U.S. Firms by Japanese Firms, in: Journal of Financial Economics, 34(3), pp. 345-371.

KANG, J.-K./SHIVDASANI, A. (1997): Corporate Restructuring During Performance Declines in Japan, in: Journal of Financial Economics, 46, pp. 29-65.

KASCHKE, M./PHILIPP, U. (2005): Carl Zeiss Vision – A Merger of the Carl Zeiss Eyeglass Division with Sola International, Inc., in: Lucks, K. (Ed.), Transatlantic Mergers & Acquisitions, Erlangen 2005, pp. 110-124.

KAYE & SCHOLER (2002): The Exon-Florio Process, Foreign Investment Update, http:// library.findlaw.com/2002/Jan/22/132588.pdf.

KERLER, P. (2000): Mergers & Acquisitions und Shareholder Value, Bern 2000.

KIESO, D./WEYGANDT, J. (1998): Intermediate Accounting, 9th edition, New York 1998.

KINDLEBERGER, C.P. (1969): American Business Abroad: Six Lectures on Direct Investment, New Haven 1969.

KING & SPALDING (2000): Hart-Scott-Rodino Premerger Notification Requirements Amended by New Legislation, http://www.kslaw.com/library/pdf/ hartscott.pdf.

KIRCHHOFF, M. (2005): Sirona übernimmt amerikanischen Röntgenspezialisten, in: Frankfurter Rundschau, September 27, 2005, p. Wirtschaft 13.

KIRCHNER, M. (1991): Strategische Akquisitionsmanagement im Konzern, Wiesbaden 1991.

KITCHING, J. (1973): Acquisitions in Europe – Cause of Corporate Successes and Failures, Geneva 1973.

KIYMAZ, H./MUKHERJEE, T.K. (2000): The Impact of Country Diversification of Wealth Effects in Cross-Border Mergers, in: The Financial Review, 35, pp. 37-58.

KLEBNIKOV, P. (2000): Auf Wiedersehen to Germany Inc, in: Forbes Magazine, May 1, 2000, p. 162.

KLEINERT, J./KLODT, H. (2002): Fusionswellen und ihre Ursachen, in: Franz, W./Ramser, H.J./Stadler, M. (Ed.), Fusionen, Tübingen 2002, pp. 27-52.

KLEINWORT, M. (2000): BASF sticht Bayer bei Agro-Geschäft aus; Übernahme der AHP-Agrochemiesparte verstärkt die Konzentration im weltweiten Pflanzenschutzmarkt, in: Financial Times Deutschland, March 22, 2000, p. Unternehmen 3.

KNICKERBOCKER, F.T. (1973): Oligopolistic Reaction and the Multinational Enterprise, Cambridge 1973.

KNÜSEL, D. (1994): Die Anwendung der Discounted-Cash-Flow-Methode zur Unternehmensbewertung, Wintherthur 1994.

KOCH, W./WEGMANN, J. (2002): Praktiker-Handbuch Due Diligence, Analyse mittelständischer Unternehmen, 2nd edition, Stuttgart 2002.

KOGELER, R. (1992): Synergiemanagement im Akquisitions- und Intergrationsprozess von Unternehmungen: Eine empirische Untersuchung anhand branchenübergreifender Fallstudien, München 1992.

KOGUT, B./ZANDER, U. (1992): Knowledge of the Firm Combinative Capabilities and the Replication of Technology, in: Organization Science, 3(3), pp. 383-396.

KOHERS, N./KOHERS, T. (2000): The Value Creation Potential of High Tech Mergers, in: Financial Analysts Journal, 56, pp. 40-50.

KOLBE, C. (1993): Anmerkungen zur Untenehmensakquisition als Form des Markteintritts, in: Frank, G.-M./Stein, Ingo (Ed): Management von Unternehmensakquisitionen, Stuttgart 1993, pp. 187-199.

KOTHARI, S.P./WARNER, J.B. (1997): Measuring Long-Horizon Security Price Performance, in: Journal of Financial Economics, 43, pp. 301-339.

KOUTSOYIANNIS, A. (1982): Non-Price Decisions: The Firm in a Modern Context, London et al. 1982.

KÜBLER, R. (1994): Management strategischer Akquisitionsprojekte: Ein prozessorientierter Ansatz zur Durchführung von Unternehmenskäufen, Bergisch Gladbach 1994.

KUHNER, C. (2000): Beitraege zum Thema - Zum Sinn und Zweck von Unternehmens-zusammenschlüssen aus gesamtwirtschaftlicher Sicht, in: Betriebswirtschaftliche Forschung und Praxis, 4, pp. 333-344.

KUIPERS, D./MILLER, D./PATEL, A. (2003): The Legal Environment and Corporate Valuation: Evidence from Cross-Border Takeovers, Working Paper Rawls College of Business Administration Texas Tech University Lubbock, 2003.

KUMMER, C. (2005): Internationale Fusions- und Akquisitionsaktivität, Wiesbaden 2005.

KPMG (1999): Merger & Acquisition Integration: A Business Guide, 1999.

KPMG (2001): World Class Transactions. Insight into Creating Shareholder Value Through Mergers and Acquisitions, 2001.

KPMG (2002a): Transactions in Germany - Success or Failure?, KPMG Deutsche Treuhand-Gesellschaft, Berlin and Frankfurt, May 2002.

KPMG (2002b): Implementing IAS. IAS Compared with US GAAP, KPMG International 2002.

KPMG (2003): Rechnungslegung nach US-amerikanischen Grundsätzen, 3rd edition, Duesseldorf 2003.

KPMG (2004a): Beating the Bears. Making Global Deals Enhance Value in the New Millennium, 2004.

KPMG (2004b): M&A-Geschäft zieht weltweit wieder an – Aber: Deutschland fällt weiter zurück, Pressemitteilung, 12. Dezember 2004.

KPMG (2005): see ECKER AND HECKEMÜLLER (2005).

KRÄKEL, M. (1999): Organisation und Management, Tübingen 1999.

KREUZ, W./ROTHENBÜCHER, J. (2005): Acquisition of Systematics by EDS – the first 100 days, in: Lucks, K. (Ed.), Transatlantic Mergers & Acquisitions, Erlangen 2005, pp. 162-166.

KRÖGER, F. (2005): Success and Success Factors of US-German Mergers, in: Lucks, K. (Ed.), Transatlantic Mergers & Acquisitions, Erlangen 2005, pp. 51-57.

KRÜGER, W./MÜLLER-STEWENS, G. (1994): Matching Acquisition Policy and Integration Style, in: Krogh, v. G./Sinatra, A./Singh, H., The Management of Corporate Acquisitions: International Perspectives, London 1994, pp. 50-87.

KRUG, J.A./NIGH, D. (1998): Top Management Departures in Cross-Border Acquisitions: Governance Issues in an International Context, in: Journal of International Management, 4, pp. 267–287.

KRUG, J.A./NIGH, D. (2001): Executive Perceptions in Foreign and Domestic Acquisitions: An analysis of Foreign Ownership and its Effect on Executive Fate, in: Journal of World Business, 36(1), pp. 85–105.

KUIPERS, D./MILLER, D./PATEL, A. (2003): The Legal Environment and Corporate Valuation: Evidence from Cross-Border Mergers, Working Paper Texas Tech University, January 2003.

KUSEWITT, J. (1985): An Explanatory Study of Strategic Factors Relating to Performance, in: Strategic Management Journal, 6, pp. 151-169.

LAHEY, K.E./CONN, R.L.(1990): Sensitivity of Acquiring Firms' Returns to Alternative Model Specifications and Disaggregation, in: Journal of Business Finance and Accounting, 17, pp. 421-439.

LAJOUX, A./ELSON, C. (2000): The Art of M&A Due Diligence: Navigating Critical Steps & Uncovering Crucial Data, New York 2000.

LAJOUX, A./NESVOLD, H.P. (2004): The Art of M&A Structuring: Techniques for Mitigating Financial, Tax, and Legal Risk, New York 2004.

LAMONT, O.A./POLK, C. (2002): Does Diversification Destroy Value? Evidence from the Industry Shocks, in: Journal of Financial Economics, 63(1), pp. 51-77.

LAMOUREAUX, N.R. (1985): The Great Merger Movement in American Business, 1895-1904, Cambridge 1985.

LANDLER, M. (2004): German Weighs Taking Stocks off Wall Street, in: The New York Times, November 20, 2004, p. C1.

LAUBE, H./OTTOMEIER, M. (2005): Oracle sticht SAP im Übernahmekampf um Retek aus, in: Financial Times Deutschland, March 23, 2005, p. 1.

LAUSBERG, C./ROSE, S. (1995): Merger Motives in European Banking Results of an Empirical Study, in: Österreichisches Bankarchiv, 3, pp. 177-186.

LEONTIADES, M. (1986): Managing the Unmanageable: Strategies for Success Within the Conglomerate, Melno Park 1986.

LEWELLEN, W. (1971): A Pure Financial Rational for the Conglomerate Merger, in: Journal of Finance, 26, pp. 521-537.

LEWELLEN, W./HUNTSMAN, B. (1970): Managerial Pay and Corporate Performance, in: American Economic Review, Papers and Proceedings, 60 (4), pp. 710-720.

LICHT, A.N./GOLDSCHMIDT, C./SCHWARTZ, S.H. (2003): Culture, Law and Corporate Governance, Working Paper Radzyner School of Law Interdisciplinary Center Herzliya 2003.

LINN, S./MCCONNELL, J. (1983): An Empirical Investigation of Anti-Takeover Amendments on Common Stock Prices, in: Journal of Financial Economics, 11, pp. 361-399.

LORANGE, P./KOTLARCHUK, E./SINGH, H. (1994): Corporate Acquisitions: A Strategic Perspective, in: Rock, M./Rock, R./Sikora, M. (Ed.), The Mergers and Acquisitions Handbook, 2nd edition, New York, 1994, pp. 3-14.

LORIE, J./HALPERN, P. (1970): Conglomerates: The Rhetoric and the Evidence, in.: Journal of Law and Economics, 13, pp. 149-166.

LOUGHRAN, T./VIJH, A. (1997): Do Long-term Shareholders Benefit from Corporate Acquisitions?, in: Journal of Finance, 52(5), pp. 1765-1790.

LOVE, J.H./SCULLER, J. (1990): Growth by Acquisition: The Lessons of Experience, in: Journal of General Management, Spring, pp. 4-19.

LOWENGRUB, P./LUEDECKE, T./MELVIN, M. (2003): Does Corporate Governance Matter in the Market Response to Merger Announcements? Evidence from the U.S. and Germany, Working Paper Arizona State University, January 2003.

LOWINSKI, F./SCHIERECK, D./THOMAS, T.W. (2002): 114 Weddings in the Mountains – Engagement Effects of Mergers and Acquisitions in Switzerland, IMA Working Paper No. 04/02, University Witten/Herdecke, October 2002.

LOWINSKI, F./SCHIERECK, D./THOMAS, T.W. (2004): The Effect of Cross-border Acquisitions on Shareholder Wealth – Evidence from Switzerland, in: Review of Quantitative Finance and Accounting, 22, pp. 315-330.

LOY, C. (1985): Die Entwicklung des Amerikanischen Antitrustrechts – Ein kurzer Überblick, in: Pohl, H. (Ed.), Kartelle und Kartellgesetzgebung in Praxis und Rechtsprechung vom 19. Jahrhundert bis zur Gegenwart, Nassauer Gespräche der Freiherr-vom-Stein-Gesellschaft, Vol. 1, Stuttgart 1985, pp. 318-327.

LUBATKIN, M./O'NEILL, H.M. (1987): Merger Strategies and Capital Market Risk, in: Academy of Management Journal, 30(4), pp. 665-684.

LUCKS, K. (Ed.) (2005a): Transatlantic Mergers & Acquisitions, Erlangen 2005.

LUCKS, K. (2005b): Introduction, in: Lucks, K. (Ed.), Transatlantic Mergers & Acquisitions, Erlangen 2005, pp. 9-15.

LUCKS, K. (2005c): Siemens Power Generation – Transatlantic M&A in a Consolidation Industry, in: Lucks, K. (Ed.), Transatlantic Mergers & Acquisitions, Erlangen 2005, pp. 144-154.

LUCKS, K. (2005d): Management of Complex M&A Projects: Challenges in Transatlantic Deals, in: Lucks, K. (Ed.), Transatlantic Mergers & Acquisitions, Erlangen 2005, pp. 246-260.

LUCKS, K./MECKL, R. (2002): Internationale Mergers & Acquisitions - Der prozessorientierte Ansatz, Berlin 2002.

LÜCKE, W. (1983): Maßstäbe des Erfolgs, insbesondere die Wertschöpfung, in: Die Fortbildung, 4, pp. 105-112.

LUTZ, H. (1984): Entscheidungswerte im Planungsprozess der Unternehmensakquisition, München 1984.

LYON, J./BARBER, B./TSAI, C.-L. (1999): Improved Methods for Tests of Long-run Abnormal Stock Returns, in: Journal of Finance, 54(1), pp. 165–201.

MACKINLEY, A.C. (1997): Event Studies in Economics and Finance, in: Journal of Economic Literature, 35, pp. 13-39.

MAGENHEIM, E. (1986): The Gains to Acquisitions, Acquisitions Premia, and the Theory of the Firm: A Theoretical and Empirical Analysis, Maryland 1986.

MALATESTA, P.H. (1983): The Wealth Effect of Merger Activity and the Objective Functions of Merging Firms, in: Journal of Financial Economics, 11, pp. 155-181.

MANDELKER, G. (1974): Risk and Return: The Case of Merging Firms, in: Journal of Financial Economics, 1(4), pp. 303-335.

MARCHICK, D./PLOTKIN, M./FAGAN, D. (2005): National Security Regulation of Foreign Direct Investment in the United States, Covington & Burling, http://www.cov.com/publications/ download/oid46912/561.pdf.

MARGOTTA, D.G. (1988): Takeover Premiums: With and Without Shareholder Rights Plans, in: The Georgeson Report 1, 6 (4th Quarter, 1988).

MARKIDES, C.C./ITTNER, C.D. (1994): Shareholder Benefits from Corporate International Diversification: Evidence from US International Acquisitions, in: Journal of International Business Studies, 25, pp. 343-366.

MARKIDES, C.C./OYON, D. (1998): International Acquisitions: Do They Create Value for Shareholders?, in: European Management Journal, 16, pp. 125-135.

MARKOVITZ, H. (1952): Portfolio Selection, in: Journal of Finance, 7, pp. 77-91.

MARTEN, K.-U./KOEHLER, A. (1999): Due Diligence in Deutschland – eine empirische Untersuchung, in: Finanz-Betrieb, 1(11), pp. 337-348.

MARTIN, J.D./SAYRAK, A. (2003): Corporate Diversification and Shareholder Value: A Survey of Recent Literature, in: Journal of Corporate Finance, 9, pp. 37-57.

MAS-COLELL, A./WINSTON, M.C./GREEN, J. (1995): Microeconomic Theory, Oxford 1995.

MASULIS, R. (1980): The Effects of Capital Structure Change on Security Prices - A Study of Exchange Offers, in: Journal of Financial Economics, 8, pp. 139-178.

MATHUR, K./RANMGAN, N./CHACHI, I./SUNDARAM, S. (1994): International Acquisitions in the United States: Evidence from Returns to Foreign Bidders, in: Managerial and Decision Economics, pp. 107-118.

MATTHIESSEN, J./BAILEY, A./DUCK, J. (2005): The Impact of Management and Leadership Behaviours on German-American M&A, in: Lucks, K. (Ed.), Transatlantic Mergers & Acquisitions, Erlangen 2005, pp. 274-284.

MAYDEW, E./SCHIPPER, K./VINCENT, L. (1999): The Impact of Taxes on the Choice of Divestiture Method, in: Journal of Accounting and Economics, 28, pp. 117-150.

MCCANN, M. (2001): Cross-Border Acquisitions – the UK Experience, in: Applied Economics, 33, pp. 457-462.

MCKINSEY (2001): Why Mergers Fail, McKinsey & Co. Quarterly, 4, 2001.

MCWILLIAMS, A./SIEGEL, D. (1997): Event Studies in Management Research: Theoretical and Empirical Issues, in: Academy of Management Journal, 40, pp. 626-657.

MEIER, W. (2005): Die US-Pensionsreform kommt nicht vom Fleck, in: Neue Züricher Zeitung, October 19, 2005, p. 21.

MERCER CONSULTING GROUP (1995): see ZWEIG (1995).

MERCER CONSULTING GROUP (2001): Transatlantic Mergers & Acquisitions: Review of Research Findings, November 14, 2001.

MERKT, H. (1991): US-amerikanisches Gesellschaftsrecht, Heidelberg 1991.

MERKT, H. (1994): Internationaler Unternehmenskauf und Einheitskaufrecht, in: Zeitschrift für vergleichende Rechtswissenschaft, 1994, pp. 353-378.

MIDDELMANN, U./HELMES, M. (2005): Due Diligence in den USA, in: Berens, W./Brauner, H./Strauch, J., Due Diligence bei Unternehmensakquisitionen, 4th revised and enhanced edition, Stuttgart 2005, pp. 651-688.

MIKKELSON, W.H./PARTCH, M.M. (1997): Ownership and Operating Performance of Firms that go Public, in: Journal of Financial Economics, 44, pp. 281- 307.

MIKKELSON, W.H./RUBACK, R.S. (1986): Targeted Share Repurchases and Common Stock Returns, Working Paper No.1707-86 Massachusetts Institute of Technology, Sloan School of Management, June 1986.

MITCHELL, M./MULHERIN, J. (1996): The Impact of Industry Shocks on Takeover and Restructuring Activity, in: Journal of Financial Economics, 41, pp. 193-209.

MITCHELL, M./PULVINO, T./STAFFORD, E. (2004): Price Pressure Around Mergers, in: Journal of Finance, 59(1), pp. 31-63.

MITCHELL, M./STAFFORD, E. (2000): Managerial Decisions and Long-Term Stock Price Performance, in: Journal of Business, 73(3), pp. 287-329.

MÖLLER, H.P. (1985): Die Informationseffizienz des deutschen Aktienmarktes – eine Zusammenfassung und Analyse empirischer Untersuchungen, in: Zeitschrift für betriebswirtschaftliche Forschung, 37, pp. 500-518.

MÖLLER, W-P. (1983): Der Erfolg von Unternehmenszusammenschlüssen, München 1983.

MOELLER, S./SCHLINGEMANN, F. (2005): Global Diversification and Bidder Gains: A Comparison Between Cross-Border and Domestic Acquisitions, in: Journal of Banking & Finance, 29, pp. 533-564.

MOELLER, S./SCHLINGEMANN, F./STULZ, R. (2004): Firm Size and the Gains from Acquisitions, in: Journal of Financial Economics, 73, pp. 201-228.

MORCK, R./SCHLEIFER, A./VISHNY, R.W. (1990): Do Managerial Objectives Drive Bad Acquisitions?, in: Journal of Finance, 45(1), pp. 31-48.

MORCK, R./YEUNG, B. (1991): Why Investors Value Multinationality, in: Journal of Business, 64(2), pp. 165-187.

MORCK, R./YEUNG, B. (1992): Internalization: An Event Study Test, in: Journal of International Economics, 33, pp. 41-56.

MORGAN, LEWIS & BOCKIUS (1996): Handbook of Foreign Investment in the United States, Philadelphia 1996.

MORGENSOHN, G. (2005): What are Mergers Good for?, in: The New York Times Sunday Journal, June 4, 2005, pp. 56-63.

MORIYAMA, H. (1994): Risk Management: Environmental Liabilities, in: Rock, M./Rock, R./Sikora, M. (Ed.), The Mergers & Acquisitions Handbook, 2nd edition, New York 1994, pp. 353-362.

MORRIS, J. (2000): Purchase Accounting, in: Morris, J. (2000), Mergers and Acquisitions – Business Strategies for Accountants, New York 2000, pp. 225-266.

MORRISS, J./JOLIN, B. (2004): Dealing with Environmental Issues in the Acquisition of Industrial Facilities: Answers to Buyers′ Frequently Asked Questions, http://www.mondaq.com/article.asp?articleid=26707&searchresults=1.

MOXTER, A. (1991): Grundsätze ordnungsmäßiger Unternehmensbewertung, 2nd edition, Wiesbaden, 1991.

MUELLER, D.C. (1969): A Theory of Conglomerate Mergers: in: Quarterly Journal of Economics, 1969, pp. 643-659.

MUELLER, D.C. (Ed.) (1980): The Determinants and Effects of Mergers, Cambridge, 1980.

MUELLER, D.C. (1997): Merger Policy in the United States: A Reconsideration, in: Review of Industrial Organization, 12, pp. 655–685.

MÜLLER-STEWENS, G./.LECHNER, C. (2001): Strategisches Management, Stuttgart 2001.

MÜLLER-STEWENS, G./SPICKERS, J./DEISS, C. (1999): Mergers & Acquisitions. Markttendenzen und Beraterprofile, Stuttgart 1999.

MUKERJEE, T./KIYMAZ, H./BAKER, K. (2004): Merger Motives and Target Valuation: A Survey of Evidence From CFOs, in: Journal of Applied Finance, Fall/Winter, pp. 7-24.

MULFORD, C./COMISKEY, E. (2002): The Financial Numbers Game: Detecting Creative Accounting Practices, New York 2002.

MULHERIN, J./BOONE, A. (2000): Comparing Acquisitions and Divestitures, in: Journal of Corporate Finance, 6, pp. 117-139.

NAHAVANDI, A./MALEKZADEH, A.R. (1988): Acculturation in Mergers and Acquisitions, in: Academy of Management Review, 13(1), pp. 79-90.

NEW YORK STATE BAR ASSOCIATION (2005): Report On Proposed Regulations Regarding Cross-Border Mergers, Report No. 109, http://www.nysba.org/Content/ContentGroups/Section_Information1/Tax_Section_Reports/1094rpt.pdf.

NIELAND, M. (2001): Financial Due Diligance bei Unternehmenstransaktionen, in: Scott, C. (Ed.), Due Diligence in der Praxis, Wiesbaden 2001, pp. 91-109.

NIEWANDT, H./SEIBERT, D. (2004): Prognose des bewertungsrelevanten Cash Flows, in: Richter, F./Timmreck, C. (Ed): Unternehmensbewertung, Stuttgart 2004, pp. 21-40.

NOCERA, J. (2005): For All Its Costs, Sarbanes Law is Working, in: The New York Times, December 3, 2005, p. C1.

NOLEN, G. (2005): Investing Locally to Grow Globally: Siemens M&A Strategy in the U.S. Market, in: Lucks, K. (Ed.), Transatlantic Mergers & Acquisitions, Erlangen 2005, pp. 135-144.

NUPPONEN, P. (1995): Post-Acquisition Performance: Combination, Management, and Performance Measurement in Horizontal Integration, Helsinki 1995.

OEHLRICH, M. (1999): Strategische Analyse von Unternehmensakquisitionen. Das Beispiel der pharmazeutischen Industrie, Wiesbaden 1999.

PACK, H. (2002): Due Diligence, in: Picot, G. (Ed.), Handbuch Mergers & Acquisitions, 2nd edition, Stuttgart 2002, pp. 267-301.

PALAZZO, B./DEFOREST, G./PELZER, B. (2005): How to Merge German and American Talents to Achieve a Cross-Atlantic Culture of Understanding and Shared Success?, in: Lucks, K. (Ed.), Transatlantic Mergers & Acquisitions, Erlangen 2005, pp. 438-448.

PAPPROTKA, S. (1996): Unternehmenszusammenschlüsse: Synergiepotentiale und ihre Umsetzung durch Integration, Wiesbaden 1996.

PAUSENBERGER, E. (1989): Zur Systematik von Unternehmenszusammenschlüssen, Das Wirtschaftsstudium, 18(11), pp. 621-626.

PAUSENBERGER, E. (1993): Unternehmenszusammenschlüsse, in: Wittmann, W./Kern, W. et al. (Ed), Handwörterbuch der Betriebswirtschaft, 5th edition, Stuttgart 1993, cc. 4436-4448.

PAUTLER, P. (2001): Evidence on Mergers and Acquisitions, Working Paper Federal Trade Commission Bureau of Economics, September 2001.

PAUTLER, P. (2003): The Effects of Mergers and Post-Merger Integration: A Review of Business Consulting Literature, Working Paper Federal Trade Commission Bureau of Economics, January 2003.

PEEMÖLLER, V. (Ed.) (2001): Handbuch der Unternehmensbewertung, Landsberg am Lech 2001.

PELTZER, M: (1986): Takeovers in den Vereinigten Staaten – können ihre Spielregeln übertragen werden?, in: Knapp, U. (Ed.), Wirtschaft und Wissenschaft im Wandel, Frankfurt am Main 1986, pp. 271-286.

PERIN, S. (1996): Synergien bei Unternehmensakquisitionen, Empirische Untersuchung von Finanz-, Markt- und Leistungssynergien, Frankfurt am Main 1996.

PERRIDON, L./STEINER, M. (2004): Finanzwirtschaft der Unternehmung, 13th revised and enhanced edition, München 2004.

PETERSON, P.P. (1989): Event Studies: A Review of Issues and Methodology, in: Quarterly Journal of Business and Economics, 28, pp. 36-66.

PETTWAY, R./SICHERMAN, N./SPIESS, D. (1993): Japanese Foreign Direct Investment: Impacts of Purchases and Sales of U.S. Assets, in: Financial Management, 1993, pp. 82-95.

PICOT, G. (2002): Wirtschaftliche und wirtschaftsrechtliche Aspekte bei der Planung der Mergers & Acquisitions, in: Picot, G. (Ed.): Handbuch Mergers & Acquisitions, 2th edition, Stuttgart 2002, pp. 3-37.

PLUMMER, E./ROBINSON, J. (1990): Capital Market Evidence of Windfalls from the Acquisition of Tax Carryovers, in: National Tax Journal, 43 (4), pp. 481-490.

PORRINI, P. (2006): Are Investment Bankers Good for Acquisition Premiums?, in: Journal of Business Research, 59, pp. 90-99.

PORTER, M. (1980): Corporate Strategy, New York 1980.

PORTER, M. (1987): Diversifikation – Konzerne ohne Konzept, Harvard Manager, 9, pp. 30-49.

PORTER, M. (1989): Spitzenleistungen erreichen und behaupten. Sonderausgabe, Frankfurt am Main and New York 1989.

POULSEN, A.B./STEGEMOLLER, M.A. (2006): Moving from Private to Public Ownership: Selling Out to Public Firms vs. Initial Public Offerings, Working Paper University of Georgia, January 2006.

POUND, J. (1987): The Effects of Antitakeover Amendments on Takeover Activity: Some Direct Evidence, in: Journal of Law and Economics, 30, pp. 353-367.

PRAHALAD, C.K./HAMEL, G. (1990): The Core Competence of the Corporation, in: Harvard Business Review, 68, pp. 79-92.

PRATT, J./KULSRUD, W. (2003): Federal Taxation, Houston 2003.

PRICEWATERHOUSECOOPERS (2000): Speed Makes the Difference: A Survey of Mergers and Acquisitions, New York 2000.

RAPPAPORT, A. (1994): Discounted Cash Flow Valuation, in: Rock, M./Rock, R./Sikora, M. (Ed.), The Mergers & Acquisitions Handbook, 2nd edition, New York 1994, pp. 161-178.

RAPPAPORT, S. (1981): Selecting Strategies that Create Shareholder Value, in: Harvard Business Review, May-June 1981, pp. 139-149.

RAPPAPORT, S. (1986): Creating Shareholder Value. The New Standard for Business Performance, New York 1986.

RAPPAPORT, S. (1988): Management on Wall Street: Making Securities Firms Work, Homewood 1988.

RAPPAPORT, S./SIROWER, M. (1999): Stock or Cash? The Trade-offs for Buyers and Sellers in Mergers and Acquisitions, in: Harvard Business Review, November-December 1999, pp. 147-158.

RASCHE, C. (1994): Wettbewerbsvorteile durch Kernkompetenzen: Ein ressourcenorientierter Ansatz, Wiesbaden 1994.

RAU, P.R. (2000): Investment Bank Market Share, Contingent Fee Payment, and the Performance of Acquiring Firms, in: Journal of Financial Economics, 56, pp. 293-324.

RAU, P.R./RODGERS, K.J. (2002): Do Bidders Hire Top-tier Investment Banks to Certify Value?, Working Paper Purdue University, 2002.

RAU, P.R./VERMAELEN, T. (1998): Glamour, Value and Post-Acquisition Performance of Acquiring Firms, in: Journal of Financial Economics, 49, pp. 223-253.

RAVENSCRAFT, D.J./SCHERER, F.M. (1987): Life after Takeover, in: Journal of Industrial Economics, 36, pp. 147-156.

REED, S./LAJOUX, A. (1999): The Art of M&A. A Merger, Acquisition, Buyout Guide, 3rd edition, New York 1999.

REICHE, L. (2005): Einmal Wall Street, immer Wall Street?, in: manager-magazin online, January 28, 2005, http:/www.manager-magazin.de/geld/artikel/0,2828, 338983,00.html.

REINECKE, R-D. (1989): Akkulturation von Auslandsakquisitionen, Wiesbaden 1989.

REINEKE, B. (2001): Vertriebsintegration im Rahmen von Unternehmenszusammenschlüssen, St. Gallen 2001.

REIẞNER, S. (1992): Synergiemanagement und Akquisitionserfolg, Wiesbaden 1992.

RESNIKOW, N./RATHKOPF, C. (2002): Legal Due Diligence, in: Rosenbloom, A. (Ed.), Due Diligence for Global Deal Making, New Jersey 2002, pp. 149-208.

REUTER, T./THOMA, G. (1999): Shrinking the Atlantic, Practical Law Company, May 1999, http://www.practicallaw.com/7-101-0014.

RHOADES, S. (1994): A Summary of Merger Performance Studies in Banking, 1980-93, and an Assessment of the "Operating Performance" and "Event Study" Methodologies, Working Paper Board of Governors of the Federal Reserve System, 1994.

RHODE, H. (2005): Die Kriegserklärung, in: Börsen-Zeitung, March 23, 2005, p. 8.

RICHTER, F. (2002): Unternehmensbewertung, in: Picot, G. (Ed.), Handbuch Mergers & Acquisitions, 2nd edition, Stuttgart 2002, pp. 301-333.

RICHTER, F. (2004): Relativer Unternehmenswert, in: Richter, F./Timmreck, C. (Ed.), Unternehmensbewertung, Moderne Instrumente und Lösungsansätze, Stuttgart 2004, pp. 367 – 380.

RICHTER, F. (2005): Mergers & Acquisitions Investmentanalyse, Finanzierung und Prozessmanagement, München 2005.

RIFKIND, N. (1998): Should Uninformed Shareholders be a Threat? Justifying Defensive Action by Target Directors in Delaware: "Just Say No" after Moore v. Wallace, in: Boston University Law Review, 78, p. 105.

RIPIN, R./GEYRHALTER, V. (2005): Delisting – the US and the German Perspective, in: Lucks, K. (Ed.), Transatlantic Mergers & Acquisitions, Erlangen 2005, pp. 301-310.

ROBERTS, T./BOONE, M. (1998): Techniques and Strategies in Protecting an Acquisition Transaction, Hayes & Boone, 1998, http://www.haynesboone.com/FILES/ tbl_s12 PublicationsHotTopics%5CPublicationPDF60%5C162%5C02_20_1998_Boone.pdf.

RÖLLER, L-H./STENNEK, J./VERBOVEN, F. (2000): Efficiency Gains from Mergers, Working Paper No. 543 The Research Institute of Industrial Economics, Stockholm 2000.

ROLL, R. (1986): The Hubris Hypothesis of Corporate Takeovers, in: Journal of Business, 59(4), pp. 197-216.

ROLL, R. (1988): Empirical Evidence on Takeover Activity and Shareholder Wealth, in: Coffee jr., J.C./Rose-Ackerman, S./Lowenstein, L. (Ed.), Knights, Raiders, and Targets. Oxford University Press, New York und Oxford 1988, pp. 241-252.

ROLL, R./ROSS, S. (1980): An Empirical Investigation of the Arbitrage Pricing Theory, in: Journal of Finance, 35, pp. 1073-1103.

ROOT, F. (1987): Entry Strategies for International Markets, Lexington 1987.

ROSEN, V. R./SEIFERT, W.G. (1998) (Ed.): Zugang zum US-Kapitalmarkt für deutsche Aktiengesellschaften, Schriften zum Kapitalmarkt, Band 1, Eschborn 1998.

ROSENBLOOM, A. (Ed.) (2002a): Due Diligence for Global Deal Making, New Jersey 2002.

ROSENBLOOM, A. (2002b): Due Diligence in the Global Economy, in: Rosenbloom, A. (Ed.): Due Diligence for Global Deal Making, New Jersey 2002, pp. 1-12.

ROSENGREN, R. (1988): State Restrictions of Hostile Takeovers, in: Publius: Journal of Federalism, 18(3), pp. 71-73.

RUBACK, R.S. (1987): An Overview of Takeover Defenses, in Auerbach, A. (Ed.) Mergers and Acquisitions, Chicago 1987.

RUEGGER, P. (1999): Structuring International Acquisitions, Part 1, Thomson FindLaw, September 1999, http://library.findlaw.com/1999/Sep/1/130897.html.

SANDLER, G.G.R. (1991): Synergie: Konzept, Messung und Realisation, Bamberg 1991.

SAUNDERS, A./SRINIVASAN, A. (2001): Investment Banking Relationships and Merger Fees. Working Paper University of Georgia Department of Banking and Finance, 2001.

SAUTTER, M.T. (1989): Stragtegische Analyse von Unternehmensakquisitionen, Frankfurt am Main 1989.

SAYRAK, A./MARTIN, J.D. (2001): Corporate Governance and the Performance of Diversified Firms, Working Paper Baylor University, February 2001.

SCHENCK, M./RICHTER, F./JUNG-SENSSFELDER, K. (2005): Capital Market – Hurdle or Help in Transatlantic M&A, in: Lucks, K. (Ed.), Transatlantic Mergers & Acquisitions, Erlangen 2005, pp. 32-44.

SCHERER, F.M. (1988): Corporate Takeovers: The Efficiency Arguments, in: Journal of Economic Perspectives, 2, pp. 69-82.

SCHERER, F.M./ROSS, D. (1990): Industrial Market Structure and Economic Performance, 3rd edition, Boston 1990.

SCHIERECK, D./STRAUSS, M. (2000): Zum Ankündigungseffekt großer Bankfusionen, in: M&A Review, 11/2000, pp. 421-425.

SCHIERECK, D./WEBER, M. (2000): Finanzaktivpreise: Theorie und Evidenz. in: Hagen, J./Stein, J.H. (Ed.), Geld-, Bank- und Börsenwesen, Handbuch des Finanzsystems, 40th edition, Stuttgart 2000, pp. 270-298.

SCHMIDT, D./FOWLER, K.L. (1990): Post-Acquisition Financial Performance and Executive Compensation, in: Strategic Management Journal, 1990, pp. 559-570.

SCHMIDT, P. (2001): Understanding American and German Business Cultures, Meridian World Press 2001.

SCHMIDT, P. (2005): Bridging the Intercultural Gap: Non-Conventional Truths About American-German Business, in: Lucks, K. (Ed.), Transatlantic Mergers & Acquisitions, Erlangen 2005, pp. 429-438.

SCHMIDT, V. (2005): Is Small Cap Private Equity an International Business? – Differences in the U.S. Versus Continental Europe, in: Lucks, K. (Ed.) Transatlantic Mergers & Acquisitions, Erlangen 2005, pp. 222-233.

SCHNITZER, M. (1995): "Breach of Trust" in Takeovers and the Optimal Corporate Charter, in: Journal of Industrial Economics, 43, pp. 229-260.

SCHOLES, M./WOLFSON, M. (1992): Taxes and Business Strategy, A Planning Approach, Englewood Cliffs 1992.

SCHROEDER, L./SJOQUIST, D./STEPHAN, P. (1986): Understanding Regression Analysis, Beverly Hills 1986.

SCHUBERT, W./KÜTING, K. (1981): Unternehmenszusammenschlüsse, München 1981.

SCHULTZE, W. (2001): Methoden der Unternehmensbewertung, Gemeinsamkeiten, Unterschiede, Perspektiven, Düsseldorf 2001.

SCHWEIGER, D.M/WALSH, J.P. (1990): Mergers and Acquisitions: An Interdisciplinary View, in: Rowland, K./Ferris, G. (Ed.): Research in Personnel and Human Resources Management, Greenwich 1990, pp. 41-107.

SCHWEIGER, G.C. (2005): Cross-Border Due Diligence and Beyond, in: Lucks, K. (Ed.), Transatlantic Mergers & Acquisitions, Erlangen 2005, pp. 357-364.

SCOTT, C. (2001): Due Diligence in der Praxis, Wiesbaden 2001.

SECURITIES AND EXCHANGE COMMISSION (1979): Securities and Exchange Act Release No. 16385, November 20, 1979.

SELLMANN, J./MAIER, O (2005): Degussa's Execution Experience with Transatlantic M&A Projects, in: Lucks, K. (Ed.), Transatlantic Mergers & Acquisitions, Erlangen 2005, pp. 196-209.

SERFLING, K./PAPE, U. (1995): Theoretische Grundlagen und traditionelle Verfahren der Unternehmensbewertung, in: WirtschaftsStudium, 1995, pp. 808-819.

SERVAES, H./ZENNER, M. (1996): The Role of Investment Banks in Acquisitions, in: Review of Financial Studies, 9, pp. 787-815.

SETH, A. (1990): Value Creation in Acquisitions: A Re-examination of Performance Issues, in: Strategic Management Journal, 11, pp. 99-115.

SETH, A./SONG, K.P./PETTIT, R. (2000): Synergy, Managerialism or Hubris? An Empirical Examination of Motives for Foreign Acquisitions of U.S. Firms, in: Journal of International Business Studies, 31(3), pp. 387-405.

SHAPIRO, S./STRAUSS, J. (1987): Appraisal Rights Breathing New Life Into State Takeover Statutes, Mayer, Brown & Platt, http://www.appellate.net/articles/takeover799.asp.

SHARPE, W.F. (1963): A Simplified Model for Portfolio Analysis, in: Management Science, 9, pp. 277-292.

SHELTON, L.M. (2000): Merger Market Dynamics: Insights into the Behavior of Target and Bidder Firms, in: Journal of Economic Behavior and Organization, 41, pp. 363-383.

SHESKIN, D.J. (1997): Handbook of Parametric and Nonparametric Statistical Procedures, New York 1997.

SHIELDS, R. (1994): Closing Services, in Rock, M./Rock, R./Sikora, M. (Ed.), The Mergers & Acquisitions Handbook, 2nd edition, New York 1994, pp. 319-330.

SHIMIZU, K./HITT, M./VAIDJANATH, D./PISANO, V. (2004): Theoretical Foundations of Cross-Border Mergers and Acquisitions: A Review of Current Research and Recommendations for the Future, in: Journal of International Management, 10, pp. 307-353.

SHLEIFER, A./VISHNY, R.W. (1991): Takeovers in the `60s and `80s: Evidence and Implications, in: Strategic Management Journal, 12, pp. 51-59.

SHLEIFER, A./VISHNY, R.W. (2003): Stock Market Acquisitions, in: Journal of Financial Economics, 70(3), pp. 295-312.

SHRIEVES, R.F./LUBATKIN, M. (1990): An Analysis of Merger-Induced Nonstationarity in Market Model Parameters of Acquiring Firms, in: Quarterly Journal of Business and Economics 29(3), pp. 56-89.

SIDEL, R. (2002): Volatile US Markets and Global Slowdown Cool Corporate Desire to Merge, in: The Wall Street Journal, January 2, R10.

SINGH, H./MONTGOMERY, C.A. (1987): Corporate Acquisition Strategies and Economic Performance, in: Strategic Management Journal, 8(4), pp. 377-386.

SINGH, H./ZOLLO, M. (1998): The Impact of Knowledge Codification, Experience Trajectories and Integration Strategies on the Performance of Corporate Acquisitions, Academy of Management Proceedings, 1998.

SIROWER, M.L. (1997): The Synergy Trap: How Companies Lose the Acquisition Game, in: New Strategic Management Journal, 9, pp. 173-184.

SLUSSER, W.P./RIGGS, R. (1994): Payment Modes and Acquisition Currencies, in: Rock, M./Rock, R./Sikora, M. (Ed.), The Mergers & Acquisitions Handbook, 2nd edition, New York 1994, pp. 209-218.

SODERQUIST, L.D. (1987): Understanding Securities Laws, in: Practicing Law Institute, July 1987, p. 236.

SOUDER, W.E./CHAKRABARTI, A.K. (1984): Acquisitions, Do they Really Work?, in: Interfaces, 14(4), pp. 41-47.

SPENDER, J.C. (1996): Making Knowledge the Basis of a Dynamic Theory of the Firm, in: Strategic Management Journal, 17, pp. 45-62.

SPREMANN, K. (Ed.) (1987): Agency Theory, Information, and Incentives. Agent and Principal, New York 1987.

STEGER, U./KUMMER, C. (2003): M&A Activity in the New Competitive Milieu, in: Steger, U./Morisini, P. (Ed.): Managing Complex Mergers: Real World Lessons in Implementing Successful Cross-cultural M&As, London 2003, pp. 1-29.

STEIN, I. (1992): Motive für internationale Unternehmensakquisitionen, Wiesbaden 1992.

STEINEBACH, L./BLUM, S./NUHN, H. (2005): Henkel's Acquisition of the Dial Corporation, Scottsdale, USA, in: Lucks, K. (Ed.), Transatlantic Mergers & Acquisitions, Erlangen 2005, pp. 97-110.

STELLINGWERF, F./MANTESE, G. (2000): Letter of Intent, in: Michigan Bar Journal, Online, November 2000, 79(11).

STERN, J. (2004): United States: Recent Trends and Changes in Merger and Acquisition Activities, Foley & Lardner LLP, New York 2004.

STEWART, T./O'BRIAN, L. (2005): Transforming an Industrial Giant, Interview with Heinrich von Pierer, in: Harvard Business Review, 83(2), pp. 114-122.

STORCK, J. (1993): Mergers & Acquisitions – Marktentwicklung und bankpolitische Konsequenzen, Wiesbaden 1993.

STRUNCK, W. (2003): Strategien für Mergers & Acquisitions in der Medienindustrie, Bamberg 2003.

STURM, N. (1999): Doch Computer können nicht lächeln Bertelsmann-Chef Wössner setzt auf das Internet, in: Süddeutsche Zeitung, November 13, 1999, p. Wirtschaft 28.

SUDARSANAM, S. (1995): The Essence of Mergers and Acquisitions, London, 1995.

SÜVERKRÜP, C. (1992): Internationaler technologischer Wissenstransfer durch Unternehmensakquisitionenen: eine empirische Untersuchung am Beispiel deutsch-amerikanischer und amerikanisch-deutscher Akquisitionen, Bern 1992.

SURA, M. (2005): The Role of Third Party Interveners in Merger Investigations Before the Competition Authorities and in Judicial Review Proceedings, in: Lucks, K. (Ed.), Transatlantic Mergers & Acquisitions, Erlangen 2005, pp. 388-394.

TANKERSLEY, M. (1999): Buying and Selling the Private Company, Bracewell & Patterson, L.L.P., Chicago 1999.

TAYLOR, A. (2001): Can the Germans Rescue Chrysler?, in: Fortune, April 30, 2001, pp. 52-56.

THELEN, REID & PRIEST (2004): Doing Business in the United States of America, New York: http://www.thelenreid.com/practice/Doing_Business_in_the_USA.pdf.

THOMSON FINANCIAL (2000): Datastream Definition Manual. Thomson Financial Datastream Publication.

TIERNEY, C. (2000): Defiant Daimler, in: Business Week, August 17, 2000, pp. 24-29.

TIGGES, M. (2005): Due Diligence und Gewährleistung im Unternehmenskauf, in: Finanz-Betrieb, 2, pp. 95-105.

TIMMRECK, C. (2004): Bestimmung der Eigenkapitalkosten, in Richter, F./Timmreck, C. (Ed.), Unternehmensbewertung, Moderne Instrumente und Lösungsansätze, Stuttgart 2004, pp. 61-76.

TISCHENDORF, S. (Ed.) (2000): Strategies for Successful Acquisitions in Germany, London 2000.

TOYNE, M.F./TRIPP, J.D. (1998): Interstate Bank Mergers and Their Impact on Shareholder Returns: Evidence from the 1990s, in: Quarterly Journal of Business and Economics, 37, pp. 48-58.

TRAUTWEIN, F. (1990): Merger Motives and Merger Prescriptions, in: Strategic Management Journal, 11, pp. 283-295.

TRAVLOS, N.G. (1987): Corporate Takeover Bids, Methods of Payment, and Bidding Firms' Stock Returns, in: Journal of Finance, 1987, pp. 943-963.

TURCON, R. (Ed.) (1994): Grundlagen des US-amerikanischen Gesellschafts-, Wirtschafts-, Steuer- und Fremdenrechts: rechtliche Rahmenbedingungen für ausländische Direktinvestitionen in den USA, München 1994.

TZERMIAS, N. (1995): Interesse von Hoechst and Marion Merrell Dow, in: Neue Züricher Zeitung, March 1, 1995, p. 27.

UNCTAD (2000): World Investment Report 2000: Cross-Border Mergers and Acquisitions and Development, New York and Geneva 2000.

U.S. DEPARTMENT OF LABOR (2003): Employer's Guide to Advance Notice of Closings and Layoffs, http://www.doleta.gov/layoff/pdf/EmployerWARN09_2003.pdf.

VERNON, R. (1966): International Investment and International Trade in the Product Cycle, in: Quarterly Journal of Economics, 80, pp. 190-207.

VERY, P./SCHWEIGER, D.M. (2001): The Acquisition Process as a Learning Process: Evidence from a Study of Critical Problems and Solutions in Domestic and Cross-border Deals, in: Journal of World Business, 36(1), pp. 11-31.

VILLALONGA, B. (2000): Does Diversification Cause the "Diversification Discount"?, Working Paper University of California, 2000.

VILLALONGA, B. (2004): Diversification Discount or Premium? New Evidence from the Business Tracking Series, in: Journal of Finance, 59(2), pp. 479-506.

VINER, N./RHOADES, D./DUMAS, D./IVANOV, S. (2000): Making Mergers Work: Turning a Big Deal into a Good Deal, Boston Consulting Group, Boston 2000.

VOGEL, D. (2002): M&A Ideal und Wirklichkeit, Wiesbaden 2002.

WALDENMAIER, M./BACH-ALEXANDER, I./BADER, T./EBERT, M. (2005): Outsourcing of Pension Obligations by German Corporations Through Implementation of a Contractual Trust Arrangement (CTA), in: Lucks, K. (Ed.), Transatlantic Mergers & Acquisitions, Erlangen 2005, pp. 402-411.

WALKER, M. (2000): Corporate Takeovers, Strategic Objectives, and Acquiring-firm Shareholder Wealth, in: Financial Management, 29(1), pp. 53-66.

WARLIMONT, G. (2000): Global um jeden Preis, in: Financial Times Deutschland, July 25, 2000, p. 29.

WEBER, Y./SHENKAR, O./RAVEH, A. (1996): National and Corporate Cultural Fit in Mergers & Acquisitions: An Exploratory Study, in: Management Science, 42(8), pp. 1215-1227.

WERNERFELT, B. (1984): A Resource-based View of the Firm, in: Strategic Management Journal, 5, pp. 171-180.

WESTON, F.J./CHUNG, S. (1983): Some Aspects of Merger Theory, in: Journal of Midwest Finance Association, 12, pp. 1-33.

WESTON, F.J./SIU, J.A./JOHNSON, B. (2001): Takeovers, Restructuring, and Corporate Governance, 3rd edition, New Jersey 2001.

WHITE, D.J. (2001): The Top Ten Mistakes in Negotiating Acquisition Agreements, http://www.zag-sw.com/in_the_news/publications/Top_Ten_Mistake_Agt.pdf.

WHITED, T. (2001): Is it Inefficient Investment that Causes the Diversification Discount?, in: Journal of Finance, 56, pp. 1667-1691.

WIDENER UNIVERSITY SCHOOL OF LAW (1999): RAG American Coal versus AEI Resources, Inc., http://corporate-law.widener.edu/documents/opinions/16728-077.pdf.

WIEANDT, A./SANTIAGO, R. (2005): Growing in the U.S.- Review of Deutsche Bank's M&A Strategy in North America, in: Lucks, K. (Ed.), Transatlantic Mergers & Acquisitions, Erlangen 2005, pp. 85-97.

WILLIAMSON, O.E. (1964): The Economics of Discretionary Behavior: Managerial Objectives in a Theory of the Firm, Englewood Cliffs 1964.

WILLIAMSON, O.E. (1973): Markets and Hierarchies: Some Elementary Considerations, in: American Economic Review, Papers and Proceedings, 63, pp. 316-325.

WILLIAMSON, O.E. (1996): The Economic Institutions of Capitalism, Firms, Markets, Relational Contracting, New York 1996.

WIRTZ, B. (2003): Mergers & Acquisitions Management – Strategie und Organisation von Unternehmenszusammenschlüssen, Wiesbaden 2003.

YAGO, G./BATES, M./HUANG, W./NOAH, R. (2000): Tale of Two Decades: Corporate Control in the '80s and '90s, Working Paper Milken Institute, November 2000.

YATES, C. (2002): Recent Decline in U.S. Cross-Border Activity - A Short-term Phenomenon?, in: M&A Monitor, May 13, 2002, http://www.piperjaffray.com/info2.aspx?id=473.

YOOK, K./MCCABE, G. (1996): The Effect of International Acquisitions on Shareholders' Wealth, in: The Mid-Atlantic Journal of Business, 32(1), pp. 5-17.

ZAHEER, S. (1995): Overcoming the Liability of Foreignness, in: Academic Management Journal, 38, pp. 341-363.

ZEHETMEIER-MÜLLER, R./DOERR, I. (2005): Thin Capitalization Rules in Germany and the United States, in: Lucks, K. (Ed.), Transatlantic Mergers & Acquisitions, Erlangen 2005, pp. 330-340.

ZELGER, H. (2005): Purchase Price Allocation nach IFRS und US-GAAP, in: Ballwieser, W./Beyer, S./Zelger, H. (Ed.), Unternehmenskauf nach IFRS und US-GAAP, Stuttgart 2005, pp. 91-140.

ZIESCHANG, P. (2000): Akquisition von Asset Management Unternehmen in den USA, Bern 2000.

ZIMMERER, C. (1993): Unternehmensakquisition, in: Wittman, W./ Kern, W. et al. (Ed.), Hand-wörterbuch der Betriebswirtschaft, Band 3, 5th edition, Stuttgart 1993, pp. 4294-4306.

ZINN, M. (2004): Taxation of Cross-Border Mergers and Acquisitions, July 2004, http:// www.us.kpmg.com/microsite/mergersandacquisitions/united_states.asp.

ZSCHÄPITZ, H. (2006): Fusionsfieber erfaßt die Aktienmärkte, in: Die Welt, February 22, 2006, p. Wirtschaft 1.

ZUMWINKEL, K. (2005): Integration at its Best – the Takeover of AEI by Deutsche Post World Net, in: Lucks, K. (Ed.), Transatlantic Mergers & Acquisitions, Erlangen 2005, pp. 170-178.

ZWAHLEN, B. (1994): Motive und Gefahrenpotential bei einer Unternehmensakquisition: Eine erfolgreiche Akquisitions- und Integrationsstrategie einer multinationalen Unternehmung am Fallbeispiel „Nestle-Rowntree", Zürich 1994.

ZWEIG, P. (1995): The Case Against Mergers, in: Business Week, October 30, 1995, pp. 122-30.

- U.S. Statutes

Clayton Act of 1914: 15 U.S.C.A. §§ 12 ff.

Comprehensive Environmental Response, Compensation, and Liability Act Of 1980: 42 U.S.C. §§ 9601 ff.

Consolidated Omnibus Budget Reconciliation Act of 1985: 29 U.S.C. §§ 1161 ff.

Defense Production Act of 1950: 50 U.S.C. §§ 2061 ff.

Employee Retirement Security Act of 1974: 29 U.S.C. §§ 1001 ff.

Exchange Act of 1934: 15 U.S.C. §§ 78a ff.

Hart-Scott-Rodino Act Antitrust Improvements Act: 15 U.S.C. § 18a.

Internal Revenue Code as of 1986: 26 U.S.C.

National Labor Relations Act of 1936: U.S.C. 29 §§ 151-169.

Sarbanes-Oxley Act of 2002: 15 U.S.C. §§ 7201 ff.

Securities Act of 1933: 15 U.S.C. §§ 77a ff.

Sherman Act of 1890: 15 U.S.C.A. §§ 1 ff.

Williams Act: 15 U.S.C. §§ 78m(d)–78m(e), 78n(d)–78n(f).

Worker Adjustment Retraining and Notification Act of 1988: 29 U.S.C. §§ 2101 ff.

- U.S. Accounting Standards

AICPA Accounting Research Bulletin 43: Restatement and Revision of Accounting Research Bulletins, Chapter 4, Inventory Pricing.

AICPA Statement of Positions 97-2: Software Revenue Recognition.

AICPA Statement of Positions 98-9: Modification of SOP 97-2.

FASB Emergence Issues Task Force 99-17: Accounting for Advertising Barter Transactions.

FASB Emergence Issues Task Force 00-10: Accounting for Shipping and Handling Fees and Costs.

FASB Statements of Financial Accounting Standards 5: Accounting for Contingencies.

FASB Statements of Financial Accounting Standards 87: Employer's Accounting for Pensions.

FASB Statements of Financial Accounting Standards 88: Employer's Accounting for Settlements and Curtailments of Defined Benefit Pension Plans and for Termination Benefits.

FASB Statements of Financial Accounting Standards 106: Employers' Accounting for Postretirement Benefits Other Than Pensions.

FASB Statements of Financial Accounting Standards 112: Employer's Accounting for Postemployment Benefits.

FASB Statements of Financial Accounting Standards 131: Disclosures about Segments of an Enterprise and Related Information.

FASB Statements of Financial Accounting Standards 132: Employers' Disclosures about Pensions and Other Postretirement Benefits.

FASB Statements of Financial Accounting Standards 141: Business Combinations.

FASB Statements of Financial Accounting Standards 142: Goodwill and Intangible Assets.

FASB Statements of Financial Accounting Standards 144: Accounting for the Impairment or Disposal of Long-Lived Assets.

FASB Statements of Financial Accounting Standards 151: Inventory Costs - an amendment of ARB No. 43, Chapter 4.

SEC Staff Accounting Bulletin 101: Revenue Recognition in Financial Statements.

FSC
www.fsc.org
MIX
Papier | Fördert gute Waldnutzung
FSC® C083411

Kolibri 360 GmbH
Ferdinand-Jühlke-Straße 7
99095 Erfurt, Deutschland
produktsicherheit@kolibri360.de